ENTERPRISE UNIONISM IN JAPAN

Hirosuke Kawanishi

Translated by Ross E. Mouer

KEGAN PAUL INTERNATIONAL
London and New York

First published in 1992 by
Kegan Paul International Ltd
PO Box 256, London WC1B 3SW, England

Distributed by
John Wiley & Sons Ltd
Southern Cross Trading Estate
1 Oldlands Way, Bognor Regis,
West Sussex, PO22 9SA, England

Routledge, Chapman & Hall Inc
29 West 35th Street
New York, NY 10001, USA

The publishers gratefully acknowledge the assistance of the Japan
Foundation in the publication of this volume.

Phototypeset by Intype, London

Printed in Great Britain by TJ Press, Padstow

British Library Cataloguing in Publication Data
Kawanishi, Hirosuke, *1942–*
  Enterprise unionism in Japan. – (Japanese studies).
  1. Japan. Trade unions
  I. Title II. Series
  331.88′0952
  ISBN 0–7103–0341–6 $c\ \upsilon$

Library of Congress Cataloging-in-Publication Data
Kawanishi, Hirosuke, 1942–
  Enterprise Unionism in Japan / Hirosuke Kawanishi: translated
from the Japanese by Ross E. Mouer.
    465pp. 216 cm. – (Japanese studies series)
  Includes bibliographical references and index.
  ISBN 0–7103–0341–6
  1. Company unions – Japan. I. Title. II. Series: Japanese
studies series (Kegan Paul International)
  HD6490.C612J35   1991   90–5050
  331.88′34′9052 – dc20   CIP

ENTERPRISE UNIONISM
IN JAPAN

Japanese Studies
General Editor: Yoshio Sugimoto

Contents

Figures

Tables

Author's Preface

During the 1980s many Japanese began to feel the pressures of 'internationalizing.' At the same time, Japanese-style industrial relations came to receive wide international attention. For most people 'Japanese-style industrial relations' came to mean the 'three sacred treasures': lifetime employment, seniority wages and enterprise unionism. Since the first OECD report on Japan's system of industrial relations in the early 1970s, Japanese-style industrial relations have been seen as a major factor accounting for the rapid economic growth that propelled Japan into becoming a major economic superpower. Although those writing favourably about Japanese-style management and industrial relations could be said to be in the mainstream both inside and outside Japan, the truth of the matter is that very few of those advocating that approach to industrial relations have done any empirical research on the actual working conditions of Japanese employees on the shop floor. Instead, they have simply created an abstract model of industrial relations which holds true as a set of logical interconnected propositions.

This book is based on several empirical investigations into the workings of enterprise unionism in a number of Japan's major firms. It has been common for critics of Japan's industrial relations to point to the dual structure which provides generous benefits to workers in Japan's large firms at the expense of workers in Japan's smaller firms. However, the real task for those wishing to study the merits of Japanese-style industrial relations is to consider how well they function even in their own citadel, the large firm itself.

As one of the 'three sacred treasures,' the enterprise union exists primarily in Japan's large firms. However, one sign of the uninformed observer is the tendency to equate Japanese unionism with enterprise unionism, and the enterprise union with the company union. For some reason the view seems common that Japan's enterprise unions are established on the principle that all employees of a given firm will automatically join that firm's enterprise union. In the literature praising Japanese-style industrial relations, another view also seems to be quite common. That is the view that unions in Europe and North America have worked to protect and to enhance the working conditions of their members at the expense of growth in the national economy. In contrast, Japanese unions are seen as having been able to promote the growth of Japan's national economy while also contributing greatly to the improved working conditions of the ordinary employee.

The problem with these kinds of assessments is that they generally fly in the face of the facts. This volume argues that Japanese unionism is the product of several different types of organizational principles, and distinguishes these from purely political or ideological orientations. Enterprise unions are shown to exist along with industrial unions, occupation-based unions, and geographically based unions. It is also argued that the enterprise union, which today is the most common form of unionism statistically, is a mixed category which includes not only those company unions to which all employees of a single firm must affiliate, but also multiple enterprise unions (which coexist at the same place of employment) and several new types of enterprise union for employees with special distinguishing characteristics such as being handicapped. A third argument is that the enterprise union has not adequately demonstrated its ability to improve the working conditions of the average employee, even in Japan's large firms. Out of these arguments a new theory of the enterprise union is formulated. If unions form one cornerstone of the industrial relations system, a new theory of the enterprise union will require some revision to theories of Japan's industrial relations.

The ideology associated with the enterprise union in the commonly cited model of Japanese-style industrial relations might be labelled 'cooperative industrial relations' or 'collaborative industrial relations.' In looking at union ideologies, it is useful to distinguish between four types. One is the unitarian ideological position which posits that labor and management share the same interests both in production and in the distribution of surplus output. Another is the cooperative or collaborative ideology which forwards the notion that labor and management have a similar interest in obtaining efficiencies in production but have different interests when it comes to distributing surplus output. The third would be an ideology which sees labor-management in a fundamental conflict both in terms of how production is organised and in terms of how surplus output is distributed. Finally, class conflict ideologies reject outright the very premises on which capitalist society is based.

Although the enterprise union associated with a peculiarly Japanese style of industrial relations is conceived primarily in terms of the second of these ideological stances, these four types of ideology can be found in most other industrialized societies. Moreover, advocates of each of the four types of ideology can be found in most other industrialized societies. Moreover, advocates of each of the four types can be found in Japan. That raises the question as to why the second type has come to be known as 'Japanese.' I suppose this reflects the commonly held view that the distinctiveness of industrial relations in Japan lies in the belief that the driving force behind the Japanese union movement is in the enterprise-level organization. It is at this level, many observers would argue, that the cooperative or collaborative ideology manifests itself most vividly in Japan. There is also an assumption that this ideology, to the extent that it can be found, manifests itself more at the national or industrial level in most European and North American societies. However, one might say the same thing about the locus of conflict-orientated ideologies. While the lines of conflict tend to be formulated at the national level in some societies, they too appear at the enterprise level in Japan. However, when conflict-oriented ideologies are found at the enterprise-level in Japan, they are referred to simply as 'union ideology advocating labor-management conflict' without reference to them as a peculiarly Japanese phenomenon.

It is useful to move away from ideological criteria in defining 'Japanese-style industrial relations.' We can identify a system of organization in which the primary locus of the authority to make decisions about leadership, financial matters, and membership criteria and recruitment lies basically at the enterprise-level of the organization. By distinguishing between the ideological principles and the organizational principles, a more accurate picture of what is truly 'Japanese' might be obtained.

Looking at the organizational principles of the enterprise union, it has been common for writers dealing with Japanese unionism to refer to the 'enterprise union' as a union which organizes all permanent employees at one firm regardless of whether they are blue- or white-collar. Although this definition does not adequately capture the state of the union movement at this level in contemporary Japan, it has set the research agenda for many studying Japan's industrial relations. To the extent that the above definition of organizational principles has been adopted, a number of enterprise-level phenomena have been overlooked in the writings about Japan's industrial relations. This bias may be corrected some by realizing that the main organizing principle is simply that the enterprise union draws its members from the same firm. From this perspective, the union which is able to organize all employees at the same firm can be said to be a special type of enterprise union. By equating this special form of enterprise unionism with the enterprise union, many observers have tended to imply that some special kind of a consensus orientation is also a feature of Japan's industrial relations.

The tendency to define the enterprise union in terms of ideological criteria and then to equate that form of enterprise unionism with unionism in Japan has made it difficult for many observers to explain the postwar history of unionism in Japan. A major fact of that history is the prevalence of union schisms which have demonstrated clearly that more than one union and several ideologies have come to coexist at many of Japan's firms. Even the most superficial look at that history reveals that the division of some of Japan's important unions in the 1950s and the relative success of competing enterprise unions in the decades that followed can only be understood in terms of the power relations between management and each of the competing unions. That history also reveals that it is possible for an enterprise union to adhere to an ideology based on the notion that labor and management have distinctly different interests in organizing production and in distributing the surplus output.

By limiting our criteria for defining the enterprise union to the simple condition that all union members must come from the same firm (as opposed to requiring that an enterprise union include all employees within its membership), we are able to incorporate a wider range of union phenomena into our analysis of the enterprise union. For example, we can find examples of enterprise unions in prewar Japan which organized certain types of employees at the same firm. We can find examples of two enterprise unions existing at the same firm. We then see in a different light the movement to include all employees (e.g., both blue-collar and white-collar) in the same union in postwar Japan and the sharp increase after 1948 in the number of instances where more than one enterprise union exists at the same firm. In all of these cases, enterprise unions were formed around the notion that members were to be drawn from the same firm. Recognition of this fact provides us with the basis for developing a more general theory to explain the rise and the functioning of the enterprise union in Japan.

In recent years unionization rates have been falling, dropping to 25.2 percent in 1990. The elitist and closed nature of the union movement is cited as one source of the problem. Another cause would seem to be the growth of the peripheral labor market and the employment of persons who do not become 'regular employees.' In order to raise the organization rate enterprise unions will have to start thinking of organizing non-regular employees at their firms. This is presently the major challenge facing the labor movement in Japan.

We can now see a number of 'new-type unions' responding to this challenge. Some are organized on an enterprise basis, but others supersede the enterprise and promote an ethic tied to broader notions of working-class solidarity. If the term 'enterprise' is to be a heuristic device for labelling Japanese unionism as a form of unionism distinct from forms found abroad, then it is important to consider the ways in which enterprise unions go about organizing the full array of employees which make up the business enterprise in Japan. To do otherwise will lead us to confuse the principle of elitism (which characterizes many enterprise unions at Japan's largest and most successful firms) with the principle of enterprise-level organization.

The preceding discussion can be summarized in the accompanying Table P.1. The table suggests that there are at least six ideal types of enterprise union which a theory of the enterprise union ought to be able to explain. Obviously, box A consists of the mainstream enterprise union. However, there are a good many unions which coexist in the same firm and they would be of the type indicated by box B. The coexisting enterprise union might be either a majority or a minority union, and it might be right-wing conservative or left-wing radical in its ideology.

In considering the union movement in postwar Japan, the reader should be aware that there are many unions which are not of the enterprise type. The industrial unions come immediately to

Table P.1 *A framework for categorizing Japan's enterprise unions*

Membership criteria	Competitive position	
	The only union at a given firm	One of a plurality of unions at a given firm
Includes all regular permanent employees	A	B
Limited to all non-regular employees	C	D
Open to all employees regardless of employment status	E	F

mind. Examples would be the All Japan Seaman's Union, Zensen Dōmei (for textile workers), Zenzōsen (for shipbuilders) and Zenkoku Kinzoku (for metal workers). As occupational or trades unions, those for office workers in schools (Gakko Jimu Rōdō Kumiai) and for maritime communication technicians (Senpaku Tsushinshi Rōdō Kumiai) might be mentioned. As for geographically defined unions, we have Zenkoku Ippan (for all kinds of workers in all industries), the various regionally based unions and community unions. There are also unions based on other criteria such as gender and ideological stance, and those which incorporate some mixture of the criteria applied by the unions mentioned just above. These examples include some unions which have a long history extending back to the prewar period, some which came into existence just after the war, and some which have come into existence much more recently in the late 1970s and the 1980s. Those which have been formed more recently are quite varied in terms of their organizational principles, and they might most usefully be grouped together into a category referred to simply as 'the new unions.' The new unions include enterprise unions of the subtypes C, D, E and F in the table.

In 1983 I was asked by Professor Yoshio Sugimoto whether I would be interested in submitting a manuscript for this series of publications. His idea was that the work I had been doing on the enterprise union might be broadened somewhat to obtain an alternate view of industrial relations in Japan. At the same time, I was beginning to have misgivings about the way in which an idealized stereotype of Japanese industrial relations and the mobilization of Japanese society for economic growth was being disseminated abroad as a kind of political ideology. As one among a large number of Japanese scholars doing research on industrial relations in Japan, I felt the offer provided me with an opportunity to 'set the record straight.' Upon agreeing to the project, I was able to obtain the services of Professor Ross Mouer, a sociologist with an imtimate knowledge of Japan who is now Director of the Japanese Studies Centre at Monash University. This was particularly auspicious since he and Professor Sugimoto had worked together on so many projects in the past which had on a more general level come to undermine many of the stereotypes of Japanese society commonly found in the literature on Japanese society written both by Japanese and non-Japanese scholars.

Although I had at first imagined that I would simply get a fairly straightforward translation of some of my earlier work, I soon found myself in an on-going dialogue with the translator. As a result, the original text was considerably revised and expanded. The dialogue continued for some six years before the final manuscript was completed. The dialogue took me on a long journey. As the work progressed, the draft of one chapter after another was mailed to me with a seemingly endless list of questions and requests for theoretical or logical tightness. By repeating this process through three drafts and perhaps as many as 200 letters, I was able to better articulate a number of points and to set the work in a broader context. Professor Mouer's own illnesses and my own schedule meant that the work progressed at an uneven pace. However, in the end a new work was created. That was to form the basis for another volume which was published in Japanese, *Kigyobetsu Kumiai no Riron – Mō Hitotsu no Nihonteki Roshi Kankei* (A Theory of the Enterprise Union – Another View of Peculiarly Japanese Industrial Relations) (Tokyo: Nihon Hyoronsha, 1989). That volume parallels this translation rather closely.

In bringing this volume into print, I must thank a number of individuals. First is Professor Sugimoto who provided me with the opportunity to have this work published. Second is Professor Mouer whose intellectual debate and warm friendship I have received. Numerous other persons have lent various forms of support along the way: Professors Koji Taira, Hazama Hiroshi and Shiobara Tsutomu. Finally, there are the readers of my work in Japanese who have communicated to me various criticisms and points of view which have helped to sharpen my arguments over the years. To these and to many others I wish to express my deeply felt appreciation.

Translator's Preface

It is generally accepted that the written histories of the victors and the elites shape our images of most societies. Views of the enterprise union in Japan have tended to be based on rather narrowly prescribed accounts of what happens in the large majority enterprise unions that organise the aristocracy of labour in Japan's largest firms. The view of the enterprise union provided in this volume will serve to correct a number of common misnomers as to how the enterprise union is organized and how it functions.

In the chapters that follow Professor Kawanishi compares the major enterprise union with the minority enterprise union. He argues that both types of union have coexisted through much of the postwar period in many of Japan's firms. It has been common for students of Japan's industrial relations to dismiss the minority union as a remnant of Japan's militant unionism immediately after the war, an aberration inspired by left-wing ideologues but out of step with the needs and the thinking of the ordinary Japanese worker. In examining the rise and fall of Japan's industrial unions, Professor Kawanishi puts the rise of the enterprise union into its proper historical context. It is a context in which class consciousness is seen as being much more fluid than is normally thought to be the case.

In much of the writing on Japan's industrial relations, the enterprise union continues to be confused with the company union. The large number of case studies in this volume illustrate the fact that the enterprise union is not a union of all employees at one company. Nor does such a union consist of employees bound together by some sense of loyalty to their firm. The author develops his arguments around more universally recognized motivational structures, avoiding the pitfalls of excessively cultural explanations. Nor does he rely on the assumption that worker motivation can be explained by reference to a single value such as material gain or higher wages. The picture painted by Professor Kawanishi shows that some workers strive for more income, others for power or status within the large corporate enterprise, and still others for the simple sense of comradeship with workmates.

This volume brings together nearly two decades of research which Professor Kawanishi has published in several books and a number of articles. The carefully documented case studies are drawn both from the core labor force and from the peripheral labor force. One argument is that the future of labor movements which fail to embrace Japan's peripheral labor force is doubtful. Despite the apparent success of the dominant enterprise unions in obtaining for their members a higher standard of living through improved productivity, Kawanishi argues that the declining organization rate of Japan's union movement must in part be attributed to its failure to obtain significant concessions for large portions of the Japanese labor force. This is an important line of questioning at a time that unionization rates are falling around the world and labor's malaise is being attributed largely to structural changes in the composition of the labor force.

The need for this kind of questioning is especially felt in Australia, where the translator lives and works. Australia is currently in the midst of an exercise known as 'restructuring,' an attempt to implement a program of union-lead micro-economic reform. There are a number of interesting parallels which link the dynamics of change in contemporary Australia to the Japanese experience: the ways in which the wage system is being altered to provide for more incentive-linked remuneration, the attempts to involve the union in productivity-raising exercises in cooperation with management at the place of work, the shift to enterprise-based wage agreements, the introduction of extensive subcontracting and the 'just-in-time systems' in certain industries, the moves to restrict the rights of unions to strike, the clearer segmentation of the labor force into core and peripheral sectors, concerted efforts to generate an extensive middle-class consciousness and a sense of embourgeoisement, and the general appearance of nationalistic sentiments and frequent references to the need to tighten discipline at work in order to rescue a floundering national economy. Throughout this volume Professor Kawanishi explores these sorts of issues as they relate to the functioning of the enterprise union in the Japanese context.

An important focal point in Professor Kawanishi's analysis is the role of power relations. Much of the work on Japanese-style management has attributed the success of Japan's industrial relations to the maintenance of a delicate balance between the forces for democracy and those for productivity. However, that emphasis appears primarily in analyses based largely on the situation in Japan in the late 1960s and early 1970s. As Professor Kawanishi shows, that was a period when there was a relative balance between (i) management and the conservative unions as a force for productivity improvement, and (ii) the socialistically inspired leftist unions as a force for democracy. However, that brief period must be seen as an interlude – a period of transition in which the forces for democracy were eventually overwhelmed by the forces for productivity. Professor Kawanishi challenges us to think about the consequences for the ordinary Japanese worker of not having maintained the balance between those two forces. Just as the writings of those in the anti-pollution movement of the 1970s served to present Japan as an example to the world of what the excessive concentration of industrial activity can produce, so too does Professor Kawanishi's work cause us to reflect on the costs of excessively gearing our industrial relations to serve unquestioningly the interests of the forces for higher productivity. While Professor Kawanishi looks for possibilities, he is in the end not optimistic about the ability of 'the system' to regain that balance once it is lost. The enterprise union is not everything it is made out to be. Its introduction represents a kind of Rubicon to be crossed only with great care by those responsible for designing industrial relations systems for the twenty-first century.

If there is a note of optimism in Professor Kawanishi's thesis, it may be in his suggestions about the possibility of developing a system of dual unionism – one in which unions for productivity and those for democracy coexist. It would seem obvious that unions of the latter type still have an important role to play as a champion for the various minorities which account for a good portion of those in the peripheral labor market. At a time of heightened international competition, an infatuation with technical solutions, and a renewed confidence in capitalist institutions, a number of socialist states have come to confront a number of seemingly intractable difficulties. It is easy in the circumstances to be drawn into a celebration of the virtues of unrestrained competition. At a time when there seems to be a new form of solidarity emerging among the techno-professional classes of the world, it may be time for workers to reconsider the wisdom of having 'peoples' unions' committed largely to democratic and egalitarian ideals. The optimistic note in Professor Kawanishi's work is in the invitation to make that reassessment.

This volume draws from manuscripts written between 1977 and 1984. The translation is the result of fairly intensive interaction between the translator and the author over a four-year period. In the process of elucidating the detail of the case studies and the overall argumentation, Professor Kawanishi has expanded on various points and added others anew. During the four years, I was impressed time and again by his ability to recall minute details and to locate the rather obscure handouts, posters and notices which he had painstakingly collected over the years. His patience in supplying further detail and elaboration meant that a new work has been produced. Realizing that, Professor Kawanishi reorganized the Japanese-language material and produced a new volume, *Kigyobetsu Kumiai no Riron: Mō Hitotsu no Nihonteki Roshi Kankei* (A Theory of the Enterprise Union: Japanese-Style Industrial Relations on the Other Level), published by Nihon Hyōronsha in 1989. At the end of that volume he provides full information on where each of the original publications appeared.

1 Introduction

I Common Perceptions of Japanese Labor Unions

Since the early 1970s it has been fashionable to credit the Japanese system of industrial relations and the Japanese enterprise union with having made a major contribution to Japan's postwar economic growth. These evaluations of industrial relations in Japan highlight several features commonly seen as being peculiar to the way Japan's labor unions are organized. One is the fact that the Japanese labor union is an enterprise or company union which has facilitated the implementation of company policies designed to promote the firm's expansion and, thereby, the growth of the national economy. Japan's form of unionism is seen as having contributed significantly to the improvement of the working conditions and the standard of living of the ordinary employee. This view can be seen in the writings of the OECD (1973), Vogel (1979), Reischauer (1979), Koike (1977) and Shirai (1979 and 1980). It is also commonly alleged by these observers that the enterprise union is wholly company-based, consisting only of persons who are directly employed as 'regular employees' (*seiki shain*). Accordingly, it is held that unionism in Japan rests primarily on the principle of 'one firm, one union' (*ichikigyō ichikumiai*).

This volume argues that the above views greatly simplify the way in which Japanese labor unions are structured. In the chapters which follow, the author's own empirical studies of Japanese labor unions will be introduced as a basis for critically evaluating the standard views presented above. In doing so, three arguments are put forward. The first is that Japanese unions have not been particularly effective in securing the worker's standard of living. The second is that, as a social phenomenon, the 'enterprise union system' in Japan included not only (i) situations in which all employees belong to the same union (*zenjūgyōin ikkatsu kanyū*), but also (ii) situations in which several 'enterprise unions' compete within a single firm (*fukusū kumiai heizon*), and (iii) situations in which employees have joined the 'new unions' (*shingata rōdō kumiai*). The view presented here is that the 'enterprise union' is not defined by the principle of 'one firm, one union', but by the less restrictive criterion that a union draws its membership from one firm. This allows for the existence of two enterprise unions in the same firm and contrasts the principle of 'intra-firm

Table 1.1 *The evaluation of Japan's industrial relations over four decades: 1945–85*

Period	Evaluation	Major assertion	Major factor initiating the period	Representative scholars
1945–55	–	stress on the feudalistic aspects of Japan's industrial relations	GHP policy emphasizing democratization	Ōkōchi Sumiya Ujihara Ariizumi Isoda
1955–65	+ –	emphasis on rational functions of Japan's industrial relations	Abegglen's *Japanese Factory* (1958)	Abegglen Hazama Matsushima
1965–75	+	recognition of the contributions of Japan's industrial relations to economic growth	OECD's report on Japan's industrial relations (1973)	
1975–85	+ +	promotion of Japan's industrial relations as the model for Europe, America, Southeast Asia and Australia	Vogel's *Japan as Number One* (1979) Reischauer's *The Japanese* (1979)	Ouchi Shirai Koike Kōshiro

Note: − = a negative evaluation
   + = a positive evaluation

unionism' with that of 'supra-firm unionism' (which might take
the form of occupational, trade or industrial unionism, on the
one hand, or general unionism, on the other). The third argument is that a careful analysis of these other forms of enterprise
unionism will help to provide a new framework for analyzing the
union movement in postwar Japan.

In considering changes in the way Japan's industrial relations
have been evaluated in the postwar period, four periods can
be identified. The periods correspond roughly with the decades
following Japan's independence in the early 1950s. The periods
are shown in Table 1.1 and the views characterizing each period
are discussed briefly below.

A   The first postwar decade (1945–55)

During the 1950s many of the features of Japan's industrial
relations seen as being peculiarly Japanese were criticized as
feudalistic. At that time people spoke of the two-stage revolution
(*nidankai kakumei ron*). Taking advantage of the various reforms
introduced by the Occupation authorities as part of its larger
program of democratization, it was argued, efforts should be
made to go beyond democratization so that a socialist revolution
would occur. The slogans were 'From Pre-Modern to Modern!'
(*zenkindaiteki kara kindaiteki e*) and 'From Feudalism to Democracy!' (*hōkensei kara minshusei e*). 'Modernization' and 'democratization' meant Westernization. In other words, Europe and
America were seen as providing the ideal model toward which
Japan ought to move. Peculiarly Japanese features were seen as
burdens which needed to be discarded. Given this typology, the
goal of democratization was to move Japan along the continuum
from the feudalistic pole toward the modern-democratic pole.

This view of the world can be seen in a number of academic
works which appeared during the period. The report of the
Jinbun Kagaku Iinkai (The Human Sciences Coordinating Committee)[1] argued in 1949 that the origins of Japan's feudalistic
system of land tenure were in the small number of wealthy
absentee landlords who owned large tracts of land which were
worked by a large number of very poor tenant farmers. Because
Japan's industrial labor force drew heavily from the strata of
tenant farmers living in serf-like conditions, it was argued,
Japan's 'modern' wage laborers found it natural to accept slave-

like working conditions and a feudalistic style of industrial relations. The report had been prepared by a committee consisting of Ōkōchi Kazuo, Sumiya Mikio, Ariizumi Tōru and Isoda Susumu.

Elsewhere Sumiya (1950) took a similar line, arguing that the feudalistic aspects of wage labor in Japan were themselves the major structural contradiction in capitalism. He claimed that this situation arose out of the close linkages between the feudalistic relations at work and the pre-modern human relations which traditionally characterized life in Japan's agricultural sector. Wage labor in Japan's industrial sector was seen as being provided by a semi-proletarian labor force which was essentially agricultural but which also, because of the poverty produced by the feudalistic relationships in the agricultural sector, had to find other employment to supplement family income.

The Nihon Jinbun Kagaku Kai (The Japan Association of the Human Sciences)[2] and the Shakai Seisaku Gakkai (The Society for the Study of Social Policy)[3] were the major driving forces in academic circles during the 1950s. In the research published by scholars associated with these groupings, three points seem to have been reiterated with regard to the feudalistic nature of Japan's industrial relations. One was that the feudalistic nature of industrial relations was being reproduced not by wage laborers in Japan's factories, but by the way in which labor was reproduced in Japan's agricultural communities. Another was that the feudalistic relationship at work (meaning a type of relationship in which particularistic personalism rather than contractual notions was the dominant feature) could be seen in the system of lifetime employment, in seniority-merit wages, and in the emphasis on the enterprise as an organic community. The third was that feudalism in the labor market precluded the development of nation-wide labor markets for different skills or occupations and opened the way for a vertically segmented labor market where the emphasis was on personal connections and various forms of favoritism. During the 1950s, then, Japan's labor relations were characterized as being at odds with what might exist in Europe and North America. The view of feudalism presented here was subscribed to by nearly all Japanese scholars working on Japan's industrial relations.

B The second postwar decade and a half (1955–70)

Abegglen's *The Japanese Factory* (1958) paved the way for a change in the thinking about Japan's industrial relations. Abegglen sought to highlight the way in which peculiar features of Japan's industrial relations functioned to ensure that a certain measure of rationality prevailed in terms of how work is organized in Japan. As a social anthropologist, Abegglen was interested in how a group of people structured their lives. He looked for patterns in the behavior, the ways of thinking, the emotions and the motivations of the people he studied. Along with other anthropologists, he inquired about the changes occurring within and without Japanese society and speculated about their effect on Japan's industrial relations. Anthropologists seemed to believe that the accommodation of Japanese social structures to those changes would occur gradually, and that the sudden imposition of change on Japanese society by outside parties would simply disrupt the society, destroying its social fabric and causing considerable social upheaval.

Within this framework of the anthropologist, Abegglen sought to uncover peculiarly Japanese features in Japan's system of personnel management. He looked at various employment practices – hiring, promotion and personnel evaluation, the wage system and relations between the company and the employee. In looking at the unique features of Japanese management as forming an integrated system of management, Abegglen referred to the configuration as something approximating 'a family grouping'. However, rather than evaluating this familism negatively as a remnant of Japanese feudalism, he underlined the contribution it made to Japan's rapid industrialization. At the same time, Abegglen also argued that Japan's experience with industrialization should not be used as a model for other developing societies. Rather, each country was seen as having its own unique tradition which would have to be mobilized in order to achieve its own form of industrialization. In other words, Abegglen was emphasizing the need for 'a pluralistic approach to development' (*tagiteki bunka ron*).

At about the same time, two Japanese scholars, Matsushima Shizuo and Hazama Hiroshi, were engaged in their own empirical studies of how Japanese management served to promote economic rationalization. Matsushima's study (1972) of poor miners from rural Japan led to a volume emphasizing as a special feature of Japan's personnel management practices the antagonism between unions and management with regard to livelihood guarantees for the workers whom he described as empty-handed laborers (*toshu kūken no rōdōsha*). In their poverty the miners had given up their land and left their home towns. Their sense of insecurity came from three sources: they were workers with nowhere to return; their working conditions were poor and they had to lead a hand-to-mouth existence; they never knew when an industrial accident would bring death or a crippling injury, leaving them without even that source of income.

Hazama's research (1964) was more historically focused, and dealt with the emergence and formation of Japanese management as a product of the way capitalism developed in Japan. His research highlighted the way in which the commercial ideology developed by the merchant class during the Tokugawa period was adapted to meet the needs of Japanese capitalism. Management paternalism (*keiei kazokushugi*), which was seen as being consistent with the demands of personnel management, appeared to provide a basis for promoting in employees a strong sense of loyalty to their firm and a commitment to their work.

Taken together, the work of Abegglen, Matsushima and Hazama served to provide a corrective to the earlier studies which took Western models as the norm, and which evaluated Japanese management in terms of the extent to which it deviated from the Western model, the extent to which it was 'behind the times,' and the time which would be required for Japan to 'catch up.' Based on empirical research and considering some of the rational aspects of Japanese management, the research conducted during this period brought a new perspective to the study of Japanese management.

C The 1970s

As Japan entered the 1970s, foreign interest in Japan's economy increased sharply. As part of the overall interest in Japan, foreign attention came to focus on Japan's system of industrial relations as a source of economic growth. This new interest from abroad was symbolized by the publication of the first OECD report on Japan's industrial relations in 1973. The report highlighted the so-called three pillars or sacred treasures of Japanese industrial relations: lifetime employment, seniority wages and the enterprise union. In seeking to explain how Japan had weathered the oil shock of 1973 while most other advanced industrialized nations experienced an extended period of stagflation, the OECD later published a second report in 1977 which added a fourth pillar: Japan's social norms, which were seen as including the emphasis on vertical social relationships, the commitment to consensus-oriented decision-making, and the value placed on the enterprise as a corporate body equally involving all employees in the achievement of its goals.

D   The 1980s

By the end of the 1970s, recognition of the positive way in which Japanese-style management and industrial relations had contributed to Japan's rapid economic growth gave way to outright adoration. Books such as Vogel's *Japan as Number One* (1979), Reischauer's *The Japanese* (1979) and Ouchi's *Theory Z* (1981) became best sellers over night. In Japan a similarly approving view was presented by Shirai (1980), Koike (1977), Kōshiro (1982) and others who tended to emphasize the importance of internal labor markets from the point of view of labor economics. They tended to argue that a similar pattern was emerging throughout the world as capitalism entered its more advanced stages. They suggested that seniority-based wages, seniority-based promotions and enterprise unionism were becoming a fairly universal phenomena in all industrialized societies. It is a view which adds to Dore's earlier notion (1973) of reverse convergence and underlines the importance of Japan as a model for other industrialized societies.

II   Some Focal Points for Research

The preceding discussion suggests that the view of industrial relations in Japan has changed over time. To some extent it could be said that the image of Japan's industrial relations has changed with the times and at any particular time has reflected the intellectual climate of the times more than it has the actual realities of Japan's industrial relations. This is partly because most of the persons writing about Japan's industrial relations, and especially about its unions, have not developed an appropriate framework for analyzing the phenomena they are writing about. Moreover, research has been carried out without a strong commitment to first ascertaining carefully all of the objective facts.

Among the viewpoints discussed above, the changing emphasis in the writing on Japan's industrial relations can perhaps best be seen in the notion of 'real efficiency' (*jisshitsu gōrisei*). The notion is associated with an approach which has two shortcomings. One is the assumption or perception that all the phenomena being observed function positively (e.g., that they serve some useful end such as promoting higher productivity or economic growth itself). The result is a built-in bias towards accepting the status quo, a view which predisposes the investigator to see eufunctions rather than dysfunctions. It is a perspective which does not promote the imaginative perspectives necessary to consider how phenomena change as a result of the processes involved in resolving and in generating internal contradictions in the system itself. A second difficulty is that this view of reality tends to treat cultural configurations as holistic entities. Attention is directed to explanations which emphasize the importance of cultural uniqueness and national character. The corollary is that Japan's industrial relations are an inevitable outcome of Japan's cultural uniqueness. Such explanations, however, are static, often treating historical events superficially and not leaving much room for considering how the power-based relationship between labor and management has served in a dynamic fashion to mediate the impact of culture.

Rather than looking for functions which are presumed to exist, the approach taken here focuses on simpler kinds of 'facts.' The aim is to develop a perspective for understanding the existence of structural contradictions or paradoxes within Japan's industrial relations. This perspective on industrial relations, then, comes with a 'built-in' interest in the on-going conflict of interests between labor and management. To grasp fully the special features of industrial relations in any given country, one must confront directly the issue of the power relationship between labor and management in terms of the historical, cultural, economic, and social milieu. The rules and practices which constitute a system of industrial relations constantly change as the structural contradictions between labor and management are resolved. Accordingly, I use 'the theory of structural contradictions' to refer to an analytical approach which places emphasis on (i) 'structural contradictions', (ii) power relationships, and (iii) the dynamics of change which result from attempts to resolve the contradictions.

When examined in terms of the 'theory of structural contradictions,' Japan's industrial relations can no longer be understood either as a model for Western societies or as a remnant of Japanese feudalism which must be reformed. Industrial relations in all societies are characterized by strengths and weaknesses. Industrial relations are constantly changing as certain structural contradictions are resolved and others are created.

When Japan's industrial relations are analyzed within this framework, the notion of consensus-based Japanese-style management can be seen for what it is – one solution to the various structural contradictions built into Japan's industrial relations which has been designed and implemented by management in the interests of management. However, because the contradictions are in turn the product of Japan's social history, its culture and the current social milieu, it is quite possible that Japan's 'conciliatory industrial relations' would give way to a period of acrimonious industrial relations and open conflict between labor and management should the current power relationship between labor and management change.

Reference to the existence of structural contradictions will move us away from static notions which posit that there is a peculiarly Japanese approach to industrial relations. Such a perspective would also allow us to view Japan's industrial relations in a more dynamic fashion. That in turn would mean a renewal of the broader emphasis on the dynamics of social change, power relationships and historical context – an emphasis which characterized earlier scholarship on Japan's industrial relations during the 1950s and which remained important in the 1960s and 1970s.

III Problem Consciousness and the Focus of Research on Japanese Labor Unions

This volume provides a broader perspective of the enterprise union in Japan by setting it within the larger confines of the Japanese labor movement. There is more to the labor movement than the enterprise union. This is particularly true if we take an historical view of the movement over the entire span of forty years since the end of the war. To be sure, the enterprise union is the most basic autonomous unit in the union movement. As such, it has nearly full control over what it does. In the case of Japan, the predominant unit of organization is the business firm (*kaisha*) or place of business (*jigyōsho*), either being referred to as the 'enterprise' (*kigyō*). It is at this level that one must first come to grips with Japan's industrial relations. For this reason, Japan's industrial relations are fundamentally different from those in the countries of Europe and America where the unions have been able to bridge across individual enterprises to establish themselves on a horizontal basis independent from the management of the specific firms which hire their members. This is explained in more detail below.

Figure 1.1 shows one way of portraying the structure of Japan's labor unions. The union movement is structured around the enterprise or place of work as the main organizational unit. The enterprise union (*kigyō betsu kumiai*) may be either a unit union (*tanso* or *tan-i kumiai*) or an enterprise federation (*kigyōren*). Many large firms carry on activities at several places of business which may each have a distinct legal identity. In such cases it is common for there to be a unit union at each place of business, with their activities being coordinated through an enterprise-wide federation (known as '*kigyōren*' for '*kigyōnai rōdō kumiai rengōtai*').

Even when the enterprise union is affiliated with a larger organization (such as a national center, an industrial federation, or a regional body), it still remains very independent and continues to have full jurisdiction over its own affairs. It does not receive orders from these other umbrella organizations; nor is it under their control in a legal or constitutional sense. Of course, there may be moral sanctions. However, seldom is an enterprise union excluded from membership or sanctioned in any serious

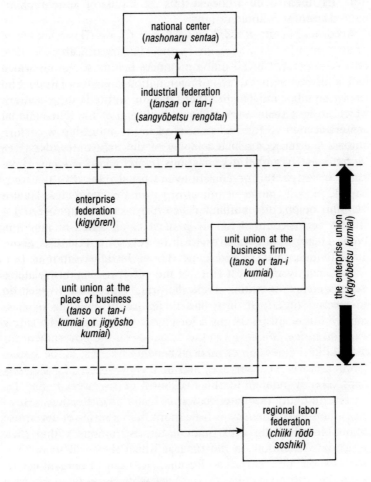

Figure 1.1 *The organizational structure of Japanese labor unions*

manner by an umbrella organization. If that did somehow happen, the enterprise union would simply disassociate itself. Given (i) that its goals are narrowly defined in terms of negotiating with management for better working conditions within the firm, and (ii) that its existence depends on conditions within the firm, its need to be affiliated with an industrial federation or national center is limited.

According to the *Rōdō Kumiai Kihon Chōsa* (Basic Survey of Trade Unions) taken annually by the Ministry of Labor, in 1986 only 65.6 percent of all union members belong to unions which had affiliated with the four major national centres (Rōdō Shō 1978). Unions affiliated to other types of umbrella organizations which are not themselves affiliated with one of the four national centers accounted for 30.4 percent of the membership in Japan's unions. These bodies include some of the industrial federations (*tansan*) and regional organizations (*chiiki rōdō soshiki*). However, these types of organizations are usually so weak that they have little pull (moral or otherwise) over their affiliates. Unionists who belong to unaffiliated enterprise unions numbered 1.4 million and accounted for 8.4 percent of all union members in 1986. These facts permit us to draw several conclusions about the activities, finances and leadership of Japanese labor unions.

First, nearly all the activities of the enterprise unions relate to issues which arise within a specific firm. Three issues which do go beyond the single firm and relate to the building of class consciousness are (i) the push for higher wages during the spring wage offensive (*shuntō*), (ii) the demands on the government for changes in the pension or medical benefits systems, in the system of unemployment insurance, and in the provision of other services directly related to the livelihood of the worker and his family, and (iii) the mobilization of voters for elections. However, the spring offensive is little more than a series of enterprise unions coordinating with other enterprise unions within their industrial federation on the time at which they will serve their demands on the enterprises. Because the right to bargain collectively, to strike, and to reach agreements is retained by each enterprise union, each union goes about organizing itself in its own way, getting what it can from its own firm and not worrying about how the unionists at other firms may fare. Commonly referred to as 'enterprise egoism', this approach reflects the fact that it is the unions at the large prosperous firms which are able to look after the interests of their own member-employees. The concern with helping workers in less prosperous firms is minimal. Policy-related campaigns and election-related activities tend to involve only the union leaders, and the ordinary rank-and-file unionists play almost no role at all. Although May Day might be cited as another example of an exercise involving class consciousness, most observers have tended to dismiss it as a kind of party or ceremony limited to one day.

As for union finances, in Europe and North America unionists pay dues directly into the larger union which is organized across a number of enterprises, and part of those funds are then automatically paid back as a subsidy to the lower organizational units. In Japan, however, the union members pay their subscriptions directly to the enterprise union. The enterprise union then passes on 10–20 percent of its revenue to the industrial federation. In terms of the organizational framework given above in Figure 1.1, the financial wealth of the unions in Japan is concentrated at the enterprise level, whereas in Europe and America the industrial federation tends to have the ultimate control over union finances. Accordingly, it is not unusual in Japan to find large enterprise unions which are better off financially than the industrial federation to which they are affiliated with several dozen other enterprise unions.

Finally, the differences with regard to leadership need to be considered. In Europe and North America, the amalgamated federations are able to hire their own full-time leaders. In Japan, however, the leaders at this level have been dispatched (or loaned) to the federation by the individual enterprise unions. In other words, the enterprise unions usually have the right to control the selection of the leadership. The enterprise union also has the right to recall someone it has sent to work in an upper-level umbrella organization at the industrial or regional level. In most cases, it may also replace 'its leader' in the industrial federation with another member from the same enterprise union. Accordingly, there is a built-in tendency for union leaders of the industrial federation to pursue policies which reflect the interests of their own enterprise union.

Several concrete examples might be given. Around 1970 Gōka Rōren (the Federation of Chemical Workers) began to be carried along by the development of the anti-pollution movement and had begun to respond on its own, having decided to demand that management in all firms in the chemical industry be asked to restrict their emissions of poisonous gas and other harmful waste products. However, owing to the opposition of union officials from the largest firms in the industry, the policy was never implemented.

At about the same time a locally based confederation of enterprise unions in Kawasaki also decided to become involved in the anti-pollution movement. However, before an official announcement of the policy could be made by the confederation there was a leak in the media which created quite a stir, with the union receiving favourable feedback from the ordinary public. As soon as management in the large firms got wind of the idea they put pressure on 'their unionists' to have the decision rescinded. The confederation retreated on the issue. It was clear that the confederation had come to feel threatened by the possibility that the large enterprise unions would recall 'their leaders' and replace them with someone else more favorably disposed to management's views.

IV Issues Requiring Further Research

In considering the role of the enterprise union within the broader context of Japan's postwar system of industrial relations, the discussion in this book is focused on three questions. First, what is the enterprise union, and what are its main distinguishing features? Second, to what extent can Japan's cooperative approach to industrial relations be said to be democratically based on a relationship of equality or parity between labor and management? In other words, is there anything useful that Japanese-style industrial relations might offer which would help advance the cause of democracy within the world today? Or is it possible that Japan's industrial relations represent a step away from democracy? Third, how are Japanese labor unions changing at the present time? Is it possible to make some informed guesses about the structure of Japanese unionism in the near future?

In using 'democracy' in the context of industrial relations, above all else reference is made to a situation in which there is a balance of power between the unions and management, and among the unions themselves when various unions exist at the same enterprise. Reference is also made to the guarantee of certain minimal civil rights on behalf of employees. These include the freedom of thought, belief and speech. Also included is the freedom from management's interference in the private lives of workers outside of working hours. Finally, 'democracy' refers to the absence of discrimination based on gender, ethnicity or race, and personal background (including the various dimensions related to socio-economic status). With reference to democracy in the unions themselves, the emphasis is on the notion that the right to make policy resides with the workers themselves.

V The Structure of this Volume

The two chapters in Part One of this volume focus on defining the enterprise union and on identifying its salient features. There is an attempt to trace the development of research on the enterprise union. In addition to highlighting the main debates over this period, attention is directed at the development of a new theory of the enterprise union.

The chapters in Part Two consider the second set of issues raised above. The discussion in Part Two begins by considering the actual situation which is so often characterized as being typical of Japan's cooperative approach to industrial relations. The subjects of the analysis are the historical setting and processes by which that approach was institutionalized and the bearing of the present situation on the future of that form of unionism. With that as a basis, the discussion shifts to examine the balance of power between labor and management in order to highlight the extent to which scales are tipped in the favor of management and the degree to which the enterprise union has lost nearly all its bargaining power. Here again, the emphasis is on placing the analysis of the present situation within an historical context.

In considering the potential of the Japanese union movement to revitalize itself, reference is made to the likelihood that unions will (i) actively involve unionists in the affairs of the union, (ii) achieve and maintain a balance of power with management, and (iii) improve the working conditions of union members through negotiations with management. The five chapters in Part Three concern themselves with the third topic for research listed above. Here attention is given to current developments over the past decade or so, in particular two trends. One is the growing importance of the minority unions (*shōsūha kumiai*) at firms where two or more unions coexist. The second is the emergence of the new-type unions (*shingata rōdō kumiai*) which are being formed by previously unorganized workers. The examination of these two new forms of unionism are then used as a basis for speculating about the future of the labor union movement in Japan toward the end of the century.

PART ONE

A THEORETICAL STARTING POINT

2 Common Theories of the Enterprise Union

Most researchers dealing with Japanese labor unions have been economists. A close examination of their work reveals four concerns. The first is with identifying the structural peculiarities which characterize union organization in Japan (*soshiki keitai ron*). Second is with accounting for the emergence of those peculiarities (*keisei yōin ron*). Third is with the extent to which certain features of Japanese labor unions in the postwar period may be understood as being carry-overs from the prewar union movement (*renzokusei ron*). Fourth is a concern with how Japanese labor unions function (*kumiai kinō ron*).

The answers to these kinds of questions have varied over time. Table 2.1 indicates how the answers to these questions have changed in each of four periods corresponding roughly to those discussed above in Chapter 1 (cf. Table 1.1). The views of the major scholars associated with each period are briefly discussed in this chapter.

I The 1950s: The Initial Formulation of Ōkōchi's Theory of the Enterprise Union

The first materials on the postwar union movement in Japan were published in 1950 by the Social Science Research Institute affiliated with the University of Tokyo (Tokyo Daigaku Shakai Kagaku Kenkyujo). Based on survey data, the report contained a basic overview of the four areas just mentioned. The survey results were published in a separate volume edited by Ōkōchi (1956), a scholar who stated his views about the enterprise union in numerous publications.

With regard to peculiarly Japanese features, Ōkōchi (1956b: 6) writes that the 'enterprise union' is 'a union of all employees within a particular firm who become members of the union

Table 2.1 *An overview of theories of Japan's industrial relations in the postwar period*

Area of concern → / Period and theory →	the 1950s Ōkōchi theory	the 1960s theory of the enterprise union	the 1970s the theory of internal labor markets	the 1980s	Kawanishi's view
(1) Structural peculiarities of Japanese unions	All in one union (*zen-in ikkatsu ka-nyūgata*)	All-in-one union	the theory that all employees are in the same enterprise		(1) part of employees belong to the same enterprise union (2) part of employees belong to competing unions within the same enterprise
(2) Factors accounting for the emergence of peculiarly Japanese organizational forms	migrant worker theory (*dekasegi chinrōdō ron*)	(1) labor movement theory (*undō ron*) (a) Ōtomo Fukuo (b) Takahashi Kō (2) Seniority system theory (*nenkōsei ron*) (a) Fujita Wakao (b) Tsuda Masumi (c) Shirai Taishiro	the theory of internal labor markets		(1) importance of Japanese culture (2) movement theory
(3) Functioning (a) theory of the postwar union movement	feudalistic hangover	real productivity	theory of high economic growth rates	the European-American model	theory of structural contradictions

Table 2.1 *continued*

Area of concern → / Period and theory →	the 1950s Ōkōchi theory	the 1960s theory of the enterprise union	the 1970s the theory of internal labor markets	the 1980s	Kawanishi's view
(b) evaluation	negative	positive/negative	positive	very positive	positive/negative
(c) catalyst	GHQ		OECD	Vogel	
(d) scholars	Ōkōchi Kazuo Sumiya Mikio	Abegglen Matsushima Shizuo Hazama Hiroshi	Taira Kōji Koike Kazuo Shirai Taishiro Kōshiro Kazutoshi		Kawanishi
(4) Origins of Japanese labor unions in postwar Japan	Postwar theory	Postwar theory *sengo ron*	Postwar theory	Postwar theory	Prewar theory

regardless of their status within the firm.' In other words, the enterprise union subsumes various occupational groupings. Ōkōchi emphasizes that all employees at a given firm belong to the same union. He frequently wrote that the enterprise union is almost without exception a union formed by all the enterprise's employees, and that it is not the case that some employees belong to one union and others to another union (e.g., cf. Ōkōchi 1955: 87–8). He also writes that 'the enterprise union refers not only to a situation in which each union is organized at only one enterprise, but to there being a situation in which all "employees" of the firm or enterprise together form the union' (Ōkōchi 1961: 2). This constant insistence on the importance of the 'all-in-one enterprise union' tended to transform a general principle for membership into an unbending 'law.'

With regard to factors leading to the formation of the enterprise union, the points made in the original publication from the Social Science Research Institute were repeated in other contexts. Most immediate was the wretched poverty experienced during the first few years after the war. In such circumstances the most obvious way to ensure survival was to control the resources closest to hand. This was done by forming enterprise-based organizations which could become involved with production control (*seisan kanri*), a step which resulted in the workers and their union taking over an enterprise from its owners and from the management and then assuming responsibility for running all aspects of the enterprise's operations. The idea was that any surplus (profits) generated would be distributed as wages to the employees.

In addition to the postwar poverty, attention was given to the impact of migratory wage labor (*dekasegi-gata chinrōdō*) on the consciousness of the labor force. Ōkōchi argued that Japan's enterprise unions arose out of the special Japanese conditions which seem to have characterized the labor problem in Japan from the Meiji period until the present (Ōkōchi 1952: 7). He referred to this as being the 'special structure of wage labor' in Japan (Ōkōchi 1955: 3), and as being a phenomenon 'which for better or for worse determined the fate of the Japanese economy and which was basic to all labor problems in Japan' (Ōkōchi 1952: 7). It was his view that this peculiarly Japanese form of wage labor gave rise to the enterprise union.

Ōkōchi explained the relationship between the enterprise

union and the *dekasegi*-type labor supply as follows. In England, which is his example of how capitalism developed in its classical form, the supply of labor came largely from the poor urban stratum, with whole families being pushed out of the agricultural villages and into the cities as a result of the enclosure movement in the seventeenth century. In Japan, however, families remained in the rural villages, while individuals left. It was single males, the second and third sons of agricultural households, and young daughters, still to be married, who came to the cities to work leaving behind their families in the rural villages. They were the supply of labour for Japan's growing capitalist economy. They are the workers Ōkōchi referred to as the *dekasegi*-type of wage labor. In his view, this type of labor was an important component in the labor force from the Meiji period up until the late 1950s. For this reason, the position and consciousness of Japan's wage laborers cannot be understood without reference to this basic fact.

Ōkōchi's *dekasegi*-type wage labor remained with 'one foot firmly planted in the agricultural economy' (Ōkōchi 1952: 9), moving back and forth between the factories and the agricultural villages. Accordingly, a stable supply of labor did not accumulate in the urban areas and a 'horizontal' labor market did not develop; instead, workers came to be procured on a firm-by-firm basis. In this way, labor came to be supplied through labor recruiters or other connections of one sort or another. Working conditions varied from worker to worker and from firm to firm. This 'vertical disaggregation' of the labor force by firm was seen as having shaped the workers' consciousness and the structure of labor-management relations, and as having facilitated the development of a 'vertical consciousness.' For this reason, even if labor unions were formed, they existed only at the firm level. In Ōkōchi's view (1952: 14), they would be unable 'to develop horizontal structures which would bridge across firms.' It was in this regard that he referred to 'the strength of the intrinsic tie between the enterprise union and the *dekasegi*-type of wage labor' (Ōkōchi 1955: 99).

Given that view, it was only logical that readers would see in Ōkōchi's writings the argument that the enterprise union was the general form of unionism in both the prewar and the postwar period. This interpretation of Ōkōchi's views became rather widespread in the postwar years. Based on extensive research on the factors accounting for the peculiar dimensions of the 'labor problem' in Japan from the Meiji period onwards, Ōkōchi concluded that the major key to understanding the prevalence of the enterprise union as the major form of union organization in postwar Japan would be found in the existence of the *dekasegi*-type wage labor (Ōkōchi 1952: 141–2). However, his writings contain reference to the Thought Police. For example, he wrote, 'throughout the prewar period, there were times when the labor movement was under the careful surveillance of the Thought Police (*tokkō keisatsu*) and even enterprise unions were not formed' (Ōkōchi 1955: 99). In other words, he was saying that although one might have expected the enterprise union to be formed even in the prewar period, they were in fact not formed. With the Peace Preservation Laws in 1900 and 1925, attempts to provide socialist revolution aimed at overthrowing the social order came to be a serious crime, drawing punishment as severe as the death penalty. Ōkōchi argued that union leaders were not able, therefore, to make any inroads into the large enterprise where the surveillance of the Thought Police was particularly thorough.

Around 1960 Ōkōchi changed his views about the importance of the *dekasegi*-type wage labor. In essence, his attention shifted from the supply side of the labor market to the demand side. In the 1960s he came to emphasize the extent to which management had taken the initiative in establishing practices which would encourage the long-term employment of the most important group of employees. Some time ago Takahashi (1965: 52) noted that this 'redirection of Ōkōchi theory' had occurred in 1963. Although he had shifted his attention to the vertical structure of factory committees (*kōjō iinkai*) and had labeled them the 'forerunner of Japanese-style labor-management relations' (Ōkōchi 1963), he remained committed to the view that enterprise unions did not exist in the prewar period. By 1970 Ōkōchi is writing that 'throughout the prewar period unions were unable to break through the 'iron wall' of the large enterprises and organize themselves' (1970a: 169–70). Accordingly, we can say that Ōkōchi came to take the view that the origins of the enterprise union lie in the postwar period (Ōkōchi 1970b: 353–4).

As for the functioning of the enterprise union, Ōkōchi noticed some of the positive features of the enterprise unions even in the early 1950s. For example, Ōkōchi (1956b: 74) wrote that the enterprise union had both eufunctions and dysfunctions as a labor union, and 'it is now time to think about how the demerits of the system might be converted to advantage.' He mentioned three strengths of the enterprise union. One was its destruction of the status system (*mibunteki chitsujo*) which had existed in the prewar period and continued to be found in the postwar period. Another was the democratization of management (*keiei minshuka*). Third was the effectiveness of enterprise unions in bargaining with management during the period of rapid inflation owing to their ability to coopt employees in key posts within the organization and to obtain accurate information about the firm's generation of profits (Ōkōchi 1956b: 68–70).

However, Ōkōchi's appraisal of the enterprise union changed as the union movement began to stagnate in the 1960s, and the apparent strengths came to be regarded as weaknesses. There seemed at times to be a certain fatalism in his writings, and one can detect a sense of urgency in his pointing to these negative features. He came to refer to the enterprise unions as having a certain 'brittleness,' as facing a 'crisis,' as possessing 'defects,' as suffering from a certain 'fate,' or as being characterized by certain 'limitations.'

For Ōkōchi the greatest shortcoming of the enterprise union was the tendency towards 'enterprise egoism' (*kigyo egoizumu*). In other words, the enterprise union had come to include only regular employees and core factory workers, leaving outside its organization those workers who were employed by other firms in the industry, especially subcontractors. It also excluded employees of the same firm who had been hired on a temporary basis. Rather than incorporating workers and developing a consciousness of workers in the broadest sense, the enterprise unions came to focus their attention on improving the working conditions of the firm's regular employees. Accordingly, the enterprise union came to engage in 'struggles which were aimed solely at securing the employment of the regular long-term career employees. This could be seen in their demands for higher annual wage increases and their opposition to any form of dismissals' (Ōkōchi 1961: 8–9). Although these reservations are clearly stated after the redirection in his original theory, Ōkōchi's ideas about the shortcomings of the enterprise union can be found earlier when he was formulating his theory of the *dekasegi*-type wage labor.

25

To summarize, Ōkōchi stressed that the enterprise union was based on the idea that there would be one union at each firm which included all regular employees, that the enterprise union emerged out of a labor market in which *dekasegi*-type wage labor was an important component, and that the enterprise had certain functional or structural weaknesses. Further, if these structural weaknesses could be understood as being the outcome or dependent variable, the basic independent variables would be the existence of *dekasegi*-type wage labor and management initiatives to introduce personnel policies which would encourage long-term employment among a certain portion of the labor force. The intermediate variable would be the formation of vertically structured union organizations.

II The 1960s: A Theoretical Shift and the Establishment of an Accepted Theory of the Enterprise Union

While Ōkōchi's theory began to be criticized from a number of angles, the enterprise union remained the central concern of those interested in Japanese labor unions, and later research came to focus almost exclusively on that level of Japan's union organization. Moreover, subsequent researchers came to accept Ōkōchi's formulation as to how the enterprise union should be defined. In the paragraphs below, a brief account is given of how that research developed with regard to the other three areas of interest indicated above in Table 2.1.

Ōkōchi's ideas about the origins of the enterprise union came under heavy criticism, and few today would accept his views about the importance of *dekasegi*-type wage labor as the determining factor accounting for the emergence of the enterprise union. One critic was Fujita Wakao (1968a). He argued that there was a labor surplus in the prewar period, and that it was management which could set the conditions according to which labor was hired. He thus emphasized the importance of management's personnel practices, and pointed to the development of the seniority-oriented personnel system as a means by which management sought to establish and to maintain control over its employees (Fujita 1961: 4–34; Ōkōchi, Ujihara and Fujita 1959:

3–57). Although he did not produce empirical evidence that there was a direct link between the seniority-oriented personnel system and the enterprise union, Fujita did develop a logical framework which linked the two. He argued that the introduction of the seniority-oriented personnel system in Japan's large firms at the end of the Meiji period resulted in labor identifying more strongly with their firm, and that their consciousness of the firm as employees tended to be reinforced at the expense of their sense of working-class solidarity. His argument, then, was that enterprise unionism was an easy form of organization for workers to adopt in the postwar period.

From another angle, Hazama (1964) drew attention to the idea that management ethos and worker morale had become intrinsically interwoven. He argued that the ethos of Japan's managerial stratum came to be embodied in its paternalistic ideology (*keiei kazokushugi*), and that personnel practices based on that ideology were readily accepted by Japan's workers who had been imbued with the desire to have the various livelihood guarantees associated with Japan's family system (*ie seido*). This ideology, he reasoned, contributed to raising morale among the workers. However, he did not comment on this form of paternalism as a major variable accounting for the formation of the enterprise union. Thus, while Ōkōchi's theory of the origins of the enterprise union was criticized from a number of perspectives, another theory has not emerged to replace it. That is a task to which our attention will be turned in Chapter 6 of this volume.

Ōkōchi accepted such criticism; as suggested above, from around 1960 he began to emphasize the importance of personnel practices on the supply side and to advocate his 'long-term employment theory' (*chōki koyō ron*). For example, he wrote that 'one of the factors encouraging the formation of the enterprise union is probably the existence of the employment practice of long-term employment which began to appear primarily in the large enterprises from the beginning of the Shōwa period onwards' (Ōkōchi 1961: 13).

For a long time, Ōkōchi's view that the enterprise union was a postwar phenomenon was accepted by all scholars working in the area. As I have summarized elsewhere (Kawanishi 1974), the view was basically that unions in the prewar period had all been horizontally organized whereas the enterprise union did not make

27

its appearance until after the war. However, Komatsu's more recent and very detailed research (1971) on the existence of enterprise unions in the prewar period has tended to undermine that view. Based on his examination of the functions and structure of workers' organizations in the prewar period, Komatsu argued that Japan's unions evolved into vertically structured organizations after the First World War. He cites the appearance of independent enterprise unions (*jishuteki kigyōbetsu kumiai*), company unions (*kaisha kumiai*), company workers' councils (*kaishateki kōjō iinkai*), independent factory committees (*jishuteki kōjō iinkai*), and enterprise branches of the horizontally organized unions (*ōdantekikumiai no kigyōnai shibu*).

In dealing with the role of anarchism as an ideology in the labor movement, Komatsu simply mentions it as an example to be found in the prewar enterprise union. However, Marxism was the main ideology in the prewar union movement, and the question of whether any of the enterprise unions subscribed to that ideology remains a topic for future research. My own research (1974) suggests that many of the prewar enterprise unions, especially those in the public sector and those in large private firms, did subscribe to Marxist ideas. It also suggests that enterprise unionism and industrial unionism often existed side by side in the same industry and in the same firm and that there were often repeated struggles and conflicts between these two forms of unionism. The result was that the tension between the forces for enterprise unionism and those for industrial unionism can be traced into the prewar period.

Ōkōchi's appraisal of the enterprise union's structural weaknesses tended to be accepted throughout the period being discussed, and much discussion has been directed to finding a way to overcome those weaknesses. One can mention the efforts of Ōkōchi and his associates to study empirically the possibility of overcoming those shortcomings by restructuring the enterprise union at the shop level (Ōkōchi, Ujihara and Fujita 1959). They sought to survey the way enterprise unions functioned in a few enterprises in steel, in the private railways, and in coal mining. Enterprises with fairly active unions were selected. Their conclusion was that the union which gave priority to safety, to the control of work loads, and to raised wage rates at the shop level were relatively more successful in organizing the workers and in maintaining their momentum.

To summarize, Ōkōchi's definition of the enterprise union and the weaknesses he uncovered seem to have been pretty much accepted at face value throughout the 1960s. However, Ōkōchi's views about the formation of the enterprise union and its existence exclusively as a postwar phenomenon came under considerable criticism, and other researchers have contributed to our knowledge in these two areas. Nevertheless, while the prewar existence of enterprise unions has been fairly well established beyond doubt, there is still a need for further research on why the enterprise union came into existence. Moreover, as a later chapter in this volume explains, there is also room to question Ōkōchi's views about the nature and functioning of the enterprise union.

III   The 1970s and the 80s: The Enterprise Union on the Ascendancy and Internal Labor Markets

In recent times a new theory of the enterprise union has appeared. Emphasizing the importance of internal labor markets, this view has been put forward by scholars such as Shirai (1980) and Kōshiro (1978). Since Ōkōchi's work, many Japanese scholars in the field have accepted the proposition that the formation of the union movement will be influenced directly by the structure of the labor market. In Ōkōchi's case, the link was between (i) the *dekasegi* type of wage labor and the existence of premodern (*hōkenteki*) company-based labor markets and (ii) the enterprise union. In contrast to his theories, the theory of internal labor market posits (a) that the advanced development of capitalism has, as a global phenomenon, been accompanied by structural changes which have hampered the free movement of labor, and (b) that enterprises have increasingly come to fill their labor requirements by recruiting labor from within their own organization. Not only is this process of the labor market being internalized as a world-wide phenomenon, but with advanced capitalism the organization of labor unions is converging toward becoming enterprise entities.

Within this framework Koike (1977) conducted an international comparative study and concluded that the employee organizations in the advanced economies of Europe and North America were quite similar to the enterprise union. Taira's view (1977) has been that the enterprise union in Japan is most suited to advanced forms of capitalism, and that it would serve as a good model for the other advanced economies as their union structures begin to come into line with the enterprise union. In the view of these scholars, the 'all-employees-together' enterprise union should only become stronger over time, and there is no indication whatsoever that the enterprise union might prove to be unsatisfactory in any way.

The theory of internal labor markets tends to support Ōkōchi's view that the enterprise union incorporates all employees at a given firm. Built into the theory is the idea that higher levels of capitalism will result in global convergence in terms of career employment and seniority wages. These practices, it is argued, will promote the introduction of enterprise unionism (Taira 1977). Applying this theory to Japan, the argument is that the enterprise union in Japan really appeared only in the 1960s during the period of extremely high economic growth. However, there remains the fact that career-employment and the seniority wage system appeared in Japan around the time of the First World War when Japanese capitalism was still in a rather under-developed state (cf. Hazama 1964). It was at that time also that the enterprise union emerged. Those propagating the internal labor market theory have overlooked these facts.

In contrast with Ōkōchi's view, the theory of internal labor markets tends to stress the favorable way in which the enterprise union has functioned. Shirai (1980: 179–91), for example, cites five contributions of the enterprise union to Japan's rapid economic growth. First, being free of the problems of demarcation, the enterprise union is seen as facilitating the introduction of new technologies and as accommodating well to change in the industrial structure. Second, the enterprise union has served well in improving the working conditions of Japan's employees, including better working hours and a nominal wage rate above that found in England, France and Italy. Third, in the aftermath of the 'oil shocks', at a time when the economic growth rates plunged to low levels, enterprise unions were able to come to grips with the situation and the danger of inflation was avoided. Moreover, by cooperating with management to adjust the size of the enterprise's labor force – through such strategies as leaving vacant positions unfilled, recruited retirement, internal rotations, and secondment to other firms – massive unemployment was also avoided. Fourth, the union has played a strong role in expanding the opportunities for participation with regard to decisions affecting working conditions and employment. Fifth, in comparison with the unions in Europe and the United States, Japanese unions had done a much better job of keeping their movement democratic.

In conclusion, we can perhaps conclude that the proponents of the theory of internal labor markets have blurred the distinction between (i) identifying the conditions which facilitated the emergence of the enterprise union, and (ii) evaluating the actual functioning of the unions. There is a tendency in the literature on internal labor markets to overlook problems intrinsic to the enterprise union and to see only its merits. Although we will consider the formation of the enterprise union in more detail in Chapter 6, in the next chapter we shall look more carefully at this question of how to evaluate the enterprise union.

3 Towards a New Theory of the Enterprise Union

I The Question of Organizational Structure

The commonly accepted theories of the enterprise union fall short on several counts. In this chapter some of the difficulties confronting proponents of such theories will be examined.

The most important oversight in many writings on the enterprise union is that no distinction is made among several types of enterprise union. As mentioned above, at least three types exist. They are (i) the enterprise union which incorporates all employees at a single firm, (ii) the enterprise union which shares the employees at a particular firm with one or more other enterprise unions of this type, and (iii) new types of unions. Figure 3.1 gives some idea as to how employees are distributed among these three.

As the figure shows, 70 percent of Japan's employees in the outer ring are not organized in any union. Systematic surveys have not been conducted to provide accurate statistics on the proportion of employees belonging to the various new forms of union organization (Type III). However, rough estimates would suggest that about 60 percent of those in enterprise unions are in an enterprise union which represents all employees in the specific firm at which it is organized (Type I). The other 40 percent are in an enterprise union coexists with one or more other enterprise unions within the same firm (Type II). About 20 percent of the organized employees in the private sector belong to Type II unions, whereas all union members in the public sector belong to Type II enterprise unions.

The first type of union (which incorporates all employees at a single firm) is the most prevalent form of enterprise unionism in Japan's core industries in the private sector. However, the notion that Type I will become even more dominant in the future is misleading. It simply ignores the role and the importance of the second type of enterprise union. Even more telling, the 'new

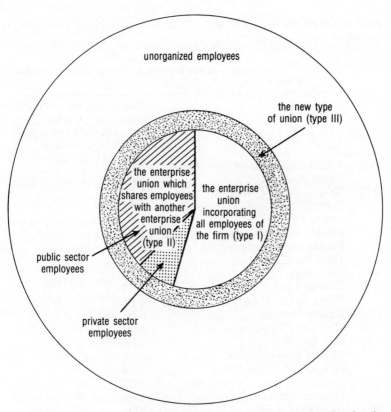

Figure 3.1 *The composition of Japan's labor union membership by the union's organizational type*

type' (Type III) is gradually increasing its numbers. Below a summary of arguments made earlier by Kawanishi (1981) and others is provided.

One conspicious feature of labor unions in postwar Japan is the large number of union schisms (cf. Kawanishi 1977). Table 3.1 provides a list of some of the major schisms. Figure 3.2 is Fujita's diagram showing how the process occurs. In most firms with two or more unions, there is usually a dominant enterprise union (which organizes the majority of the employees at the firm) and one or more minority enterprise unions. However, when schisms have occurred, it has been common for the minority unions to continue existing for a long time afterwards. If this fact were more openly recognized, more attention would be

Enterprise Unionism in Japan

paid in Japan to the existence of the second type of enterprise union.

Table 3.1 *Major labor disputes in the postwar period and the formation of second unions*

Year	Dispute	The emergence of type II enterprise unions (i.e., the occurrence of a split in the type I union
1945	Yomiuri Newspapers (first dispute)	NO
	Keisei Railways	NO
1946	Tōshiba Electric Machine	NO
	Yomiuri Newspapers (second dispute)	YES
	Japan's Seamen's Union	NO
	Electric power industry	NO
	Tōyō Tokei	YES
1948	Tōhō Eiga	YES
1949	Tōshiba Electric Machinery	YES
	Nihon Seikō (Hiroshima factory)	YES
1950	Hitachi Sōrengō	NO
1951	Mitsukoshi Department Store	NO
1952	Ube Kōgyō	YES
	Electric power industry	YES
	Coal Miners Union	YES
1953	Nissan	YES
	Tōhōaen Chemical	YES
1954	Amagasaki Seitetsu	NO
	Ōmi Kenshi	YES
	Employees in the financial sector	YES
	Local bank employees	YES
1955	Nihon Seikō (Muroran Factory)	YES
1956	Nihon Seikō (Akabane Factory)	YES
1958	Ōji Seishi	YES
1959	Shufu to Seikatsusha	YES
	Tanrō (Mitsubishi, Sumitomo, Furukawa and Yūbetsu mines)	YES
	Hokuriku Tetsudō	NO
1960	Mitsui Miike	YES
1961	Hospital employees	YES

Source: The data has been put together from various parts of Ōkōchi and Matsuo (1969 and 1973), Fujita and Shiota (1963) and Kawanishi (1986).

Because examples of the second type of enterprise unionism have largely been ignored, their actual numbers have not been carefully estimated. Nevertheless, if various surveys of the situ-

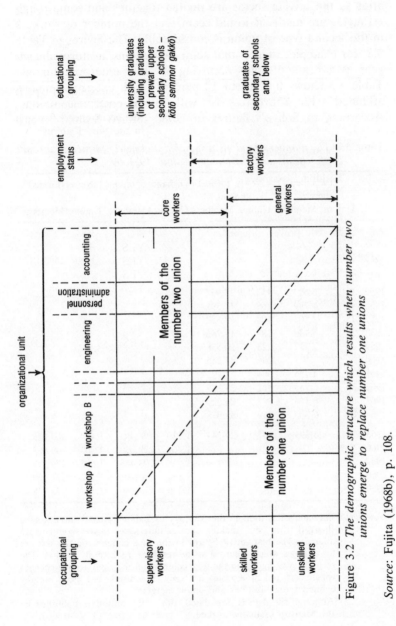

Figure 3.2 *The demographic structure which results when number two unions emerge to replace number one unions*

Source: Fujita (1968b), p. 108.

ation in the private sector are pooled together and some rough estimates are made, it would seem that the number of workers in the second type of union is considerable. The figures in Table 3.2, for example, suggest that some 300 unions are formed each year as a result of splits occurring in other enterprise unions. Table 3.3 shows that about 12 percent of all enterprise unions affiliated with Sōhyō coexist with other enterprise unions. According to Sōhyō's figures for 1980 (Sōhyō Soshiki Kyoku

Table 3.2 *The number of unions disbanded and newly formed as a result of schisms and their membership: 1951–69*

Year	Disbanded unions		Newly formed unions		Disbanded unions		Newly formed unions	
	Unions	Members	Unions	Members	Unions	Members	Unions	Members
1951						960		
1952						497		
1953	79					868		149,913
1954	18	2,433						
1955	16	6,699	152	23,957				
1956	42	4,799	168	17,597				
1957	15	2,104	108	9,552				
1958	26	3,130	189	19,786				
1959	25	3,717	223	20,538				
1960			346	37,255				
1961	37	4,756	304	32,795				
1962	50	5,183	381	35,189				
1963	67	6,134	367	26,529				
1964	89	6,300	459	35,075				
1965	74	5,393	337	29,744	1,619	196,493	1,438	203,623
1966					1,769	229,030	1,700	249,082
1967					1,638	293,443	1,582	279,548
1968					1,144	170,901	1,137	171,260
1969					1,156	273,206	1,197	272,938

Notes: (1) The categories used in the Ministry of Labor's annual surveys have changed over time, making careful time-series figures comparisons difficult. The first set of figures in the four columns on the left are for changes which occurred as the result of a schism in a union. The second set of figures in the four columns on the right are for changes which occurred as a result not only of schisms, but more broadly defined reorganizations and union mergers.

(2) Although the data is now dated, this is the only data published by the Ministry of Labor to date.

Source: Rōdō Shō (Ministry of Labor), *Rōdō Kumiai Kihon Chōsa Tōkei* (Statistics from the Basic Survey of Trade Unions), from the annual reports.

1982: 32–5), 768 type II enterprise unions were affiliated with Sōhyō. Although more recent figures are not available, Nikkeiren's figures for the same year show that 15.1 percent of the firms affiliated with it had two or more enterprise unions. The figures in Table 3.4 show for an extended period of time that consistently about 40 percent of the disputes dealt with by the Central Labor Relations Commission (Chūō Rōdō Iinkai) have involved the second type of enterprise union.

Table 3.3 *The number of 'coexisting unions' (type II unions) affiliated with Sōhyō by industrial federation: 1976*

Industrial federation	Number of affiliated enterprises unions (A)	Number of affiliates which are type II enterprise unions (B)	Percentage 100 × B/A
Zenkoku Kinzoku	1,300	130	10
Kagaku Dōmei	130	35	27
Shitetsu Sōren	243	20	8
Kamipa Rōren	116	8	7
Gōka Rōren	128	25	20
Zenzōsen	35	11	31
Zendenryoku	3	3	100
Total	1,955	232	12

Source: This data was collected by the author in a series of interviews and questionnaires which were administered in 1976. A fuller explanation of the data is given in Kawanishi (1977), Chapter 3, p. 78.

These facts suggest that the second type of enterprise union is not insignificant in the private sector. If we consider the public sector, the case is even clearer. Employees of the Japan National Railways have been organized by six unions;[1] postal workers, by four unions; and teachers in the nation's public schools, by five unions. Nearly every area of employment in the public sector is organized by the second type of enterprise union. Because employees in the public sector account for about 30 percent of all organized employees in Japan, a rough estimate of the percentage of union members in the second type of enterprise union would be about 40 percent. The figure is not negligible, and it is for this reason that any attempt to portray the union movement by referring only to the first type of enterprise union would be seriously misleading.

Table 3.4 *Tabulations on the union background of disputes handled by the Central Labor Relations Commission in the private sector*

Year	A Total number of disputes handled by the Central Labor Relations Commission	B Disputes in firms with two or more enterprise unions	Percentage 100 × B/A
1967	509	219	43.0
1968	503	212	42.1
1969	489	229	46.8
1970	513	236	46.0
1971	495	219	44.2
1972	650	307	47.2
1973	564	244	43.3
1974	625	263	42.1
1975	745	268	36.0
1976	675	228	33.8
1977	615	213	34.6
1978	634	262	41.3
1979	529	222	42.0
1980	474	193	40.7
1981	540	197	36.5
1982	524	183	34.9
1983	483	177	36.7
1984	402	165	41.0
1985	405	134	33.1
Yearly average	546	220	40.1

Source: Chūō Rōdō Iinkai (Central Labor Relations Commission), *Rōdō Iinkai Nenpō* (Year Book of the Central Labor Relations Commission), as reported in the annual volumes.

A full reappraisal of the union movement in Japan must consider the newly emerging third type of union. This type of unionism is particularly noticeable among workers in the medium-sized and small firms and includes unions organized on various principles (cf. Kawanishi 1981). Some are organized on an occupational basis and others on the basis of employment status. There are unions for temporary workers (*rinjikō*), for part-time employees (*pāto-taima*), and for the unemployed. Still others are organized according to personal characteristics which set their members off in the labor market. Examples include a women workers' union, a union for physically handicapped workers and a union for middle-aged workers. The principle of organization and the interests which they pursue supercede the individual enterprise. In many cases the driving force can be found in the reaction against the prevailing ideology in the enterprise unions which has tended to close off the enterprise union as an elitist organization working for a small group of privileged employees but discriminating against those who have joined the third type of union. These are the peripheral workers concentrated in Japan's smaller firms or in non-permanent positions within the large firms. In other words, these unions have been formed as a reaction against the 'elite' in the labor force – male employees who have permanent or regular employment status in Japan's large firms in the private sector. The elite type of enterprise union, which accounts for the largest number of union members, excludes many workers who are not unionized at all. The declining organization rates for the unions in general reflects the declining rates for the type I union. This is because it excludes part-timers, subcontractors and other casual employees who are increasing as a proportion of the labor force owing to structural changes in the economy. Accordingly, it appears that the new unions are responding to a need which previously unorganized workers have felt. If this analysis is correct, there is considerable room for type III unions to organize whereas the type I union has already organized all the elite workers and there is little leeway for it to expand.

For these reasons, the commonly accepted concept of the enterprise union has limited utility as a heuristic device for understanding the union situation in Japan. On this point, it is interesting to observe Kōshiro's estimates (1982: 36) that only about 3,980,000 employees (one fourth of all employees) are (i) in the large firms listed on either the upper or lower sections of the Tokyo Stock Market, (ii) in the national or local public services, or (iii) in medium-sized and smaller firms which can be said to have a reputable standing. For these reasons, it is extremely misleading to generalize from the experience of type I unions about Japanese unionism as a whole.

II Union Functions

Most writings on the enterprise union emphasize the eufunctions which type I unions perform. However, a close look at those writings reveals that few provide any evidence for the claim that such unions perform useful functions for their members. An examination of the realities clearly shows that the type I enterprise union functions in a manner which is very different from the picture presented in the idealized accounts.

There are some limited studies of the enterprise union and its functioning in some of Japan's largest firms in a few industries central to Japan's postwar industrialization and rapid economic growth. The industries include automobiles (Yamamoto 1981), steel (Matsuzaki 1982), steel and telecommunications (Inagami 1981), and electrical machinery and chemicals (Kawanishi 1981). Inagami is the only scholar among those mentioned who has favorably evaluated the enterprise union. However, it should be noted that Inagami's study was based wholly on questionnaire surveys which are a fairly simplistic way of trying to assess the situation and the consciousness of workers. The carefully conducted studies by the other three authors who used participant observation and other qualitative techniques have provided much more careful analyses of the situation and have not led their authors to draw favorable conclusions about the functioning of the enterprise union. The three careful studies provide information about the functioning of the enterprise union in four areas: wages, employment, hours of work and personnel practices. In the subsections below, I wish to introduce briefly some of those findings.

A Wages

The contribution of the enterprise union to its members achieving a higher wage income can be considered in terms of the rate of increase in wage levels and the overall trends in labor's share. In doing this, it is useful to refer to Table 3.5.

1 The rate of increase in wage income Although the level of wages has steadily risen in postwar Japan there is no apparent relationship between the rate at which wages have increased and the presence of the enterprise union. Although too many factors are involved for firm conclusions to be drawn, the data in Table 3.5 suggest that the highest rate of increase were not registered during the decade after 1955 when the enterprise unions in Japan's major manufacturing industries were coming into their prime. Moreover, the relative absence of the enterprise union in the first period did not preclude sizeable wage hikes which averaged 13.8 percent annually in nominal terms.

Table 3.5 *Labor's share, increases in productivity and increases in wage rates: 1951–79*

Specifics of the sample	Variable	Period					
		I 1951–1954	II 1955–1959	1960–1964	III 1965–1969	1970–1973	IV 1974–1979
employees in firms with 1000 or more employees	(1) labor's share	39.1	37.6	31.4	31.7	32.9	38.3
	(2) annual rate of increase in labor productivity as measured by value added	12.0	9.5	10.1	13.4	7.0	4.9
	(3) annual rate of increase in average cash wages	13.8	5.4	8.3	10.6	11.5	5.8
employees at a specific automobile manufacturer	(1) labor's share	70.5	38.4	20.9	30.4	37.9	55.2

Note: Labor's share = $\dfrac{\text{Cash wage payments to employees}}{\text{value added (profits + cash wage payments)}}$

Sources: Yamamoto (1982), p. 114.
Yamamoto (1981), p. 17.

The need for more research is obvious. On the other hand, one could argue that it became increasingly difficult to achieve further improvements in the living standard over time, and that the smaller rates of increase became more significant over time. It is also true that the rate of increase was more pronounced in the late 1960s when the enterprise unions were more entrenched.

Finally, it must be pointed out that the rates of increase that were achieved were greater than those in similarly advanced countries. Nevertheless, a more careful study taking into consideration the rate of inflation and inter-industry differentials must be undertaken before we can conclude that the enterprise union has accounted for the growth in Japan's wage levels.

2   Labor's share   The figures in Table 3.5 suggest that labor's share declines during the period of rapid economic growth in the 1960s and then rises again in the 1970s as the economic growth rate slows down. It is important to note here that the processes affecting the distribution of income seem to be fairly universal; they are found in other economies and cannot be linked in time series data with the changes in the influence of the enterprise union.

These general conclusions are firmly supported by Yamamoto's findings for the Nissan Automobile Company. It seems to be highest in the first period, but then dropped considerably as a more conservative 'number two union' came to replace the more radical unions and the 'ideal type' of enterprise union began to emerge. Of course the very low 20.9 percent for the early 1960s in part reflects the tremendous increases in capital investment which have been crucial in raising productivity in the automobile industry. Yamamoto (1981: 17) estimates that productivity rose over an eighteen-year period at an average annual rate of 15.6 percent and gross profits rose 24.6 percent, while the workers' real wages rose only 4.5 percent. These figures suggest that it is difficult to argue that the enterprise union developed a strong bargaining position with regard to the division of the additional surplus generated by improved productivity.

3   Summary   The preceding discussion suggests that we do not as yet have sufficient data to support the argument that the enterprise union was the key variable accounting for the increased wage levels of the Japanese employee whom they represented. It is more likely that the rise in the absolute wage rates reflected the increase in the size of the pie owing to other factors, and that the increase of labor's share obtained in the 1970s reflected the labor shortage. In the period of low economic growth rates, there are numerous other reasons for believing that the bargaining power of the enterprise union was not all that great.

B   The maintenance and expansion of employment
    opportunities

The problems of elitism and the weakness of the enterprise
union become more obvious when the matter of employment
is considered. Two issues in particular highlight the difficulties
confronting the enterprise union. One concerns those who are
excluded from membership and the other is the inability of the
enterprise union to deal with the retrenchment of employees
which has accompanied management in most large firms.

1   Rinjikō and the subcontractors   Although the period of
high economic growth resulted in higher levels of employment
and many new jobs being created, the distribution of jobs by
employment status changed. It is hard to attribute to the enterprise union jobs which are created either for non-unionized
workers being employed by subcontractors or for temporary
workers who were excluded from joining the enterprise union. To
do so we would need to argue that the jobs of a small aristocracy
of labor were being protected at the expense of others in the
economy, that by limiting the number of highly paying jobs the
union was contributing to the creation of many poorly paid jobs
for the rest of the population.

On this point some data is presented in Tables 3.6 and 3.7 for
the major industries which were the backbone of Japan's 'economic miracle' – automobiles, shipbuilding, steel and chemicals.
The tables show clearly that in three of the four industries most
of the expansion in employment occurred in the form of more
temporary workers and subcontracted workers. The only exception was chemicals. The increase in the employment levels for
regular workers (*honkō*) was rather small. Particularly noticeable
is the increase of temporary workers in the automobile industry
and of subcontractors in shipbuilding.

The figures presented in the two tables are for the early period
of rapid growth. To be sure, in the late 1960s and early 1970s
there was a decline in the number of peripheral workers, and
many temporary workers were given status as regular employees.
However, by that stage it seems likely that employers were motivated to move in that direction more by the labor shortage than
by union pressure. Thus, leading up to the first oil shock in the

Table 3.6 *Index of employment levels in four key industries from the early 1950s to the early 1960s (employment levels in 1952–4 = 100)*

Industry and employment status	Period I 1952–4	Period II 1955–9	1960–2
Automobile industry			
Regular workers	100	99	125
Temporary workers	100	307	487
Total	100	109	174
Shipbuilding industry			
Regular workers	100	101	104
Temporary workers	100	187	124
Subcontracted workers	100	236	237
Total	100	126	123
Steel industry			
Regular workers	100	102	133
Temporary and daily workers	100	129	163
Total	100	105	136
Chemical industry			
Regular workers	100	131	136
Temporary workers	100	95	45
Total	100	125	112

Source: The above figures have been taken and rearranged by the author from Yamamoto (1967), pp. 72–3.

mid–1970s it is difficult to identify a clear-cut employment effect which can be attributed to the unions.

2 Downward adjustments in employment levels When the economy faced recession following the oil shock, rather than protecting employment levels, the enterprise union cooperated with management in the implementation of policies to cut personnel levels. As Table 3.8 shows, between 1974 and 1980, many persons in the shipbuilding industry were laid off. White-collar employees were reduced by 30.6 percent, regular factory workers by 36.7 percent, temporary workers by 44.0 percent and subcontractors by 52.8 percent. In each firm, the minority union (usually Sōhyō affiliated) sought to resist such moves, but the dominant enterprise union (usually Dōmei affiliated) went along with the plans handed down by management. Some of the dominant unions even took the initiative in proposing such reductions.

Table 3.7 *The percentage composition of the labor force in four key industries: 1960–2*

Industry	Regular workers	Temporary workers	Sub-contracted workers	Total (numbers)
Automobiles	63.3	36.7		100.0 (36,312)
Shipbuilding	66.8	8.5	24.8	100.0 (107,404)
Steel	87.2	12.8		100.0 (204,572)
Chemicals	93.9	6.1		(100.0 (36,946)

Source: Taken and rearranged by the author from Yamamoto (1967), pp. 72–3.

One example would be Sumitomo Heavy Machinery. With 12,409 employees and an enterprise union in 1977, it was able to reduce employment levels by 31.3 percent (3879 persons) over the succeeding two-year period (Kamata 1980: 202). During two years from 1977 the six major firms in the shipbuilding industry reduced their employment levels 22.7 percent from a level of 44,259 in 1977. Sumitomo prepared a set of criteria for laying persons off; priority was given to the release of (i) older

Table 3.8 *Changes in the number of persons employed in the shipbuilding industry by employment status: 1974 and 1980*

Employment status	Number of employees 1974 (A)	1980 (B)	Number of laid-off workers (A-B)	The percentage decrease (A-B) (A)
Supervisory personnel	63,148	43,796	19,352	30.6
Regular workers	117,605	74,470	43,135	36.7
Temporary workers	3,445	1,928	1,517	44.0
Subcontract workers	89,706	42,386	47,320	52.8
Total	273,904	162,580	111,324	40.6

Source: Zennihon Zōsen Kikai Rōdō Kumiai (1981), from p. 74 onwards. The data was originally taken from *Kaiji Tōkei Geppō* (the Monthly Report of Maritime Statistics) and *Zōsen Kikai Tōkei Geppō* (Monthly Report on Shipbuilding and Related Equipment) which are published by the Un-yu Shō (the Ministry of Transportation).

employees, (ii) those who had a spouse also working in the same firm, and (iii) union activists. In particular, seventeen members of the minority Sōhyō-affiliated union were singled out to head the list of those to be fired. The majority Dōmei-affiliated union willingly went along with management's plans. In fact, to pressure some employees into leaving, some of the union's members participated with management in harassing 54 workers who had resisted dismissal and had tried to remain on the shop floor (Kamata 1980: 120–1).[2]

This kind of behavior on the part of the enterprise union has not been limited to the shipbuilding industry. In 1978 Oki Denki (Oki Electrical) fired 93 of its 13,000 employees for political reasons (cf. Nakayama 1987; Kenmochi 1979: 136–52).[3] They were members of the company's number one union. Those fired had been members of the Socialist and Communist Parties or otherwise associated with the 'new left'. That was the first red purge in twenty years, the last having been in 1960 with the Mitsui Miike coal miners' struggle. The majority enterprise union did not resist these dismissals, and looked on with approval.

C Shorter hours of work

Although hours of work gradually declined in Japan following the period of high economic growth as the two-day weekend began to be introduced, it is important to note that they actually rose during the period of rapid economic growth. The failure of the enterprise union in shortening hours of work becomes clear if we examine the processes by which hours have been shortened (i.e., the introduction of the two-day weekend), the union position on overtime, and the findings of several case studies.

1 The two-day weekend In considering the motivation behind the introduction of the two-day weekend, it is important to recognize that management gave up nothing. The findings of one survey on the goals of management in introducing the two-day weekend, taken by the Ministry of Labor in the early 1970s, are presented in Table 3.9. Among the six considerations raised in the survey, the only one which seems to reflect union bargaining power is that given in column C. Only 11.8 percent of the firms

Table 3.9 *The goals to be achieved by introducing the two-day weekend (unit: percentage of firms)*

Size of enterprise (number of employees)	Lower rates of absenteeism	Higher productivity	The distribution of benefits of higher productivity	Increased safety at work	Improved health among employees and more leisure for employees	Less time spent commuting
TOTAL for all firms	26.9	35.3	11.8	48.5	76.6	2.1
5,000+	13.2	40.7	20.4	41.9	86.2	3.0
1,000–4,999	19.2	42.5	13.7	42.5	85.1	4.6
500–999	22.7	40.9	13.6	42.7	76.8	3.6
300–499	32.6	41.3	14.1	44.6	77.2	5.4
1–299	30.0	32.1	10.2	51.5	73.5	1.0

Notes: (1) Because multiple answers were accepted, the totals do not equal 100.0.
(2) The percentage of firms giving other goals as an answer was no more than 8.6 percent for any of the firm-size groupings.
(3) The percentage of firms answering 'unclear' or 'not known' was no more than 1.8 percent for any of the firm-size groupings.
Source: Rōdō Shō (Ministry of Labor), *Shūkyū Futsukasei Jittai Chōsa* (Survey of the Actual Situation Regarding the Two-Day Weekend) (Tokyo: Rōdō Shō, 1973).

claimed that the introduction of the two-day weekend was aimed at sharing increases in productivity with employees (although one could argue that consideration seems to have been more pronounced in the largest firms where the unionization rate would have been highest). The other reasons, which were mentioned much more frequently, were clearly related to management's attempts to raise productivity or to secure labor (at a time when the labor shortages were most seriously felt).

2 Overtime Although there has been a reduction of the standard workweek over time, management has been able to offset the loss of hours worked as part of the normal day simply by increasing the number of hours worked as overtime. In manufacturing as a whole, the monthly average number of hours of overtime between 1950 and 1963 was 18. The average for chemicals was 12; for automobiles and electric machinery, 17; for steel, 25; and for shipbuilding, 30 (Yamamoto 1982: 237–40).

In Japan the Labor Standards Law has provided for an ordinary workweek with a maximum of 48 hours, and for labor and management to negotiate a shorter week if they wish to do so. However, the law also allows for labor and management to negotiate concerning the conditions under which any overtime will be worked, stipulating only that overtime will attract a minimum premium of 25 percent (Article 36). Given the general weakness of the enterprise union, however, the premium is seldom set above the 25 percent minimum required by law, and management can fairly freely impose upon employees to work longer hours. The law does not restrict the number of hours of overtime which management can ask employees to work.

The problem of working hours becomes even clearer if international comparisons are made. As Table 3.10 indicates, Japan compares poorly on all measures related to hours of work.

3 Some case studies A detailed study of the steel industry by Matsuzaki (1982) lends support to the argument that enterprise unions have not done much to lessen the workload of their members. In 1970 Japan's major steel firms altered the shift system which had been followed for some fifty years. Three shifts came to be manned by four teams instead of three. The unions boasted that this was the result of their bargaining power, and observed

Table 3.10 *International comparisons of the annual hours of work of production workers in manufacturing: 1983*

Variable	Unit of com- parison	Japan	United States	England	West Germany	France	Italy
A Total hours worked (B+C)	hours	2152	1898	1938	1613	1657	1622
B Standard hours of work	hours	1950	1742	1798	1535	1579	1577
C Overtime	hours	202	156	140	78	78	45
D Regular days off during the week	days	83.8	104.0	104.0	104.0	103.3	104.0
E Other days off during the year	days	18.1	9.1	8.0	9.9	7.9	10.0
F Days off on annual holidays	days	9.7	19.4	22.5	30.9	25.9	20.0
G Other days away from work	days	4.2	8.3	-	20.5	19.1	21.0

Source: Figures produced by Japan's Ministry of Labor which were published in *Asahi Shinbun* (April 22, 1986).

that the change would result in an additional fifteen days off for its members, thereby lowering fatigue levels. Other things being equal, a decrease in hours of work would obviously result in a rise in labor costs in order that the same production target be achieved. However, Matsuzaki's analysis reveals that management offset these costs by intensifying the work load.

One piece of evidence he presents concerns the staffing levels for each shift. In order to have the fourth team of workers while retaining the same work loads, he argues that the number of workers should have been increased by one third. Table 3.11 gives the data for Japan's largest and technologically most advanced plant belonging to a steel company with 40,477 employees. Although an additional 1813 persons (33.3 percent of 5438) should have been hired to set up the fourth team, in fact only 246 workers were hired, an increase of 4.5 percent. In making the changes, management took considerable pains to see how the work could be reorganized in order to lower the number of persons who were necessary. One measure was automation. Another was lowering the standard number of workers from the number required at peak production times to the average number required for the entire shift. A third was to reduce the number of employees at places of work where output had gone down. Other workers were removed by reorganizing the work groups, by increasing the frequency of certain operations, and by sending some work outside to subcontractors. The end result was that work loads were intensified.

Table 3.11 *Changes in the size of the labor force and shift teams as a result of introducing a fourth shift team (unit: number of workers at work during a single shift)*

	(A) The old shift system	(B) The new shift system	(C) (B)-(A)
Number of workers on the shift team	4,464	5,124	+660
Number of workers on the 'meal-time team'	201	96	−105
Additional reserve of replacement	608	278	−330
(Foremen)	(628)	(734)	(+106)
Chief workers	165	186	+21
Total number of employees	5,438	5,684	+246

Source: Matsuzaki (1982), p. 221.

When three work teams manned the three shifts, there had also been a small team of workers to keep operations going during meal times. The size of this team was greatly reduced. In order to keep the mills running 24 hours a day in the steel industry, a shift team was divided into six subgroups which rotated in taking a 45-minute meal break. It had been the practice to use the following formula to calculate the number of additional persons (the meal-time team) which were necessary to continue operations.

A	B	C	D
the size of the meal-time team	number of persons on the regular shift	$\dfrac{1}{\text{number of meal rotations}}$	number of teams

with = and × signs: $\text{A} = \text{B} \times \text{C} \times \text{D}$

Using this formula, management was able to reduce the size of the meal-time replacement team (i) by dividing the shift team into eight subgroups rather than six and (ii) by reducing the meal time from 45 to 25 minutes.

Finally, a number of innovations were introduced to ensure that labor productivity increased during the time that employees were 'on the job.' The total time to be spent on breaks was reduced from 60 to 45 minutes. The amount of overlap time at the beginning (10 minutes) and the end (5 minutes) had previously been part of the regular hours of work. Under the new arrangements the overlap time came to be part of overtime (with pay at the overtime rate as a kind of compensation), but management required workers to make the changeover from one shift to another within the ordinary hours of work, and the responsibility for recording hours of work was shifted from the office to the shop floor. Also, management began to stipulate that workers would have to take their paid holidays not at a time they wanted, but at a time which would be set according to a plan devised by the company. This allowed management to spread out the leave and lower the number of reserve workers it needed to relieve vacationing workers. In essence, this meant that workers were being coerced to give up the freedom of choosing when to take their paid holiday leave, and that they were having to take on the work load normally carried by their fellow workmates whenever they went on leave.

As a result of these various measures, weekly hours of work were officially cut by 64 minutes, a reduction of 41 hours 45 minutes per year. This reduction in hours of work was much less than half of the reduction of 98 hours demanded by the union.

4 Summary Matsuzaki's study of the steel industry shows how established customs and practices with regard to hours of work were changed, and how a certain price was extracted from the employees in exchange for shorter hours of work. By giving workers shorter hours of work, management was able to develop a technique for intensifying the work load. Rather than relaxing the overall work load, the control over work was increased and the work experience only became less pleasant. The international competitiveness of Japan's steel industry needs to be understood in light of the system of labor-management relations which made this intensification of work possible. The enterprise union must, in the end, bear some of the responsibility for the introduction of this kind of system.

D   The enterprise union as an arm of management

The most significant deficiency of the enterprise union is the extent to which it has become a kind of extra-managerial body which assists management in the implementation of its personnel policies.[4] Two issues in particular require attention. One is the shop-floor organization of the enterprise union and its relationship to the institutionalization of a system of joint labor-management consultations (*rōshi kyōgisei*); the other concerns democracy.

1   Labor-management   consultations   and   shop-floor organization   A system of joint consultations between labor and management began to develop between the second union and management in the early 1960s. Although reference is made to 'the system of joint consultations,' in fact there were many systems and the term 'system' has come to refer to a general relationship between labor and management in which the emphasis was on cooperative arrangements. As Mitsufuji (1965), Nakayama (1974) and Rōdo Shō (1973) have noted, there is a great variety of possible ways in which cooperative relations developed. Leftist unions in general and less-conservative minority unions in particular (who did not participate in consultations) have been critical of that approach, often referring to it as 'cooptation' rather than 'cooperation'.

The following account of labor-management consultations on the shop floor is taken from Kawanishi's study (1981: 113–55) of the Hitachi Electric Company, a large electrical goods manufacturer with about 65,000 employees. The major thrust of the firm's personnel policies was to organize the worker's life in a way which would reconstitute, even if in an artificial way, a sense of belonging to a *gemeinschaft*-type community and thereby produce a fuller sense of commitment to the firm than would otherwise have existed. In order to implement its policy, the firm sought to incorporate the union as part of the 'enterprise community,' giving it important functions in the area of personnel administration. To achieve those ends, an elaborate system of joint labor-management consultations was established.

The system allowed for management to take the initiative in informing the union of all management plans and then seeking feedback and approval from the union. The system was conceived so that the union would comment publicly only on the issue of job security and wage rates. The structure provided management with a means of obtaining the union's acquiescence in rationalizing various production processes. The union came to fulfil a managerial decision-making function by being party to an arrangement which was given the appealing label 'workers' participation in management.' The end result was a set of parallel structures for implementing policies designed to raise the productivity of the workers.

The organizational structure which emerged served as an excellent means of mobilizing union members to support management's schemes for raising productivity. Consideration of the union's activities in two different shop-floor organizational units is instructive. The two are (a) the strongest unit, the electrical workers, and (b) a unit of ordinary strength, the foundry workers.[5] In both cases, the section chief (*kachō*) participated in the selection of the shop stewards (*shokuba yakuin*) to head each work team. Although the section chief was a member of management, his views of the production situation and the political situation outside the firm became important considerations in the selection of the shop-floor stewards. His involvement was informal and came basically in the form of 'suggesting' a 'suitable' candidate. It was common for his nomination to be officially presented to the workshop committee (*kumiai shokuba iinkai*) by the head of that body. A climate in which several persons could easily have been nominated was altered and the election became a mere formality. The final product was a system of self-nomination, and the chain of authority set up by management on its side (i.e., foreman → assistant foreman → ordinary factory worker) tended to be duplicated in the selection of persons to serve as union officials on the shop floor (chairman of the workshop committee, secretary of the workshop committee, and ordinary committee members).

The working of this system can be seen in the handling of grievances. When grievances did arise, it was not uncommon for the shop stewards to take the viewpoint and to have the consciousness of a management supervisor. After all, they were members of management's front-line supervisory staff. Their interest was not in opposing management in order to improve the working conditions of the individual worker. Rather, for better or for worse, they took the narrow view which saw the workers' interests only in terms of whether productivity levels were being improved.

In the case of the electrical workers who probably formed the union's strongest units in the factory, the workers had three major concerns, all related to their hours of work: excessive overtime, their inability to take their annual paid holiday leave freely, and definition of the time set for the various standard production processes. Union representatives at the shop level made the following points in discussing these concerns:

(i) Although the union members at the shop floor were concerned about the hours worked as overtime, which averaged 75 hours per month, the shop stewards did nothing to improve the situation. The head of the *han* committee argued that the system was such that the right to negotiate about such matters rests with the union's executives, and that the union was interested in cooperating with management to raise productivity and was not inclined to confront management on that particular issue.

(ii) With regard to paid annual leave, the shop stewards again looked at the problem from the point of view of management. At the workshop in question, a system of accounting for the actual time worked had been instigated. Each minute was counted and a work-time coefficient (*shūgyōritsu*)[6] was calculated. The total time worked by each employee was calculated down to the last minute; since part of the worker's wage came in the form of a lump sum paid to the team and the calculation of that sum included the relative value of the work-time coefficient attained by each team, the workers were made to compete as teams and any time off – whether for annual paid leave or for sick leave – came to affect the income received by other members of one's team. The shop stewards viewed anyone taking their annual paid leave as simply being lazy.

(iii) The problem of the standard hours of work concerned the assembling of large electric motors, an operation which required the careful attention of the skilled workmen. The time set for completing certain operations was simply not enough for the job to be adequately completed. Because the assembly operation took more time than was allowed, the workers found that their wages were docked. The workers asked their shop stewards to consult with management to set a more reasonable time standard for the assembly operation. Here too, however, the shop stewards tended to show their color as members of the management team. One shop steward even showed up at the shop floor with a stop watch and ordered the union members to perform their tasks 'on schedule.'

(iv) In addition to the points just made, it should be noted that the shop stewards also participated in evaluating the worker's performance as it relates to the setting of his wage rate and to his promotion. However, the shop steward's participation in ranking employees for management flies in the face of the notion of equality which is a fundamental part of union philosophy. Again, although this comment arises from this particular case study, it seems typical of that found in many Japanese firms.

The above findings suggest in the case of Japan's largest manufacturer of electrical goods that the enterprise union was unable to function independently from its role as an administrative arm of management.

2   Union democracy   Yamamoto's study (1981) of Nissan, the large automobile manufacturer, raises further questions about the extent to which the enterprise union is democratically organized. His analysis begins with a distinction being drawn between three types of union officials. The first is the 'career employee' who comes from a prestigious university and has already been singled out for a management position in the future. The second, labeled 'non-career A,' is a graduate of a 'run-of-the-mill' university or even of a high school. This type will eventually be a middle- to lower-level administrator or a technician. The third, referred to as 'non-career B,' will eventually fill supervisory posts (*yakutsu-kekō*) at the lowest level within the factory.

Figure 3.3 shows the composition of the union executive of the company-wide federation in terms of each member's career path and his location within the overall organization. It is readily apparent that most of the top union officials are of the career type. Moreover, most of these career types had worked in the company for about seven years in positions related to personnel affairs.

They would work for several years in the union and then return to the personnel divisions at their respective factories as section chiefs (*kachō*) or even as heads of the divisions themselves (*buchō*). This is possible because each factory has its own personnel division headed by an executive officer in charge of personnel affairs who is complemented by several section chiefs, depending on the size of the factory. It needs to be emphasized that career types are usually responsible for planning and hammering out union policy. Even the head (*kaichō*) of the company-wide federation must thus wear two hats – one as a future member of management and as a union official with a company career, and the other as a representative of the workers and as a member of the union team consisting largely of non-career types.

Although the union's constitution provides for union officials to be elected, the procedure is not really followed. Table 3.12 provides some figures on the election of the union's full-time officials (*jō-nin iin*). The first fact to notice is that the number of candidates is the same as the number of positions. This is because the executive committees do the nominating. An atmosphere is created in which it is very difficult for ordinary members to take the initiative in making their own nominations. Although Japan is famous for the alleged emphasis on consensus, this finding is extraordinary from the point of view of union democracy. The fact is that the balloting is not done in secret. Yamamoto reports that both management and union officers supervise the voting and that dissenting ballots are even inspected to determine the handwriting of the voter in question. The result is that union members have neither the right not to vote nor the right to cast dissenting ballots.

Yamamoto's careful case study provides us with an example of how management has stepped in to appropriate the leadership positions in the union. Most of the important positions are filled by career types who are extremely thorough in their control of union affairs. Although the end result has been higher levels of productivity, the improved ability of many firms to compete in international markets cannot be understood apart from their involvement in the enterprise union and its loss of autonomy in many spheres of activity.

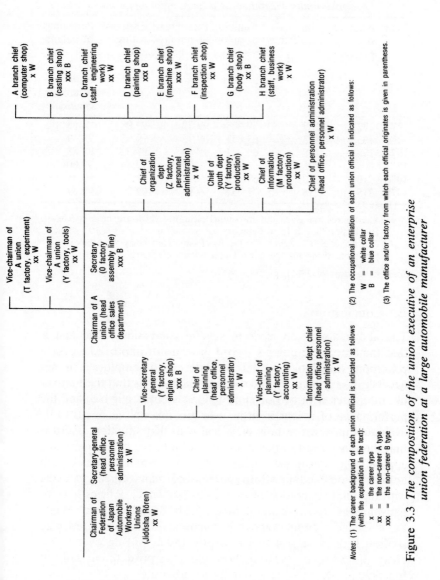

Figure 3.3 *The composition of the union executive of an enterprise union federation at a large automobile manufacturer*

Source: Yamamoto (1981), p. 223.

Notes: (1) The career background of each union official is indicated as follows (with the explanation in the text):

  x   = the career type
  xx = the non-career A type
  xxx = the non-career B type

(2) The occupational affiliation of each union official is indicated as follows:

  W = white collar
  B = blue collar

(3) The office and/or factory from which each official originates is given in parentheses.

Chairman of Federation of Japan Automobile Workers' Unions (Jidōsha Rōren) xx W

Secretary-general (head office, personnel administration) x W

- **Vice-secretary general** (Y factory, engine shop) xxx B
- **Chief of planning** (head office, personnel administrator) x W
- **Vice-chief of planning** (Y factory, accounting) xx W
- **Information dept chief** (head office personnel administration) x W

Chairman of A union (head office sales department)

- Vice-chairman of A union (T factory, experiment) xx W
- Vice-chairman of A union (Y factory, tools) xx W

Secretary (0 factory assembly line) xxx B

- **Chief of organization dept** (Z factory, personnel administration) x W
- **Chief of youth dept** (Y factory, production) xx W
- **Chief of information** (M factory production) xx W
- **Chief of personnel administration** (head office, personnel administrator) x W

- A branch chief (computer shop) x W
- B branch chief (casting shop) xxx B
- C branch chief (staff, engineering work) xx W
- D branch chief (painting shop) xxx B
- E branch chief (machine shop) xxx W
- F branch chief (inspection shop) xx W
- G branch chief (body shop) xx W
- H branch chief (staff, business work) x W

57

Table 3.12 *Data on the election of full-time union officials in an enter-prise union federation at a large automobile manufacturer*

Year	Number of positions	Number of candidates	Number of union members eligible to vote	Percentage of union members actually voting	Effective voting rate	Percentage of ballots cast received by the winning candidate
1972	182	182	59,908	99.72	99.08	98.58
1973	193	193	63,653	99.75	99.08	98.59
1974	198	198	65,131	99.78	99.32	98.83
1975	205	205	66,115	99.94	99.44	99.00
1976	210	210	67,719	99.97	99.74	99.48
1978	218	218	71,737	99.96	99.90	99.69

Note: The figures are given for the annual elections which are held in August. By-elections are held in February for a small number of seats (about 10); although the figures for the by-elections are not given, they are similar to those for the much larger annual elections.

Source: Yamamoto (1981), p. 237.

E Conclusions

The above discussion leads to several conclusions. The first is that the enterprise union's record in terms of improved working conditions and looking after the interests of employees is not necessarily a good one. The second conclusion is that the number of enterprises with two or more unions is not negligible, and the performance of unions in firms with multiple unions needs to be evaluated in terms of how they deal with that situation. Third is that there is a need to pay more attention to the decision-making apparatus in enterprise unions and to the extent to which such unions become administrative organs of management to assist with the implementation of its various personnel policies – 'company unions' (*goyō kumiai*) in the truly negative sense. While the evidence presented above is patchy and based on a few case studies, it does suggest that in-depth studies will uncover a rich array of examples showing how the enterprise union fails to function in the way made out by its advocates.

III Towards a New Perspective in the Study of Japanese Unions

For the reasons stated above, there is room for skepticism in evaluating the popularly accepted theories of the enterprise union. This is particularly true regarding explanations about its structure and propositions about how it functions. Enterprise unions are not simply unions organizing all the employees at a particular firm. Some enterprise unions are organized in that way, but others organize only a portion of the employees at a particular firm and compete for their membership with one or more other unions. The evidence from case studies lends support to the view that the enterprise union has not been effective (a) in obtaining a larger share of the value added for its members, (b) in negotiating for an easing of the work load of its members, or (c) in improving the ability of its members to participate in decision-making related to the organization of their work.

To move beyond the presently formulated theories, two steps must be taken. One is to pay more attention to the contradictions which are born out of a situation in which three types of unions seem to 'coexist.' Particular attention should be given to the processes of change which affect the relative balance among these types. The second is to face up to the shortcomings of the enterprise union and to differentiate clearly between (i) unions which can satisfactorily perform the functions generally assigned to unions and (ii) unions which cannot do so.

Despite their importance, however, almost no research has been conducted on the multiple enterprise union. There is, of course, the work of Fujita (1955, 1959 and 1968b), but his focus was largely on the sources of union schisms and on the processes whereby number two unions were established. We know very little about what happens to each of the unions after the split, and very little about how they function today.

Following the split and the erosion of support for its views, the number one union has had to struggle to survive. As part of that process, it has had to consider carefully its own short-comings. Having done that, however, it has been able to develop its ability to serve as a 'class-based organization' and has gradually evolved into being a union oriented to the overall needs of workers and their families. For this reason, it has been able to remain true to the principles of the labor movement, principles which have largely been abandoned by the one-firm-one-union type of enterprise union. Their success in doing this has been linked closely with their ability to involve their members in the organization and to reflect fully the consciousness of the members and their families. Moreover, they seem to have a certain appeal to the younger workers who have grown disillusioned with the status-quo oriented unionism of the majority unions. Their appeal lies in the minority union's critical stance toward the number two union, the apparent earnestness which seems to have been born out of its earlier role as a kind of martyr, its ability to incorporate members with a wide variety of value orientations, and its overall vitality. For these reasons, the potential of the minority union to bring about a change in the enterprise union movement deserves special attention.

In the 1950s, when union splits were rampant, the opportunity to establish right-wing number two unions was created. Once the left-wing number one unions had been relegated to the status of being minority unions, many of them threw away their established principles and merged with the number two unions. At that time, the leftist unions had adopted the ideology of the World Federation of Trade Unions which called for a strategy of having a very centralized and hierarchically organized labor union movement, with one enterprise union at each enterprise, one industrial federation in each industry and one national center. The motto was 'unification and solidarity.' It was natural, then, that many of the union leaders adopted the view that schisms in the labor movement would result in the total defeat of the labor movement and that minority unions would have no real future. Those who remained loyal to the minority unions were severely criticized and labeled 'union splitters.'

Once into the 1960s, however, the situation began to change. There were a number of unions which simply refused to go along with the times, and their members made it clear that they intended to continue as a minority union. Moreover, their members came to believe that their type of movement was a meaningful one in terms of the overall situation confronting labor in Japan.

By the 1970s, it had also become clear that some of the number one unions would be able to retain their dominance. Also, some number one unions which had become minority unions were able to reassert themselves and successfully absorb number two unions. Furthermore, a good many young workers who had become disillusioned with the conservative drift of the labor movement as a whole came to embrace the movement of the number one unions quite enthusiastically. Rather than simply becoming alienated and joining the ranks of the apathetic, they took the initiative in setting up their own leftist unions.

By the time Japan was entering the 1980s, the idea of merging with the conservative unions was quite far from the minds of those in the minority unions, and they had become quite committed to the view that their unions fulfilled a useful function for their members and that their unions had an important role to play in the Japanese union movement.

The argument advanced in this chapter is that the minority enterprise union has over time taken on a renewed importance in Japan's key industries and that it now has a unique role to play. The author would also add that the minority union holds one of the keys to the future of the enterprise union movement in many of the large firms which form the backbone of Japan's main industries. This assessment is based on the author's earlier research on enterprise unions (1977 and 1981). It is to that research that our attention is turned in the next four chapters which constitute Part Two of this volume.

PART TWO

THE LIMITATIONS OF THE
ENTERPRISE UNION: THE
DYNAMICS OF ATROPHY

4 A History of Industrial Disputes in Postwar Japan

The chapters in Part Two consider the second set of issues raised above. The discussion begins by considering how the cooperative approach to industrial relations (*kyōchōteki rōshikankei*) actually functions. Chapters 4 through 6 focus on the historical setting and the processes by which the cooperative approach was institutionalized. Chapter 4 provides a brief overview of how that approach to industrial relations was established in postwar Japan. Chapter 5 focuses on the workshop, providing a general discussion with some concrete examples of how that approach was imposed from above by management. Chapter 6 introduces a case study to illustrate how management carefully designed a strategy to break up Japan's militant industrial unions and paved the way for a more cooperative form of unionism based on the independent enterprise union. Chapter 6 argues that the 1952 strike in the electric power industry was a major watershed for the union movement in postwar Japan.

With Chapters 4 through 6 in the background, Chapter 7 examines the balance of power between labor and management. Based on a case study the analysis shows how management has substantially increased its power by gaining control of the shop floor. The lesson is that the enterprise union loses nearly all of its bargaining power when it is coopted on the shop floor. Chapter 7 utilizes field notes from the same factory study which Dore (1973) utilized to write about Japanese industrial relations, but with very different conclusions. Underlying the analysis in Chapter 7 is the argument that specific instances of Japan's industrial relations must be understood within a broader historical context.

I Introduction

The preceding chapter considered several case studies pointing to shortcomings of the enterprise union. These become more obvious if we consider briefly the experience with strikes. The enterprise union's inability to engage successfully in disputative action is one key to understanding its overall weakness. This chapter deals with the union movement in fairly general terms, considering both industrial federations and enterprise unions. To understand a specific dispute in a given firm, it is necessary to place it in the larger context of industrial relations in postwar Japan. One needs to have a time perspective – to see the ebb and the flow in the power relationship between labor and management. Especially important is the long-term decline in the bargaining power and in the solidarity of the union movement as the enterprise union became the dominate form of unionism after the mid-1950s.

To understand the choices unionists are making today, one must begin by studying the larger forces in society which determine parameters at the macro-societal level. The individual worker's decision to join a particular enterprise union in a specific firm needs to be analyzed in terms of conditions which he cannot easily determine. Although the discussion does not go the the next step and analyze the forces which ultimately shape the Japanese economy (e.g., changes in the world economy, the internal dynamics of the Japanese economy, structural forces in Japanese society, and the formation of Japan's industry policies), it does identify the roles played by the main actors. Because labor, management and the government set the tone for Japan's industrial relations in the 1960s, 1970s and 1980s, it is useful to consider the power balance among these actors. This can be done by examining Japan's major industrial disputes during the first three decades after the war.

Industrial disputes (*rōdō sōgi*) often produce social changes which transform social relations at work. They frequently occur when the various contradictions produced by industrial society and the business firm begin to appear in the behavior of the main actors. Although labor disputes emerge from a set of social relations which have evolved out of the past, they often become a major force shaping social relations for the future, sometimes producing completely new relationships and sometimes reinforcing the status quo. Accordingly, we can see in the resolution of social contradictions a certain continuity, a history which links together the past, the present and the future (cf. Kawanishi 1986: 22–6).

From this perspective, industrial disputes may be regarded as the normal state of affairs. Industrial relations without labor disputes are rare even in Japan. It is inevitable that labor-management relations will include the behavior and the sentiments of labor and management, and that they in turn will emerge out of the various strategies which the two parties have institutionalized as a means of resolving those contradictions. Industrial disputes represent one way of dealing with the social contradictions in Japan's economic organizations.

Before proceeding further it should be noted that the term 'labor disputes' (*rōdō sōgi*) is used in Japan when referring to industrial disputes. Use of the term 'labor disputes' continues the prewar practice of referring to work-related problems as part of 'the labor problem' (*rōdō mondai*). In Japan 'labor disputes' have been presented by the government, business and the mass media as something which are caused by the unions. This kind of campaigning to turn public opinion against socialistically inclined unions was particularly obvious from 1981 onwards in the moves to disassemble and privatize the Japan National Railways (JNR). The huge losses of the JNR were attributed to the strike records of the railway unions, to the protection they afforded workers who would not work, and to the unions' failure to cooperate with management in implementing various programs to rationalize the railways' operations. Dissolution and privatization were presented to the Japanese people as a means of solving 'the labor problem' in that sector. The goal was to eliminate illegal strikes and to foster 'responsible unionism.'

The analysis of industrial disputes ought to begin by asking, 'Who has engaged in what disputative action with which objectives in mind?' Three steps are required. First, the principal actors (*shutai*) must be identified. Second, the points of conflict (*sōten*) and the outcome (*kekka*) must be made explicit. Third, careful attention must be paid to the processes (*keika*) by which the conflict develops and is resolved. The importance of identifying the principal actors lies in the fact that unions are not the only party initiating industrial disputes. Management-led disputes include instances where management has fingered certain employees for dismissal, locked employees out of their work place, or refused to bargain collectively with a union. There are also cases where employees independently participate in sabotage, insubordination and sit-ins.

This chapter identifies the principals in Japan's major postwar disputes with attention being given to the overall outcome. The analysis reveals five distinct periods; the major characteristics of each are discussed. The major variable delineating the periods is the power relationship between labor and management. The periods are also defined by the strategic importance of the dispute and by the party who took the initiative.

An initial summary of 23 major disputes between 1945 and 1980 is presented in Table 4.1. The disputes are classified first in terms of where the initiative came from and then in terms of the general objectives which the party initiating the dispute sought to achieve. This resulted in four types of disputes. One type includes disputes in which labor (in the form of a union or some kind of joint struggle committee) took the initiative in trying to obtain higher wages or to restrict a previously recognized right of management. This kind of dispute might be called the 'labor-offensive type' (*rōdōsha kōseigata*). The second type consists of disputes which were initiated by labor to express its dissatisfaction over a perceived deterioration in working conditions as the result of an explicit management policy being introduced. This kind of dispute may be referred to as the 'labor counter-offensive type' (*rōdōsha hankōgata*). A third type consists of disputes in which management takes the initiative by announcing large layoffs (or some other sudden change in the accepted working conditions), and may be labeled the 'management-offensive type' (*keieisha kōseigata*). The fourth type occurs when management tries to regain a prerogative which had been lost to labor. An example would be the management's reassertion of its right to hire or to fire. That might be done by firing all union officials. Such disputes belong to the 'management counter-offensive type' (*keieisha hankōgata*).

Several conclusions can be drawn from Table 4.1. First, with a few exceptions, the disputes won by the unions occurred in the first one or two years after the war. After 1950 the record shows management taking the initiative to restore what was lost during the years immediately after the war. Second, contrary to the suggestion made by the term 'labor dispute,' many of the disputes resulted from action initiated by management. In a number of cases management openly provoked the unions. In half the disputes management successfully took the initiative in regaining its rights (i.e., when making a counter-attack). More-

Table 4.1 Twenty-three major labor disputes in the postwar period by outcome and by the locus of the initiative: 1945–80

Party instigating the dispute	Aim	Outcome won by the labor union	Outcome won by management
the labor union	attack	first Yomiuri dispute (SK) (1945) – A Toshiba dispute (SK) (1946) – B October struggle in Electric Power (Densan) (SK) (1946) – D (1982)	February 1 General Strike (SK) (1947) – C (1949, 1979 and 1981)
	counter-attack	Ōmi Kenshi dispute (Z) (1954) – I anti-rationalization struggle in the JNR (S) (1971) – E (1982) Japan Seamen's Union struggle for human dignity (D) (1972) – F Saseho Shipbuilding dispute (D) (1979–80)	Strike for the Right to Strike (S) (1975) by workers in the public sector – E (1982)
management	attack	struggle against firings in the JNR (SK) (1946) – C (1949, 1979, 1987) Seaman's struggle against firings (SK) (1946) – F	*second Yomiuri dispute (SK) (1946) – A *Tōhō dispute (SK) (1948) – D (1986) *Tōshiba dispute (SK) (1949) – B *dispute over personnel adjustments in the JNR (SK) (1949) – C (1981) *Coal/Electric Power dispute (Densan) (S) (1952) – D (1982a)

69

Table 4.1 *continued*

Party instigating the dispute	Aim	Outcome	
		won by the labor union	won by management
	counter-attack	*Nissan dispute (S) (1953) – G Amagasaki Steel dispute (S) (1954) – H (1973)	Nihon Seikō Muroran dispute (S) (1954) – H (1973) *JNR Niigata dispute (S) (1957) – H (1973) Steel Workers' Federation dispute (S) (1957) – E (1982) *Mitsui Miike Mine dispute (S) (1960) – J *Zeneraru Oil Refinery dispute (C) (1970) – D (1981)

Notes: (1) *　　= dispute resulting in a split in the union
　　　　SK　= Sanbetsu Kaigi
　　　　S　= Sōhyō
　　　　Z　= Zenrō
　　　　X　= Dōmei
　　　　JNR = Japan National Railways
　　　(2) At the end of each entry following the date of the dispute and the dash is a letter indicating one of the sources.

Sources: A Masuyama 1976
　　　B Ishikawa 1986
　　　C Suzuki 1949, 1979, 1981
　　　D Kawanishi 1979b, 1981, 1982a, 1986
　　　E Shimizu 1963, 1982
　　　F Numata and Sasaki 1972
　　　G Saga 1983
　　　H Ōkōchi and Matsuo 1969, 1973
　　　I Takita 1972
　　　J Ōta 1975

over, nearly all of management's counter-offensives resulted in a split in the enterprise's union and in the establishment of more conservative number two unions. An implicit goal of management in those disputes was the destruction of the number one union. In other words, there was a disinclination to recognize the rights of the workers to be represented by a militant union. Few number two unions emerged without the interference of management.

The various case studies show clearly that management took the initiative in carefully developing a comprehensive strategy to undermine socialistically oriented unions. By isolating Japan's more militant unions and winning a number of small but strategically important disputes, management accumulated a certain momentum. After the Densan dispute in 1952 (the topic for discussion in Chapter 6), management began to consolidate its position in the private sector, moving wherever possible to replace socialistically inclined unions with conservative company-oriented enterprise unions. With management having succeeded fairly well in the private sector by the end of the 1960s, the government began to use the same tactics to step up pressure on left-wing unionism in the public sector in the 1970s. The recent dissolution and privatization of the JNR in 1987 marked a major turning point in the public sector. Although the table shows that labor sought to launch a counter-attack of its own in the 1970s, it was unable to turn the tide. Management has had the upper hand in most of Japan's industrial relations since the late 1960s.

Some important differences by national center also deserve attention. In the early years after the war, unions affiliated with Sanbetsu Kaigi, which was inagurated on August 19, 1946, took the initiative with 'labor-offensive' type disputes. However, before long they were on the defensive, becoming involved in disputes which management had initiated to recover ground lost immediately after the war. A study of the disputes at this time reveals how Sanbetsu Kaigi lost the battle with management and thereby its vigor. One can see very little activity on the part of Sanbetsu Kaigi after its fifth national convention in February 1949; it disbanded in February 1958.

In the meantime Sōhyō was formed in July 1950. It soon became the driving force in the Japanese labor movement, coordinating the annual Spring Offensive and dominating even the private sector for a while. However, management's success in fostering number two unions produced a split in the labor movement: Sōhyō continued to dominate in the public sector, but Dōmei came to the fore in the private sector. Unions affiliated with Sōhyō absorbed the brunt of management's counter-offensive, nearly always coming out on the losing end. These loses went hand-in-hand with Sōhyō's deteriorating position in the private sector.

On the other hand, many of the unions affiliated with Dōmei (formed in April 1962) and its predecessor (Zenrō from 1954 to 1962) have engaged in struggles to regain ground lost to management. Their action can be seen as a kind of second labor offensive. And, it should be noted, they have generally been successful. This type of dispute occurred as the result of a build-up of dissatisfaction on the part of workers who felt the pressures of aggressive personnel policies on the part of management. Although they do not have the magnitude of the major disputes shown in Table 4.1, smaller disputes of this type arise frequently in Japan's small and medium-sized firms.

In order to have a better understanding of the 'behind-the-scenes' processes accompanying these shifts, it is useful to discuss the changes which have occurred in each of the five time periods. The periods correspond roughly with those identified by Japan's political and social historians. Although the difficulties of delineating one period from another are obvious as most significant social change occurs gradually over time (cf. Nakayama 1975: 167–75), social scientists have found it useful to symbolize a series of changes by pointing to particular events which seem to have jarred the consciousness of a people. The periodization used below follows in that tradition.

II   The Period of Upheaval: 1945–50

The first period lies between the end of the war and the outbreak of hostilities in Korea. It was a period of struggle between the forces which wanted Japan rebuilt as a capitalist society and those which pushed for the reconstruction of Japan along socialist lines. The development in Korea seemed to inject a sense of urgency and crisis into the Occupation's policy which was reflected in an increased readiness to maneuver in a way that was advantageous to the forces for capitalism. The red purge in the late 1940s and early 1950s was one indication of that readiness.

The postwar years were a period of great social unrest. With many social changes being imposed upon Japan by the Occupation, it was a period when the main social actors in the industrial arena competed with each other to gain the political initiative. The prewar power bases of the establishment had been seriously weakened by the war and by postwar reforms. While it was clearly on the defensive and could do little more than engage in rearguard action, the establishment fought tenaciously as the leftist or anti-establishment forces sought to take as much advantage of the situation as possible.

The first major postwar labor dispute was waged by the workers at the Yomiuri Newspaper Company in October 1945 (Masuyama 1976). The union demanded that those responsible for the war be held to account, that the firm provide relief from starvation and that the firm be democratized. The dispute terminated with a complete victory for the workers. Two techniques were used to appropriate the prerogatives of management: production control (*seisan kanri*) (which called for workers to control editorial policy) and the establishment of a management consultative group (*keiei kyōgikai*). The techniques were soon adopted elsewhere throughout the country. The disputes at Tōshiba in December 1945 and October 1946 were along these lines (Ishikawa 1986). At Tōshiba, through the management consultative group the union was able to have a strong influence over management policy in general and on the setting of working conditions in particular. Dismissals and the redeployment of employees came to require the agreement of the union.

The production control movement spread to workships throughout the country, action was taken to expose persons hoarding goods, people gathered together to organize 'people's food harvests,' and a 'Food May Day' was planned (Ōkōchi and Matsuo 1969: 142–4). The 'people's food harvests' were organized in many localities throughout the country, but the movement reached its culmination on May 12, 1946 when 1000 people in Tokyo's Setagaya Ward marched on the Emperor's palace carrying the Red Flag and demanding that food stored for the royal family be distributed to the people. On Food May Day (May 19) 250,000 people gathered in front of the palace and demanded that the control of food supplies be turned over to the people. They also called for a people's government. The move to set up a peoples' democratic government gained momentum, and a climate emerged which made a (full-scale) revolution a very real possibility (Yamamoto 1977a). Such a revolution would have further weakened the position of the capitalists.

At this juncture, the Japanese government and the Occupation authorities departed from their previous policy. On May 20, 1946 MacArthur issued his statement prohibiting mass demonstrations. On May 31 he ordered the Minister of Welfare to draft legislation for the settlement of labor disputes. On June 13 the government issued a declaration on the maintenance of social order which spelled out steps for dealing with mass demonstrations and indicated that production control would be considered illegal. The second Yomiuri dispute was launched in June 1946 in response to management's firing of six union leaders who were held responsible for the workers' attempt to promote the 'peoples' democracy' by publishing their own paper to criticize the 'democracy from above' approach which seemed to characterize political developments at that time (Masuyama 1976).

In October 1946 the twenty-one industrial federations affiliated with Sanbetsu Kaigi decided to oppose those moves (Masuyama 1976). As a kind of skirmish leading to a much larger showdown, labor was successful in combating the dismissal of 75,000 in the National Railways and 43,000 employees in shipping (Suzuki 1979). The two victories seemed to pave the way for a general strike. However, the leading union in Sanbetsu Kaigi, the Tōshiba Labor Federation, was unable to make any headway with its management (Ishikawa 1986) and the Yomiuri union was badly routed in its second dispute with management. A schism developed in the Yomiuri union which resulted in a number two union being formed (Masuyama 1976). In these circumstances, the unions affiliated with Densan in the electric power industry took the lead, pushing for an age-based wage system in October 1946 and coming out victorious with the famous '*Densangata* wage system' by the end of the year (cf. Ayusawa 1966: 280–4, Kawanishi 1989: 177–9). It seemed that the balance of power had again shifted to labor's favor (Kawanishi 1979b). Pushing this advantage, public sector employees rallied behind workers in the National Railways to develop their own struggle aimed at obtaining their 'right to a minimal livelihood' (*seikatsuken kakutoku tōsō*) (Suzuki 1979).

With this development behind them, the unions decided to launch a general strike the following year. A major objective was to promote the establishment of a peoples' democracy. However, the movement was again set back by MacArthur's order prohibiting the general strike scheduled for February 1. With the cold war developing in the background, the GHQ began to implement a policy in line with the directives of the US Secretary of the Army, and pressure was increased to bring Japan's unions 'into line' (Ōkōchi and Matsuo 1969: 217). It was important that Japan's factories be ready to supply the American army with various goods for its upcoming campaign in Korea. On January 6, 1948 General Royal, Commander of the US Army, referred to Japan as 'the fortress against Communism in Asia' and the need to make Japan into a huge munitions plant for the US forces in Asia (Ōkōchi and Matsuo 1969: 217).

With these developments the power balance shifted yet again, and disputes were touched off by management at Tōhō Motion Pictures (1948), at Tōshiba (1949) (cf. Ishikawa 1986) and at the National Railways (when management began to retrench personnel) (cf. Suzuki 1986). In each of these instances, management took the initiative and labor suffered clear defeats. With the beginning of hostilities in Korea, there came the red purges which were aimed at some 40,000 activists, many of whom filled key leadership posts in all the major industrial federations. As a result, the ability of Sanbetsu Kaigi to function was seriously undermined (Takemae 1982: 340–86). As Japan approached independence in 1952, an era in Japan's industrial relations came to an end.

III The Period of Economic Recovery: 1950–5

The turbulent years immediately after the war saw the power balance swing back and forth several times, but by the end of the period the balance finally came to favor management and the course for the economic recovery seems to have been set.

With the start of the Korean War in 1950 and the signing of the San Francisco Peace Treaty in 1951, Japan's importance for the Western camp in Asia had become clear, and its economic course seemed to be set. Japan was to reindustrialize while the Americans looked after the country's national defense.

Although the balance of power in Japan's industrial relations seemed clearly to have shifted to management, the political scene remained somewhat confused. The conservative camp was divided into the Jiyūtō (the Liberal Party) and the Minshutō (the Democratic Party). On the other side of the political spectrum, Shakaitō (the Socialist Party) had split as opinion divided over the position the party ought to take with regard to the signing of a peace treaty which did not include all of the belligerents. However, on October 13, 1955 the socialist parties united and the two conservative parties quickly followed suit on November 15. In the same year the Japan Communist Party was able to bring its internal bickering to an end. Finally, in 1955 Japan experienced its first real postwar boom, known as 'the Jimmu Boom'; the infrastructural foundations had been laid for what became two decades of sustained rapid growth. For these reasons, 1955 can be seen as another watershed (Masumi 1985: 29–38).

During this period, management came to the fore as the force which seemed likely to take the initiative in moving Japanese society. Having been successful in its efforts to retrieve some of its prerogatives during the latter part of the first period, management was able to use the profits generated during the Korean war to bolster its financial base. The period was also a time when the Japanese economy began to put itself on an independent footing, with an emphasis on chemicals and the heavy industries and with the reconstitution of the large enterprise system. So that the economy could move ahead and the gains made during the Korean war could be consolidated, the leading management organizations pushed in the power industry, steel and other core industries for management to take the initiative in restructuring their industrial relations (Hazama 1981: 287–90).

For its part, labor was regrouping under a new national center. Sōhyō sought to recapture the earlier momentum of the labor movement by focusing on two issues: (i) the political relationship with the United States which had emerged under the San Francisco treaty and was seen as having capriciously made Japan a pawn in the cold war, and (ii) higher wages. The positive attitude in confronting management with new wage demands was symbolized by one union leader as a process whereby 'clucking chickens would become quacking ducks' (Takano 1952 as quoted in Takano Minoru Chōsakushū no Henshū Iinkai 1976: 451–4).

With the ascendency of the left-wing group within Sōhyō resulting in Takano Minoru becoming its General Secretary in March 1951, the national center decided to pursue policies in line with the Four Principles of Peace: a peace treaty with all the belligerents (including the Soviet Union), neutrality, no foreign bases in Japan, and no rearmament. The Takano line called for Sōhyō to assist in organizing mass demonstrations in support of the Four Principles. On wages, the left wing pushed for a militant line. 'The duck' was seen as being a much more aggressive, persistent and noisy creature than 'the chicken.'

Management focused its counter-offense on the industrial federations in the electric power industry (Densan) and in mining (Tanrō). By the late 1940s Densan had become the central locus of power in the newly formed national center. Management's counter-offensive manifested itself in two disputes in 1952. Pressure came to be put on Tanrō (the miners' union) when management sought to constrict wages in order to move ahead with its own plans to rationalize operations. A similar strategy was pursued in the electric power industry, although in that case there was the added aim of smashing Densan, the powerful industrial federation (Kawanishi 1982a: 407–44). This intention was clearly stated in the Diet by Takase, the Minister for International Trade and Industry (Rōdō Sōgi Chōsakai 1957: 107) and by the Japan Federation of Employers' Associations (Nikkeiren 1952).

Management clearly perceived the industrial federations to be a major source of the postwar labor movement. The Federation of Electrical Power Workers (Densan) was singled out as the major driving force promoting the industrial orientation and sense of solidarity among Japan's workers. The ultimate goal, then, was to alter that consciousness and to cultivate a climate in which enterprise unions would develop. The enterprise union was seen as being the form of unionism most suited to a system of industrial relations in which management would be able to guarantee itself the initiative in personnel administration. The two unions were put in a position of having to fight a defensive battle. The subsequent strike in the coal industry lasted for 63 days; that in the electric power industry, 86 days. Each union suffered defeat.

With roughly the same goals in mind, the management at Nissan Motors followed suit in 1953. Its workers had been affiliated with the All-Japan Industrial Union of Automobile Workers (Zennihon Jidōsha Sangyō Rōdō Kumiai) which had negotiated an industry-wide agreement. Regardless of the firm, it had set industry-wide rates for six classes of workers which also reflected each worker's length of employment with the same firm. The six groupings were unskilled, semi-skilled, first-grade skilled, middle-grade skilled, upper-division skilled, and senior skilled. This had been no mean achievement and was a considerable source of pride to the federation. It was in response to this situation that management sought to undermine the industrial federation and to gain back some of its own prerogatives. The dispute resulted in the union splitting, and the federation's Nissan branch suffering defeat (Saga 1983). The federation dissolved itself the following year. Following these major setbacks, the union movement began to drift away from the notion of industrial unionism and those pushing for enterprise unionism started to come to the fore.

The next industry selected by management was the steel industry. The disputes at Amagasaki Steel and at Nihon Seikō's Muroran plant in 1954 were also management-led efforts to recoup earlier loses, but in these instances we see a new tactic developed by Sōhyō. The leaders of Sōhyō had come to be quite conscious of the weaknesses of the enterprise union which seemed destined to be the major organizational unit in the labor movement following the defeats in the electric power and automobile industries. Under the leadership of Takano Minoru, the idea of organizing local support for beleaguered unions took hold (cf. Takano 1958b). Following the 'Takano Line,' the defensive struggles at Amagasaki Steel and at Nihon Seikō's Muroran plant developed into a 'family and community struggle' (*kazoku gurumi-machi gurumi tōsō*). Again, long battles were waged over 53 days and 193 days respectively. In both cases, however, the unions lost. With these victories under its belt, management can be said to have cleared the core industries of industrial unionism and to have paved the way in industrial relations for the period of high economic growth which followed.

One dispute with a different coloring during this period

occurred at Ōmi Kenshi in 1954. Already there had been rum-
blings within Sōhyō. A number of industrial federations with
more conservative leanings began to complain openly that Sōhyō
had become too oriented to political goals. Four industrial federations (the textile workers, the seamen, the broadcasting workers
and the second federation of film-makers) issued a joint declaration (*yon tansan seimei*) on October 23, 1952. They withdrew
from Sōhyō on October 20, 1953 and then established their own
national grouping, known as 'Zenrō Kaigi', on April 22, 1954.
The struggle at Ōmi Kenshi, which was involved in the spinning
of silk thread, was the first dispute that Zenrō became involved
in after its formation. Billed as a fight for 'human rights in the
face of feudalistic personnel practices,' the union was able to
generate fairly broad support and emerged with a victory after
a 106-day strike.

The experience at Ōmi Kenshi provided the impetus for a
number of similar struggles in small and medium-sized firms.
Focused on the demand that personnel management practices be
modernized, these struggles often provided an opportunity for
across-the-board improvements in working conditions. Many in
the labor movement saw this struggle as a model for launching
labor's counter-offensive against management (Takita 1972 and
Kawanishi 1986: 273–319).

IV   The Early Years of High Economic Growth: 1955–60

During the late 1950s economic growth became a social priority
widely accepted by the populace. Many Japanese came to believe
that economic growth would automatically result in improvements in all spheres of life. Having generated a small surplus of
capital through its favorable trade balances during the early
1950s, management was able to pursue a policy of capital investment in new machinery and it began to import new technologies
in major industries such as steel, automobiles, shipbuilding and
chemicals. This can be said to have launched the economy into
the period of high economic growth. With the unification of the
political parties on the right and on the left, the political situation
stabilized as the two major parties (the Liberal Democratic Party

and the Japan Socialist Party) came to dominate the political scene and the '1955 arrangement' became institutionalized (cf. Masumi 1985: 29–38).

During this period, the strategy of labor shifted and the Takano Line came to be replaced by the Ōta-Iwai Line at Sōhyō's Sixth National Convention in July 1955. Attention shifted from individual plant struggles to the nationally coordinated spring wage offensive which came to be known as '*shuntō*.' The *shuntō* formula called for labor (i) to cooperate with management in raising productivity and (ii) to seek an enlargement of their own share through negotiations with management which would focus on the 'base-up' (an across-the-board hike in the wage base) (cf. Ōta 1975).

Because economic growth proceeded at a rapid pace, and the improvements in productivity allowed management to meet the annual demands of labor for higher wages, the *shuntō* formula was seen as having been rather successful; the standard of living of nearly all Japanese improved steadily throughout this period. In this climate, Japan's postwar democracy began to take root, a development which was reflected in the popular struggles against the police law (*keishokuhō*) in 1958, the introduction of the teacher evaluation system (*kinpyō*) in education during the years 1957–60 and the mutual security treaty with the United States (1959–60). Particularly noteworthy was the linkage which developed in 1960 between the struggle at the Mitsui Miike mines and the movement against the security treaty. The result was the largest series of mass demonstrations in postwar Japan (Shimizu 1963).

Although the idea of *shuntō* was based fundamentally on the notion of cooperation between labor and management, there were some rather fierce struggles between labor and management during this period. In particular, Tekkōrōren continued to be a formidable industrial federation with particular strength at Fuji steel and at Nihon Kōkan. Accordingly, those became the firms where management next sought to concentrate its efforts which took the form of the 'management rationalization offensive' (*keiei gōrika kōgeki*) (Ōkōchi and Matsuo 1973: 192–213).

The Tekkōrōren strikes in steel occurred in 1957. Taking advantage of the spring offensive, ostensibly to obtain higher wages and an increase in retirement pay, the affiliated unions

A History of Industrial Disputes in Postwar Japan

decided to give Tekkōrōren the authority to call strikes. A joint struggle committee was established, and eleven strikes of 24–48 hours' duration were organized. However, management resisted, claiming that 'steel was the most important business of the nation' (*tetsu wa kokka nari*) and that 'the management in steel would be the champion of Japanese management.' In the end it got its own way, taking advantage of the federation's weaknesses and maintaining its refusal to pay any more than workers were currently receiving (the '*zero kaitō*') (Ōkōchi and Matsuo 1973: 314–16). Following its defeat in that struggle, Tekkōrōren turned to take a cooperative line with management.

The 'one-shot formula' (*ippatsu kaitō*) (according to which management gave one final answer) became the accepted practice in subsequent spring offensives as the agreements in the core industries moved away from demands for industry-wide minimal standards and came to reflect inter-firm differences in profits, productivity and the ability to pay. As the unions in the private sector were defeated in one struggle after another and came to adopt a stance which was open to cooperation with management, it was the public sector unions, led by Kōrōkyō and its most powerful affiliate, Kokurō, which were able to continue the fight with management. However, even Kokurō received a heavy blow in its defeat in the Niigata National Railways struggle in 1957 (Fujita and Shiota 1963: 317–68).

Although Kōrōkyō had not been able to obtain a wage increase over the four years leading up to the spring offensive in 1957, with four waves of strikes in 1957 it was finally successful. However, management retaliated by handing out massive punishments to the leaders of Kōrōkyō under provisions in the law which made strikes by workers in the public sector illegal. Kōrōkyō then responded with its struggles against disciplinary action (*shobun hantai tōsō*). Its strategy called for the Niigata branch of Kokurō (one of the unions organizing the National Railways) to take the lead. The branch had already become a focal point in the struggle with management owing to a series of altercations concerning the running of workshops (*shokuba tōsō*). Kokurō's strategy was for workers to make demands about various conditions of work on the shop floor and then to negotiate directly with management at the shop-floor level (Fujita and Shiota 1963: 330–7). The National Railways called in armed police (*busō keikan*) on the grounds that the trains were being paralyzed by

81

the disputing workers. The dispute received nation-wide attention in the mass media, but in the end the union lost with four leaders being fired and 46,734 members receiving disciplinary action. As had happened earlier in the private sector, this kind of dispute provided an opportunity for management to cooperate in efforts to establish a second union, which became known as 'Tetsurō.' The way in which the dispute was resolved also came to symbolize management's determination to punish public sector unionists who engaged in strike activity. The result was the Kōrōkyō came to face an insurmountable barrier.

Although the union movement came to lose much of its earlier vitality, one union of considerable strength remained. That was the union at the Mitsui Miike Mines. Having taken a fairly moderate line on cooperating with management, the union came to be known as one of Japan's strongest unions after its '113-day strike without heroes' in 1953, and had used various tactics at the work place to improve safety, to control production and the shift system, and to involve the workers more generally in the setting of personnel practices related to work and wages. Recognizing that these developments represented an erosion of its prerogatives, management took the unprecedented step of firing 2000 employees, including 300 union activists. This action was obviousdly aimed at retrieving management rights and bringing the union to its knees (cf. Shimizu 1963 and Hirai 1979). The union response was to launch a strike which developed into the largest struggle of the postwar period and also at the time came to be referred to as a struggle against the Mutual Security Treaty with the United States. After 282 days, the result was a bitter defeat for the union. A schism developed and a number two union was established.

The Mitsui Miike struggles were the last great dispute for more than a decade, and represented another important watershed in the history of the labor movement in postwar Japan. It was the last instance of a 'family and community struggle,' an approach developed by Tanrō during its 63-day strike in 1952. At that time 77,000 wives of the striking miners formed their own organization, the Collective Committee of Wives of Japanese Miners (Nihon Tankō Shufu Kyōgikai). At that time most miners lived in company housing and it was easy to get the wives together. Their sense of solidarity grew out of the process of giving each other mutual support with the running of their households on an everyday basis. During the Mitsui Miike dispute families were again mobilized through this organization (Shimizu 1963). The Mitsui Miike dispute more or less brought an end to a strategy which had emerged after the war as a response to popular demands for a more democratic approach to the organization at work.

With the defeat of the unions in the Mitsui Miike dispute, management's ascendency in industrial relations was fully achieved in the private sector (cf. Shimizu 1973 and Hirai 1979). Politically, the leftist forces in Japan were able to force cancellation of Eisenhower's visit to Japan, but were unable to stop ratification of a ten-year extension for the treaty with the United States. The Socialist Party split shortly afterwards and it was not long before Zenrō formalized its organization as a national center and became Dōmei. In the union movement itself the 'political unionism' of the left had clearly given way to the growth-oriented 'business unionism' of the right.

V   The Latter Years of Rapid Economic Growth: 1961–73

As Japan's economy continued to grow, the economic growth and the prosperity it brought with it came to be widely accepted in society as primary goals. With IMF-JC and the Dōmei unions at the forefront of the labor movement, a policy of cooperating with management to increase productivity came to be adopted by Japan's mainstream unions. The number of employees apathetic to the union movement increased. As long as economic growth continued, it seemed everyone would receive higher wages regardless of whether they joined a union or not. This view was particularly widespread among the younger workers (cf. Ishikawa 1975 and Inagami 1982).

As the process of cooperating with management came to be institutionalized in the private sector, the number of disputes naturally declined. Through various forms of participation in management, the unions were able to maintain some influence. During this period both Sōhyō and Dōmei strengthened their activities related to policy formation, and their views came to be considered by the government when new legislation and administrative guidelines were being drafted. Finally, the growing involvement of the national centers in the international labor movement and their contributions at that level also deserve attention.

The only major dispute during this time was Kokurō's struggle against the introduction of sweeping rationalizations in the National Railways. The Railways moved ahead with its efforts to raise productivity by nurturing the number two union, Tetsurō, and by taking advantage of whatever opportunities there were to discriminate against the members of Kokurō and Dōrō. However, with their organizations seriously threatened, the leadership and members of Kokurō and Dōrō decided that they would stand up and fight. In doing so, they aimed to put a full stop to the rationalization movement and to have earlier disciplinary action rescinded. The JNR authorities eventually admitted that its rationalization program and subsequent actions had constituted unfair labor practices and apologized to the unions. In achieving their goals, the unions in the National Railways sprung back to life. In doing so, they also provided inspiration to the other public sector unions, and there seemed to be new hope for Kōrōkyō as its affiliates took a more forward-looking approach in designing policies to maintain its strength (Hyōdō 1981).

Another focal point during this period was the Seamen's Union. A strong industrial federation with roots going back to the prewar period, it had adopted a cooperative stance toward management in order to raise productivity and was one of the main pillars of Dōmei. However, these policies had resulted in an extreme intensification of work for the seamen and a growing burden being placed on their families. The pressures of work manifested themselves in growing dissatisfaction with working conditions (which often required the seamen to put up with excessively long separations from their families). This feedback was incorporated into the union's policies, and in 1972 the union took decisive action with a 92-day strike. Called 'the struggle to recover humanity,' the strike was successful in that working conditions were altered significantly and the outcome can be said to have had a subtle influence on the labor movement as a whole (Numata and Sasaki 1972). The struggle reminded all of those involved with industrial relations that a broadly based movement can succeed. If a union is willing to consider the demands of the families of its members and has the means of injecting their demands into its decision-making process, even a fairly conservative union which is used to cooperating with management can generate considerable popular support and, in the process, move to an ideological stance which is very antagonistic towards management.

VI The Period of Slower Growth: 1973–86

The oil shock in 1973 ended the period of unbroken rapid economic growth. Not only did the economy decelerate; a social concern with obtaining a more balanced type of growth surfaced. People became more 'multi-dimensional'; their concerns broadened and came to encompass more than is implied by the straight-forward materialism which seemed to prevail during the period of high growth rates.

During this period, a growing number of workers became disinterested in unionism. The labor movement stagnated. With structural changes in the economy, the number of males employed in Japan's key industries as regular employees declined as a percentage of the entire labor force. As these were the workers who had formed the nucleus of the union membership in Japan, the importance of the enterprise union declined. Japan's unionization rate dropped, falling from 35.4 percent in 1970 to 34.4 percent in 1975 and then to 30.8 percent by 1980, reaching a postwar low of 29.7 percent in 1983 before falling to 25.2 percent in 1990.

Reflecting the times, large labor disputes disappeared, although Kokurō, Dōrō and Zentei engaged in a 'right-to-strike strike' in 1975. The illegality of their action was again duly noted by the authorities who took disciplinary action against 15,000 members of Kōrōkyō and fired 1016 persons. Kōrōkyō then launched an eight-day strike to press its demands for the right to strike. However, the move backfired. Not only did the unions fail to obtain the right to strike; they also alienated a large segment of the public who had become critical of public servants engaging in such behavior. The mass media portrayed the workers as being irresponsible in taking advantage of the fact that their employer, the state, would not go bankrupt like a private firm, no matter how lazy they were or how often they refused to work. The unions also came to be the focus of critical public opinion when the government set in motion its plan for administrative reform. In particular Kokurō was criticized for taking a slack attitude toward work following its victory in the anti-rationalization campaign at the beginning of the 1970s. It was also blamed in the media for causing the tremendous annual deficits which the National Railways had been recording (e.g., cf. *Asahi Shimbun*, September 13, 1981). Little attention was given in the media to the role that politicians played. Political expedience resulted in many non-economical lines and stations being established with no planning or feasibility studies. Expansion occurred simply to please local constituencies which supported conservative candidates. The executives of the JNR, which themselves had been appointed by the government, were repeatedly compelled to borrow for such development, obviously adding to the debt burden of the JNR. The political solution was to blame left-wing unionism and recalcitrant workers for the JNR being unable to rationalize at the pace necessary to cover the costs of such irrational expansions.

While an analysis of JNR's financial straits requires a close examination not only of the impact of strikes on JNR revenue but also of the impact of political interference (e.g., Hyōdo 1982, Takagi 1984, Kōshiro 1980), the fact remains that Kokurō became increasingly isolated in the media and increasingly out of favor with public opinion. Faced with internal divisions, the growing strength of Tetsurō, and the government's determination to divide and to privatize the National Railways, the union seems to have been drained of its vigor. As the last stronghold of militant unionism, Kankōrō will be entering a long winter period.

At the same time, developments among unions in the private sector under the leadership of IMF-JC and the Seisaku Suishin Rōsō Kaigi point toward the formation of a new national center for unions in the private sector and in 1983 Zenminrōkyō was established to coordinate the moves in that direction. Although there has been a good deal of discussion about what the character of Zenminrōkyō will be, it is still too early to tell whether this new organization will be able to develop into a body which will restore political influence and bargaining power to the labor movement in Japan (Yakabe 1985). It is, however, a period during which management and the government have been taking the initiative. It is also a period where the appeal has been to nationalistic slogans, with frequent references being made to 'national interest' (*kokueki*) and to the notion of the 'enterprise as a collectivity sharing a common fate' (*kigyō unmei kyōdōtai*). With these developments, Japan's industrial relations enter a new era.

VII The Period of New Nationalism: 1987–

As government and management came increasingly to dominate the industrial relations scene, the conservative elements in the union movement have come to be coopted into the overall scheme. The new nationalism will gradually be implanted deep in the consciousness of the ordinary people. This phenomenon has already commonly been referred to 'Japan's neonationalism'. The new ethos has come to be embodied in Zenmin Rōren which was established on November 20, 1987. It evolved into Rengō on November 21, 1989.

At the same time, to obtain the full picture one must still pay attention to those opposing this shift to the right. They have moved to form their own competing national centers. Zenrōren was formed on November 21, 1989 by elements in the labor movement which are close to the Japan Communist Party. Zenrōkyō was formed on December 9 by those associated with the left wing in the Japan Socialist Party, the new left and various independents.

VIII Conclusion

The preceding discussion is summarized in Table 4.2. The fortunes of the labor movement are clear. For about ten years after the war, labor was able to hold sway over management, although its advantage began to slip in the late 1940s. Within the union movement itself, the left-wing factions (which took a confrontationalist line with management) held the initiative. In the first

Table 4.2 Five periods of disputation in postwar Japan

Period (years)	Major balances of power	Major events	Major industrial disputes	Type of industrial relations
I 1945–50	(1) GHQ // mgmt unions >> mgmt (2) Sanbetsu Kaigi >> Sōdōmei	End of the War 15.8.45 Sōdōmei established 1.8.46 Sanbetsu Kaigi established 19.8.46 General strike planned for February 1, 1947	Yomiuri 1945–46 Tōshiba 1945–46 Seamen, JNR, Densan (electric power workers)	consolidation of union-led industrial relations
	(1) GHQ / mgmt unions > mgmt (2) Sanbetsu Kaigi > Sōdōmei + Sanbetsu Mindō		*Tōhō 1948 *Tōshiba 1949 *JNR 1948	
II 1950–5	(1) Government / mgmt unions > mgmt (2) Sōhyō >> Sōdōmei + Zenrō	Beginning of Korean war 25.6.50 Sōhyō formed 11.7.50 Sōdōmei reconstituted 1.6.51 San Francisco Peace Treaty 8.9.52 red purge 24.7.50	Tanrō, *Densan 1952 *Nissan steel 1953–6	reordering of union-led industrial relations
			Amagasaki Steel 1954 Ōmi Kenshi 1954	
		Zenrō Kaigi established 22.4.54	Nihon Seikō Muroran 1954	

Table 4.2 *continued*

Period (years)	Major balances of power	Major events	Major industrial disputes	Type of industrial relations
III 1955–60	(1) Government $\diagdown\!\!\!\diagdown$ unions – mgmt	announcement of 8 industrial unions' joint struggle (*shuntō*) 22.1.55 Japan Productivity Center established 14.2.55 '1955 political arrangement': JSP's first national convention 13.10.55 LDP's first national convention 15.10.55		reordering of union-led industrial relations
			*JNR Niigata struggle 1957 Tekkōrōren's 11-wave strike 1957 struggle against the police law 1958 struggle against teacher evaluations 1958 *Ōji Paper 1958	
	(2) Sōhyō > Zenrō			
IV 1961–73	(1) Government $\diagup\!\!\!\diagdown$ unions < mgmt	AMPO and Miike 1960 Dōmei formed 26.4.62 IMF-JC formed 1964	*Mitsui Miike Mine 1960 Kokurō's struggle against removing assistant drivers 1969	consolidation of the newly established industrial relations

Table 4.2 *continued*

Period (years)	Major balances of power	Major events	Major industrial disputes	Type of industrial relations
	(2) Sōhyō = Dōmei + IMF-JC		Zen-gunrō, *Zeneraru Oil Refining 1970 Kokurō against rationalization 1971 Seamen (to recover humanity) 1972	
V 1973–86	(1) Government ╲╱ union << mgmt (2) Sōhyō < IMF-JC + Dōmei	Oil Shock 1973 Seisaku Suishin Rōsō Kaigi formed 1976 Zenminrō formed 14.12.82	Kōrōkyō 'right-to-strike strike' 1975 Saseho Shipbuilding 1979–80	consolidation of management-led industrial relations
VI 1987–	Government ╲╱╱ union <<< mgmt Zenrōren, Zenrōkyō << Zenminrōren	Japan National Railways dissolved and privatized (1.4.1987) Zenmin Rōren formed (20.11.1987) Rengō and Zenrōren formed (21.11.1989) Zenrōkyō formed (9.12.1989)		

Notes:

(1) * union split occurred
   – weak interaction
   = close interaction
   ≡ symbiotic relationship

(2) Power relations are expressed as follows:
   A = B   A and B are equally powerful
   A > B   A is somewhat more powerful than B
   A >> B   A is considerably more powerful than B
   A >>> B A is able to dictate fairly freely to B

Sources: The table was constructed by the author drawing from the wide range of sources cited in Table 4.1.

five years Sanbetsu Kaigi was the leading center; in the second half of the decade, Sōhyō.

Although from 1955 onwards the right-wing unions could be seen coming to the fore, the key event was the Mitsu Miike Coal Mine Dispute in 1960. Once Japan's strongest industrial union had been defeated, the conservative forces were able to ride the wave of rapid economic growth which swept over Japan during the 1960s and the early 1970s. The presence of the cooperatist union leadership was greatly reinforced by the sense of crisis which swept Japan following the oil shocks in 1973 and the lower growth rates later in the decade. Japan was able to survive the 1970s with low rates of inflation and relatively low levels of unemployment, at least in official terms, and large firms were able to maintain their systems of career employment. These achievements were in no small way due to the role of the con-servative unions. One can safely say that the right-wing unions have completely dominated the union movement in Japan since the late 1970s.

The rise of the right wing in the labor movement can be easily traced in Table 4.2. The key turning point was 1987, when the Japan National Railways was privatized and Rengō was first formed. Those events followed a period of growing neonational-ism, and the sense of a new era was perhaps also articulated by the passing of the Emperor who had come to symbolize postwar Japan. While there continues to be opposition to the new indus-trial relations, management has won out. The large industrial disputes of the postwar period have skillfully been turned against labor. In the final analysis we would have to conclude that they have been cleverly manipulated so that they would function to strengthen the hand of management. The development of man-agement's basic strategy can be seen in the creation of the number two union. The division of the union movement has served to create a framework in which worker-oriented unionists could easily be isolated while an environment conducive to the development of cooperative relations between labor and manage-ment was also being promoted.

The record shows clearly in each period that management has doggedly pursued the leading left-wing unions. In a society which is consistently portrayed as a consensus-based society, the unwill-ingness of management to live and let live needs to be under-lined. Of course, where one decides that the status quo lies –

whether it was the state of industrial relations in 1935, 1955 or 1985 – is quite arbitrary. However, management has had a very clear idea about its rights *vis-à-vis* employees and has moved quickly to maintain and even to enhance its domain.

Industrial relations in contemporary Japan reflect the status of the union movement. They are the product of the power balance not only between labor and management, but also between left-wing and right-wing elements within the labor movement. There are in both dimensions strong ideological differences. It is not surprising, then, that some scholars will see trends over the past three decades as a healthy development, while others see it as a weakening of democracy in Japan. The former group of scholars include Koike (1977), Shirai (1980) and Kōshiro (1982). The later group includes Kawanishi (1977, 1981 and 1986), Yamamoto (1977a), Shimizu (1982), Totsuka (1977), Kumazawa (1983) and Hyōdō (1983).

5 A History of Labor-Management Relations on the Shop Floor

I Introduction

The previous chapter introduced some reasons for eschewing overly enthusiastic appraisals of the enterprise union. This chapter builds on that overview by discussing in more detail the development of industrial relations at the shop level. Careful analysis of how the enterprise union functions at the micro level will further highlight the inability of enterprise unionism to serve the interests of Japan's employees.

The organization of work at the shop level is of special importance to management, to the union and to the employees. For the worker the workshop is a multi-functional social group, a community which shapes both his well-being at work and his private life outside the firm. In all ages, workers have been tightly bound to the primary work group at the place where work is being carried out on an everyday basis. Their consciousness and outlook at work and in their daily lives have been greatly influenced by interpersonal relationships at their place of work. The shop-floor group functions to meet the various needs of the workers. These include (i) friendly relations with others, (ii) mutual assistance in times of physical and psychological need, (iii) the joy of doing their work, (iv) equal opportunities for promotions, and (v) other socially recognized needs. In meeting these needs the dynamics of the workshop group are such that strong bonds emerge among the workers. Japan's large firms are characterized by the strong ideological emphasis on 'working for the good of all' – an emphasis which is said to reflect the 'group orientation' of the Japanese. The influence of work groups does not stop at the factory gate; it extends to the lives of employees even when they are away from work.

Although the relationship between labor and management is seen in theoretical terms as being antagonistic, collaborative relationships between labor and management emerge in many of

Japan's large firms, in part because of the special way in which the enterprise union is organized. In these firms the union's structure parallels that of management: the two overlap and over time there is a tendency for the union structure to be subsumed within and subordinated to the organizational framework established by management. In terms of Figure 5.1, there is a shift from the arrangement shown in part A to that shown in part B as the workshop group (*shokuba shūdan*) comes to reflect the fact that the two work together when it comes to personnel administration in the enterprise. The three-way interaction between labor, management and the employees has grown out of the tug-of-war between labor and management over who will control the workshop group; and it is out of that interaction that the history of the group evolves into a concrete set of practices. As long as the union is able to stand up to management and retain its independence, it will be able to maintain the structure shown in part A of the figure. However, once it loses its independence from management, the original structure gives way to the arrangement shown in part B. The structural features shown in A make the enterprise union especially susceptible to this form of degeneration.

After Japan began to experience low economic growth in the late 1970s, the union found that it was even more difficult to maintain an antagonistic relationship with management. The shop floor has increasingly become subject to the control of management hierarchies. Over time there has been a general shift in the structures from the pattern shown in Part A of Figure 5.1 to that shown in part B. Workers have come increasingly under the influence of management-inspired personnel policies designed to heighten the worker's sense of attachment to the firm (*kigyō kizoku ishiki*).

What is the process by which this transition has occurred? What kind of ideology and what personnel practices has management adopted to gain control of the workers' groups at the shop level? Further, how have workers and their shop-floor groups responded to management initiatives in this area? With these questions in mind, this chapter discusses the way in which labor-management relations developed at the shop floor during the period of high economic growth. The chapter begins by providing a brief overview of the major developments; it then considers the major characteristics of labor-management relations on the

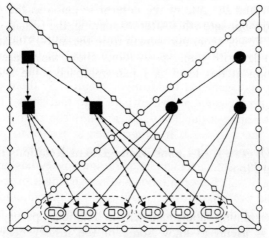

A The theoretical idea of a cooperatist structure at the beginning

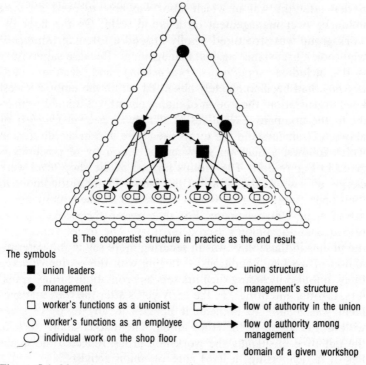

B The cooperatist structure in practice as the end result

The symbols

■	union leaders	◇—◇—◇	union structure
●	management	○—○—○	management's structure
□	worker's functions as a unionist	□—▶	flow of authority in the union
○	worker's functions as an employee	○—▶	flow of authority among management
⬭	individual work on the shop floor		
		- - - - -	domain of a given workshop

Figure 5.1 *Management structure and its counterpart in the enterprise union*

95

shop floor and the role of the enterprise union in the period of rapid economic growth. After examining the situation in the period of slower economic growth from the mid–1970s, the chapter concludes with some speculations about the future of work organization at this level as Japan approaches the end of this century.

II An Overview of Labor-Management Relations on the Shop Floor

Before examining labor-management relationships on the shop floor, it is useful to know some of the history behind those relations. The initial postwar period (cf. Table 4.2) was the only period after the war in which labor was able to exert a strong influence over management on a grand scale. On the floor the work group was structured wholly around a foreman (*kumichō*) who took a firm stance against management. Because supervisory staff, including supervisors (*kakarichō*) and section chiefs (*kachō*), had been completely absorbed within the union's lowest level organization, the notion of management was limited primarily to the company executives at the division level (*buchō*) or above. (To understand the terms used here and in the discussion which follows, a diagram showing the hierarchy of positions is given in Figure 5.2.) The groups formed at the shop level were clearly an asset in the hands of the union. Quite autonomous in their operations, the groups were renowned for their spontaneous action against management. For that reason the workshop was regarded as the union's sacred territory. The major concern of the unions in those days was in securing more say in the determination of working conditions – starting with the setting of wage rates, but also including such matters as promotion, hiring, transfers, layoffs, and firings. In the early years after the war, management was unable to implement policies in any of these areas without the assent of the labor union. The union's ability to take the initiative in shaping the workshop group reflected the qualities of its leadership, a hard core of union activists.

Given this situation, the only way for management to strengthen its hand was by removing these activists from the shop

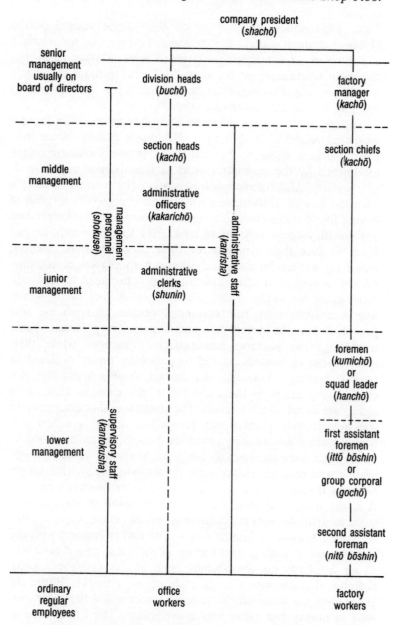

Note: The reader should remember that terminology developed here is only an example. The use of titles varies considerably from firm to firm and is often a very complex matter. The greatest care is required to avoid confusion.

Figure 5.2 *The organization of management: a diagrammatic definition of some key terms*

floor. Management set out to do this in the second period (1950–5) through massive firings, the red purge, and the outright expulsion of activists from the place of work. Having recovered the 'right to manage' on the shop floor, management at Japan's large firms began to introduce new technologies, thereby paving the way for Japan's economic takeoff.

Ujihara (1966) conducted some interesting research on Japan's industrial relations at that time. His major findings were five. First, workers came to be bound up in the social structures established by the mammoth firms as management regained its prerogatives. Ujihara reports how workers have come to have a common feeling of alienation within that framework, a sense of having found themselves in a position where they no longer had anyone they could rely on to look after their interests or any place to take their demands or their dissatisfactions. Second, based on a very bureaucratic approach to personnel administration, a system of strict seniority was introduced to maintain order in the workshop. Third, while the practice of having someone in a supervisory role continued unchanged from the first period, it must be noted that such supervisory personnel came increasingly to perform administrative functions while their involvement in matters related to personnel policy declined to almost nothing. Although the formal arrangements did not change very much in the early 1950s, the changes were quite significant in substantive terms. The result was that management was able to take a small step forward in removing union personnel from policy-making positions. Fourth, unionists in supervisory roles were increasingly educated to see the value of cooperating with management to raise productivity. They were taught that any threat to the firm was a threat to the worker's income. A result of this education was that the attention of union leaders came to focus on working conditions, which meant almost exclusively an emphasis on higher wages. The earlier concern with the relative size of each person's share of the value added gave way to an emphasis on the absolute size of the entire pie (and, thereby, the absolute size of each person's share). Fifth, the generation gap between the younger workers and the older persons in managerial ranks was considerable. The former recognized the importance of having the unions. However, only half of the younger workers felt the union was doing the right thing; the other half did not approve of the policies which the union was pursuing. There was also a strong feeling that unions had come to rubber stamp management policies rather than reflecting worker sentiments on the shop floor. Moreover, this dissatisfaction was not reflected in the direction which the unions took.

As unions increasingly cooperated with management to raise productivity, the workshop came to be the 'sacred territory' of management. Nevertheless, within this milieu a few unions continued to stand up to management, and in some firms the workshop group was able to maintain its autonomy. Ōkōchi, Ujihara and Fujita's research (1959) showed that the workshop groups in such firms continued to maintain close ties with the union.

As the economy continued to expand in the subsequent period of high economic growth, even the workshops which had remained relatively independent gradually came to see their autonomy eroded. By the late 1960s in very few shops were workers' organizations able to stand up to management. During the 1960s the workshop came to be closed off from outside observation and few scholars were able to study how industrial relations at the shop-floor level had changed. For this reason, the reports by journalists such as Kamata (1973) and Saitō (1974) provide valuable insight and deserve careful attention.

With this introduction to the situation in the 1960s, I wish now to discuss briefly industrial relations at the shop level as I have seen them in my own research during and after the period of high economic growth.

III Shop-Level Industrial Relations in the Period of Labor's Initiative

A Characteristics of the strong unions

Any assessment of the unions' efforts to revitalize their movement must begin by examining the historical significance of the period of high economic growth for the unions and for Japan's workers in general. Did the rapid growth facilitate the formation of stronger unions, or was it detrimental to the formation of such unions? As the preceding chapter concluded, answers to this question conflict, reflecting a difference in the philosophical or ideological orientation of those making the assessment. Here the term 'strong unions' refers to any form of unionism which can stand up to management when it comes to protecting the interests and working conditions of workers in the broad sense, but particularly with regard to wages, employment security, and job content. The tenacity with which a union can stand up to management is dependent upon the strength of union activity at the shop-floor level.

B Union goals and structures

One argument advanced in this volume is that ideology matters, and that one's analysis of unions in Japan is facilitated by classifying unions according to their ideology. In the most general terms, it is useful to distinguish between (i) unions which subscribe to an ideology emphasizing basic conflicts of interest with management and the need to confront management on various issues in order to look after the workers' interests, and (ii) unions which pursue a cooperative line with management. This approach goes against those taken by Shirai (Hōsei Daigaku Kokusai Kōryū Sentā 1979) and others who seem to argue that ideology is not important. Their analysis tends to treat all unions in Japan as being similar, considering only whether they function successfully or not. However, 'success' is narrowly conceived in terms of productivity and the adherents to that approach have not engaged in empirical studies to determine why some unions are successful and others are not. The position taken here is that ideology is an important factor explaining not only differences in terms of such narrowly defined success, but also in terms of the general climate at work, the relationships among union members and the overall level of each member's commitment to the union. Ideology is seen as an important phenomenon affecting the health of any union organization. For these reasons, the history of labor-management relations on the shop floor must begin by considering changes over time in the union's ideology.

During the first five years after the war, Japan experienced a rather unique situation. For the only time in the nation's history the 'working class' was able to dominate the 'capitalist class.' In this period there were a number of strong unions which might provide us with a model (or ideal type) of shop-level phenomena when the 'strong union' is present. We can, for example, look at the three unions involved in the October struggle organized by Sanbetsu Kaigi in 1946. They were the Newspaper Employees' Union (Masuyama 1976; Yamamoto 1978), Densan (Kawanishi 1978 and 1979b) and Tōshiba Rōren (Ishikawa 1986; Yamamoto 1983). All three unions (i) focused their demands on guaranteeing the livelihood of the workers and (ii) sought to promote equality among all the workers.

1 Guarantees of livelihood   The 'guaranteeing of livelihood' meant that company profits were to be given less priority than improvements in the workers' living standards. A certain minimum wage was set and profits were to be generated because workers were sufficiently supported. Management too had a right to this minimum wage in return for its labor, but the firm should be seen as a collective where the goal was to achieve that minimum for all employees before anyone took away profits. In other words, workers should not be obliged to supply management with luxurious homes before they themselves have access to the basic necessities of life. This setting of priorities was basic to the philosophy of the unions mentioned above. The emphasis on wage hikes in exchange for cooperation with management in raising productivity (and profits) is contrary to this kind of thinking. This view of things is perhaps based on an ideological stance which assumes that labor-management relations are antagonistic as long as management is bent on taking a profit before each worker is provided with a minimal standard of living – which means a living wage and humane working conditions.

2 Egalitarianism   As a central organizational principle, 'equality among the workers' (*byōdō shugi*) means (a) that workers do not have to compete among themselves and (b) that equality among the workers is promoted (cf. Kumazawa 1978: 166). This stands in direct opposition to the approach of management which segments the labor force according to gender, employment status, occupation, qualifications and educational background, and uses these divisions to promote competition among workers, especially among those in the more privileged categories.

To illustrate how the effort to implement policies based on these two principles shape a union's organization, it is useful to consider the wage system which emerged out of the October Struggle in 1946.

C The world of the *Densangata* wage system

The '*Densangata* wage system' refers to the wage system which the electrical power workers won as a result of the October Struggle. The Federation of Electrical Power Workers (Densan) had been formed in March 1946 when individual unions at the power companies brought together their 120,000 workers under the same industry-wide organization. Although Kawanishi (1979b, 1989: 177–9) writes in more detail about the system elsewhere (in English also cf. Ayusawa 1966), it is common knowledge that the *Densangata* wage system was widely referred to as a model for wage negotiations both by labor and by management in other industries in the late 1940s.

The *Densangata* wage system was popular with the workers for several reasons. Of course, the negotiations brought with it a four-fold increase in wage levels. As one measure to control inflation the government had begun to issue new yen notes, and set a ceiling on the salaries of employees of ¥500 in the new currency. Densan sought to test the reasonableness of that amount in terms of the cost of living for a standard family (*hyōjun kazoku*) consisting of a breadwinner aged 35 and three other persons. By using data from surveys of household budgets, it established that the absolute minimum costs in the new currency would be ¥2000 per month. During the October Struggle its estimates were officially recognized by government and by management in the electric power industry. More important, however, was the wage system it devised and imposed on management.

For the preceding eighty years of Japanese capitalism, capitalists and their managers had taken the initiative in establishing wage systems which facilitated their control of the workers. Then, for the first time in the history of Japanese capitalism, workers introduced a wage system which would serve their needs and interests. It should be noted, however, that the system was introduced only through struggle. As a new force in industrial relations, union leaders began to acquire a certain amount of self-confidence and self-awareness. Masuyama (1978: 181–5) describes the ground swell which followed throughout Japan. In other industries throughout the country unions launched joint struggles to implement a similar system of wages. A number of writers have also written about how the momentum generated by Densan's success in establishing this new wage system carried through to the planning of the General Strike for February 1, 1947 (Masuyama 1978: 208–9; Suzuki 1979: 103–4; Katayama 1946).

As a wage system inspired by labor, it embodied several principles of importance to the workers. In saying that wages were based on the logic of labor, weight was given first to guaranteeing that each worker would receive a minimum wage which would allow him and his family to maintain a 'culturally acceptable standard of living' regardless of the worker's educational background, his job qualifications, his occupation, employment status, or gender. In implementing what they considered to be a fair wage system, the electrical workers utilized a survey of their members to find out about their living conditions and salary intake. (Actually management had taken the survey to provide a basis for asking the government for a hike in electricity rates, but the union obtained the data and was able to use it for its own purposes.) With this kind of information, the Engels Coefficient could be calculated. Finally, reference was made to the consumer price index. Accordingly, the notion of a 'livelihood guarantee' was given a practical meaning which reflected fairly accurately the worker's needs and actual standard of living. The idea of considering the level of internal reserves as the first priority and then distributing what was left over to augment the workers' standard of living was far from the minds of the labor leaders.

A major goal of the *Densangata* wage system was an easing of the competition which was stimulated among the workers by management's approach to the assessment of work performance. In place of criteria which depended on the subjective and arbitrary judgment of management, the *Densangata* wage system attached weight to the fairly objective criteria associated with need. Age and family size (*setai seiinsū*) were the major variables determining a worker's wage income. Densan's agreement with management called for the complete abolition of 'wage inequality based on qualifications, class and educational background' (Nihon Denki Sangyō Rōdō Kumiai Kyōgikai 1946). From the union's point of view it was crucial that the wage system be seen as being fair. This meant that management's discretion to inject its own subjective likes and dislikes concerning a worker's personal beliefs be severely limited.

Under this system it seems likely that union members in supervisory positions and university graduates in management-track positions were unhappy with the new system. For it was they who would have benefitted from a wage system which (a) gave them managerial discretion in dealing with subordinates and (b) rewarded educational background, employment status, and one's age-linked merit rating (*nenkō*). If there was to be no concern at all with the way individuals worked it would have been possible to criticize the system as producing 'the worst kind of equality' or even inequality itself. For this reason, the Densan leadership sought an approach which would allow their brand of 'egalitarianism' to fit with the realities of life. Accordingly, the system also called for an 'add-on wage' which was tied to ability, length of continuous employment, and diligence. The result was that reference was also made to '*nōryokukyū*' (ability pay) which placed emphasis on the level of skill one possessed but which was to be distinguished from '*nōritsukyū*' (efficiency pay), a rather subjective concept amenable to manipulation by management. *Nōryokukyū* was not on the average to account for more than about 20 percent of the total wage packet, and each individual's skill classification was to be decided in negotiations between the union and management.

The third point which deserves mention when discussing the *Densangata* wage system is that notions of egalitarianism and livelihood guarantees were not simply abstractions. The new wage system reflected the unionists' commitment to a particular goal. Putting that commitment on the line against the power of SCAP, the union threatened to bring the whole country to its knees with an unlimited shut-off of electric power, and five-minute power blackouts were scheduled throughout the country, starting with the imperial palace. The willingness to engage in that kind of disruptive action is evidence of the workers' commitment to the new wage system. This commitment of the workers to the principle of egalitarianism has been amply documented (e.g., see Kawanishi 1978, 1982a, 1984 and 1985).

D   The shop floor with strong union leadership

The shop floor was shaped by the presence of a strong union movement in the first five years after the war. Four important characteristics stood out.

1   The role of supervisory personnel   In leading the shop-floor group, the *kumichō* (foreman) and other supervisory personnel took a stance independent from management. One of the big questions of the times was whether the unions could come in and overnight totally replace the workshop group as it had been previously established by management. Of course, this is what the unions wanted to try with their newly acquired influence. At Yomiuri, all management staff were judged to be unacceptable because they had been appointed by the company's president who was seen as being one of those responsible for the war. The idea was to replace all management staff with ordinary employees, and thereby to strengthen the union's hand *vis-à-vis* management. The intent is clear from the report in *Tōsō Nippō* (The Struggle's Daily Reporter) (no. 11: November 6, 1945), a newspaper published by the employees' union at Yomiuri (Yomiuri Jugyōin Kumiai) (cf. Tokyo Daigaku Shakai Kagaku Kenkyūjo 1973: 83). Densan also dismantled the old system of job classifications, and attempted to establish its own system of job categories.

Although the unions decided that 'the old system' of job classifications should be completely discarded, it was impossible to establish a system of job categories based on 'the logic of the workers' (*rōdōsha no ronri*) and the above-mentioned report concluded that 'it would be impossible to gain a full consensus on any given system.' The end result was that the old system of job classifications continued both in the electric power industry and at Yomiuri Newspapers, and union leaders opted for a strategy of building their own structures on top of the existing system (Masuyama 1979: 28).

While the limitations of these strong unions became obvious, their ability to generate sufficient strength can also be seen. The important point to be made, I believe, is that the union did not implement unreasonable strategies. Although the system of *kachō* and *kakarichō* continued to exist, the lower-level supervisory staff were brought fully into the union's organization on the shop floor. Only the company executives could clearly be identified as 'management.'

During the struggle for production control at Yomiuri in 1945, all management personnel below the level of division director (*kyokuchō*) participated in the joint struggle committee. The struggle was lead by commentators (*ronsetsu iin*), section chiefs (*buchō*) and their assistants (*jichō*) in the editorial divisions and by the team chiefs (*hanchō*) and the supervisors (*shunin*) in the printing division (cf. Masuyama 1976: 50). In the electrical power industry, 60 percent of union leaders at the workshop level were subsection heads (*kachō*), chief clerks (*kakarichō*) or shop supervisors (*shunin*) (Ōkōchi, ed. 1954: 106–10).

2 Workshop autonomy The second characteristic is that workshops in which the supervisors were closely aligned with union leadership had a strong degree of autonomy. Moreover, that autonomy tended to be particularly conspicuous in activities organized at the workshop level. The shop-floor struggle launched by Tōshiba Rōren was characterized by frequent shop-wide meetings of workers. The meetings' resolutions were taken directly to the factory manager (*kōjōcho*). Another approach was to get the personnel manager (*kinrō buchō*) to attend the shop-wide meeting and then negotiate directly with him while the workers were assembled. These activities were repeated as one working condition after another was negotiated (Yamamoto 1983: 59).

The results achieved in one shop often affected the outcome of negotiations at other workshops. By initiating a round of negotiations and obtaining significant gains in a particular workshop, the union was able to maximize the spill-over effect, and thereby the overall level of benefits received by the unionists. For this reason, the union leadership attached considerable importance to the promotion of struggles at the shop level. Although management criticized these activities as 'wild-cat strikes,' the union saw them as an effective means of exposing the incompetency of supervisory staff and raising the consciousness of union members (Yamamoto 1983: 60). In promoting shop-floor activities, the union's leadership sought to highlight the efficacy of spontaneously and autonomously motivated employees in the workshop rather than the need to strengthen its control over the union membership by introducing more bureaucratic mechanisms or by further centralizing the organization. Even at Yomiuri Newspapers, it was through the spontaneous workshop struggles that the union came to control the workshop. On December 12, 1945 the paper's editorial proclaimed that the Yomiuri newspaper 'would henceforth align itself with the people and forever be a paper of the people' (cf. Masuyama 1978: 129–32).

3   Influence in personnel affairs   As the result of shop-floor struggle, the union was able to acquire considerable say in personnel administration. It could provide considerable protection to unionists whose well-being and livelihood would otherwise have been vulnerable to the arbitrariness of management's personnel assessment systems. By placing an emphasis on egalitarianism, the unions were successful in developing and maintaining a strong sense of solidarity among their members.

The collective bargaining agreements negotiated by the Densan unions required that management receive their approval in implementing policies concerned with hiring, firing, remuneration, other working conditions, and job categories. The unions decided not only the criteria for promotion, distributing bonuses, disciplinary action, transfers and similar matters, but also the employees to be considered for such treatment. Accordingly, the unions became involved in resolving each individual's case as it arose (Tokyo Denryoku Rōdō Kumiai 1975: 53–4).

The union's control over personnel affairs was particularly pronounced at Tōshiba. In addition to requiring union approval for the firing or transferring of staff, one agreement from a collective bargaining session called for management to obtain union agreement through a process of workshop-wide meetings before personnel decisions could be made concerning factory managers (*kōjōchō*), division heads (*buchō*) and section chiefs (*kachō*) (Ishikawa 1986: 54). On the shop floor the authority of the union's central committee was more decisive than that of the division heads (*buchō*) and section chiefs (*kachō*) who ran the factory (Yamamoto 1983: 52).

4   Order at work   The sudden changes introduced by the union did not result in anarchy at the workshop. Rather, as the main actor the union had its own autonomous power and was, of its own accord, able to generate a new set of rules for guiding behavior at work. Many reports support this interpretation.

Under the leadership of the foremen at Tōshiba, the workshop groups were successful in their 'production recovery struggle.' A perusal of the union's official history reveals a number of instances of how factory management and the on-line supervisors were able to work within the framework provided by the union (Tōshiba Rōdō Kumiai 1963: 91).

Another example of how new work rules were generated can

be seen in the 'work control' (*gyōmu kanri*) introduced in December 1945 by the Union of Electrical Workers of the Kantō Electrical Power Authority (Kantō Haiden Rōdō Kumiai), another affiliate of Densan. In assuming certain managerial functions, the union's Central Struggle Committee (Chūō Tōsō Iinkai) took the lead in revising the work schedule so that the daily 12-hour shift could be replaced by an 8-hour shift. The union also came to control the records on work attendance, and changed the ordering of names from a status-based ranking to an alphabetical system. Like many other changes, the measure was introduced to enhance the sense of egalitarianism on the shop floor (cf. Kawanishi 1984). Union members also worked hard to improve services to the consumer of electricity. Particular mention was made in one newspaper of 'their strenuous efforts to install street lighting, to repair broken power lines and poles, and to regulate the flow of electricity for commutation and for factory operations' (*Asahi Shimbun*, January 17, 1946). The result was an overall improvement in the efficiency with which electricity was supplied to the nation.

E The struggle between labor and management on the shop floor

Because the strength of the unions rested firmly on their organization on the shop floor, management's counter attack was aimed at restoring management's control of the workshop. In its attack management received the support of the Occupation authorities. The union's 'struggle against the company's adjustment measures' (*kigyō seibi hantai tōsō*) at Tōshiba in 1949 was one indication of the changes occurring in this regard. Management was particularly anxious to restore its control over personnel affairs, and the union realized that 'to lose control of the workshop was to lose everything' (Rōdō Shō 1949: 821). Although the union launched its own 'counter-counter-offensive', 6681 union activists were fired and the union lost control of the workshop.

In the electric power industry as well, management's counter-offensive was aimed at the workshop. In 1950, 2183 activists were dismissed as part of the red purges; the result was the total collapse of the union movement at the workshop level. Then, in 1952, management sought to dilute the '*Densangata* wage system' by providing 'job-based responsibility pay' (*shokumukyū*).

Densan tried to oppose those moves, but it too was defeated. In industry after industry the unionists met with setbacks on the shop floor. The period of union dominance thus came to an end. In coming to put pressure on the union movement, the main strategy adapted by management was first to foster schisms in the union movement, and then to promote the formation of second unions. Schisms could be seen in the Yomiuri Employees Union in 1946, in the Tōshiba union in 1949, and in Densan in 1949 and 1952.

Under management's control, the way was paved in the workshop for the introduction of new technologies and the rationalization of management systems. These changes in turn made Japan's 'takeoff' to high economic growth possible. The workshop was no longer the 'sacred territory' of the union; it had come to fall fully within the domain of management.

IV Labor-Management Relations in the Period of High Economic Growth

As the previous chapter suggested, during the early 1950s the socialistically inspired industrial federations began to lose their influence. In the private sector, the enterprise union began to emerge as a competitive form of unionism in the large firms. The 1950s were characterized by the struggle between the old form of unionism, strongest in the public sector and declining in the private sector, and the new form emerging in the private sector. This period deserves careful attention if we are to understand the dilemma faced by the labor movement and the enterprise union in contemporary Japan.

A Some general characteristics of Japan's new enterprise unions

Four characteristics distinguished the enterprise union in the large private firms from other forms of unionism. First was the ideological emphasis on the importance of cooperative relations between labor and management. Second was the priority given to the use of joint labor-management consultations rather than collective bargaining as the major form of resolving differences between labor and management. Right after the war labor-management relations took place mainly in collective bargaining and in consultations. However, the consultations of the late 1940s were quite different from those which were occurring with the enterprise unions during the period of high economic growth. In the early years, consultations were a part of the process of collective bargaining, although there was a tendency for the collective bargaining sessions to deal primarily with wages and other working conditions and for consultative sessions to deal mainly with production planning and manpower strategies.

In the 1960s, however, the two forms of interaction came to be very clearly differentiated. Collective bargaining came to focus exclusively on working conditions. A basic assumption was that disagreement could result in a strike. However, although consultations continued to serve as a forum for reviewing management's policies and manpower strategies, the union seems to have lost its sense of 'rights' in those areas. Management was free to consult or to inform the union, but the right to make decisions was clearly with management. Union dissatisfaction in these areas was no longer to lead to disputative behavior. During the years of rapid economic growth, the system of joint consultations was expanded and institutionalized, and in many firms decisions concerning even basic working conditions were brought within its jurisdiction. In the process, the 'moral right' to strike was lost, and the apparatus for collective bargaining was put on the back shelf, as though it was only an antique machine from a bygone era.

Third was the adjustment of union goals in a way that legitimized an exchange of (i) the union's cooperation in raising productivity for (ii) the higher wage income which improvements in productivity made possible. The idea was that higher wages be paid only after a certain level of profits had been achieved. The result was a view of things in which the workers' wages were raised only as a result of increasing the size of the pie, not as a result of changes to the distribution of shares received by labor and management. Fourth, the enterprise unions brought with them a new rationale – higher monetary income – for the union movement. Given this emphasis, the enterprise union as an organizational form attracted widespread support among many members, and the egalitarian organizational principles on which

110

the industrial unions had been based were soon forgotten by the rank and file. The result was that the earlier sense of union solidarity declined. Many years later this change in principles would be reflected in Japan's large number of apathetic unionists.

B The actual situation on the shop floor of Japan's large firms

How were industrial relations on the shop floor affected by the new form of unionism? Here the results from a specific case study at a factory of Hitachi Company are introduced to facilitate our understanding of the realities. At the height of Japan's economic growth in 1967 a survey of workshops was made by this author at an electrical goods manufacturer (hereafter referred to as 'Hitachi') organized by one of the unions affiliated with Denki Rōren (the main industrial federation in Chūritsu Rōren and one of the four major bodies constituting IMF-JC). Although the survey's findings and methodology are reported elsewhere in detail (Kawanishi 1981: Part I), and a fuller analysis is presented below in Chapter 7, the reader should know that the study consisted of a series of interviews with management at all levels of the firm and a survey of 300 employees. Also interviews with seven operatives in the section assembling electric generators were supplemented with nonparticipant observation. As for union activity, officials of the factory's union were interviewed while studying a large amount of the union's written material. Finally, the union's organization in two further workshops – one with a strong union organization and one with a weak organization – were observed.

The union being studied was not a weak union, having a reputation in the union movement as a rather strong union on the left. The union had striven conscientiously to develop its activities within the particular political and historical context which was shaped by Japan's rapid economic growth. Accordingly, this case study serves as a suitable means to learn about the activities of the enterprise union on the shop floor in its formative period.

The union at Hitachi had earlier gained its reputation as one of the strongholds of left-wing unionism when it was affiliated with Sanbetsu Kaigi. It had been affiliated with Sanbetsu Kaigi through one of the strong industrial unions which emerged after the war, Zenkoku Kikai Kinzoku Sangyō Rōdō Kumiai Rengōtai (Zenkikin) (the National Confederation of Labor Unions in the Machinery and Metals Industries). It later left Zenkikin, and in 1955 it affiliated with *Denki Rōren*. In the late 1940s the union had many of the features associated with the strong unions described above in the preceding subsections – Densan and the unions at Yomiuri and Tōshiba. In 1950, however, management sought to regain the upper hand by dismissing about 6000 employees. The exercise was used to 'weed out' shop-floor activists. The union launched an eighty-day strike, but was decisively defeated. The strike is one of the last great strikes of the first postwar period of industrial relations. With that defeat, the labor union at Hitachi followed the footsteps of other unions which it had earlier criticized for engaging in struggles which sacrificed large numbers of union members. It had struggled to develop a different type of movement in which such sacrifices could be avoided. After its defeat, the union adopted the three characteristics cited above as later being common to most unions at Japan's large firms during the period of rapid economic growth.

First, the emphasis on cooperative labor-management relations was coupled with the hope that higher wages would best be obtained by cooperating with management-inspired rationalizations and programs to raise productivity and total output. However seriously labor might have wanted to oppose management, leaders came to believe that further sacrifices could not be justified. Management had taken the reins and militant unionism was clearly on the defensive. The only acceptable strategy was to avoid further attacks by management while also trying to secure better living conditions for its members. The decision to cooperate with management in raising productivity was seen as being inevitable, and therefore as being practical.

Second, the union leadership reflected on the past strategy which emphasized shop-level struggles and cohesiveness among the union's members. Decision-making was shifted away from the shop floor, and soon came to be concentrated in the enterprise federation (*kigyōren*). The result was that the 60,000 unionists at Hitachi came to belong to an increasingly bureaucratic organization.

Third, the system of collective bargaining (*dantai kōshōsei*) tended to give way to a system of joint consultations (*rōshi kyōgisei*). This drift was accepted by a union leadership which believed the power relations were such that the union could no longer successfully engage in strikes and other disruptive action.

The management at Hitachi welcomed this change in direction. Like many other Japanese firms, Hitachi began to export during the period of high economic growth and soon found itself engaged in a battle to cut costs on all fronts in order to compete internationally with Europe and North America. The strategy was simple; it called for the introduction of new technologies and industrial diversification based on the development of an elite core of workers. In order to achieve these goals, it was essential that industrial relations be 'normalized' and put on a good footing. On the surface, the union's acceptance of the approach as the most practical or expedient policy seems to have been the correct strategy.

However, while contributing to higher incomes for employees, there were also a number of built-in contradictions. Along with the push for more and more output, overtime increased, the shift system was introduced to maximize the return to machinery and other overhead investment, and the intensification of the work load became more pronounced as management began to release all surplus labor. Although union members gradually became dissatisfied with these developments, union leaders sought to persuade workers that such measures had to be implemented and were in their long-term interests as long as the drive to rationalize did not result in more industrial accidents. The leadership bit its lip and argued that this was the only way.

With the centralization of functions and negotiations, wage rates and other working conditions came to be negotiated by the company-wide federation (*kigyōren*). This meant that the local factory's union office (*tanso*) lost its functions. No longer could it do much about an individual member's problem, and it was not long before the member lost interest in the union.

In the search for a meaningful role to play, the local unit (*tanso*) came to be a first-line shock absorber for grievances which resulted from management-inspired rationalizations. Its other main function was to check for excessively intensified work loads. It became the job of the local union leadership to circulate around the workshops to listen directly to the complaints of the union's members in that particular factory. However, that show of interest proved to be 'too little too late.' The spread of apathy among the membership could not be stemmed. Although grievances from the workshops were passed on to the management consultative council (*keiei shingikai*) which had been set up as part of the system of joint consultations, and even though serious problems with rationalizations were brought to its attention, the union continued to be oriented to a policy of production first. Grievances were always dealt with in an *ad hoc* manner. In the eyes of the rank and file, it seemed that the union was being used by management only to extract further effort from the workers. It is not surprising, then, that union executives should confide to this researcher that their members seemed never to appreciate the role of the union in handling grievances and always to think that the company had solved the workers' problems on its own. The consequences for industrial relations on the shop floor were considerable.

C Personnel administration and the workshop group

Management's rationalization program was accompanied by huge changes in personnel policies on the shop floor. The earlier emphasis on 'seniority-based workshop groups' (*nenkōteki shūdan*) gave way to an emphasis on the 'achievement oriented workshop' (*nōryokushugiteki shokuba*). The immediate goal was a more qualified labor force. Hiring policies called for middle-school graduates to be replaced by graduates from industrial high schools. In some workshops only high school and junior college graduates were considered for jobs as manual operatives.

There were also changes in the structure of the workshop group. In the past workshop groups had been organized around a number of persons with different skills. Through cooperation the group as a whole strove to raise its productivity. The new approach, however, called for those with less skill to be weeded out. Stragglers were branded and some were even transferred to other companies or to the more monotonous jobs requiring less skill.

The role of the foreman (*kumichō*), who was the leader of the workshop group, also changed. Previously, the foreman had typically been a middle-school graduate who had received special training and then gone through an apprenticeship on the shop floor. He would eventually become the 'god of a particular skill' (*ginō no kamisama*). However, with the rapid transformation of the technological base, the old type of foreman lost his ability to cope with the demands of the workshop. Management therefore redefined the position. The new model foreman would be a graduate from a technical or industrial arts high school. He would have a broad understanding of all the skills required in the workshop and would have outstanding leadership skills, judgment and intellect.

The problem was that the company's skilled personnel did not fit the newly defined position. In order to reshape those currently serving as foremen, a rigorous retraining program was established. In addition to learning new technical skills, the new foremen were also imbued with the philosophy and procedures of 'ability-oriented management' (*nōryokushugi kanri*). Those judged to be unqualified for the new role were demoted to ranks of the ordinary operatives.

Those who had become foremen under the old system endeavored to meet the expectations of management, but in many cases their efforts were seen by management as being insufficient. Many came to lose their self-confidence as the number of high-school graduates increased. The situation was redefined so that it became nearly impossible for the old type of foreman. While his authority was based on his own skill and he could lead the workshop group into battle with management, the authority of the new foreman was backed up by his legal position as a member of management rather than by his own skills *per se*. No longer was the foreman the boss of the workshop group (*shokuba shūdan no bosu*) or the spokesman for workers in the group. He had become the lowest-level administrator for management.

With the introduction of new technologies, control of the technical processes shifted upward in the organization. The foremen were removed from that function; their primary responsibility came to be personnel administration in the form of simply assisting with interpersonal relations among the workers. They were to look after each employee's personal needs at work and in his private time as well. This form of total control (*zenjinkakuteki kanri*) resulted in all aspects of the thinking and behavior – not only of the employee but his family as well, at work, leisure, and school – coming under the purview of the company. By doing this, management hoped that a high level of worker motivation could be maintained among employees on the shop floor. In this role, the foreman became the lowest level representative of the personnel manager – his front-line supervisor or administrator – on the workshop floor.

In the past the foreman spent a good deal of time looking after the interests of the workers in his own workshop. He was interested in their private lives to the extent of intruding. At times he organized social gatherings for the workers and took it upon himself to make arrangements for their weddings and funerals. Through these activities a 'family-like atmosphere' was created. The final product was a workshop group with a strong sense of community which reflected the group's autonomy from management.

The new foreman, however, contrasted sharply with his forerunner. Because his authority was backed by the power of management rather than his own demonstrated skill, the best that could be achieved was an artificial sense of community which was subsumed within the larger bureaucratic structures of the firm. Even if the workshop was given some autonomy, it was not enough for it to be able to 'stand up' to management.

The principle of organization had shifted from skill to 'ability' (*nōryoku joretsu*). The larger occupational groupings which located the employee within the firm no longer reflected age or years of service with the firm. For example, high-school graduates under thirty came to be earning the same as middle-school graduates aged over forty. Among the younger workers there was a very clear hierarchy based on skill differentials (*nōryokusa*). As a personnel administrator, the new foreman's power came to be in the discretion he was given to decide where such differentials lie. He was the first point of reference in evaluating those under his jurisdiction. Accordingly, ordinary workers intent on promotion and on up-grading their qualifications could not ignore the 'political' presence of the foreman. The result in many cases was that workers came to compete by being solicitous to the whims of the foreman (who in turn was able to utilize that obsequiousness to his advantage in running the workshop to management's specifications).

Finally, it should be noted that foreman was the top position to which operatives could aspire. Regardless of how much they studied or matured, operatives had no hope of being promoted to staff positions. They were locked into a very short promotion scale and were forced to compete 'all out' for the few positions that were available. By skillfully manipulating this competition management was able to maintain discipline among the labor force at the shop-floor level.

D The labor union on the shop floor

The obvious outcome of the above developments was that the unions became little more than an administrative arm of management in the area of personnel affairs. Most of the union's workshop committees came to be headed by the new type of foreman. The committee's secretary would be the first assistant foreman (*ittō bōshin*), and the other committee members would be drawn from among those next lower in rank, including the second assistant foreman (*nitō bōshin*). The structure of the union at the shop level came to parallel that of the management's administration. It thus became impossible for younger workers who were at the bottom of the new job hierarchy to 'break through' and become union officials.

When someone from the workshop stood for election to a position as a full-time official on the union's factory executive (*tanso shikkōbu*), it became common practice that the section chief be consulted beforehand to be sure that the member's absence from the workshop would not interfere unduly with the attainment of the plant's production goals. In other words, to participate in union affairs, union members needed management's approval. When the section chief's approval had been obtained in the union's selection of personnel, it was generally the case that the union's activities could be smoothly carried out. The result has been the total emasculation of the union official as an independent spokesperson for the ordinary worker.

Many problems in the workshop required an independent union. The intensification of work resulting from management-inspired rationalization provides one set of concrete examples in this regard. Diversification based on a small elite of core workers meant an increase in their monthly overtime up to an average of 75 hours per worker. The families of these core workers soon came to expect, and even to depend upon, this overtime. Overtime became necessary to repay housing loans, and the effort required to work such long hours pushed many workers to their physical limit.

To do away with surplus labor on the shop floor, management introduced the 'minute accounting system.' Management published the average time (in minutes) workers in each workshop spent away from their work station (*riseki jikan*). As all leave was counted and active work groups docked for 'excessive' leave (based on a comparison with other work groups), workers soon found themselves unable even to use their annual holidays.

Workers were particularly unhappy with the use of computers to calculate standard operation times, claiming that the time expectations of management were unrealistic. Displeasure was also expressed with regard to (i) the discretion given the foreman in evaluating skill differentials, and (ii) the way in which job-based pay differentials were awarded. Although there was a system for handling grievances, it was seldom used. If it were used, the problem raised would appear on the agenda of one of the meetings in the system of joint labor-management consultations and the name of the person who raised the issue would be made public. Since that person would be made to appear as a 'complainer' or a 'whinger,' given the system of 'total person (personality) management' (*zenjinkakuteki kanri*), an employee required an extraordinary amount of determination and courage to withstand the peer-group pressure which such a system generated. In short, the kinds of 'grievances' which the system was designed to deal with were mainly environmental matters which could be connected with improving levels of productivity. The workers were presented with a suggestion system rather than a grievance system.

It is instructive to consider briefly how the chairman of the union's workshop committee (*shokuba iinchō*), who was also the foreman, dealt with real complaints. With regard to overtime, the chairman could negotiate directly with his supervisor, the section chief. However, when the section chief simply replied that 'overtime was necessary because of heavy demands,' the union's commitment to cooperating with management to raise productivity made it difficult for the union to turn around and restrict overtime. In fact, as an administrative arm of management, the union leaders often found themselves persuading their members to work even harder.

With regard to the willingness of workers to forego their paid annual leave, the chairman of the union's workshop committee found himself with a conflict of interest since his role as foreman brought him to give priority to maintaining as full a staff as possible on the production line. Work schedules were so organized that the absence of one employee, even if planned ahead of time, would result in added work loads for other workers, which would in turn take them beyond the breaking point. The other workers were encouraged to feel that they were being 'whipped' to work harder while one of their workmates was having a free ride and enjoying himself. The end result would ultimately be open dissension on the shop floor and disruption to the cadence which management had struggled to establish. The ability of the foreman would come to be questioned for having allowed the employment utilization rate (*shūgyōritsu*) (see the definition above in Chapter 4) to fall.

The chairman of the union's workshop committee also held the right to evaluate the employees under his mantle in the workshop. But he did not evaluate them evenly or fairly in line with the union's original aims of promoting 'egalitarianism.' If he had, he would have been judged by those further up in the hierarchy as being incapable or as being a recalcitrant foreman. Accordingly, he took the initiative in employing the evaluation system to differentiate among union members. According to one foreman, it was a process of sometimes raising an employee's personal evaluation dramatically and at other times dropping it dramatically in order to keep the workers 'fired up.' It was the discretion of the chairman to raise or to lower the evaluation of employees which ensured him his influence.

Sometimes a union member will cynically state that 'it's foolish to participate in union affairs.' Because union officials have to be absent from the workshop some of the time, the employment utilization rate (*shūgyōritsu*) for their workshop drops and their workmates have to pay 'the price' one way or another. More-over, a fall in the *shūgyōritsu* will have ramifications, for the committee chairman is also the foreman. If a committee member in the shop (*shokuba iin*) is too enthusiastic it is likely that the chairman cum foreman will give him a low evaluation. In other words, union officials are asked to spend time going through the motions, but not too seriously, a kind of hypocritical behavior which is ultimately alienating. Those able to perform the job are quick to develop a very thick skin which is calloused by the constant cynicism attached to his interactions with others.

Members of the union committee are likely to have less over-time as their 'free' time is taken up with the affairs of the union. However, the foreman, who is responsible for the personnel evaluations, is the first person to know whether a worker has 'enthusiastically' been doing overtime. Failure to carry a full workload will work to the disadvantage of anyone serving as the shop-floor representative (*shokuba iin*). If overtime decreases, so too does one's income and the pinch is felt immediately in one's finances at home. With the artificially created sense of community strongly implanted in the minds of the employees, they come to regulate their own involvement in union activities. This self-censoring results in the worker concluding that 'it is silly to engage in union activity as long as everyone else is engaged in overtime.'

The end result is that the union members come to know the parameters for union activity which are set by the committee chairman who is also a foreman, and to realize that it is in their own interests to engage in union activity only to the 'proper' extent. As the committee chairman in turn knows what is expected by his immediate boss, the section chief, he too will behave 'properly' in accordance with those expectations. In this manner, the union's organizational unit at the level of the work-shop came to be subsumed within the personnel administration structures of management. No longer could the union's executive committee control its workshop organization, for the workshop has clearly become the domain of management.

The case study at Hitachi indicates how industrial relations on the shop floor have been shaped by the redefined balance of power. With the scales tipped in favour of management, the union came to accept the 'logic of the larger pie' (*pai no riron*) as the rationale for its strategies. In doing so, it lost its ability to pursue an independent policy *vis-à-vis* management. However, union members on the shop floor had depended upon the union to look after their interests by providing a buffer between the worker and management. Failure of the union to maintain an independent presence meant that the worker came ultimately to be at 'the mercy of management.' Regardless of whether the union was able to win or lose on certain issues, and despite whatever shift might have occurred in the balance of power owing to the rapid growth of the economy, had the union, in the eyes of the members, been able to maintain a constant stand against the intensification of work loads, it is unlikely that it would have been annihilated so thoroughly on the shop floor.

V   The Changing Face of Japan's Industrial Relations

The tragedy of the labor movement in general during the period of high economic growth rates is that union members did not feel that they had lost anything with the demise of the union's workshop activities. For workers in Japan's large firms, intensification of work loads was offset by the increase in their incomes. Considering their previous standard of living, they were decidedly better off. Moreover, their wages were suitably above those of their counterparts in Japan's smaller firms. This would be how those surviving the increased competition in the workshop would have seen things. To the extent that their standard of living could be achieved without reference to the union – indeed, even because of its loss of power – workers had little reason to turn to the union.

Although union leaders in Japan's large unions were willing to concede that unions had lost their previous status in terms of the power relationship, they argued that the goal of securing a minimal standard of living for union members had been achieved by the new form of enterprise unionism. What more, then, was there that the union should be doing? The idea that industrial relations was about power relationships lost its appeal, although much later in the 1980s there has been a renewed interest in reassessing the trade-off between income and power which had occurred with the rise of the enterprise union.

At this point it is useful to reconsider the significance of having chosen Hitachi as the firm at which to conduct the case study. Although the enterprise union at Hitachi took a relatively cooperative stance *vis-à-vis* management, it was nevertheless known as a strong union with a decidedly left-wing orientation. Accordingly Hitachi was chosen to gain an idea about how an active enterprise union had positioned itself at one of Japan's largest firms in one of Japan's core industries. At most other large firms the enterprise union played an even less active role on the shop floor. In fact, there would be many firms where the union played no role at all on the shop floor. This would seem obvious from other case studies by Kamata (1973), Saito (1974), Matsuzaki (1982) and Kawanishi (1981).

VI The Future

The union's emasculation on the shop floor has not yet been seen by most workers as a serious problem. Their attention has been on the relatively high standard of living which Japan's large firms can provide. Although competition among employees had increased, employees could blindly devote themselves to the competition for promotion without having to worry about the consequences of losing. To a considerable extent their wages and employment seemed guaranteed. Of course, it was possible during the period of rapid economic expansion for management to retain less efficient workers and continuously to be paying higher wages. Accordingly, workers were willing to devote their full energies to the competition to obtain the best evaluations possible. In a very real sense there were no losers.

However, the times have changed. No longer can employees rest assured that their job is secure, for employees are now divided into two groups. One consists of a small core of elites who fill the key positions; the other consists of the non-elite workers who have been placed on the periphery. For the second group, competition has meant a relative loss of employment, security, and income. These workers hold one key to the future of the enterprise union and industrial relations in Japan. Will they continue to sacrifice themselves to the competitive principle and come to differentiate their own self-interest from the interests of their workmates? Or will they embrace the principle of 'equality' to the extent that everyone will have a guaranteed minimum? At present, the choice between these two is being forced on many workers. Although it is too early to say which consciousness will dominate the minds of most workers in Japan, the potential for the union to play a role in influencing that choice seems greater now than during the period of rapid growth. It is certain that employees can no longer indulge in the simple belief that their livelihood is guaranteed by management regardless of whether the union exists or not.

But can the unions recover? For over thirty years they have steadily been losing their ability to stand up to management. In order to revive themselves the unions will have to reassert themselves on the shop floor. In looking for the way ahead, at least three policies would facilitate the survival of the union movement in Japan.

The first is for workers to develop their own culture on the shop floor, and for the union to develop its activities on that basis. The concept of a 'workers' culture' (*rōdōsha bunka*) might be defined as 'a comprehensive set of ideas concerning the approach to human relationships, the life-style, behavior and consciousness which are suited to the needs of workers.' It is a culture distinct from that of the managerial class and the 'middle class.' During the period of high economic growth, Japan's workers forsook their own culture and sought to adopt the norms and patterns of behavior associated with the other two classes. The idea of guaranteed livelihood minimums which evolved out of the value placed on equality during the period of labor's offensives provides a good example of a 'workers' culture' appropriate to the times.

Is it possible to create a 'workers' culture' appropriate to the current social milieu? The example of the number one union at Zeneraru Oil Refineries provides a useful point of departure (cf. Kawanishi 1981: Part III). Eight years after a second union was formed in 1970, the first union's struggle against 'the system' resulted in 11 firings being withdrawn while 42 disciplinary cases were dropped and 69 incidences of unfair labor practices were corrected. In addition, inappropriate wage differentials were abolished. Accounting for the success of the number one union was its strategy of building a 'workers' culture.' Following the schism, nearly 90 percent of its members left to join the number two union. The first union ended up with about 100 members in their late teens or early twenties who styled themselves as being the most outspoken workers at Zeneraru Oil Refineries. However, they made a pact among themselves and confronted the 800-member strong number two union. There was a shared belief that 'each member would not stab his mates in the back' and a philosophy which was wary of 'getting ahead by oneself at the expense of others' and of outdoing one's mates in a competition for the fruits of everyone's labor and cooperation. There was a determination not to leave one's place of work no matter how unpleasant the work experience became. The number one union's goal was to change the place of work fundamentally. The work was monotonous and boring. Working on one of two 12-hour shifts, the employees were required to keep watch on lots of meters. The work was physically and mentally exhausting. Having become members of a minority union which represented only 10 percent of Zeneraru's total workforce, unionists in the number one union were ostracized by management and by those employees who had joined the number two union. They were interfered with and constantly discriminated against. It was not surprising, then, that some of the unionists who remained in the number one union were 'buying time' – waiting for an opportunity to find other work so that they could 'escape' the place of work they had come to despise.

However, many realized that to leave Zeneraru would only mean moving to another firm and another work situation which would be similarly depressing. Accordingly, most of the employees decided to stay put and to use the force of their minority union to improve working conditions on the shop floor at Zeneraru. In doing that, a new sense of workers' solidarity emerged. It was from this kind of approach that Japan's unions can perhaps find a measure of inspiration.

Two facets of the minority union's experience at Zeneraru stand out. One was linked to the refusal of the unionists simply to quit and move away. The minority union cultivates a sense of proprietorship in the workshop – a certain pride in their work which meant they could not be removed at management's request. A long struggle ensued. The unionists had to put up with various forms of discrimination and the lower material standard of living that implied. However, their consciousness as employees was heightened, thereby cutting them free from the self-denial which characterized the attempts of mamy employees who left the union to aspire to the competitive life-style of the 'middle-class.' The workers in the number one union may not have been as well off materially, but they enjoyed a life-style with which they were comfortable psychologically.

The second facet was the union's involvement in issues of direct relevance to its members. In the areas relevant to the workers' careers, the reassertion of the principles of equality in policies for promotion, job transfers and dismissals allowed the union to maintain the support of its members. During the late 1970s several unions in the Japan National Railways were successful in their activities largely because members felt that the union's philosophy of equality gave them a 'stake in things' (cf. Rōshi Kankei Chōsakai, 1981: 335–511; and Inagami 1981: 227–350).

Koike (1977) suggested that the unions ought (i) to try to limit the extent to which management can arbitrarily determine evaluations (*satei*), and (ii) to propose concrete criteria and rules by which workers will be evaluated. Koike (1977) argued that American unions had been able to consolidate their positions against management by controlling the evaluation of union members. The experience of Japan's unions right after the war also reveals that this is an effective measure. During the immediate postwar years, the labor unions made control over personnel policies the basis for their power. If that is the case the immediate goal should be the rebirth of the ethos that characterized the labor movement and the working class immediately after the war. The idea of seeking personal gain only needs to be replaced by the broader sense of solidarity among all workers, a commitment to a selfless struggle on behalf of the welfare of all workers.

Finally, it is perhaps time that the union paid attention to those who have been placed beyond the scope of its interests: female workers, temporary and part-time employees, those employed by small subcontractors, and middle-aged and older workers. By organizing their own unions it is possible that these workers will exert some influence on the enterprise unions which emerged in the 1950s and 1960s almost exclusively for the core or career employees in Japan's large firms. As Chapter 8 suggests, such moves began to appear in the late 1970s (cf. also Kawanishi 1970). Considering that the 25.2 percent of Japan's employees presently organized in 1990 tend to constitute the upper echelons of the labor force, it is impossible to talk about the revival of Japan's labor unions without there being some movement to organize workers who are not employed on a tenured basis by Japan's large firms.

The strategies discussed immediately above require a return to some kind of egalitarian philosophy which rejects the notion of discriminatory employment practices. As long as the union movement cannot resurrect its visions of an egalitarian society of and for the workers, it is unlikely that a unified labor movement will emerge in contemporary Japan. Despite the ideological emphasis on homogeneity, there are too many inequalities for the underprivileged workers to accept.

In the preceding chapter, the history of industrial disputes in postwar Japan was discussed. Attention was paid to the way in which the unions lost their initiative and management came to win battle after battle. In this chapter the discussion highlighted the consequences of management's supremacy for the way in which industrial relations are carried out on the shop floor. In the next chapter attention is shifted to consider the way in which the union structure was changed from that of the industrial union to that of the enterprise union. The argument is that the strength of Japan's unions immediately after the war lies to a considerable degree in their form of organization. It was for this reason that management sought to rebuild its position in the early 1950s primarily by undermining the industrial union and striving to nurture the enterprise union in its place. That transformation was symbolized by the demise of Densan – the powerful industrial union in the electric power industry. The next chapter tells the story of the rise and fall of Densan, focusing on its famous dispute late in 1952.

6 The Establishment of the Enterprise Union: An Examination of the 1952 Densan Dispute

This chapter focuses on the processes which gave birth to the form of enterprise unionism prevalent in Japan today. By examining a specific dispute in the power industry, it seeks to elucidate how enterprise unionism came to replace industrial unionism as the major form of organization in the Japanese labor movement.

In this chapter 'enterprise unionism' is used to refer to an approach to union organization that limits membership to employees of a single enterprise and formulates demands to promote only the welfare of those employees at the one firm. 'Industrial unionism' is used to refer to a form of organization that allows for the equal participation of all employees in an entire industry and that formulates demands on the basis of the needs of all employees in the industry. The 'ism' in each term implies that each form of organization is accompanied by an ideological stance or philosophical outlook which attaches a normative value on a particular approach to organizing employees.

As Kawanishi (1981: 6–9) has argued elsewhere, enterprise unionism has not been an unchanging union philosophy with a long, unbroken tradition in Japan. First, 'industrial unionism' was the prevalent philosophy in the years immediately after the Second World War. Second, enterprise unionism came to displace industrial unionism during the 1950s. Third, the change from one philosophy to the other was not inevitable; rather, it occurred as the result of a tremendous struggle between the two philosophies *cum* ideologies.

From this perspective, then, enterprise unionism is a way of thinking which emerged out of a particular conflict relationship between labor and management. Because the philosophy of enterprise unionism is not a cultural given and has the potential to change again, as do all ideas, enterprise unionism needs to be understood within the broader historical context which has produced it. This chapter utilizes findings from a case study of unionism in the power industry to examine the processes by which the above-mentioned conflict was generated and resolved. It concludes by considering the significance of the findings for assessing the way organizational philosophy is likely to evolve in Japan's labor movement over the last decade of this century.

I   Theories on the Formation of the Enterprise Union

Numerous theories have been advanced to explain the emergence of the enterprise union in Japan. However, none of the theories have been adequately substantiated. In the paragraphs below, two general categories of theory are introduced. One may be called the cultural approach. The other is the labor-market approach.

A   Cultural explanations of the enterprise union

Many observers have emphasized features such as lifetime employment (*shūshin koyō*), the seniority-merit ranking system (*nenkō joretsu seido*) and the enterprise union (*kigyōbetsu kumiai*). Such phenomena are seen as being a natural, even inevitable, outcome of a peculiarly Japanese frame of mind which is embedded in the culture. Such views can be found throughout much of the literature on Japanese-style management. In its most stark form, the argument is that Japanese-style management was born directly out of the Japanese national character. However, the most serious deficiency of this literature is the nearly complete absence of anything we could call 'an academic orientation.'

One exception to this generalization is Hazama's research (1964) on the origins of Japanese-style management. Having compiled a full historical account, Hazama argued that the basic social structure in prewar Japan was the *ie* or household system. He maintained that the core structure of that system was implanted in Japan's commercial establishments at the end of the Edo period – establishments which later became the driving force behind Japanese capitalism in the Meiji era. In that fashion, he seeks to uncover the origins of Japan's style of paternalistic management. Hazama argues that paternalistic management became somewhat established as a management system and ideology about the time of the First World War. Paternalistic management was an approach to human organization which extended the *ie* ideology to serve the needs of the enterprise as an on-going commercial operation. In other words, the *ie* ideology was useful in mobilizing the symbols associated with society's basic social unit in order to enhance the work group's ability to act as an organic functional body. In simple terms, the firm was presented as a family household. The metaphor suggested that the hierarchical class relationship between management and employees was the same as the relationship between parents (especially the head of the household) and their offspring (who were seen as the legitimate successors). The ideological emphasis on the likeness of the firm and the family has been given a touch of reality by the institution of various personnel practices. They include the seniority-merit wage system, career employment, and a comprehensive set of additional provisions for employees. 'Japanese-style management' tends to be vindicated to the extent that such practices have been successfully implemented. Moreover, as a kind of 'self-fulfilling prophecy' the direction of attention to those successes tends to produce fairly high levels of employee morale and a strong sense of identification with their firms. This process, then, further facilitates the institutionalization of such practices.

To be sure, Hazama's concern is with the origins of paternalistic management, and he did not write about the formation of enterprise unions *per se*. Nevertheless, it is easy to see from his research how Japan's paternalistic style of management could facilitate the emergence of a strong sense of identity with their firm on the part of Japan's employees. Once the existence of such a consciousness is established, it might be argued there would be a logical basis for concluding that a class-based unionism cutting across the firm would have a difficult time developing. At the very best, one might argue, under such circumstances activists in the labor movement would have to settle for a form of company unionism which rested primarily on the maintenance of interpersonal relationships within the paternalistic framework of the firm.

B Internal labor markets

The origins of Japan's enterprise unionism have been viewed from another angle by labor economists. Their view is that the enterprise union is a logical outcome of certain ways in which the labor market is structured. When the market is vertically structured, they argue, it is reasonable to expect that unions too will be so organized. Those reaching this conclusion can be further subdivided into two subgroupings.

One subgrouping follows the lines of Ōkōchi (1972). As explained above in Chapter 2, Ōkōchi emphasized the uniqueness of the peculiarly Japanese labor market which emerged during the Meiji period. Central to this approach is Ōkōchi's theory of the migrant wage laborer (*dekasegi-gata chinrōdō*) and the vertically structured labor market which resulted from that type of labor. For Ōkōchi the logical outcome was enterprise unionism.

A second subgrouping includes Shirai (1980), Taira (1977) and Koike (1977). These writers point to more universal phenomena in explaining the emergence of the enterprise union. According to them, the maturation of capitalism is accompanied by the growing importance of internal labor markets in any society. The internationalization of labor markets brings with it career employment and seniority-merit wage systems. The result, they argue, is a form of enterprise-oriented unionism in which all employees have a mutually interdependent stake in the organization to which they are affiliated.

C The power relations in labor-management relations

There is another approach to labor-management relations which highlights the dynamics of power, authority and hierarchy. Although each of the two approaches mentioned above offers valuable insight for understanding labor-management relations in Japan, neither explains directly how or why the enterprise union was established at a given firm. They provide explanations which do not contradict the existence of the enterprise union, but they really do not specify the mechanism or actual procedures by which the enterprise union is established. They tend to be historical explanations devoid of human actors. Although the two theories may point to some background factors facilitating the formation of the enterprise union, organizations are born out of a complex of behavior. The ability of the organization to function, indeed its basic structure, is determined by the way its members behave. Accordingly, there is a need to go beyond the basic preconditions which Hazama, Shirai, Taira and Koike wrote about.

The enterprise union which developed in Japan is the product of two conflicting forces and the outcome of decisions made by the major actors – the human individuals who have shaped the conflict. On the one hand, there is management. Its interests are not served by the development of horizontal unionism which supersedes each enterprise's organization. On the other, there are the unionists who see their interests being promoted by such unionism. The approach utilized here assumes first that management forms a coherent stratum in society. Management is seen as being motivated by the pursuit of profit. Profit is maximized by organizing individual members of the working class into a large number of separate organizations known as 'business firms' and then setting them into competition against each other. This can be seen as a general framework in which employees are mobilized. The idea was that large, vertically structured enterprise groupings competed one with the other. To win the competition, each enterprise tried to garrison itself against other competitors in an all-out struggle to survive. Each firm wanted employees who would work blindly to achieve its goals. Unions which reached across firms were seen as a threat to this kind of ideology and to structures contrived by management to promote this kind of commitment from employees. Accordingly, management found that the spread of industrial unions would not be in its interests. Instead, it pushed for some form of vertically structured enterprise-based unionism (which emphasized the primacy of enterprise unions, employee associations, mutual amity meetings and employee credit unions). At this point one might well ask, 'Why does management push for any union at all?' 'Why does management in Japan's large firms not simply push for a situation where there would be no unions at all, as is the situation in most smaller firms in Japan?'

To answer this sort of question, one must return to the historical context. First, to have been actively against all forms of unionism would have allowed the critics of capitalism too easily to accuse management of being 'undemocratic.' 'Democracy' has been a key word in postwar Japan, and the label 'undemocratic' had come to mean 'feudalistic,' 'anachronistic,' 'outdated.' To appear progressive, management felt it must accept unions as a necessary evil. With that as a given, management's strategy was to encourage the form of unionism most amenable to its goals. It was quick to see that there were likely to be fewer disadvantages in having to deal with enterprise unions than in having to deal with industrial unions. Moreover, with the cultivation of the enterprise union as a body which could assist in administering management's personnel policies, certain types of enterprise unions might even have been seen as making a positive contribution to the achievement of the firm's goals which could not be expected of the industrial union. For example, Article 36 of the Labor Standards Law allowed management to have overtime agreements with unions which organized 50 percent or more of their employees. With such an agreement, any amount of overtime could be requested of employees.

The approach adopted here further assumes that Japan's employees have an interest in the developing mechanisms to improve their working conditions and to limit the extent to which their labor is 'unfairly' appropriated by management. From that perspective, one decisive measure they can take is to join hands on an industry-wide basis in order to act collectively as a cohesive class. The approach workers will take in any specific society will depend upon a variety of factors in that particular society at that particular time. In England there are the shop steward committees; in West Germany, the *betriebsträt*; and in Italy and France, the enterprise committees. However, regardless of the organizational form taken, employee organizations based within the firm will not be effective in limiting the arbitrary employment practices of management unless they have an awareness of themselves as 'intervening' or 'temporary-support' organizations bent on achieving some kind of industry-wide or society-wide standard. To possess an adequate amount of bargaining power, such an employees' association would need at least some kind of organization on which it could rely when heavily pressed by management. Such an organization would need a base broader than that of the individual enterprise or firm.

In a capitalist society there is a basic dynamic which is set in motion by the conflict between the 'enterprise principle' (*kigyōb-etsu shugi*) of management and the 'horizontal principle' (*ōdan-*

shugi) of the working class. If we can accept this framework as one way of analyzing changes in industrial relations, a careful examination of the power relationship between labor and management becomes one's starting point. Such an examination requires that we look separately at the power of each party. The discussion below focuses on the labor union and its structure as one means of assessing the power of Japanese employees.

II The Case Study

The analysis proceeds with a careful examination of the 1952 Densan dispute (Densan Nijūnananen Sōgi). Nihon Denki Sangyo Rōdō Kumiai (the Japan Electrical Power Workers' Industrial Labor Union), more commonly known simply as 'Densan,' was organized in 1947 by 120,000 employees at ten electrical power companies. In late 1945, employee unions were formed separately at each place of work in all the power companies. Before long, the workshop-based organizations began to form company-wide federations. The logical extension of those moves was the formation of an industry-wide council of electrical power workers in 1946. The council evolved into Densan the following year. The industrial federation had no sooner been formed than it began to come under pressure from management. It was then only a matter of time before 'number two unions' began to appear as a result of schisms.

Although Densan played a major role in the union movement in postwar Japan, less than ten years after its formation the Central Executive was rendered inoperative. The rise and fall of Densan came to symbolize the rise and fall of industrial unionism in postwar Japan. Accordingly, a careful examination of Densan may give some insight into the transformation of Japan's union movement from industrial unionism to enterprise unionism. From this perspective, the 1952 Densan dispute serves as a watershed – a symbol both for the end of industrial unionism and for the advent of the form of enterprise unionism which became institutionalized during the period of high economic growth between the late 1950s and the early 1970s.

Densan took the lead during Sanbetsu Kaigi's October Struggle in 1946. In winning from management the epoch-making 'Densangata wage system,' Densan paved the way for the golden era of industrial unionism in the hard years after the war. However, only six years later it suffered a huge defeat along with Tanrō, the major industrial union in the coal mining industry, as the major driving force behind the fall offensive organized by Sōhyō in 1952. Known more generally as 'the dispute of 1952,' the confrontation with management deserves careful analysis because it was one of the stepping stones to the introduction of enterprise unionism into Japanese industry. Four years of wavering between 'industrialism' and 'enterprisism' in the electric power industry finally led to the triumph of those favoring the latter. By that time the writing was clearly on the wall. Several years later, in 1956, Densan's Central Executive was dissolved. 'Enterprisism' spread and the enterprise union came to take firm root in the private sector.

For this reason the 1952 Densan dispute is relevant not only to understanding the history of Densan itself, but for understanding how industrialism came to be replaced by 'enterprisism' in the labor movement as a whole. Accordingly, the dispute provides the basis for an important case study of the actual circumstances under which enterprise unionism emerged in postwar Japan (cf. Shimizu 1978).

III Densan and the Ascendance of 'Industrialism'

A The 'era of industrialism'

Before looking at the issues in the 1952 Densan dispute, it is useful to survey briefly some major features of the philosophy which was developed by the Densan leadership in the years after the war. At the same time, it is important to keep in mind the well known fact that the unionization rate in Japan jumped from nought to about 40 percent in the first year after the war, reaching a high of 55.7 percent in 1949, a sharp rise from the prewar high registered in 1936, 7.9 percent. Although most of the unions right after the war were of the enterprise type, they were imbued with the idea of 'industrialism' and moving in the direction of forming industrial unions. On the first day after defeat (August

16, 1945) the All Japan Seamen's Union issued its call for industrial unionism. Thereafter, unionists on the left and on the right moved to establish their own centers, but both groups had some form of industrial unionism in mind.

On the left Sōdōmei was established on August 1, 1946. Consisting of 1699 unions with about 850,000 members, it accounted for 22 percent of all unionists. It was led by a Central Preparatory Committee (Chūō Junbi Iinkai) which resolved that its members would make industrial federations and a strong national confederation their primary organizational goal (Ōkōchi and Matsuo 1969: 117). The main organizational unit was to be a prefectural-level council of unions. In order to implement their plans, the prewar activists entered factories around the country. By providing the leadership for industrial disputes, they felt that they would be able to promote the formation of labor unions. The labor movement which evolved around Sōdōmei was organized from the top down, although the movement was definitely conceived as moving toward industrial unionism in which some form of local organization would constitute the nucleus or key organizational unit.

On August 19, 1946 Sanbetsu Kaigi was formed with 21 industrial federations and about 1.63 million members who accounted for about 43 percent of all unionists. Sanbetsu Kaigi could be said to have been organized from below; enterprise-level organizations were seen as being the main driving force in creating a viable form of industrial unionism. However, at the First Meeting of Factory Representatives from Kanagawa on December 25, 1945 the principle of forming independent industrial federations was clearly enunciated. The All Japan Union of Newspaper and Communication Workers (Nihon Shinbun Tsūshin Rōdōkumiai) was formed according to that principle the following February. It provided the guiding principle for the industrial unions which formed Sanbetsu Kaigi. Of course, these developments were influenced by the resolution of the Japan Communist Party to promote the formation of national industrial unions on top of a structure of enterprise unions.

The idea of having industrial unions can be said to have been further promoted by the activities leading up to the October Struggle organized by Sanbetsu Kaigi in the fall of 1946. The labor movement, which had began to develop quite vigorously from late in 1945, entered a kind of lull after May. Overall there was a drop in the number of disputes, and the production control movement began to wane. These changes reflected changes in the policies of the Occupation. Although the Occupation seemed, on the whole, to have pursued a policy supporting the development of the labor movement, a number of developments later led it to restrict the labor movement. The reconstruction of Japanese industry within the overall framework of a capitalist social structure (cf. Yamamoto 1977a) required that industrial production be lifted. The Occupation soon became concerned about the detrimental effects of the production control movement. In the streets, the struggles to expose hoarding, the large gatherings to demand food rations and the mass demonstrations were seen as further destablizing the situation. In the political arena, the Occupation authorities were troubled by the temporary vacuum which had been created by the resignation of the Shidehara cabinet. In this climate the October Struggle was seen by the leaders of Sanbetsu Kaigi as a means of crystallizing the class consciousness of the working class which was facing its first reversal in the postwar period. The feeling that a working-class movement was being achieved was further promoted by the participation of the unions affiliated with Sōdōmei in the second phase of the struggle.

In the early stages of the October Struggle many unions, including the Struggle Group at Yomiuri and the Tōshiba Union, found themselves unable to realize their demands for higher wages and for the reinstatement of all employees who had earlier been fired. However, just as the union movement seemed to be on the verge of collapse, the electrical power workers were able to achieve all their demands, including the famous *Densangata* wage system. Their success reinvigorated the entire labor movement.

Following the victory of the electrical power workers, unions in the private sector were able to move ahead with their counter-offensive. This in turn created an environment which inspired the wage demands of workers in the public sector. The end result was the decision of the unions to organize a General Strike on February 1, 1947. Accordingly, the new year saw labor riding another wave of intensive activity. With the successes in late 1946 Sanbetsu Kaigi reached its zenith. Densan had provided a powerful model for the other industrial unions.

B The distinguishing characteristics of Densan's industrialism

As the distinctiveness of the Densan approach has been described in some detail elsewhere (Kawanishi 1979b), the discussion here focuses on four main characteristics of the 'Densan model.'

1 The industrial union as the basic organizing principle Densan is commonly regarded as the prime example of an industrial union in postwar Japan. The regional and prefectural organizational units consisted of employees from several different firms. It was only at the level of the shop committee that employees in the same firm were organized together. In Japan it is common for the organizational structure at the industrial level to be something along the lines of the loose federation of enterprise unions shown as Type III in Figure 6.1. At the extreme they might approach the second type of structure shown in Figure 6.1. Federation along the lines shown in Type III often resulted in industry-wide goals and functions being sacrificed in the compromises which were hammered out among its self-interested enterprise unions.

Densan, however, was different. This was in part because there was a national enterprise (Nihon Hassōden) (hereafter referred to as 'Nippatsu') which was responsible for distributing electrical power throughout the country. With this enterprise as the main pillar, the union was able to organize prefectural and local branches which would bring together workers in the nine power sales companies with those in the power supply companies. This approach mitigated against the union serving primarily the interests of workers in just one or two of the more influential firms.

Membership in Densan was not restricted to employees of Nippatsu and the nine local power sales companies. The door was open for employees of electrical contractors and subcontractors and for employees of construction companies which built the power plants.[1] The aim was to join all workers in the electrical power industry. It was the central organization which decided on membership. It retained fifty percent of all union fees and made the decisions to strike, to bargain, and to settle. In other words, Densan was seen as being very close to the ideal of what an industrial union should be.

137

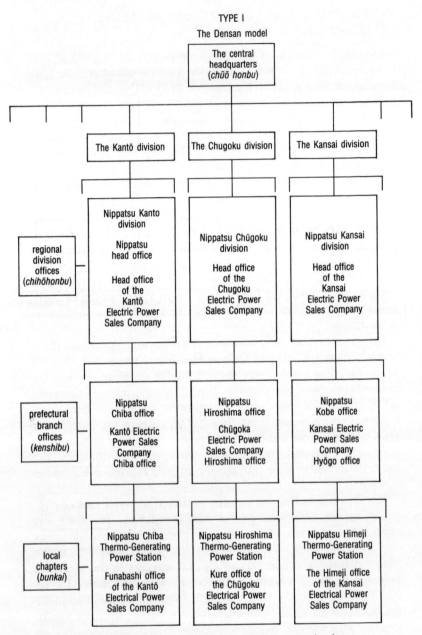

Figure 6.1 *Three types of industry-based union organization*

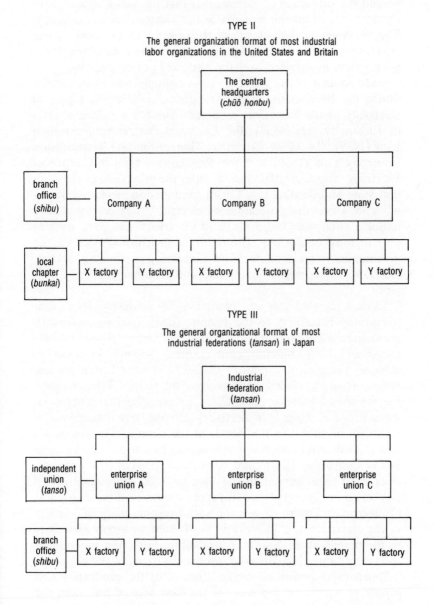

TYPE II

The general organization format of most industrial
labor organizations in the United States and Britain

TYPE III

The general organizational format of most
industrial federations (*tansan*) in Japan

2   The ideal of worker control   Another important principle
behind the formation of Densan was that the union should serve
the interests of all the workers in the electrical power industry.
The emphasis on the industry as the primary unit of concern can
also be seen in its determined fight against the control which the
government maintained over the electrical power industry.

State control of the electrical power supply was to strengthen
during the 1930s as the military sought to stabilize the supply of
electricity as the war effort mounted. The State Administration
of Electricity Act (1938), the Electrical Power Administration
Law (1939), the Japan Electricity Generation and Transmission
Company Law (1939) and the Regulations for the Control of
Electricity Supplies (1942) issued under the provisions of the General State Mobilization Law (1938) combined to produce a framework in which the generation of electricity was entrusted to a
national enterprise and the sale of electricity was given over to
nine regional authorities. The resultant structure allowed for the
government to make all decisions concerning personnel practices,
electricity rates, wages, investment and all other important matters.

Densan rejected this way of running the industry. Its slogan,
'Returning Electricity to the People' (*denkijigyō no shakaika*),
symbolized a five-point platform. First, the electrical power industry should be completely democratized. Second, in order to
achieve that goal, the industry should be removed from government control and placed in the hands of the people. Third, it called
for the industry to be rationalized by merging the generation,
transmission and supply of electricity into one large national enterprise. By placing it in the 'hands of the people,' Densan meant
that the national enterprise would be run by a tripartite Electrical
Power Committee (Denryoku Iinkai) composed of (i) representatives from management in the industry, (ii) representatives of
workers in the industry, and (iii) representatives of the consumers
of electricity. Fourth, it was the social responsibility of workers
in the electric power industry to work hard to supply electricity
to the people at the lowest cost possible. Fifth, the government
should introduce legislation to 'return electricity to the people.'

Densan's emphasis on worker control of the production and
supply of electricity was seen as the best way of providing the
people with cheap and reliable electricity. It was argued that the
government had a moral responsibility to provide electricity in

this manner, and that the union had a moral obligation to oppose the way in which the various authorities and companies in the industry were trying to make a profit at the expense of the ordinary Japanese citizen.

3 Industry-wide wage demands As the central feature of the *Densan* wage system, Densan called for industry-wide standards. It is significant that the wage system was the first in the eighty-year history of Japanese capitalism to be conceived from the 'logic of the workers' (*rōdōsha no ronri*). Wage systems had always been formulated according to the logic of management (*shihon no ronri*).

The two approaches to wage payments contrast on several points. Management's approach calls for wage payments to vary according to two principles. The first might be called the 'principle of divide and control.' This calls for the labor force to be divided into a number of cross-cutting strata according to employment status (*mibun*), qualifications (*shikaku*), occupational category (*shokushu*), educational background (*gakureki*), gender (*sei*), etc. The incumbents of each resulting grouping are then further subdivided by some form of assessment. The end product is a system which gives management full discretion to discriminate among some major categories of employment and to decide who in each category would be promoted and who would be given pay raises. The opinions of one's workmates are not paid much attention, and the individual gets ahead primarily by being subservient to management. The second principle is the ability to pay principle (*shiharai nōryoku ron*). The principle emphasizes the importance of the firm as the main organic entity and its survival is seen as the prime value. Weight is given to the size of the firm's resources *vis-à-vis* its financial requirements. The pool of resources available for distribution, the firm's surplus, is metaphorically referred to as 'the pie.' It is only by increasing the size of the pie that employees may obtain higher wages. This view, then, tends to shift attention away from the question of distributive justice and goals in production other than the survival of the firm in an abstract and ambiguously defined fashion. This approach to structuring the wage system places emphasis on the coherence of the firm as the social unit of prime significance in the consciousness of the workers and tends to conceive of workers in other establishments as the 'enemy.' It results in a system which increases the extent to which the worker's livelihood is made to depend on the successful operation of the enterprise and the extent to which the worker is willing to be subservient to the demands, even the whims, of management.

In contrast to systems conceived by and for management, the '*Densangata* wage system' was founded on the notion of age-linked needs and merit in work. The first component evolved out of a consideration of the worker's needs in maintaining a reasonable standard of living. The second reflects the importance attached to the worker's development of skill. Figure 6.2 shows how these two concerns were integrated into the *Densangata* wage system. The 'workers' logic' appears in several ways. First, the principle of egalitarianism, is enhanced by making the criteria for promotion objective. By removing the room for management to pass arbitrary judgment on employees, the *Densangata* wage system prevented management from using its discretion to play one worker or one set of workers off against another. In the *Densangata* wage system, the basic component (*kihonkyū*) of the wage package was determined by the worker's period of employment (which was seen as being fairly equivalent with age) and the size of his family. Room for discretion on the part of management was removed. Second, in conceiving of the livelihood guarantee, reference was not made to the ability of the firm to pay but to the wage necessary to provide workers with a civil minimum in terms of their standard of living. According to the *Densangata* formula, the livelihood component (*seikatsukyū*) accounted for 80 percent of the total wage package. Third, the payment for ability, defined as skill (*ginō* or *jukuren*), was seen as being a 'flow-on' or 'add-on' which was paid over and above the livelihood component. By tying this payment directly to years of experience in the firm, the discretion of management was further removed so that the inclusion of this component also came to be seen as legitimate in the eyes of the workers.

Given this framework, the *Densangata* wage system can be understood as providing an industry-wide minimum standard of living for all employees within the industry, a standard appropriate to the industry's position in the national economy. It represented an approach which superseded the concerns of management within a particular firm and sought to implant a socialistically inspired notion of distributive justice.

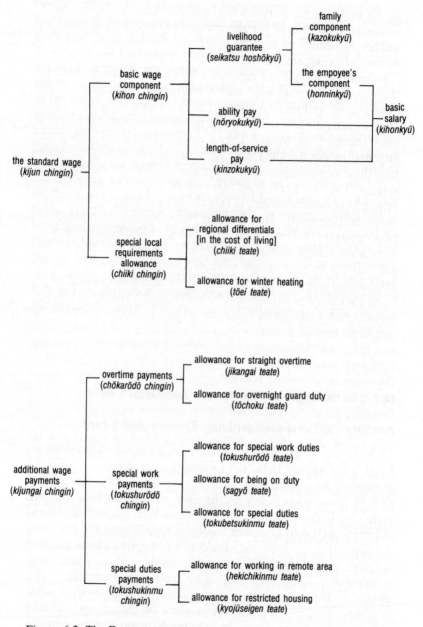

Figure 6.2 *The* Densangata *wage system*

4 Industry-wide negotiations and industry-wide agreements To develop further its ability to function as an industrial union, the leaders of Densan sought to develop an arrangement whereby wage negotiations were to be negotiated for all firms in the industry through collective bargaining sessions between Densan and an employers' association for the industry. In the October 1946 struggles, Densan caused management in the industry to set up a group of top representatives drawn from each of the firms in the industry. From 1947 onwards, Densan negotiated directly with the Management Association for the Electrical Power Industry (Denki Jigyō Keieisha Kaigi = Denkei Kaigi).

For the reasons just explained, as an industrial union in the true sense Densan could be seen as having been at the forefront of the labor movement. The philosophy behind it clearly called for industry-wide standards in the area of personnel management and remuneration and for workers to be represented through negotiations at the industry-level. One could even say that its very success in bringing together workers in the industry served only to strengthen the resolve of management to destroy it. For that was the aim of management in the activities which led up to the dispute in 1952.

IV The Struggle to Dissolve the Industrial Union

A The 1952 dispute involving Densan and Tanrō

Although the initiative in the labor movement was with Sanbetsu Kaigi from August 1946, the Occupation interceded to stop the general strike planned for February 1, 1947. With the general shift in Occupation policy as the lines of confrontation became more clearly drawn in the emerging Cold War, a quick succession of events served to undercut Sanbetsu Kaigi's position. One was the appearance of Sanbetsu Mindō as a competing national center on the right. Another was the Dodge Plan which was implemented along with the 'Nine Economic Principles.' The dismissals and other steps to rationalize the allocation of labor in private firms put tremendous pressure on the unions affiliated with Sanbetsu Kaigi. Then, in 1950 the Korean War brought the 'Red Purges.' In its wake, Sōhyō was formed on July 11, with strong backing from the GHQ. On August 30 the GHQ ordered that Zenrōren be dissolved. The subtle changes occurring in the labor movement signalled the end of Sanbetsu Kaigi's role as the dominant national center. The 'Age of Sōhyō' had arrived.

Sōhyō represented an interesting mixture of forces in the union movement. Its core consisted of the 'Shokusei Mindō faction,' a loose and informal grouping of unions which were basically oriented toward some form of enterprise unionism. This faction was formed primarily by lower-level office workers in lower supervisory positions. The new leaders were firmly against the values inherent in the type of unionism which Sanbetsu Kaigi had promoted. They opposed the egalitarianism built into the seniority-merit wage system which Densan had forged. Rather, they advocated a framework which would recognize the validity of inter-firm wage differentials and the legitimacy of an occupationally based wage system. It was inevitable, therefore, that the birth of Sōhyō would serve initially only to strengthen right-wing unionism.

To be sure, the left-wing forces within Sōhyō were able to dampen somewhat the enterprise egoism of the Shokusei Mindō group at Sōhyō's Second General Congress in March 1951. This was the transformation from 'being a quiet clucky chicken to being a noisy quacking duck' that Takano Minoru had pushed for. Those advocating this kind of change felt that the union movement needed to speak out against the GHQ, the government and management in general. One resolution of the congress called for Sōhyō to serve as a means of bringing together a number of industrial federations in order to develop an effective campaign responsive to the needs of workers within the overall class structure in Japanese society. The policy on wages called for the establishment of minimal livelihood guarantees and a weakening of inter-firm and inter-industry differentials. At the Third General Congress, Sōhyō's wage policy came to be formulated in terms of the 'market basket.' It is particularly important to note on this point that Sōhyō's emphasis came to be placed (i) on lifting the workers' overall standard of living and (ii) on implementing a minimum wage system. The congress positioned Sōhyō squarely against the view that the calculation of wages should be tied to the profits of the enterprise. This brought it into conflict with management and with unionists in Sōdōmei.

Both groups argued that the major consideration should be the firm's ability to pay.

Densan played a major role in fostering this reorientation of Sōhyō to the left. Although there had been a shift in the Executive Committee of Densan, with the Mindō forces replacing the Communist Party forces in 1949, there was no change in the commitment to industrial unionism. Given the ability of its 140,000 members to launch effective disputative action at any of Japan's power stations and the generally well developed philosophy behind its policies, Densan was a powerful force within Sōhyō. This fact was symbolized at the Third General Congress in 1952 when the Chairman of Densan's Central Executive, Fujita Susumu, was elected to head Sōhyō.

With this background in mind, it is easy to see the significance of the dispute which Densan launched late in September 1952 with Tanrō (the industrial union for workers in coal mining), another powerful industrial union in a closely related industry supplying the major source of energy to the Japanese economy at that time. The aim was clearly to regain the initiative which had been lost owing to the Red Purges and the consequent reorganization of the labor movement.

B   The authority's plans to break Densan

The GHQ, the government and management kept a step or two ahead of developments in Sōhyō as the latter moved to the left, and their coordinated strategy to repress the left-wing union movement unfolded swiftly. It soon became clear that Densan was to be the focus of the establishment's counter-offensive. There were several reasons why they chose Densan.

First was the key importance of the electric power industry in the Japanese economy. Given the shift in Occupation policy as the Cold War progressed and the desire of the American government to see Japan become America's 'fortress against communism in Asia,' Japan's elites pushed ahead with a policy for reindustrialization. Economic leaders saw the stable supply of electricity as being a critical ingredient in any recipe for rapid economic recovery and growth. However, having been placed under direct state control as mentioned above, management had become bloated with incompetent bureaucrats who had come to their position as a result of *amakudari*. The end of the war found the state enterprise some 800 million yen in debt, a situation which progressively deteriorated in the years which followed. Accordingly, political and industrial leaders felt a pressing need to rationalize the industry. However, it was also known that Densan would fight tooth and nail against the type of rationalization which management had in mind.

A second reason lay in the symbolic importance of Densan which was seen as the irreconcilable enemy of the 'ruling class.' Not only did the *Densangata* wage system result in a high standard of wages for workers in the power industry. Given the hierarchy of firms in terms of their productivity, the industry-wide approach to negotiating industry-wide wage rates (*tō-itsu kōshō tō-itsu chingin*) inevitably curbed the ability of many firms to maximize their profit. Moreover, by increasing the sense of worker solidarity on an industry basis, Densan was seen as under-mining each worker's commitment to his firm's management. This solidarity was seen as the decisive factor determining the outcome of industrial relations in the industry.

Finally, at the macro-level any move to 'socialize the supply of electricity' (*denki jigyō no shakaika*) was seen by conservatives as the first step toward changing the entire social system and introducing some form of socialism. It is not surprising, then, that Densan became the target of management's animosity toward labor, for it was necessary to dismantle the industrial union and its philosophy of industrial unionism if management was to win the minds, if not the hearts, of Japan's workers.

For these three reasons, political and industrial leaders planned for the inevitable showdown. From their point of view, the status quo had to be changed. Their trump card was a shrewdly designed plan to divide Nippatsu into nine regional enterprises which would then be married to the corresponding firm respon-sible for selling the electricity. By merging the power generation and power supply operations, it was reasoned, both the rationali-zation of the industry advocated by Densan and the dismantling of Densan could be achieved in one go. Rationalization was to be promoted by making each regional entity responsible for generating its own profits.

Pressure would be placed on Densan simply by breaking up Nippatsu, the industry-wide organizational structure for which Densan had been tailor-made. The reorganization of the power industry was designed to force Densan to adopt an organizational

147

structure more in line with the second type of organization shown in Figure 6.2. If the enterprise consciousness of the workers could then be further heightened, it was reasoned, Densan would eventually become nothing more than a loose federation of independent unions along the lines of the third type in Figure 6.2. That was the ultimate goal of the establishment. It is interesting to note over thirty years later that the same approach has been taken in destroying the powerful unions which had organized workers in the Japan National Railways. They too were divided into regional companies and privatized in order to 'disaggregate' the operation, thereby making smaller units independently responsible for their profits and losses (cf. *Asahi Shimbun*, morning edition, September 13, 1982).

The division of the power industry into nine regional enterprises moved ahead in this fashion. On April 29, 1950 the Yoshida cabinet presented its draft legislation for restructuring the power industry along with its draft of a law for public enterprises. However, the move had been uncoordinated; the specific interests of politicians both in the ruling party and in the opposition became entangled and the thinking of management as well had not been worked out beforehand. Accordingly, the bill was shelved at the last sitting of the House of Councillors. Also, the GHQ seemed to change its position. Originally it simply warned that funds would have to be cut off for the industry and that its deficits should no longer be covered with public monies. However, it moved to keep the Diet from extending its session so that the rationalization bill could be passed by the end of June. Then on November 22, 1950, the GHQ again changed its position and suddenly issued a memorandum from MacArthur ordering that Nippatsu be divided into nine regional enterprises 'according to the spirit of the Postdam Declaration.' On the next day the government issued two orders – one on the reorganization of the power industry and the other on public enterprises. The nine enterprises were to be formally established the following year on October 1, but an order from the GHQ brought that date forward to May 1. It is clear that the Japanese establishment moved with the very strong support of the Occupation authorities. Although the conservative forces were ultimately successful, the train of events clearly indicated how desperate the ruling parties were at that time. Democratic procedures were by-passed in their haste to confront Densan, and a good deal of dubious maneuvering occurred 'behind the scenes.'

The GHQ had gone about as far as it could in directing Japan's internal affairs with Yoshida firmly in office, and the return of Japan's independence on September 1, 1951 served only to strengthen the hand of the conservatives. However, as management would no longer be able to rely on GHQ to protect its interests once sovereignty had been returned, management was quick to realize that it would have to take the initiative, and the job of crushing Densan came to be given top priority. Centering around Nikkeiren, the representatives of capital set about in a resolute fashion to assassinate the 'prince of industrial unionism.'

C The preparedness of Densan for the struggle ahead

Management's timing was perfect. Strong as it was, Densan was not in a position to wage an all-out battle with the establishment. It had been seriously weakened by several developments.

1 The Red Purge The antagonism between the Communist Party group and the Mindō group was apparent from right after the formation of Densan. At its Fourth General Conference in 1949 control of the executive shifted from the first to the second grouping. Friction between the two became so pronounced that the Fifth General Conference, scheduled for May 1950, had to be called off. Occupying the majority of seats on the Central Steering Committee, the Mindō group sought, as a means of censuring the Communist Party group, to issue a special order requiring all members of the union to reregister. The written order, which was circulated to all members, contained a number of references to 'international red fascism,' 'red imperialism,' and the 'red malaise.' This was clearly the anti-communist rhetoric used by the right-wing socialists and fascists. In this regard Sakamoto (1979: 120) writes as follows:

In addition to members of the Japan Socialist Party, the 'Densan Mindo Group' also included those rightwingers or fascists who had been associated with the pro-Emperor thinkers before the war. If we exclude the Communist oriented leftwing members of the Socialist Party and the rightwing fascists, we are left with a large group in the middle which sought a middle-of-the-road policy.

Their plan was to reregister only those who denounced the communists and agreed with their position. It was a ploy to move the union away from its original vision as a mass organization set up to look after the interests of workers in the electric power industry.

These attempts of the Mindō faction within the labor movement to impose a form of self-censureship could be found in other unions as well. For example, at the Japan National Railways the Kokutetsu Mindō group issued its infamous 'Order Number Zero.' Following the Shimoyama, Mitaka and Matsukawa incidents and the framing of over twenty communists who were members of Kokurō, the JNR authorities fired seventeen employees who were on Kokurō's Central Struggle Committee (all members of the JCP). Although the events were clouded with mystery – including allegations of CIA involvement – and the only detainee convicted of involvement maintained his innocence until the end (cf. Matsumoto 1960; Satō 1976; Suzuki 1981: 202–9), the Mindō members of the committee quickly organized a by-election to replace the fired members of the committee who, they argued, could no longer be union members since they had been fired. Without convening the committee they issued under their own names an order (which did not have the committee's usual sequence number on it) instructing union members to elect replacements for the seventeen. The entire labor movement came to be politically divided by these blatant attempts at thought control.

The move to have all members reregister had the strong backing of management, and within the first month 108,095 persons had reregistered. However, 19,282 members refused to reregister under those conditions. Thereupon Densan's Central Executive responded by disassociating 411 members and suspending the rights of another 167 members. On August 26, 1950 management handed 2137 individuals dismissal notices, an act which came to be called the 'red purge' in that industry. By 1950 the dismissals and the meting out of arbitrary disciplinary measures had become management's major weapon against the unionists. Already in 1949 the government had announced its intention to implement the Dodge Plan, cutting back on expenditures by dismissing 240,000 employees in the public sector.

Rationalizations in the private sector saw one million employees retrenched. In the public sector, the JNR, with its militant unions, bore the brunt of the government's measures, with about 100,000 employees being sacked. The dismissal of 2137 individuals from the electrical power industry in mid–1950 was 'in line with the times.' However, while most strong unions would have fought the dismissals, however unsuccessfully, under the control of the Mindō faction the Central Executive of Densan issued a statement saying that it would not initiate any industrial action on behalf of any unregistered employees who happened to be fired. This represented tacit approval for management's initiatives. Indeed, there is evidence to suggest that the Mindō group took the initiative in the whole affair and went so far as to prepare for management the list of those to be dismissed (cf. Tsutsui 1961: 273; Sakamoto 1979: 144–54).

The result was that the Communist Party and its sympathizers were eradicated from Densan. For the first time since Densan's formation, the Mindō group ruled unchallenged. The incident meant not only that communists would have no place in Densan, but that activists of any kind would be dealt with in a similar manner. The campaign was not a pretty one. It was one in which activists of any hue would be colored red and smeared with innuendoes regardless of their actual convictions. In the end, many members came to feel that the safest way to protect their necks was simply to withdraw from the union movement altogether. Many dismissed unionists were branded 'red' and their families were forced to bear the stigma as a heavy social burden. The growing awareness of such circumstances simply accelerated the move of employees out of the union movement. The final analysis shows clearly that the purge left workers afraid to be identified not only with the Communist Party, but with the union movement as a whole.

In earlier times the union had been willing to pour all its energies into fighting the dismissal of even a single member. Members were able to put themselves in the dismissed member's shoes, and this gave the union tremendous credibility among its membership. After the red purges, however, union members came to suspect the union of having participated in the dismissal of its own members. There was a subtle shift in the consciousness of the workers who came gradually to feel that it was management they could rely upon when it came to guaranteeing their employment and their families' livelihood. Atrophy would, no doubt, be the fate of any union which stained its hands with the blood of its own members. Although Densan's control of the work place was gradually slipping away, as much by default as by management's conniving, the Mindō-led Executive (*shikkōbu*) seemed oblivious to its loss of influence. It became engrossed in celebrating its victory over the leftist opposition forces within Densan. But the real winner was not the Mindō group at all; it was management.

2   *The Formation of Kanpai Rōso*   Another development which had placed Densan at a disadvantage in 1952 was the move by management to encourage the growth of a competing union movement within the industry. As early as 1949 management had pointed to the impending break-up of Nippatsu into nine regional enterprises as a means of indicating to certain union members the limits of the Densan formula. Management's efforts to promote a reorganization of its labor into independent enterprise unions obviously planted the seeds of dissension within Densan while also dangling carrots in front of those who argued for the reorganization. It was this push which led to the formation of Kanpai Rōso (Kantō Haiden Rōdō Kumiai) at the Kantō Electricity Supply Company as a break away from Densan's Kantō Regional Organization. After the formation of the nine regional enterprises on August 7, 1949, the new body became known as Tōden Rōso (Tokyo Denryoku Rōdō Kumiai) – the enterprise union for workers of the Tokyo Electrical Power Authority.

By 1950 the tip of the iceberg was visible. Management was moving ahead both with its red purge and with its restructuring of the industry. On September 21, 1949 the head of the Densan's Kantō Regional Organization (Densan Kantō Chihō Honbu), Yoshida Kazukichi, and his assistant (the second in command), Katayama Takeo, suddenly resigned from Densan. Two months later, on December 13, they formed a new Kanpai Rōso, with about 5000 members. Both had been members of the Communist Party. They claimed that they had joined the Communist Party to spy on it.[2] By creating the second union and then quitting the Communist Party, they had come upon a way to escape the impending red purges and save their own skins. They claimed that the operations of the new regionally based company were quite efficient and that their profits were being eaten up by the less efficient operations of the newly formed companies in the other areas. 'The breakup of Nippatsu into the nine regional enterprises which incorporated the generation and supply of electricity is inevitable. Because profits will come to be calculated on a regional basis, employees will do better with an independent union which will be able to obtain for its members a fairly nice package of allowances).'[3] The play on 'enterprise egoism' (*kigyō egoizumu*) was clear. Ōkōchi and Shirai (1957: 108–9) wrote of the incident in a critical vein:

Yoshida and Katayama perceived that there would be significant disparity among the several resultant entities as plans to divide Nippatsu into nine regional enterprises were implemented. The two departed from the industry-wide organization and took a stance which unabashedly advocated enterprise sectionalism and promoted enterprise egoism. Because the main actors in the Kantō Regional Organization of Densan had been affiliated with the Communist Party, the split came to symbolize the moves advocated by the Mindō group within Densan. As these regional leaders were seeking to protect themselves from the imminent red purge, it is reported not that they only withdrew from the Communist Party, but that they went a step further and colluded with management in conniving to split the union membership. These two persons later worked in concert with the Chūbu Regional Branch of Densan when the schism between the Chūbu Regional Branch [the first union] and the Chūbu Electric Power Company Union (Chūbu Denryoku Rōdō Kumiai) [the second union] was coming out into the open. They finally came to occupy a very important position in Denrōren (Zenkoku Denryoku Rōdō Kumiai Renmei) [later a Dōmei affiliate], the federation of the nine company unions in the electrical power industry.

Many involved in those events have since indicated that the basic motivation was the wish to protect themselves from the red purges. Yoshida himself once confided that 'the only way to be exempted from the red purge was to have the split' (Kōyama 1981: 47). Kanpai Rōso (Kantō Haiden Rōdō Kumiai), the union of electricity supply workers at the Kantō Electricity Authority, grew rapidly to have a membership of 10,300 by the time of its Second General Congress in May 1950 and to 21,800 by the following year when its Third General Congress met in June. By that time it had organized 80 percent of the workers at the Kantō Electricity Authority, and was receiving strong support from management. As a case study, events in the power industry provide much insight into industrial relations during those turbulent years.

During a dispute with management in December 1949 Kanpai Rōso was formed. It then jumped at the chance to become the majority union and sought quickly to settle with management, obtaining an average monthly salary of ¥6000 for its members. However, when Densan later obtained ¥7000 for its members, management invited Kanpai Rōso back to the table and awarded its members an average salary of ¥7200. Management made it very clear that those who wanted higher wages ought to join Kanpai Rōso. In promoting the second union, management clearly was using money as the bait. The psychological effects were considerable and several hundred employees shifted from Densan to the union being supported by management (cf. the historical source materials in Rōdō Shō 1951: 794).

In trying to implement its special order calling for reregistration in July 1950, the Mindō group (which had just taken over the leadership of Densan) sought to establish its own branch headquarters (*daikō honbu*) within the Kantō Regional Organization (Kantō Chihō Honbu). However, already having a second union organized along the lines it advocated, management felt able to take a firm stance. It refused to recognize the authority of the special branch headquarters and refused to bargain with it. Kanpai Rōso publicized the fact, claiming that a union which could not bargain with management did not qualify to call itself a union. This propaganda served to undermine further the confidence of Densan's members and over a thousand members were said to have left the union as a result of the difficulties Densan was having in exerting its authority in the Kantō area (cf. the historical source materials in Rōdō Shō 1951: 794–5).

With the red purge dismissals on August 26, 1950, management began publicly to refer to the atrophied condition of the Densan unionists, a tactic designed to add to the demoralization of employees who were beginning to feel insecure about their jobs. The message was clear: those who remained in Densan would be fired while those who joined Kanpai Rōso would not.

The personnel manager for the Kantō Electricity Authority actively encouraged employees to join the second union and circulated that union's registry for those who wished to leave Densan. Management's use of unfair labor practices and its blatent discrimination against employees who belonged to Densan are legend. Densan's only possible response was to appeal to the Central Labor Relations Commission (Chūō Rōdō Iinkai) (cf. the historical source materials in Rōdō Shō 1951: 797–800).

Having rejected in principle the idea of industry-wide negotiations and disassociating itself completely from Denkei Kaigi, the management association Densan had organized in October 1946 for its industry-wide negotiations, management opened the door for making special arrangements with Kanpai Rōso. Management reiterated its promise that the superior record of the Kantō organization would result in higher wages for those workers who stuck by the idea of 'the enterprise first' (*kigyōbetsu yūi*) (see historical source materials on Densan in Rōdō Shō 1951).

With management's strong support, Kanpai Rōso firmly established itself. However, Densan did not respond adequately to the challenge. When Kanpai Rōso first emerged, it was dismissed lightly as having only 4000 members and Densan's leadership optimistically concluded that it had no influence whatsoever in the other regions (historical source materials in Rōdō Shō 1951: 793). The best strategy, it reasoned, was simply to wait for Kanpai Rōso to see the light; the prognosis was that it would simply die a natural death without Densan having to do anything at all. Its analysis of management's response was equally optimistic: management was seen as attaching little weight to the new union. At most, the leaders of Densan cynically argued, management would be willing 'to teach the union how to swim if it were really intent on trying to be a fish in unfamiliar waters.' In its analysis of future developments in the industry, the leadership seemed committed to the view that the generation of electric power was carried out within the framework of a controlled or centralized national economy and that the state would not consider having its financial affairs run on a regional basis in the future (cf. historical source materials in Rōdō Shō 1949: 404). Only too late did it realize how far its analysis had missed the mark. By the time that someone spoke out at the Sixth General Congress in July 1951, the die had been cast. The Kantō Regional

Organization had already lost out totally to Kanpai Rōso (which had by that time become Tōden Rōso), and behind-the-scenes activities of second unions which would seriously undercut Densan's other regional offices.

At the same time, however, it should not be forgotten that there had been movements back to Densan. For example, in the Asagaya Branch of Tōden Rōso, the leadership supported the notion of the enterprise union but sought to restructure things internally in order to overcome some of its weaknesses. They sought to move ahead by taking a critical stance, and their approach was to push for a restructuring of Tōden Rōso's organization. However, their efforts bore little fruit and they soon became disillusioned with the deterioration in Tōden Rōso's ability to meet their needs. At the end of 1951, a year before Densan's defeat, nearly all of the branch's 800 members rejoined Densan. Such was the situation in 1952 when Densan decided to launch its final offensive. The 1952 dispute can be said to have developed through four stages. Here the events at each stage are briefly traced in the following section.

V The Dispute: Management's Assault and the 1952 Power Strike

A Stage I – collective bargaining

The dispute began in an ordinary manner. The union presented to Denkei Kaigi two logs of claims, one on March 28 asking for revisions to a part of the collective bargaining agreement and the other on April 14 asking for a wage increase. The first request involved nothing more than a simple extension of the agreement which had been negotiated for six months the previous fall. The second request was for a 52 percent increase in the standard wage component (*kijun chingin*) (cf. Figure 6.2), the union arguing that the amount agreed upon at the end of the previous year (¥12,400) was insufficient and that ¥20,005 would be more appropriate. For Densan the procedure was similar to that which had been followed in the past.

Management, however, took an uncompromising stand. It presented the union with a counter-demand for a shift from what had been a union shop to an open shop. Also on its agenda was a request for a change in the provisions concerning prior notification when disputative action was being planned. Moreover, it wanted to set up an arrangement whereby certain union members would not engage in any disputative action so that power supplies could be maintained. Further, it wanted to tighten the provisions for holidays, overtime and other working conditions which related to hours of work. With regard to wages, opposition to the union position was not just in terms of the amount demanded. Management was committed to rationalizing the wage system and replacing the Densangata wage system with one which attached weight to job content (*shokkaikyū sei*). These were all changes which would have enhanced the power of management and weakened the position of Densan. Management was making a concerted push to move away from the system of industry-wide settlements, and this, it could be said, became the central issue in the months which followed.

The union's leadership seems to have been quite lethargic in responding to this change in attitude on the part of management. It simply replied to management's proposals by reiterating its own demands. Representatives from Densan and Denkei Kaigi met five times in the spring of 1952, but agreement was not reached and the matter was taken to the Central Labor Relations Commission in May. In its submission to the Central Labor Relations Commission, Densan argued simply that it was taking 'a reasonable and restrained position,' adopting 'a positive attitude,' offering 'to concede generously where concessions should be made' – in short, taking a reasonable and restrained stance (cf. the historical source materials in Rōdō Shō 1952). By taking the dispute to the Commission, however, Densan had moved the dispute into its second stage.

B Stage II – mediation

The commission received a request for mediation from both parties. On July 22 it presented its proposal on the collective agreement; its proposal concerning wages was handed down on September 6. Densan rejected both proposals and decided to show its strength. On September 16 it launched a one-day office strike and on the 28th it organized the first of a long series of power strikes. Tables 6.1 and 6.2 show the extent of the strikes.

Table 6.1 *The amount of electric power lost during strikes in late 1952*

Month	Day	Hours involved (H)	The decrease in the amount of electricity supplied (kw)
9	28	6	603,298
10	3	8	880,430
	7	8	678,473
	11	8	1,103,760
	15	8	1,090,863
	21	8	940,349
	22	8	1,551,121
	28	8	1,478,777
	29	8	1,565,445
11	6	8	1,319,942
	13	8	1,495,598
	19	5.5	1,287,255
12	2	24	649,400
	3	16	not clear, but strike similar to that held the previous day
	4	24	978,200
	5	24	780,600
	6	24	772,800
	7	24	826,000
	8	24	651,300
	9	24	499,600
	10	24	521,800
	11	24	763,000
	12	24	667,100
	13	24	648,500
	14	24	431,700
	15	8	
	17	16	488,400
	18	21	421,600
TOTALS		440.5	22,101,921

Source: Rōdō Sōgi Chōsakai (1957), pp. 305–11.

It should be noted that management also rejected the mediation proposal put forward by the commission. The result was that labor and management entered another period of strife. The commission's plans essentially called for a preservation of the status quo and were aimed simply at preserving the peace. With regard to the nature of the collective agreement, the commission rejected the position taken by management and requested that the parties continue to discuss the matter. With

158

Table 6.2 *The amount of electricity lost to stoppages: November 1952*

Day	Number of hours	Number of factories affected (targeted)	Number of factories without the supply of electricity	Amount of electricity not supplied (kW)
7	2	665	118	513,423
12	4	649	41	520,202
17	4	845	43	534,074
18	4	791	67	453,699
21	4	679	65	536,126
22	4	685	55	526,672
TOTALS	22	4314	389	3,084,196

Source: Rōdō Sōgi Chōsakai (1957), p. 305.

regard to the wage system, the commission again ruled against management, arguing that it would be premature to introduce a job-scaled pay system and recommending that current wage parity be maintained, with the *Densangata* wage system and the industry-wide approach to settlements being held intact. Thus, in two important respects, the commission ruled in favor of Densan. Nevertheless, Densan was dissatisfied with its findings on its wage demands. The Densan leadership suggested that an appropriate rate would be only a nineteen percent improvement on the December rate. This would have brought the average monthly salary of the Densan workers to ¥15,400, ¥4605 below their demanded salary. The commission reasoned that various other benefits would bring the monthly package to ¥19,250 in real terms, 44.6 percent above the average salary received in all industries and 26.9 percent above the amount received by employees in firms with 500 or more employees. In its view, the amount it proposed should have been quite fair. The commission parried the demands of management for a change in the ground rules and met the demands of the unionists for a mammoth increase in wage rates, thereby maintaining the status quo, and it was obvious that such a ruling was to the advantage of Densan. The mediation plan had a number of aspects management would have found hard to digest.

One might reasonably wonder, then, why the union would want to make such a big deal over a few thousand yen when it seems to have come out all right on the other points. The answer is not easy to find. One consideration perhaps might have related to the pride of the Densan leadership as Densan had never lost a battle since its formation. Not having reflected seriously enough about the consequences of the red purge, nor having thought thoroughly about the full intentions of management and the political establishment, it is also possible that the leadership hastily concluded that any kowtowing to management was humiliating in and of itself. In any case, the leadership reacted as it had in the past and rejected the mediation offer, apparently thinking that repeated power cuts would result in an even more favorable conciliation plan. Such was not to be the outcome.

C   Stage III – conciliation

Having rejected the mediation offer, Densan immediately launched its power strikes. Over the next two months its members struck eleven times. However, rather than weakening, management only became more resolute in its stance against the unionists. Firmly rejecting the notion of industry-wide negotiations and a standard wage rate, it insisted even more vehemently that negotiations should be carried out on a regional basis and that wage rates be determined separately for each firm and for each occupational grouping. In refusing to negotiate with Densan, it made clear its intention to foster enterprise unionism.

On October 18 management restated its refusal to negotiate on an industry-wide basis and asked for negotiations at the regional level. Densan refused. Ten days later management unilaterally gave notification that it would negotiate only on a regional basis with the regional organizations within Densan. Thereafter it negotiated no further with the Central Executive of Densan. It went a step further and dissolved Denkei Kaigi, the industry-level organization which had until then represented management in its negotiations with Densan at the industry level. In its place it set up a loose coordinating body, consisting of the enterprises in the electric power industry as independent bodies. The new body was labelled 'Denki Jigyō Rengōkai' (abbreviated to 'Denjiren') (Confederation of Electric Power Enterprises). Denjiren refused to engage in industry-wide negotiations. Meanwhile, on October 20, Nikkeiren issued its own statement which prodded management in the industry to avoid an easy settlement, indicating that management in general would lend their support.

It was clear that the powers to be were pushing for their counterparts in the electric power industry to remain resolute in the struggle with Densan.

As the parties remained stalemated, the Central Labor Relations Commission came up with a plan for conciliation on November 20. However, the conciliation offer had now become even less acceptable than that offered earlier in the mediation plan. The commission had by then been brought around to management's view regarding the organization of collective bargaining. Although it did not change the recommended salary level, it recommended an increase in the weekly hours of work from 38.5 to 42, a marked deterioration in working conditions. Nothing could have been more humiliating for the 'prince of the labor movement' than to accept a decline in the working conditions of its members. The 1952 dispute had now developed to a point where Densan's very existence was at stake. With the stakes raised, Densan decided to push on to a decisive conclusion. It rejected the offer and resolved to carry on with further power cuts. However, with the Central Labor Relations Commission backing down to pressure from the government and Nikkeiren, and with public opinion steadily mounting against Densan the outcome was inevitable. Whatever course Densan followed, its activities could be regarded as little more than a pitiful charade.

As Table 6.1 shows, the extent of the disruption decreased over time. After the first two months, the government, management and the mass media were successful in moving public opinion against Densan. Accordingly, Densan felt compelled to alter its strategy. It sought to extend the shut-down time for certain types of electricity while continuing the production of electricity which seemed vital to the well-being of ordinary households.

D   Stage IV – the finale

Under the circumstances, it was clearly to management's advantage to keep the pressure on Densan – to turn its victory into a rout. Two days after the conciliation plan was presented, management indicated its acceptance. It continued to ignore Densan's repetitious demands for industry-wide negotiations and directed its energies to destroying Densan altogether.

Reeling at the drastic defeat they had suffered through the

commission, the leaders of Densan, on the other hand, resolved to step up their efforts to cut power, hoping that some small amount of ground might be recovered, anxious that a quick settlement might somehow be achieved so that Densan itself might be rescued to fight another day. Densan launched an intensive campaign of strikes – 24 hours a day for two weeks straight. However, it stopped the supply of only certain types of electricity, and this greatly reduced the effectiveness of its actions. Moreover, management and the political establishment successfully mobilized the support of the mass media and public opinion. Whatever sympathy might have existed outside the industry was lost, and Densan became increasingly isolated. On the day that management indicated its acceptance of the conciliation offer, Densan's Kansai Regional Organization indicated its willingness to negotiate at the regional level and asked the National Executive for the right to negotiate and to decide on strikes for the members in its region. In the Chūbu region, a split occurred in the organization and a second union (the Chūbu Denryoku Rōdō Kumiai) (The Chūbu Electric Power Company's Union) was formed. Negotiations immediately began in the Kansai, Kantō and Chūbu regional offices and independent agreements were reached. And then, in the Kyūshū region, another number two company union appeared. On December 17 a schism developed in the Kyūshū regional organization. The Central Executive was left with little alternative but to accept the conciliation offer. It decided to call off the strike and on the same day signed the conciliation agreement.

The 1952 dispute ended in a mammoth defeat for Densan. In addition to accepting a humiliating agreement, it had to acknowledge that each of its regions had accepted a wage formula which was based on the regional power authority's ability to pay and attached more weight on to each individual's characteristics. For all practical purposes industry-wide negotiations had come to an end. The end was in sight: Densan was quietly dissolved some years later on March 1, 1956. With Densan went the philosophy of industrial unionism. The 1952 dispute became a major divide in Japan's postwar industrial relations. The times were changing, and with them the era of industrial unionism gave way to the era of enterprise unionism. Today the 1952 dispute has come to symbolize that change.

VI Further Schisms and the Dissolution of Densan

Densan did not die an easy death. It was not the case, as some writers such as Shirai (1979: 147) have suggested, that the 1952 dispute produced a clear-cut winner. The dispute is a watershed and has symbolic value only in hindsight. The leftists were still a very strong force in Japan up until the mid–1970s. A careful appraisal of the last few years of Densan reveal how bitter the divisions were in the labor movement. There continued to be a hard core which remained committed to the Densan ideal. They gave way very reluctantly, and then in many cases only after a tremendous amount of pressure was brought to bear on them, on their associates at work, and on their families. Even then, as we see in Part Three of this volume, many of the unionists continued to fight on in what came to be minority unions. In the Chūgoku region, Densan's regional organization remains today and its story is told below in Chapter 10. Here the story of Densan's last few years as a nation-wide union and the ramifications of its defeat for Japan's labor movement are explained as briefly as possible.

A The schisms

Although the 1952 dispute had resulted in a massive defeat for Densan, it is important to remember that Denrōren did not emerge immediately, and that it was over three years before Densan actually disbanded its National Executive. As the minority union during that period, Densan waged a bitter battle with the number two unions. It was a long four years for the labor movement as a whole, a period which left the movement scarred with the deeply felt antagonisms among those of different political or philosophical outlooks. It needs to be pointed out that workers on the shop floor did not necessarily support the enterprise unionism being promoted by the number two unions. It was for this reason that Densan was able to continue as an influence in the industry.

Following settlement of the dispute, the schisms spread to all of Densan's regional organizations. Table 6.3 shows the process of attrition. It was over a year later in May 1954 that the number two unions were able to coordinate themselves well enough to form a loose industry-wide organization, Zenkoku Denryoku Rōdō Kumiai Rengōkai (Denrōren) (the National Association of Unions in the Electric Power Industry) which later became a Dōmei affiliate.

By the time Denrōren was formed, the criticism of Densan had become a fairly coherent statement of principles. Foremost was the feeling that Densan had been too involved with political issues. Its adherence to and attempts to spread a revolutionary socialist philosophy, its blind allegiance to Sōhyō, its support for specific political parties, and its willingness to devote resources to particular political causes were all sources of dissatisfaction among some members. Nevertheless, although the number two unions called for a more business oriented unionism, the choice itself had political consequences and was simply the choice of another political philosophy. When the Mindō faction had taken over the executive of Densan following the red purge, it was the left-wing group within the faction that came to the fore. The right-wing group within the Mindō faction sought to push Densan even further toward an enterprise unionism, and then dropped out and formed their own number two unions with management's support when they proved to be unsuccessful.

The ideological differences boiled down to choices between enterprise unionism and industrial unionism, perhaps reflecting differences in the relative benefits for specific individuals of one approach as opposed to the other. The difference had always existed, but it was never obvious that one approach would win out over the other. In a very real sense, it was the involvement of management which swayed the balance. For those who sought to promote the ideology of industrial unions, that involvement was seen as being a form of unfair labor practices and a push for the political involvement of management in the political affairs of the union. In that sense, there was the charge that the decisions were made in an undemocratic fashion reminiscent of the way the 'labor movement' had been directed under the guise of Sanpō during the war.

The tension between the two ideological camps can be seen in the evolution of the Densan wage system even in its first two years of operation. Table 6.4 shows how the weight attached to each component changed over time. Two changes were important. One was the increase in the allowance for the regional cost of living. Originally the idea was that those in the six large cities

Table 6.3 The membership 'drift' from Densan to Denrō

Region	Date on which Denrō affiliate was formed	Membership of Denrō affiliate on founding	Memberships on August 7, 1953		Memberships on March 1, 1954		Memberships on January 31, 1956		Memberships on August 15, 1956		The final position of the local organization
			Densan	Denrō	Densan	Denrō	Densan	Denrō	Densan	Denrō	
Hokkaidō	27.7.1953	582	5,400	800	5,010	873	4,921	1,005	0	5,905	Densan absorbed by Denrō
Tōhoku	20.4.1953	5,770	7,800	7,100	7,189	7,720	5,267	9,048	152	14,099	Individuals continued to crossover to Denrō
Kantō	21.5.1952 Kantō Haiden Rōso 1949	17,221	8,200	21,300	5,581	23,665	5,572	23,789	0	28,564	Densan absorbed by Denrō
Chūbu	8.12.1952	12,750	0	17,200	0	17,031	0	17,058	0	16,922	Individuals continued to join Denrō
Kansai	2.5.1953	3,218	11,700	11,600	5,178	18,782	1,335	21,389	1,229	21,330	Individuals continue to crossover to Denrō
Chūgoku	28.8.1953	1,330	10,500	1,500	7,741	4,514	5,940	7,037	3,864	7,975	Situation of coexistence attained
Shikoku	31.8.1953	6,001	600	5,800	162	5,973	31	5,887	23	5,911	Individuals continued to crossover to Denrō
Kyūshū	17.12.1952	1,185	16,900	1,600	15,438	2,343	6,050	12,469	5,218	13,522	Individuals continued to crossover to Denrō
Hokuriku	18.10.1954		6,000	0	5,895	0	1,627	4,147	0	5,809	Densan absorbed by Denrō
TOTAL			67,100	66,900	52,194	80,901	30,743	101,829	10,486	120,037	

Source: Compiled from Rōdō Shō (1945: 910 and 912), and Rōdō Sōgi Chōsakai (1957: 126) as presented in Kawanishi (1981: 179).

165

Enterprise Unionism in Japan

would receive an 'add-on' of 30 percent the livelihood guarantee; those in other cities which were bombed during the war, 20 percent; and those in the other cities, 10 percent. However, since the regions really coincided with the boundaries or locations of the various power authorities, to say that one region deserved an add-on was to say that the employees at a particular power authority were to have the add-on. This meant that alterations to the formula over time reflected the competition between different power authorities to obtain more for their own employees. Obviously, the authorities in Tokyo, Osaka and Nagoya were the most successful. Because Nippatsu was a national authority, to increase the regional allowance for the workers in those areas meant decreasing the amount of wages paid to workers in the other areas. Over time, the amount of the total wages paid which was distributed according to the employees' basic characteristics on a national industry-wide formula declined and the proportion

Table 6.4 *The percentage composition of the basic wage component in the Densan wage system and changes in the importance of each sub-component: 1947–9*

Component	April 1947	March 1948	January 1949
honninkyū (the employee's component)	47.5	47.5	43.4
kazokukyū (family component)	20.7	20.7	17.6
kinzokukyū (length-of-service pay)	3.7	3.7	2.2
nōryokukyū (ability pay)	19.4	19.4	24.0
chiiki teate (allowance for regional differential)	8.0	8.0	11.4
tōei teate (winter allowance)	0.7	0.7	1.5
TOTAL	100.00	100.0	100.0
Amount paid as the standard wage (*kijun chingin*)	¥1854	¥5358	¥7100

Source: Compiled by the author from Ōkōchi (1954: 94–5).

distributed according to the place of employment increased. Whereas the regional allowance was equivalent to only a sixth of the employee's component in April 1947, it had come to account for a quarter of it by January 1949.

The other important change concerned wage differentials among workers at the same enterprise. The differentials grew as the amount of the total wage paid which was distributed according to individual 'ability' also increased. Originally, ability was to be set according to years of experience in a fairly objective manner. However, 'ability' came to be linked to the level of 'responsibility' the individual carried within each authority, and each region was to set up a system of evaluating this responsibility. Already there was a shift towards a system emphasizing firm-size differences and worker status differences. The major point to be made is that some benefitted from the change and others did not. Whether the new criteria was seen as providing a fairer means of distributing income or not is a value judgment. The struggle within Densan between those pushing for enterprise unionism and those subscribing to industrial unionism was waged in ideological terms. Each group tried to convince the membership that one set of criteria provided a fairer way of deciding the wage distribution among workers in the industry than the other set. At Densan's Sixth National Convention in 1951 there was a drawn-out debate between the two camps. The representatives from the relatively disadvantaged regions (Hokkaidō, Kyūshū, and the Hokuriku region) argued that the notion of compensating for price differentials was dubious, noting that food might be more expensive in the cities, but that clothing was more expensive in the rural areas. The representatives from the large cities remained unimpressed, arguing that the cost of living was much higher in their areas and threatening that 'workers in the newspaper industry were not divided by ideology as much as by these kinds of regional differences.' When the decision to get rid of the regional allowances was passed by about 90 percent of the vote, the representatives from the Kansai region left, and those from the Kantō region sought to disrupt the proceedings. Already there were deep divisions in Densan.

The 1952 dispute served only to exacerbate the divisions and bring them to the surface. After the settlement, the Kantō Regional Organization tried to get Tōden Rōso back into the fold. However, while sympathetic to the need for a unified labor movement, the leaders of Tōden Rōso stated the condition for returning to Densan was a commitment to the enterprise principle. With the formation of Tōden Rōso a few years earlier, the division between the two ideologies came to be widely discerned in the Kantō area.

Although the Densan's Regional Organization in the Kansai area took the initiative in moving ahead with negotiations at the enterprise level, a step which could be seen as having cast the die for Densan, that move was not immediately supported by the rank and file. Even in the Kansai's Regional Steering Committee the decision to go ahead with negotiations at the enterprise level had collapsed; the branch offices in Kyoto, Shiga, Hokuriku and Hyōgo decided to continue opposing the activity of the regional organization. The following year, about one third of the members of the regional organization still continued to oppose any moves to withdraw from Densan or to accommodate enterprise-level negotiations.

Particularly interesting is the fact that certain leaders in Tōden Rōso had become aware of the serious organizational defects which characterised the enterprise unions. They sounded out Densan about the possibility of merging back with Densan. At the end of 1952, just before the climax of that year's struggle, 302 members of the Tochigi branch of Tōden Rōso criticized the notion of enterprise unionism and rejoined Densan. They claimed that the reality with Tōden Rōso was such that 'working conditions fell far short of those negotiated by Densan,' that 'the atmosphere at work had changed for the worse,' that 'more pressure than was necessary for running the business had been placed on them,' that 'the presence of the union had diminished,' and that they 'had come to reflect seriously on what had been a mistake in leaving Densan' (quoted from a leaflet distributed in 1959 by the Tochigi branch of Tōden Rōso).

The result of these kinds of happenings was that the union movement temporarily stagnated on both sides. Densan had lost its base while the newly formed organizations did not have the full support necessary to consolidate their position. Leaders of the new unions felt that the rank and file were not participating in the activities they had planned, and that the tendency to leave things to the 'organization' was spreading. The rank and file no doubt felt that the new leadership had established itself, won the recognition it sought from management, and was then happy to forget about engaging in any further struggle for the benefit of the workers. Reflecting on the situation which had emerged after the switch to an enterprise-based union, many workers came to have a new appreciation for the stance taken by Densan. Densan was remembered fondly as an organization which had not acquiesced to agreements which are not in the interests of the workers, and had stood up to fight the battle for justice at work. From this perspective, Densan continued to be viewed as being the progressive union.

Why did the workers have second thoughts about enterprise unionism? Returning to the document just mentioned above, we can see that they seemed to find an essential truth in the sense of class solidarity which came from having a national organization. As they saw it, the choice was between an organization representing a *large class of people* who enjoyed sharing a common lot and one of many small organizations each representing only the narrowly defined interests of employees caught up in the *small world of a single enterprise* in which workers sought to escape one from another. The workers at the Tochigi branch clearly found purpose in the former. They solemnly resolved on October 18, 1956 to rejoin Densan which was determinedly fighting together with 120,000 other comrades from around the country. They argued that their decision was not based on any complicated theoretical considerations or on a particular emotional state; they simply attributed it to a 'gut reaction,' the 'common sense which goes with being a worker' and which was awakened by management's increasingly obvious use of authority in its relations with the Densan affiliates.

For these reasons, then, a strong sense of resistance and resentment was born out of the sense of class solidarity which was strengthened on an intuitive level by management's attempt to use its own authority to shove the workers back into the small world of the enterprise. The transition back to a more parochial frame of mind took four years.

B   The dissolution of Densan

During the four years leading to its disbandment, the members of Densan engaged in a large amount of self-criticism. It is instructive to reflect briefly on those discussions for what they tell us about the sources of defeat. To that end, a document tabled at the Ninth General Meeting of Densan in 1954 (held by the author) provides us with an overview which might be summarized in the following several paragraphs.

The history of Densan was the history of the fight against enterprise egoism. Using the vocabulary developed in Densan, it was a fight to change the way workers thought about their work – from a way of thinking which placed emphasis on 'our company' to one which emphasized the fact that they were part of a larger activity known as the electric power industry. If there was any meaning in that history it was in the fact that Densan had in the later 1940s pretty much lain the monster known as 'enterprise egoism' to rest. However, just when one might have thought that the monster had been slain, it was found to be lurking in the shadows.

The monster reappeared in two forms. One was in the changes to the Densan wage system which were discussed above. The other was the system of supervision which management sought to introduce at the shop level. As Ariizumi Tōru, Akita Jōju and Tosaka Ranko (cf. Ōkōchi 1954: 85) argued, most of the activists in Densan were in lower supervisory positions. The problem was seen as lying in the fact that 'unless one is extremely committed to one's purpose and mindful of the situation, through the process of assisting in the management of the enterprise it is easy for lower level supervisory staff to wake up finding themselves thinking like the managers.'

Union officials returning to their place of work were usually promoted to supervisory posts provided management was satisfied with their role in the union. It had become a situation in which those who renounced industrial unionism were guaranteed their livelihood in the form of promotions and a higher income. The end result was a union leadership unable to communicate or to empathize with the rank-and-file. Since union officials in the lower supervisory ranks formed the backbone of the union movement, their cooptation seriously undermined the authority of the unions they represented.

However, when Densan's leadership finally caught on that enterprise unionism was on the rise, it indulged in bombastic denounciations, in threatening the heretics and in launching yet another reregistrative drive. In hindsight it could be seen that such responses did little more than create anarchy at the place of work. Management was quick to note that the dissatisfaction of its lower supervisory staff with Densan's egalitarianism had not been seriously considered by the union. It was at this 'blind spot' that management 'skillfully drove its wedge' into the union movement.

Even with management's involvement as an important factor it may still be necessary to probe further. Why did these lower level supervisors shift so dramatically when they did? Although the notion of enterprise unionism was beginning to raise its head, in the year since Nippatsu had been divided into nine separate enterprises one could not say that the mood had shifted so drastically that enterprise unionism had come to undercut the worker's sense of class solidarity. In pointing to management's strong coercive influence over the employees, one must then ask why it was that the supervisors submitted to management's coercion. It is here that we return to the red purge which had been carried out two years earlier. The conclusion would be that the decisive battle was won at that time. For the red purge had made it clear to workers that those who withdrew from the union movement and contributed positively to achieving management's goals would be rewarded by the system. Looking back through the materials and interviewing those involved, my assessment is that Densan was seen by the members as having conspired with management in implementing the red purge. The result was that the members retaliated by disowning the very union which had in so many other ways looked after their interests. In the report mentioned above the leadership of Densan did not delve into this possibility (cf. Sakamoto 1979: 149; Kawanishi 1982b and Kawanishi 1983: 267).

VII The Union Movement after the 1952 Densan Dispute

A The effect on Sōhyō

Following Densan's defeat, industrial unionism gradually declined as an organizational principle within the labor movement led by Sōhyō. In 1953 the Yahata Steel Workers' Union and the Fuji Steel Workers' Union reached independent settlements with management at their firms just before the second wave of strikes planned by Tekkōrōren (the Federation of Steel

Workers). Similarly, the Jōban Miners' Union withdrew from battle half way into a strike organized by Tanrō.

The strength of enterprise consciousness was even more evident in the Nissan Dispute later in the same year. At that time Zenji (Zennihon Jidōsha Sangyō Rōdō Kumiai, the All-Japan Industrial Union of Automobile Workers) organized the workers at all the major automobile manufacturers. It had in place an industry-wide wage system known as the 'six-class unified basic wage' (*ropponbashira no tōitsu kijun chingin*). Regardless of the company to which a worker was affiliated, he was classified into one of six categories based upon his length of experience: unskilled, semi-skilled, first-level skilled, middle-level skilled, high-level skilled and top-level skilled. Entrants with no experience were given a minimum guarantee of ¥10,000. As they gained experience, their wages rose. This meant that inter-firm wage differentials did not exist and that a strong sense of worker solidarity was maintained within the industry. The Nissan branch within Zenji had a proud reputation for being the most militant branch in the organization. However, the branch's leaders were fired in 1953 and a second union was created. Shortly afterwards, the Nissan branch lost a major dispute which led to the branch dissolving. In 1954, Zenji itself was disbanded.

B The two choices

Sōhyō did not stand idly as enterprise unionism came to the fore. Rather, it saw the defeat of enterprise unionism as one of its aims and worked hard to counter the tide. Two strategies were proposed. The one pushed by the Takano faction stressed the importance of struggles at the regional level. The other advocated by the Ōta-Iwai faction placed emphasis on strengthening the functions of the industrial unions. A fierce debate occurred between the proponents of these two courses. At Sōhyō's Fourth National Convention in 1953 the Takano faction won support for its strategy of 'family-led struggles and community-led struggles' (*kazokugurumi-machigurumi tōsō*) which was adopted the following year as the model for the disputes at Amagasaki Steel Company and the Muroran Mills of Nihon Steel. However, while for a time the unions seemed to be making headway, both disputes resulted in defeats. Criticism of the regional community struggle strategy swelled, and Takano Minoru's leadership was challenged by Ōta Kaoru at the Fifth National Convention in 1954. Although Takano won a tight election, the delegates voted to revise the strategy. However, little was done in developing an alternative strategy. At the next Convention Iwai Akira became the Secretary General and Ōta became the Deputy Chairman. Accordingly, the Ōta-Iwai line was embraced. The following March saw the birth of the Spring Offensive, a coordinated push by five major industrial federations designed to strengthen the functions of the federations while also serving to offset some of the weaknesses associated with the enterprise union.

The Spring Offensive, however, seems to have had an effect opposite to that which was intended. Rather than overcoming the deficiencies of the enterprise union, it served only to promote the spirit of enterprise unionism. The major premise of the Spring Offensive was that each union would negotiate separately for an agreement based upon the ability of the firm to pay. The idea was that each industrial federation would agree upon an amount which all of its members would use as their starting demand. However, the demand was for the same amount of increase, not for the same salary level. Accordingly, even if each union obtained the agreed-upon amount, the absolute differential between firms would remain, although it would decrease in relative terms. In reality, the enterprise unions did not all achieve the same results and inter-firm wage differentials expanded considerably. This tended to focus the attention of employees on their firm's ability to pay; the bottom line became the size of the firm's pie and the willingness of employees to work hard to enlarge that pie. Rather than a sense of solidarity developing with other workers, the employees at each firm came to know that employees at other firms in the same industry were competitors (i.e., the enemy). In this manner, the Spring Offensive came only to bolster the move toward what has since come to be known as 'Japanese-style management.'

Again thinking they were successful, the leaders of Sōhyō were blinded to the further deterioration of their base of support, and thereby their ability to function as an organization existing primarily to protect the interests of workers as a social class, however amorphous that grouping might have been. With high economic growth rates receiving attention in the 1960s and 1970s, it would have seemed that the Spring Offensive formula had been successful in securing stable employment and higher wages for Japan's employees. However, there is room to argue that such benefits did not flow from the union movement, but from the overall level of economic activity and Japan's position in the world economy at a particular time. On this point, it is important to remember that only one third of Japan's employees, and less than a quarter of the entire labor force was unionized. In fact, one could argue that the period had been one in which workers increasingly came to depend on the firm, not the unions, to guarantee them their livelihood. When the successes of the Spring Offensive are extolled, we need to think carefully about the fact that the number of employees totally uninterested in the union movement has increased greatly, that the union has come to perform fewer and fewer functions at the place of work, that union democracy has become fossilized and that the rationale for its very existence seems to have evaporated. Instead of being an organization to look after the interests of the workers, the union has in many cases become nothing more than the administrative arm of management (for more detail cf. Kawanishi 1981). This was the heritage the union movement carried into the period of low economic growth at the end of the 1970s.

7 The Labor Union at the Shop Floor under the System of Joint Labor-Management Consultations

I Introduction

A central concern throughout the postwar period has been the role or function of Japanese labor unions. In the early 1970s, when the very existence of unions came to be questioned, people began to ask, 'Were unions necessary?' 'Did they perform any useful function for their members?' Serious concern was expressed about the extent to which Japan's important enterprise unions were increasingly coopted by the system of joint labor-management consultations. Many observers came to feel that many enterprise unions were functioning as administrative bodies for management. In order to achieve higher productivity, it seemed, the needs of the union members were being sacrificed. Examples of this could be seen above in Chapter 3's discussion of the situation at Nihon Kōkan, Nissan and Hitachi.

Returning to the two forms of union organization mentioned earlier, Table 7.1 explains my use of the terms more fully. In referring to an enterprise union's functioning as an employees' organization, I refer to its functioning primarily to increase the economic well-being of employees of that specific firm by cooperating with management to increase the firm's profits and thereby the 'pie' which is available for distribution to the firm's employees. To accomplish this, the union does two things. One is to cooperate in helping the firm achieve goals such as higher productivity and the rationalization of its operations. The second is to narrow the union's concerns to the working conditions of the firm's employees. This occurs when the union reaches an independent settlement with its firm's management and does not worry about workers in other firms. It is important to note that the ability even to serve only the workers in its own firm depends

Table 7.1 *The functions of the enterprise union*

Main direction of attention	Function	Type of union	
		Union which functions as an employee's organization	Union which functions as an organization of the working class
Concept of relations with outside bodies (e.g., management or a number two union)	ideology for dealing with its environment	the all-together ideology	ideology of labor-management conflict
		the ideology of labor-management consultations	ideology of class conflict
	definition of its goals	improvement of the conditions of the firm's regular employees only	improvement of the conditions for all workers in the working class
		priority to management's goals if 'necessary'	priority to union's goals and sacrifice management's if 'necessary'
concept of relations within the union (e.g., among its members)	membership solidarity	strengthen worker's consciousness as an employee	strengthen worker's consciousness as a member of the working class
	motivation principle	maximization of individual's interests as an employee	maximization of interests of the working class

wholly upon its cooperating with management to raise productivity.

These functions can be viewed from another angle. The enterprise union which functions as an employees' organization will limit its membership to the regular employees of a specific firm. In the members' consciousness priority will be given to achieving benefits only for the firm's regular employees who will among themselves feel a strong bond of solidarity. The union will promote an ideology which presents labor and management as a unified force working to enhance the benefits which accrue to the firm's regular employees. Finally, this type of union will choose as its guiding set of principles either the 'all-together ideology' or the 'labor-management collaborative ideology.'

One can distinguish between four kinds of ideology. The first I shall call the 'all-together ideology' (*rōshi ittai shugi*). Its basic assumption is that labor and management share the same interests and that there is no conflict of interest either in terms of increasing production or in terms of how the increase is distributed among labor and management. The second I shall call the 'labor-management collaborative ideology' (*rōshi kyōchō shugi*). Its basic assumption is that labor and management share a common interest in having production increased, but will part ways when it comes to how best to distribute the increase. The third I call the 'ideology of labor-management conflict' (*rōshi tairitsu shugi*). Its assumption is that the interests of labor and management are not necessarily both served by an increase in productivity and that each set of interests will be served by a different distribution of whatever increases might occur in the level of production. At the far extreme is the fourth philosophy (*kaikyūtairitsu shugi*). It posits that the working class and capitalist or management class are irretrievably in conflict and that the interests of the working class can only be advanced by the removal of the other class.

Why is the enterprise union ideologically constrained so that it will function only for the benefit of the firm's regular employees? Because the union is so defined that it would cease to exist if the firm ceased to exist and its very well-being is tied to the survival of the firm, a sense of conflict with other workers develops. Within that framework sacrificing the interests of other workers becomes conceivable. This is the logic of enterprise unionism which was described above. It is therefore inevitable that an enterprise union will veer toward either of the first two ideologies explained in the preceding paragraph. It is also inevitable that the goals of the union will be the goals of management. Basic to the union's ideology is the assumption that the functions of management and those of the union need not conflict. To the extent that management is able to attain its goal of profit maximization, the union will be able to achieve its goal of obtaining more income for its members.

The union which functions as a class organization has broader concerns. It is not concerned primarily with the interests of a particular firm's regular employees, but with the working conditions of all workers. Even where the union is organized on the basis of the enterprise, importance is not attached to the fact that the members all work for the same firm. Their demands are couched in terms which highlight their sense of oneness with the entire working class. To be sure, even with that kind of organizational framework union members will on a day-to-day basis pressure management to improve conditions at their own firm. However, moves to improve working conditions at their own firm will not be pushed in a way which disadvantages workers at other firms.

This is a particularly important point in Japan where regular employees work alongside nonregular employees and subcontracted workers. All three share the same work space, although their working conditions, especially in terms of pay, are often quite different. Unions which function only to serve the interests of the regular employee entrench status differences; this in turn undermines the sense of class consciousness and fraternity which would otherwise exist. Unions functioning as class organizations will invariably develop ideologies which emphasize the inevitability of conflict with management. From their point of view, by cooperating with management at individual firms, workers serve only to heighten competition among the various enterprises at their own expense. In that competition the attention of employees is shifted away from discovering the problems which they share in common. They are distracted from pursuing strategies aimed at improving the working class as a whole.

The result of cooperating with management is that the interests of the working class are always sacrificed or given second place to those of management. Because the union which functions as a class organization does not depend on the existence of any particular firm, it can when necessary move to promote the interests of the working class as a whole, and pursue a policy which would close down any given firm. For example, it could reasonably consider the costs to the working class of having firms which produce military supplies and armaments, or firms which pollute the environment, or firms which monopolize certain sectors of the economy. Moreover, if the union movement were to decide that a socialist arrangement was for some reason desirable, it could work for the dismantlement of all firms. In Chapter

8 I provide an example of an enterprise union which has adopted this kind of ideological outlook.

In this chapter, however, I wish to examine some of the reasons why most enterprise unions have so easily become organizations which function only to serve the interests of regular employees. The analysis is divided into two parts: (i) an examination of the impact of management's personnel policies as a variable external to the union; and (ii) consideration of the interaction between the union's workshop group and the workshop leader (shop steward) as an internal variable which the union can manipulate.

The importance of management's personnel policies lies in the link which exists between the union's existence and that of the firm. A union member is a union member only so long as he or she is an employee of the firm. The strategies which management adopts to maintain the firm's existence present themselves to the workers in the form of management's personnel practices. It is through personnel practices that the interests of the firm are most directly felt by the members of the enterprise union.

There are several reasons for looking carefully at the union's shop-floor organization. First, in a group-oriented society like Japan, the workshop group is an important focal point in the worker's life. While it is the main unit in which production is organized, it also provides a major sense of community which influences in many ways the worker's social life outside the firm. It is, therefore, the main group which links the employee both to the firm and to the union. Second, it is the major arena in which the interests of the employee as a wage laborer and the interests of management as a representative of capitalist interests are thrown into sharpest relief. The shop-floor group is the 'frontline organizational unit' for both management and the union. It is, therefore, on the shop floor that the 'skirmishes' occur most frequently between the union and management. It is on the shop floor that each seeks to 'outperform' the other, and the sense of conflict is most tensely felt. Third, the shop floor is where union democracy works itself out. In unions which place an emphasis on democratic decision-making, a number of important decisions will be made at this level and the organizational unit at the shop floor is usually where representatives are chosen for the higher decision-making bodies such as the annual convention or the various working parties. Although labor-management relations are most frequently presented in terms of the interactions between the top leadership of the union and management, it is at the shop-floor level that the day-to-day realities of a firm's industrial relations present themselves.

In considering the way in which the union organizes itself at the shop-floor level, special attention must be given to the role of the shop steward or shop-floor leader (*shokuba-yakuin*). He is the person who provides leadership at this level. It is through him and his efforts that the union's executive and the ordinary member know each other. He is the central activist who has the authority to stand up to the supervisory staff when necessary. He represents the union to the worker and the worker to the union. If the union is to function as a class organization, it is he who must take the initiative in guiding the class consciousness of the workers in his workshop. From a normative point of view which sees the union as having a mission to perform as a class organization, the evolution of the union into an employee's organization can be understood as having resulted from the failure of the shop-floor leader and a kind of paralysis of the shop-floor group. Once this paralysis sets in, it is very difficult to overcome it. Most of the enterprise unions in Japan which have developed from the mid–1950s onwards are characterized by this kind of paralysis. It is therefore necessary to examine carefully the situation at the shop-floor level. In today's world the role of the shop-floor organization of the union has been bureaucratized by the upper levels of the enterprise union. In many firms, the shop-floor organization has come to serve as a kind of administrative arm of a union committed to management goals. The inability of the union to take its own initiatives in the workshop is so widely recognized that it is not necessary to present proof of it; however, this basic fact underlines the importance of studying the leadership style at the shop-floor level.

For this reason, I wish to consider as a case study a large enterprise union at a private firm from the perspective of union democracy. The aim of this chapter, then, is to examine the general functioning of the enterprise union in terms of democracy on shop floors which are more or less controlled or structured in accordance with the needs of management.

II The Case Study at Hitachi

This case study concerns the working of the enterprise union in terms of its functions as an employee's organization and its functions as a class-based organization. The findings presented in this chapter are drawn from a survey of the labor union at the Hitachi Company's Hitachi factory. Although some of the findings were introduced above in Chapter 3, here I wish to present the findings from the Hitachi study in much more detail.

The study was carried out by Hazama, the current author (then a postgraduate student), and two undergraduate students at Tokyo Kyoiku Daigaku (Tokyo University of Education). The students participated as part of their assignment for a class on survey methods. The study was made in August 1967 and September 1969. Dore participated in the surveying for a few days in 1967. The findings from the survey have been presented elsewhere by Dore (1973) and by Hazama (1974).

A Background to the study

One of Japan's large electrical goods manufacturing companies, the Hitachi company had 32 places of business (*jigyōsho*) throughout the country. Its capital was 80 billion yen and it employed 70 thousand regular employees. Its annual sales were in the neighborhood of 300 billion yen.

The data was gathered from management through interviews. The interviewing started at the top and then shifted progressively to the lower levels of the organization. A good amount of written material was also collected. At the shop floor seven operatives involved in the assembly of electric generators were interviewed, and the researchers engaged in non-participant observation. Further, a random sample of 300 employees was chosen for recorded interviews. The union leadership was also interviewed from the top downwards and various written materials were collected. The union organizations in two workshops were chosen as case studies. Care was taken to choose one shop in which the union was very active and one in which it was relatively inactive. The union representatives at this level were interviewed and non-participant observation was utilized in each shop. The survey of management was carried out jointly by all members of the research team in 1967. The union component was carried out solely by this author in 1969. At the time of the union study management at Hitachi offered this researcher a room in its dormitory, but it was declined to maintain the researcher's neutrality, and lodgings were obtained in the Hitachi City, meaning that the researcher commuted each day to the factory for the duration of the study. A survey of unionists was attempted, but ran into various problems and the results could not be used.

The results from the union study were first brought together in the author's masters thesis, 'The Managerial Functions of the Enterprise Union and the Shop-Floor Group' (February 1970). A summary of the thesis was published later in 1970 in the journal of the Sociological Association of Japan, *Shakaigaku Hyōron* (no. 83). Hazama's report (1974) on the research project focused largely on industrial relations in England. When the situation at Hitachi was mentioned, the comments were restricted to the findings of the survey of the sample of 300 employees. Accordingly, the findings presented here and Hazama's findings are about different phenomena and there is no overlap in coverage. However, since Dore (1973) reached very different conclusions in his treatment comparing Japanese and British industrial relations when dealing with the same phenomena covered in this chapter, a few comments are in order. Dore's interpretation of the late development hypothesis and his argument that British industrial relations would converge toward those in Japan – the so-called 'reverse convergence thesis' – have been highly regarded by industrial relations experts, sociologists and students of Japanese society. In contrast to Dore's evaluation of the situation at Hitachi, the presentation in this chapter paints a rather negative view of those relations. How should the conflicting results be explained?

Although the same facts will often be interpreted differently by researchers bringing different paradigmatic assumptions to their work, we often find that those assumptions extend to methodological considerations and we can account for some of the differences in interpretation by referring to differences in the way researchers go about gathering 'the facts.' Hazama and this author spent three years of intensive work on the Hitachi study; Dore participated in that work for only three or four days. Although Hazama and I both conducted the survey of management in 1967, the union's side was handled primarily by myself.

While Dore participated marginally in some of the interviewing of the union's executive while visiting Japan in 1967, I alone did all of the interviewing at the level of the shop floor in 1969. Dore had absolutely no part in surveying the union representatives on the shop floor or the union members themselves. One of my responsibilities was to record all of the interviews of both management and the unionists.

In those days we still did not have tape recorders for interviewing, and all the information had to be written down at the time of the interviews and then edited after returning to Tokyo. The edited reports were all given to Hazama who then sent them to Dore. I imagine that Dore would have based his accounts of the Hitachi union, at least in part, on those notes. Perhaps because I was only a postgraduate student at the time and not one of the formal members of the research team, my name is not mentioned even once in Dore's book. In 1970, three years before Dore's book appeared, I completed my masters thesis and published the summary of it in *Shakaigaku Hyoron*. Neither was cited by him in 1973. However, the agreement beforehand was that all data collected in Japan and in England would be open to all involved, and that each researcher would be free to write up whatever conclusions he reached independently.

In trying to explain why Dore's account veers so far from mine, I wonder whether he read the research notes out of context. The notes were a partial record of how I subjectively reacted to the interviews. Of course, fully aware of the background and the undercurrents which provided the context in which industrial relations occurred at Hitachi, I only recorded what the interviewees themselves had actually stated. The background for interpreting the data was not included. However, without a full knowledge of that background, there is a danger in taking what was actual said at face value.

There may also be a problem in timing. Although my first summary appeared in 1970, it was not until 1981 that I felt I was able 'to tell the whole story.' Because I had been fairly critical of the way industrial relations were conducted at Hitachi, I felt it would be necessary to wait some period of time before making the case against the enterprise union. To do so earlier, I feared, would compromise some of those involved in the study.

Perhaps it is human nature that researchers fall into the trap of going easy with the unfamiliar while being overly critical in areas where they are familiar. In overly praising Japan's industrial relations while sharply critizing those of Britain, Dore may have been too familiar with Britain and not familiar enough with Japan. In the case of Hitachi, Dore did not really take the time necessary to see things with his own eyes. In reading the diaries, perhaps he was unable to read between the lines.

B   A general overview of the union at Hitachi

The labor union at Hitachi is the Hitachi Federation of Labor Unions (Hitachi Rōren) – an amalgamation (*rōren*) of local unions (*tanso* or *rōso*) at each of the places of business (cf. Figure 7.1). Hitachi Rōren embraced about 65,000 employees in the late 1960s. The main driving force in the Hitachi Federation is the Hitachi Worker's Union (Hitachi Rōso), the local union formed at the original Hitachi plant (in Hitachi City). In 1970 the Federation became a unit union (*tan-itsu kumiai*) with each of the local unions becoming branches (*shibu*).

At the time of this research Hitachi Rōso had about 10,000 members. Its contract with management called for a union shop, with all but a few specified employees belonging to the union. Hitachi Rōren was a leading affiliate of Denki Rōren (Federation of All Japan Electrical Workers), which was the major industrial federation in Chūritsu Rōren, the third largest national center for labor organizations until the formation of Zenminrōren (which was formed by the private sector unions in Dōmei, Chūritsu Rōren, Shinsanbetsu and Sōhyō) in November 1987. Hitachi Rōren is the enterprise federation which supplied the chairman for Denki Rōren and for Chūritsu Rōren. Hitachi Rōso supplied the chairman for Hitachi Rōren. Hitachi Rōren was obviously an important union playing a central role in the labor movement in Japan in the late 1960s. Its internal structure is shown in Figure 7.2. With the Federation becoming the central actor, all collective bargaining came to be concentrated at that level, although the right to strike and the right to accept a management offer remained with the local branch. It was felt that centralized negotiations would strengthen the local union's bargaining position, while union democracy would be protected by leaving the right to strike and to accept agreements to each local. (Nevertheless, since 1950 there has not been a single case in which a local had gone on strike by itself or had gone against the recommenda-

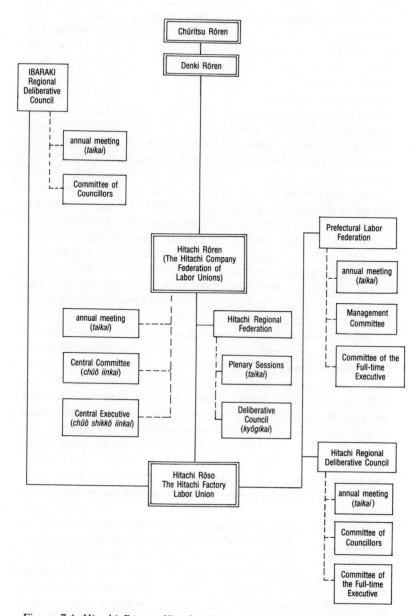

Figure 7.1 *Hitachi Rōren, Hitachi Rōso and the union movement*

tion of the Federation's Executive. Accordingly, one could say that the structures left to guarantee democracy were only of a formal nature.) The importance of the Federation is reflected in the fact that the Hitachi Factory Union did little more than handle daily administrative matters, and it was seen largely as a middle-level body in the decision-making process. Finally, the Executive of the Hitachi Factory Union consisted of the union's chairman, vice-chairman, secretary and several Executive Members. Although there were elections, only preselected candidates stood and the ballot allowed only for a vote of confidence. Each member of the executive headed a functionally defined section. However, the nomination process was not designed to choose persons who would best head the sections. Rather, a local committee of the Japan Socialist Party decided who would stand for election and then fit them into whatever sections needed a head. At the time of this study, two persons were serving their first two-year term; four were serving their second term; and one was serving a third term. One person had served previously, returned to the shop floor, and then come back for another term. The turnover was fairly noticeable, and few had any plans of becoming a career unionist. Because the local did not have the right to negotiate or decide on important matters, members of the Hitachi Rōso had little specialized knowledge of union affairs or experience in leadership positions. Most felt it would be to their disadvantage to be involved as a full-time union officer.

Because the administrative functions of the Hitachi Rōso were so great, its secretariat was extremely busy. One can gain some idea of how it served to regiment its members by examining the 37 forms used by the secretariat. In addition to the head of the secretariat there were two male clerks, nine female office workers and one person to manage the workers' hall. The sense of professional commitment to the union or to the union movement was low.

At the level of the workshop (*shokuba*) the '*han*' is the union's organizational unit which corresponds to the section (*ka*) in management's organization (cf. Figure 7.2). The *han* incorporates a number of production teams (*sagyō shūdan*). For management the *ka* is the most meaningful level at which to form its basic lower level managerial unit. Accordingly, it is not inappropriate for the union to have a corresponding organizational unit like *han*. Nevertheless, it is the production team which is most inti-

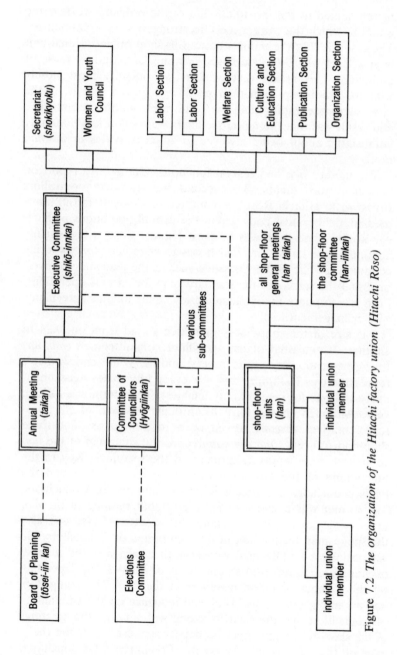

Figure 7.2 *The organization of the Hitachi factory union (Hitachi Rōso)*

187

mately linked to the day-to-day life of the ordinary worker, the group to which the worker feels his strongest sense of affiliation. The result is that the union's basic workshop organizational unit is at a level where the employee has only a secondary sense of affiliation. This means that workers will identify most closely with the union rep from their production group who is on the *han* committee rather than with the *han*'s union officers. The end result was that the union members were often less than fully enthusiastic about being involved in union activities at the *han* level.

The union's *han* had several functions. One was to report on personnel movements. The second was to elect councillors (*hyōgiin*) to Hitachi Rōso's Committee of Councillors (an intermediate deliberative body within the overall operations of Hitachi Rōren). The third was to assist Hitachi Rōso with its many administrative tasks. The fourth was to negotiate some working condition specific to the workshop such as the allocation of overtime and the setting of the standard time for various operations. Fifth was to police the implementation of the union's agreements with management.

The size of the shop-floor committee varied from one *han* to another. It consisted of the shop-floor committeemen (*han-iin*) (one person to every ten members) and the youth and women's representatives (*seifu-iin*) (one for every fifty males aged under thirty and one for every twenty females). Their term was for one year. Although chosen formally through a system of elections, representatives actually served on a rotation basis. The three shop-floor officers (*han san-yaku*) were the chairman of the *han* committee, the deputy chairman and the secretary. Key to the functioning of the *han* committee were its chairman and the *han*'s councillors on Hitachi Rōso's Committee of Councillors. The former was responsible for the smooth running of the *han* in carrying out the five functions just mentioned. He was also the spokesman for the *han* in the Committee of Councillors. He was usually a middle-aged worker with experience and a sense of presence. He received an allowance of ¥600–1000, depending on the number of union members in the *han*. The councillors had an ambiguous status. They had influence on the Committee of Councillors and the right to attend without vote the meetings of the shop-floor committee. As deputy spokesmen for the chairman of the *han* committee on the Committee of Councillors,

councillors tended to be younger workers who were being groomed for future positions in the union.

Hitachi Rōso took pride in the fact that it was a leader in developing union democracy in Japan, and was seen as being an organization which encouraged participation from below. Most unions in Japan would claim to be democratic, with the election of union officials very much influenced by the position and the role of the workshop group. This is provided for in most union charters. However, the extent to which the workshop group actually affects the outcome of the elections will depend on the daily activities of the union leadership. Among the leadership in Hitachi Rōso there were no political activists. The leadership was committed to the well-known principles of union activity. It was known for the tenacity with which it sought to develop a working relationship as an equal partner with management, and for its efforts in developing a program of education designed to foster a strong sense of class consciousness. Overall, it had worked hard to promote socialism within Japan. This is significant since by the late 1960s the number of unions which stood by the traditional principles of the union movement, even if only to give them lip service, had declined greatly.

The leadership of Hitachi Rōso had adopted the slogan, 'Any good idea will be implemented.' It had worked hard to strengthen links with the workshop group and to solve grievances which arose at that level. It had instigated a system of 'workshop patrols' whereby union officials would visit each workshop at least once every two weeks, and had put up suggestion boxes at 37 locations. It even provided a telephone answering service for members who felt they had a grievance at the workshop. The leadership also arranged numerous informal gatherings at the workshop level. In 1969 it became involved in 350 grievances. Of the 350 cases, only 50 concerned remuneration, hours of work and similar matters; the other 300 cases concerned the working environment, the provision of welfare services, company housing and the like. It is clear that the union was looking after its members in the broadest sense possible. The signs of union democracy were also evident in the term of office for those on the Executive Committee. The average length of time served was four years – two consecutive two-year terms. Pains were taken to avoid having a professional leadership which gradually got caught up with other concerns and came to be unconcerned with what was happening on the shop floor.

For these reasons the officials of Hitachi Rōso were able to avoid the path taken by the leadership in so many other enterprise unions which had coopted for a close relationship with management. This is not to say that there was not dissatisfaction with the way union leaders did things. However, the overall impression was that the leadership at Hitachi's main factory had developed an approach which emphasized the importance of the workshop and activities at that level.

C   Hitachi Rōso's functions as an employee organization

A look at the union's diary (*katsudō nisshi*) shows that the union was involved in 207 coordinated activities during the one year from August 1, 1968. However, only 31 of the activities (15 percent) could be said to have functioned to promote the interests of employees as members of the working class. Such activities would have been a city demonstration, a rally organized by the prefectural labor council, or a gathering organized by Denki Rōren. Moreover, it should be noted that Hitachi Rōso was always represented by only its leadership at these kinds of functions. None of these activities involved the participation of the rank and file. The general conclusion to be drawn is that Hitachi Rōso functioned primarily at the place of work from which its membership was drawn.

The union's leadership seemed to be tied to the labor-management collaborative ideology and the maintenance of consensus between management and the union leaders. As the Hitachi Company had evolved from a mining firm, labor-management relations in the firm were colored by a deeply ingrained tradition of paternalistic management. This tendency was strengthened in the late 1960s as the firm became more involved in international markets and began to present itself to the workers as 'Hitachi in the World.' Management sought to limit the union activities within the firm and to build it up as a 'partner in production' (*seisan kyōryokusha*). Management took pride in the 'success' it enjoyed with the union, claiming that it was able to share secrets about its financial situation with the union.

Hitachi Rōso had been formed in 1947 as a left-wing union. In its early days it had played an active role in Sanbetsu Kaigi.

However, in 1951 it lost a major struggle against the large layoffs and firings which had accompanied the Red Purge. The left-wing elements were removed in one sweep and the union adopted a conciliatory approach towards management. Ideologically it came to be guided by the right wing in the Japan Socialist Party. The leadership soon turned to cooperate with management in raising productivity, and the idea of obtaining a higher standard of living for its members through increased profits for the company came to be the cornerstone of its activities. It came to avoid political activities and followed the line associated with 'business union-ism.' However, even in pursuing economic goals, it sought to focus on concerns within Hitachi and could be said to have placed a relatively minor emphasis on the activities organized by Denki Rōren.

Both labor and management at Hitachi had come to adopt an outlook in which each existed to serve the other in a kind of daily life cooperative (*seikatsu kyōdōtai*) – the Hitachi Community – while also boilstering the international competitiveness of the firm. In practical terms, this outlook manifested itself in the establishment of an Enterprise Management Consultative Committee (*jigyōsho keiei shingikai*). All matters, including production and personnel plans, were brought before this body for joint labor-management consultations. The committee consisted of the factory head and each of the section heads from management and the entire executive committee from the union. It met every six months to examine various matters of mutual concern.

When the committee met in the second half of 1968, it discussed the amount of business Hitachi was obtaining, the extent to which it was using subcontractors, the firm's personnel plan, the construction of the budget for the first half of 1969, and a report on management's production plans. None of these were matters on which management was required to inform the union. The union officials asked a number of questions about these items, but did not seek to negotiate any of the basic parameters which defined management's production and personnel plans. The major concern seems to have been with the wages of workers in terms of production levels and with the procurement of sufficient supplies of labor.

Regular employees at Hitachi received a guaranteed base wage (*kijun chingin*) plus a contracted wage (*ukeoi chingin*). The contracted wage was a kind of regulated piece rate. So much would be set aside as pay for a particular section or work group which completed a particular job within a standard period of time (*hyōjun jikan*). If the job were not completed within the standard time, the amount set aside would be diminished. If it were completed more quickly, a bonus would be added. The method of payment has also been called the 'output wage system' (*deki-daka-chinginsei*).

For about ten years after the war this system was used with the foremen making decisions about how the contracted wage amount would actually be divided up among the individual employees in his shop. These foremen provided the leadership for the manual labor force. The standard time for each job was decided in negotiations between management and the foreman. When the foremen were also the union representatives and bargained with management as such, they were able to wield considerable influence. That was generally how things were decided at Hitachi and at many other large manufacturing firms in chemicals and heavy industry immediately after the war. The strength of the foreman as a union leader gave the union the upper hand in its relations with management in the years immediately after the war. To alter this arrangement fundamentally, the management at Hitachi decided in 1950 to dismiss 5555 employees (including union leaders at this level). In a dispute with management the following year, the union lost. There was a change in the union's leadership, and since that time management has had the upper hand. Even today the system of paying a contracted wage component remains, but management single-handedly decides the standard times and other matters related to its implementation.

At the time of this study union officials did not have any say about the contracted wage component. They were basically uninfomed and could not bargain on an equal basis with management. Moreover, nearly all the officials were from the shop floor. Following the 1951 dispute, the better educated white-collar workers had pretty much withdrawn from union activities. The end result was a tremendous gap in the intellectual capacity of management and that of the union leadership. Although the union took the attitude that it should not interfere with management's prerogatives, it nevertheless found itself in the odd situation of working within management's participatory system. The reality was that the Enterprise Management Consultative Committee did little more than direct the union with regard to management policy and served as a mechanism whereby the nod of the union might be publically acknowledged. It was not a forum where the union leadership could insist on safeguarding the interests of its members.

Told that their own representatives had participated in making the decisions, workers had little option but to go along with management-conceived plans to rationalize production processes and to intensify work loads. For management, then, the Enterprise Management Consultative Committee was the means of obtaining the consent of employees for its own initiatives. The union had basically become resigned to the view that labor intensification was all right as long as it did not result in industrial accidents. This is not to say there was not resistance to change. Prior to the introduction of the ST (standard time) system (which set standard times for each of the various operations) in 1967, the union had not opposed the plans when they were discussed in the Enterprise Management Consultative Committee. However, a good number of grievances arose on the shop floor when the system was actually implemented.

In conclusion, it could be said that the union did maneuver for improved working conditions within the cooperative framework which gave first priority to the pursuit of profit. Although specific problems were dealt with in one of the various subcommittees of the Enterprise Management Consultative Committee (see Figure 7.3), the authority to negotiate about working conditions had been lodged with Hitachi Rōren, the enterprise federation. Accordingly, Hitachi Rōso's main function was to deal with worker grievances on the shop floor. Because the firm's personnel section basically ran the workers' mutual aid society which provided workers with their basic livelihood security, the union's activities were confined primarily to matters of safety and the work environment.

These various characteristics can be seen in relief if we examine the functioning of the union's welfare committee (one of the subcommittees of the Enterprise Management Consultative Committee). The committee met twice a month and dealt with various problems arising at work and at home with regard to the provision of welfare services and the operation of the company hospital. At one of its May 1969 meetings it dealt with the following matters: a display of thermal clothing for workers on

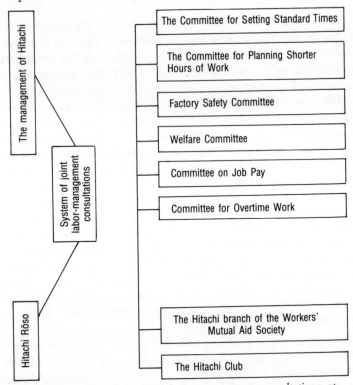

Figure 7.3 *The system of joint labor-management consultations at Hitachi*

the night shift, heating in the cafeteria, putting in automatic vending machines which sell milk, the instalment of a parking area for workers who commute by car, painting the roofs and fixing the toilets in the company housing complex, paving a road, improving the quality, quantity and price of food in the cafeteria, raising water pressure in the factory, putting in an emergency fire escape, building new toilets, improving lighting in the factory area, improving existing parking facilities, cutting the grass, repairing the cafeteria, putting new drawers in the kitchen, and getting new fans. All were small matters; none impinged on areas where there might be a conflict of interest between labor and management.

The one way in which the Hitachi union could clearly justify its own existence was in its handling of various grievances. By handling grievances expeditiously, the union was able to gain the confidence of its members and involve them in its activities. At the same time, however, it was clearly in the interests of the management at Hitachi to deal effectively with such grievances as a means of raising productivity. In order to move ahead with its various plans for rationalization, it was important that workers not be distracted by petty dissatisfactions arising from easily remedied problems. The costs of handling most grievances were small compared to the symbolic value attached to such issues by the workers. Accordingly, by being perceived as having taken the initiative in these matters, management was able to heighten the employee's commitment to the firm, thereby enhancing the willingness of employees to cooperate in raising productivity. (For that same reason, managements in many firms have taken a positive attitude toward the union's involvement in grievance procedures and have been only too ready to ensure that unionists receive wages for the time they spend in such activities. The problem is that the unions often come to function merely as communicative pipelines which effectively relay messages from the shop floor to a joint labor-management consultative body so that grievances can be solved by management. Despite the union's role in all of this, it is management which is perceived as having solved the problem, not the union.)

In summary, the union has become little more than an informant for another command. Management has over time been able to duplicate skilfully the functions of the union and thereby displace it on the shop floor where it had once reigned supreme. The examples presented above have concerned issues where the union has responded to management prerogatives. By considering areas in which the union's activities did not impinge upon management prerogatives – areas such as membership, education, the union's internal communications, or its provision of various welfare services – we might be able to uncover the possibility for union activity independent of management in which the union's ability to function as a class organization might gain ascendency over its functions as an employee organization. However, the reality in 1989 was that all indices of union activity (the energy put into its activities, the scale of its activities, enthusiasm for its activities, various measures of the members' identification with or commitment to the union, and the influence which its activities have on management) suggested that there would be little ground for believing that its functions as a class

195

organization would ever supersede its functions as an employee organization.

There are several reasons why Hitachi Rōso came to function in the service of management. A union which wishes to conceive of itself as a body independent of management and to develop as an equal in its relationship with management must choose between the philosophical orientations mentioned above. It can choose to function as a class organization and rely on an ideology emphasizing labor-management conflict (*rōshi tairitsu ideorogii*). Or it can choose to functions as an employee organization relying on an ideology stressing the fruits of labor-management collaboration (*rōshi kyōchō ideorogii*). Unions choosing the latter set of functions will inevitably come to cooperate in joint consultative arrangements. However, because such arrangements are premised on the assumption that there is consensus between labor and management, when negotiations break down, the possibility of resorting to disputative action against management is denied by the ideology of the union itself. The union is left unable to generate any real opposition to the policies which management pursues.

In the case of Hitachi Rōso, the collective agreement stipulated that there would be a clear delineation between the system of joint consultations, the system of collective bargaining, and the system for handling grievances. In reality, however, the functions of the latter two systems came to be subsumed within the first system. As a result, it became almost impossible for the union to exercise the three rights given it by the law – the right to bargain collectively, the right to engage in disputative action as a collectivity, and the right to reach collective agreements. Even at the enterprise or factory level, where there would seem to have been an opportunity to apply some kind of pressure on management with regard to working conditions, any attempt to do so was seen as running counter to the basic principle that the union ought to cooperate with management in order to raise output.

In the final analysis, it is inevitable that the enterprise union bent on benefitting only its own members (who are employees at a specific firm) will cooperate with management. By throwing away its right to strike in the name of 'management participation' the Hitachi enterprise union came increasingly to function on behalf of management as an employee organization. The union continues to develop (e.g., to have influence in the community, to achieve improved working conditions, to enjoy more social prestige and to be more institutionalized within society) by working to enhance the firm's ability to adapt to heightened international competition, to labor shortages, and to changes in the industrial structure and in society as a whole.

To isolate some of the factors shaping the activities of the union on the shop floor, it is useful to compare the way the union functions at a workshop where there is a high level of union activity and at a workshop where the union is inactive. At the Hitachi factory the electricians' workshop team (*denkōhan*) was chosen as an example of union activity. The foundary workers' workshop team (*chūzōhan*) was chosen as an example of union inactivity. In saying they were 'chosen,' some explanation may be necessary. Before deciding to gather the data from those two units, union activities in a large number of workshops were studied. Data was also gathered from Hitachi's Taga factory (which manufactured washing machines). However, the data obtained from the Taga factory (which Dore cites, thereby giving the impression that a number of factories were studied) and from a number of the workshops at the Hitachi factory were not adequate. It should also be noted that, as with any case study, the researcher was somewhat on his own to feel his way through the organization. Neither the firm nor the union would have seen it as being in its interest to admit to the researcher that some of the workshops were not 'up to scratch.' In short, in firms which operate in a very competitive environment, where profits and productivity are the sole goal, any time and money spent to help a university research project must be embarrassed and lose its competitive edge as a result of having its internal affairs made public. There is certainly no incentive to see that that the project is carried out in line with the 'scientific ideals' of an outsider researcher.

In the end five strong *han* (shop floor organizations) were identified but only one was made available for further study. Although no inactive *han* was introduced to the researcher, two 'average' *han* were and the researcher choose the weaker of the two as the one to be used for comparative purposes.

III Union Officials on the Shop Floor and Union Activity: A Look at Workshop Teams Composed of Electricians

A The structure of the union *han*

The *han* formed by the electricians was one of the five strongest *han* in Hitachi Rōso. In 1965 it had received the union's prize for being the most active *han*. The *han* was singled out for three reasons. First, since the union was formed, this *han* had produced a string of activists who had served in various positions on the union executive, including that of the General Secretary and the head of the Organization Section, and in several outside positions requiring a representative from the labor movement. Second, discussions on the shop floor were seen as occurring on a high level. Third, the reports of its members at the Hitachi Rōso's Plenary Sessions (*taikai*) and the Committee of Councillors (*hyōgiinkai*) were judged to have been outstanding.

The electricians were involved in the final stages of the manufacturing of large electric generators. The operations included manufacturing the coil, laying out the wiring, fitting the insulation, and installing the electricity supply wiring. The work team consisted of the coilers, the wire layers, the insulators, the coil assemblers and the fitters for the supply wires.

The work was skilled and was not exceptionally physically demanding. The manual processes were numerous and considerable dexterity was required. It took five or six years to become fully skilled in the work. As in other factories around Japan, here too many of the processes were being automated in the late 1960s when this study was made. The wrapping of the insulating tape around the motor coil and around the field coil had become automated. There had also been for some three years experiments with standardizing all the materials at the planning stage so that the assembly of the motor itself could be automated. Overall, the workers in this section had been fairly positively oriented towards automation. The shop-floor chiefs had formed an Automation Promotion Committee to cooperate in reorganizing the work so that it could be automated. The automation did not lead to the displacement of the skilled workers, but it did require various kinds of technological change.

Within this setting it is instructive to look at the role of the *kumichō*. Because the structure of the enterprise union tends to be shaped by the way in which management is organized, the first step in the analysis of union *han* – which corresponds to management's 'section' (*ka*) – was to examine the smallest unit of management within the *ka*, the *kumi* or production team, and its leader, the '*kumichō*' or foreman.

The second stage brought together the *kumichō* with the process planner (*tejunkakari*) to examine the production plan in the Blueprint Inspection Committee. At this level the *kumichō* had a voice in the running of things. The third stage involved the process planner (*tejunkakari*) mapping out in much more detail the exact allocation of work to the various workshops. In this regard the *kumichō* was able to provide feedback to the process planner, but he did not have the right to alter the allocations.

The fourth stage involved a look at the actual production of the generators. This was done wholly in the assembly section. On the shop floor, the *kumichō* mobilized his workforce and got the job done. He had the right to allocate work as he saw fit, and was the primary assessor of how work was performed. However, his authority was not extensive. He was constantly subjected to various kinds of checks which were carried out by the office staff. For example, the *kumichō* was called to a weekly meeting convened by the industrial engineer to answer questions about how the work was progressing. Every month the *kumichō* was required to come before the 'Output Committee' (*seika kaigi*) to be cross-examined as to whether his workers were keeping to the standard work schedule (*hyōjun sagyō jikan*). He was also expected to attend the Meeting of Supervisors which would be called by the section chief in order to ascertain whether discipline and production levels were being maintained within his shop. Management's control of workshop activities at the Hitachi factory was thorough. Working under these controls, the *kumichō* did his best to motivate the workers on the shop floor and to weld them into a cohesive work group which would effectively raise their own productivity.

The workshop was not a particularly bad environment in which to work. It was said to be about standard. Although work was not arduous and there were few serious accidents, many of the more experienced workers did suffer from a number of occupational illnesses. The use of varnish and chemical solvents had meant that finger nails became discolored and sometimes fell out. Also, the frequent handling of fibre glass had resulted in inflammation of the skin, lower blood pressure and an abnormally low level of white corpuscles.

Several characteristics of the labor market should also be noted. First, because good electricians command a good price in the open market, it was established practice that many would quit the company before mandatory retirement and set themselves up as entrepreneurs. Others would take up positions as working managers (*yakuzukikō*) for one of the subcontractors or other related firms which worked for Hitachi. For this reason, the workforce in the electrical section at Hitachi was relatively young. A second characteristic was that there were ample opportunities for young workers to be sent overseas. This was definitely an attraction; young employees would work hard to improve their skills to the level necessary for being sent overseas, and the turnover was very low. The result of the first two factors was that the workforce formed a rather well proportioned age pyramid. Finally, because the work was not particularly heavy and required considerable dexterity, fifty of the 360 employees in this section were women.

B Some characteristics of the *han* committeemen

There were 360 union members in the section. The number had been 400 until a few years earlier, but the labor shortage among the young and management's steps to rationalize the production process had meant that new graduates had not been hired for several years and the overall numbers had fallen slightly. The *han* committee consisted of 23 persons: 3 from the planning subsection and 20 from the production subsection. The three executive officers of the *han* committee were elected by the committee itself, but there had not been any times when more than the necessary number of candidates were nominated.

It was hard to get persons to volunteer to be on the *han* committee. This was true of all the workshops in the factory. Although the *han* committees were usually filled on a rotation basis, in this particular *han*, the structure of the production process meant that a simple rotation was not followed. Primary consideration was given to the functional organization of the work. In the late 1960s it was customary to elect the assistant deputy foreman (*daini bōshin*). He was second in line for the foreman's job. Three assistant deputies were aged around thirty. Work load intensification had left them with the lightest work load in the subsection (*kumi*). Moreover, since one of each committeeman's jobs was to liaise with all the workers in the *kumi*, it was possible for the assistant deputy foreman to communicate about union business while doing his job. Given the very tight control with which the workshops were structured, it would have been difficult for younger workers to have performed the job. One needed to know 'the ropes.' They also needed a measure of authority to gain a following. The assistant deputies were somewhat experienced persons who were a bit up on the supervisory ladder, but not above doing all the necessary running about which went with the position. Finally, it was not necessary for the *kumichō* to be on the *han* committee to have his views acknowledged. Since nearly all union activity was under the control of management, as explained above in the preceding section, he was able to communicate his views through the *bōshin* who was located under him in the management hierarchy. Of course, from the point of view of implementing management's personnel policies, there would always be some *kumichō* on the *han* committee. Section chiefs and other top management tried to arrange for those *kumichō* to be on the committee.

In terms of the functioning of the enterprise union, having a large number of assistant deputy foremen had several consequences. First, the committee's composition was influenced strongly by the way in which the production process was organized. Second, some persons were more likely to become committee members because of the nature of the work they did rather than because of any interest they may have had in the union or because of any innate leadership traits they may have possessed. Third, the committee reflected the management hierarchy at the place of work. Fourth, management considered it one duty of the *kumichō* that he would work to control the union's activities. The above discussion can be illustrated in more concrete terms if we introduce briefly some of the members of the *han* committee in 1968.

The head of the *han* committee, Mr Watanabe Yoshihiro, had entered the company in 1937. He had had no experience with the union movement before the war. In 1946 he was repatriated and had been involved in union activity since the inception of the union. Watanabe had been elected to the *han* committee nearly every year, but had been involved only with its shop-floor activities and had not served on Hitachi Rōso's Executive Committee. He had served as head of the *han* committee five or six times, and at the time of this study was also serving concurrently as head of the Division Liaison Committee. The leadership of Hitachi Rōso would have regarded this person as the typical shop-floor activist.

Watanabe believed that through long years of experience *han* committeemen should be able to devote themselves to looking after the welfare of others on the shop floor. He felt that the union existed not simply as an organization to improve the working conditions of the workers, but also as a kind of cooperative community which was there to assist workers with their various needs. Reflecting his strong affinity for the union, he had his eldest daughter work in the union office. He was a second generation employee; his father had also worked at Hitachi as a wire wrapper. At 51, Watanabe was a foreman. In the electricians' section there were many women in the union, and, as head of the *han* committee, Watanabe was very much respected for taking the time necessary to explain the work of the union to them.

One of the councillors (*hyōgiin*), Mr Suzuki Teruhiko, had entered the firm in 1960 and had at the time of this research been serving as a *hyōgiin* consecutively for four years. He was a graduate of the high school which had been established within the company. Believing that the graduates of that school would become the company's core employees, he had become disillusioned because of the treatment he had received. One of the older workers in the workshop persuaded him to become active in the union. After serving for three years on the Women and Youth Committee, Suzuki then worked on the Editing Committee before becoming a *hyōgiin*. At 28, he was seen by one of the leaders of Hitachi Rōso as one of the up-and-coming union activists who would later be a candidate for a position on the union's executive. His present union activities were seen as a kind of training for such responsibility. Suzuki worked in the office as an industrial engineer and was in charge of budget control at the time this research was carried out.

The secretary of the *han* committee, Mr Mabuchi Akio, was 29. A deputy foreman, he had not had previous experience with union activities, but had been approached by Mr. Watanabe who was his foreman on the shop floor.

Not having been particularly inclined toward the union and its activities, Mr Hirai Takanobu was at first surprised that he had been asked; however, because his boss offered to 'teach him the ropes,' he allowed himself to be persuaded. The Committee Member for Women and Youth, Mr Hirai Takanobu had applied to enter the engineering stream in the company's industrial arts college when he graduated from the company's high school in 1964. However, when he was not accepted he decided to enter the company. He was 25 at the time of this study.

These individual sketches illustrate how the *han* committee had come to be dominated by a veteran activist who was also the shop foreman. Watanabe had been able to use his position to mobilize younger employees under his supervision in the workshop to perform various tasks for the union. He appeared to be the sincere, hard-working employee who had a certain idealism which could be ignited by a paternalistic foreman. Two of the committeemen had graduated from the company's high school, having in common a view of themselves as members of an elite group of employees. One of the two, however, did not feel he had been satisfactorily treated as a member of the elite; the other had failed to be accepted into the company's industrial arts college. Both had been given 'another chance' by the company's internal system for off-the-job training. In the eyes of Hitachi Rōso's executive, the *han* committee was ideally structured.

C   Activity in the *han*

At the center of the production process, the electricians experienced directly the onslaught of management's programmes to rationalize production. Work loads were intensified and many of the workers were putting in 75 hours of overtime each month. The heavy work loads meant that it was difficult, if not impossible, to put much time into union activities. One could even conclude that the only activity was the all-shop-floor general meeting of the *han*. The meeting was held once a month after the meeting of Hitachi Rōso's Hyōgiinkai. Held during the 30-minute lunch break, the only items on the agenda were the councillor's report on the Hyōgiinkai and a series of announcements from the Rōso's executive made by the chairman of the *han* committee. Issues arising in the *han* itself were never considered. Although the union's by-laws stipulated that 70 percent of the *han* members be present to constitute a quorum, only 50–60 percent would attend. For the spring wage offensive and for the bonus wage campaign, however, two general meetings would be held and nearly all members would attend.

Workers seemed to be particularly interested in the issues which directly affected them, but were much less interested in meetings which concerned the local elections, revisions to the collective agreement, or retirement benefits. Members were required to pay ten yen per month to cover the cost of lunch as a small incentive to members who served on the *han* committee and attended the plenary sessions of Hitachi Rōso. Although all positions had been honorary, younger members seemed to be unwilling to volunteer for such jobs unless they were reimbursed for these kinds of small outlays.

Although the electricians were said to have had the strongest *han* in the union, union activities within the *han* lacked spontaneity. As head of the *han* committee Mr Watanabe had spent many hours agonizing over ways to improve the situation. At one stage he had attendance taken at the general meetings and sought to embarrass members into attending by asking them why they did not attend. He had also sought to change the process for selecting delegates to Hitachi Rōso's Hyōgiinkai from elections to an arrangement whereby he himself would appoint the councillors. Watanabe believed such a change would invite criticism from some quarters, but he also felt that it would allow him to involve a number of able younger employees in the union's activities. Considering the difficulties faced by this union leader in the strongest *han*, one can imagine how much more difficult it must have been in the other *han*.

There seem to be two reasons why the electricians' *han* was seen as being particularly strong. First, a large number of persons from the *han* had served on the Rōso's Executive as union officials. Second, the person from management who headed their section had always seemed to be quite understanding of union activities. On the first point, it should be noted that the electricians had been active in the leadership of Hitachi Rōso from its inception; to a certain extent the present situation was simply a 'flow-on' from the past: older leaders had nurtured younger unionists and saw that they were given union responsibilities in the different sections (see Figure 7.2) while they were still young. Members of the executive committee from the electricians' *han* often came to the *han*'s general meetings to explain union policy and they also served as a pipeline communicating grievances from the *han* directly back to the executive committee. The result was that an especially close link came to be developed between the *han* and the executive committee. Overall, one would conclude that the *han* was able to 'get on with business,' not having to waste time by going through the motions associated with union activity at the shop floor but concentrating on developing activists who could 'take care of business' at the level of the factory union and the enterprise federation itself (e.g., within Hitachi Rōso and Hitachi Rōren).

On the second point, unionists in the workshop often stated that it was easy to become involved in union activities because the manager of their section was understanding of union activities. They reported that there were a number of other *han* in which workers might have wished to stand for election to the executive committee, but had to stand down because of a manager's pressure. They claimed that unionists required the division manager's approval before they would actively participate in union affairs. This illustrates how extensive the authority of management is and how the union's ability to function is shaped by the personnel policies of management and the discretion given to middle-range management at the *kachō* level.

A few comments might now be made about the functions performed by the *han* committee. Mr Watanabe saw his own role as chairman of the *han* committee basically as being an administrator for Hitachi Rōso. It was in performing as an administrator that he tried to serve the workers in his *han*. One of his tasks was to collect and to deliver monetary contributions from unionists in his *han* as a congratulatory or condolence gift whenever weddings or funerals occurred. He would assist with the paperwork and serve as a personal guarantor when members wished to borrow money from the Workers' Lending Cooperative. Watanabe felt that it was essential for union officials in his position to do these jobs if the executive committee was adequately to serve its 10,000 members. Feeling that the members of the executive committee were extremely busy, he worked hard to see that the views of the unionists in his *han* were passed on to the *hyōgiin* and that the *hyōgiin* were pressed to speak out when necessary so that the members of the Executive Committee would be informed of what members in his *han* were thinking without having to take time from their busy schedule to tour the workshop from which his *han*'s members were drawn. He had a very deep sense of duty which 'required' him to support Hitachi Rōso's executive in this way. He was also motivated by a desire to serve those members of the executive committee who had come out of the electricians' *han*, a commitment which helped to promote a feeling that the union leadership and the rank-and-file both belonged to the same large community.

The head of the *han* committee went about gathering information on unionists' views and grievances as he carried out his supervisory tasks as foreman (*kumichō*). The workers' views were seldom expressed at the *han* general meetings, a problem which in part may have reflected the fact that there were many women in his particular *han*. Given that his job as *kumichō* required him to circulate around the section, he was able to wear two hats as he did so, and was able to spend a considerable amount of time walking around the shop floor soliciting the views of his workers and picking up criticisms of the union. His ability to fulfill both the managerial and the union roles at the same time in no small measure reflected his long years of experience at the position.

Serving as *hyōgiin*, Mr Suzuki saw his function as being a bridge to facilitate communications between the executive committee and the *han*. He emphasized two aspects of the job. One was to take the views of the executive committee to the shop floor and see if the members approved or disapproved of particular courses of action being considered by the committee. The second was to relay the feelings at the shop-floor level to the Committee of Councillors.

However, while claiming to spend a considerable amount of energy in these activities, Suzuki admitted that he was often too busy with the day-to-day requirements of his job and was, therefore, unable to engage seriously in obtaining the real views of workers on the shop floor. Instead, he would pick up in a second-hand fashion the views which surfaced at the *han* committee and pass them on to the Committee of Councillors as accurately as he could. As for the first function, he felt that the position required him to pass on as objectively as possible the views of the Committee of Councillors, but admitted that he had served in the post for four terms and had come to hold his own views on many issues, views which would invariably be interjected into his reports to the *han* on what the executive was doing or thinking. The problem of subjectivity had arisen some years earlier when the executive had decided to increase the membership contribution and the decision was then voted down by the membership. Suzuki felt that had occurred because many of the *hyōgiin* had been overly swayed by their emotional attachment to their workmates when they came to giving their report from the executive at the *han* general meetings. He reported that his stance as a councillor would be to report on the executive in a way which lent his support to its policies.

As secretary of the *han* committee Mr Mabuchi performed two tasks, one as secretary to the Chairman of the *han* committee and the other as bookkeeper for the *han*'s accounts. Most of his time was taken up with the distribution of information which had been sent to him by the executive. For example, he would be responsible for distributing and collecting ballots for all the union elections, and for mobilizing the *han*'s members to attend the *han*'s general meeting, especially right after the Executive had drawn up its strategy for the spring wage offensive. Members in the electricians' *han* were spread out in four different buildings, each about five minutes walk from the others. Mabuchi needed about fifty minutes to make the rounds of all four buildings and contact each of the *han* committeemen. However, when special general meetings were called on short notice, he had to run hard to make the rounds in thirty minutes. That was a source of his fatigue, but also an accomplishment in which he took some pride.

The members of the *han* committee served as the main conduit for disseminating Watanabe's views as chairman of the committee to the rank-and-file. Their other main function was to give feedback to the committee from the rank-and-file. That feedback would then be considered by the *han* committee and passed on to the Committee of Councillors or to the executive committee. At the time of the research, many of the rank-and-file were complaining that the executive of Hitachi Rōso was not really standing up to management the way it should.

D   Problems on the shop floor and their resolution

In interviews with union members in the electricians' *han*, the most commonly raised problems were excessive overtime, the inability to utilize their annual leave, and the unreasonableness of the standard times set for specific jobs. Each is considered briefly below.

Under the banner of developing 'small elite taskforces' (*shōsū-seiei shugi*), management pushed ahead with measures to rationalize the production processes and workers felt the pressures of work intensification. As the work loads increased and the number of persons on the shop floor was reduced to one third, production targets were achieved by having employees work long hours of overtime. The average overtime was 75 hours each month. As chairman of the *han* committee, the foreman, Mr Watanabe, had spoken to management about the problem, claiming that something would be done about it only if the union took the initiative. Although workers were guaranteed a base pay (*kihon-kyū*) (cf. Figure 6.2), workers had come to depend upon their contracted load pay (*ukeoikyū*) in settling into their life-style and covering their living expenses. However, they felt that the current levels of overtime were excessive and that they were being stretched beyond their physical limits.

As for annual leave, management had introduced the 'work attendance rate' (*shūgyōritsu*) system, with the rates achieved by each work group (*sagyōgumi*) being publicized. Although the work attendance rate was calculated for each individual, the record for each work group was made public. Each group's rate became one criteria in management's assessment of the performance of its foreman. It also became an important consideration when the group's overall work performance was judged. The work normally carried out by anyone who became absent would have to be performed by others in the work group. Given this climate, taking annual leave was simply beyond consideration. Management did not have reserve workers on the payroll for filling in when absences occurred. The end result was severe competition between groups to have the highest *shūgyōritsu*, and it came to be felt that any absence for union activity or for illness would end up as a burden for other members in one's own work group. In these circumstances, it was certainly impossible for workers to exercise their legal right to have annual holidays. Taking those days off remained a distant dream, the reality being that each employee had to repress his desire for a rest in order not to add further to the heavy work load already being imposed upon him by his workmates.

The standard time estimated as necessary for each of the production processes was churned out by a computer. However, when the computer generated unrealistic schedules, work teams were simply expected to catch up by intensifying their effort. For example, the following kind of problem often occurred with the coiling process. According to the standard process procedure, about 100 kilograms of wire was to be wound by four people before being passed to two persons who used a machine to give the coil its final shape. However, because the coil was too heavy for the latter two persons, two from the first group would have to assist them. The end result was that the first group would have to interrupt its own work temporarily while assistance was being given to the second group. The computer did not take account of this aspect of the first group's workload, and persons in that group would actually have to work unpaid 'overtime' to complete the work they had been assigned by the computer. And, for being late, the amount of their contracted load pay would be cut. The same problem seemed to exist on many other shop floors, and there was much unhappiness with the way computers were being used to rationalize work processes.

How was the union responding to these kinds of issues at the shop-floor level? According to the agreement with management, the *han* committee's chairman had the authority to oversee the overtime arrangements shown in Table 7.2. However, his authority was limited to overtime on holidays and at night. Moreover, if the executive committee of Hitachi Rōso gave its approval, management virtually had a free hand in setting overtime. Hitachi Rōso's executive often lamented the fact that it did not have an adequate policy for dealing with the sudden increases in overtime which occurred in order to meet the company's production targets. Because it had taken an ideological stance in deciding to cooperate with management to raise productivity, it was not in a good position to argue that overtime be restricted. Accordingly, the union paid little attention to the problem of overtime. The best that union members could hope for was that union officials at the *han* level would at least ensure that the few restrictions limiting overtime at night and on scheduled days off were observed. The union was not able to do more than that, and the problem remained for most workers.

The story with regard to annual paid leave is not dissimilar. The foreman heading the *han* committee was regarded as having a managerial or supervisory function. Those above him in the

Table 7.2 *The 1969 revisions to the agreement on overtime work*

The form	The previously agreed upon practice	The new agreement	The deadline for the union and management to agree on overtime	The parties among whom agreement must be reached
	(1) when overtime will exceed 4 hrs/day (8 hrs on Saturdays and Sundays) (up to two times during a week)	as in the past	4 p.m.	head of the *han* committee
	(2) Overtime at night up to once per week, overtime on days off and on the day before a holiday (up to twice a month)	as in the past	4 p.m.	
the white form	(3) work on days off (women included)	as in the past	4 p.m. of the previous day	section manager (*kachō*)
	(4) overtime between 12 and 18 hours per week	stopped		
the yellow form	(1) overtime over 4 hrs/day (when it will occur more than two times in a week)	as in the past	4 p.m.	Hitachi Rōso's executive
	(2) overtime surpassing 18 hrs in one week	as in the past	4 p.m.	the factory manager
	(3) overtime for which compensatory time off is not given (if this happens more than twice a month)	as the need arises	4 p.m.	
the pink form	(1) overtime surpassing 75 hrs/month in December, January, February, June, July or August and 65 hours during other months	as in the past	4 p.m.	Hitachi Rōso's executive

the factory manager |

management hierarchy pressured him not to take his annual leave. Because Watanabe was the one who should be getting employees to work harder, his authority would have been seen as being undermined if he himself took such leave. The foreman thus led a dual existence. On the one hand, he identified strongly with the men under his supervision, and saw himself as a member of the workshop community. At the same time, he was unable to see clearly how workers and management could have different interests, and was therefore not predisposed to confront management on the issue of work load intensification. As long as Hitachi Rōso itself was committed to a policy of cooperation to raise productivity, there was little room for union leaders at the shop floor to take the lead in encouraging employees to take annual leave at the expense of higher levels of production.

With regard to the standard time for production processes, one worker reported that

> To keep within the standard time, the foreman brought a stop watch onto the shop floor to make sure we finished within the required time. He also warned workers about having a poor work attitude and ordered that they do the work exactly according to the stipulated method. However, a number of the operatives claimed that they were able to complete their task because they performed the work in a way which was at variance with the stipulated method. This challenged the authority of the shop-floor veteran. It is likely that the foreman felt pressure from his superiors to follow the stipulated method and did not have the confidence necessary to deviate from his 'orders.' Even if the other method worked, he did not want to appear to be going against the system by himself.

The conclusion to be drawn from this episode is that the foreman could not put forward new ways of doing things on behalf of the ship-floor unionists as long as the union itself was for cooperating with management. Because the computer worked out a production plan for the entire factory based on functional premises to achieve some predetermined level of output of specified goods, it was assumed and expected that each workshop would do whatever was necessary to complete the tasks set for it. If the worker in one *han* felt the work load set for them was unreasonable and

211

refused to work harder, it meant either that more workers would need to be assigned to their workshops or that the entire production plan would have to be recalculated to their level of activity. Since management was bent on reducing personnel levels as a means of raising productivity, the only option was cutting back on output. However, workers in one workshop who brought down production levels would have been seen as being anti-social since lower overall output in the end meant lower overall income for all workers.

A look at the relationship between the shop-floor supervisory staff and the union revealed that the foreman, the deputy foreman and management's other first line supervisory staff filled most of the lower union positions at the shop-floor level. The fact is that these union officials always gave final priority to their role as management staff. This was true with regard to the problems which arose concerning overtime, annual leave and the standard times for production processes. The same consciousness could be seen in the foreman's use of the work evaluation system to differentiate between workers on the shop floor. One would have thought that the union's fundamental commitment to equality at work would have led most unionists to oppose such discriminatory behavior. However, failure to make such evaluations would have brought these lower level supervisors into conflict with management further up the hierarchy. As long as that was the situation, there was no way in which the interests of the union members could be protected. It was, in a sense, inevitable that the head of the *han* committee would continue to make personnel assessments which created inequalities among the workers, and that he would continue to exercise his right to determine who would and who would not get ahead in the company.

It is obvious that this kind of system has a number of contradictions built into it. The contradictions are seen most clearly, perhaps, when it comes to the handling of grievances. Three *han* committeemen were responsible for handling grievances. However, hardly any union members brought grievances to their attention. It was said that the positions are nearly always filled by assistant section heads (*shunin*) and the foremen (*kumichō*) because ordinary employees would not have any authority in the work place to deal with such matters satisfactorily. However, because management has a stake in hushing up such problems, the system for dealing with grievances has no independence and many union members are reluctant to use the system to resolve their problems. Indeed, if a matter was brought to the attention of one of the grievance committeemen, it seemed likely that the matter would be taken up by one of the joint consultative bodies, and that the name of the person making the complaint would be publicized in a way that would lead to that person being ostracized. The result was that the victim is victimized again without any change being made. In a system where tabs are kept on each person's behavior, it takes a lot of courage for one to stand up against the system. This is especially true if there is little or no assurance that the union will stand up to management to see that the individual is not disadvantaged simply for having spoken out.

Given this situation, what became of most grievances? To a surprising degree, they seem to have been taken directly to the union's executive committee. The committee had suggestion boxes in the workshops and it worked hard to implement its system of 'workshop patrols.' In 1968 it received about 350 complaints. Although the vast majority concerned the working environment, there were also complaints that there should be a procedure for dealing with complaints which allowed for the names of those having a grievance to be kept confidential. One unionist complained that no one would speak out about any problem because everyone knew they would have to pay a cost in personal terms for speaking out. Others quite frankly stated that the situation was such that when they had to say something they would find it necessary to go directly to the executive committee itself for that very reason. It was difficult to complain to those who at the workshop had a direct power relationship with the 'plaintiff.' Because the member's relationship with the executive committee was of a different nature, it seemed easier to broach the matter at that level.

The lessons to be learned from the preceding discussion are clear. Union members had little faith in the willingness of the union officials at the shop-floor level to solve problems which arose from workers who had a direct conflict of interest with management. Mr Watanable, who had served continuously on the *han* committee since the union's inception, summarized the situation nicely:

Until about 1950 the head of the *han* committee was about equal in influence with the section chief (*kachō*). Today nobody would seriously argue that that is still the case. The head of the Committee is not in a position where he could even hope to be viewed as an equal to the *kachō* by his own union members. Members might anticipate that the committee's head would negotiate on their behalf to a certain extent, but few would expect him to go very far on their behalf.

It seemed that workers with serious problems would not speak frankly about them. Rather, they would wait for an opportunity to bring them up in their own way with another foreman. However sincerely one might believe there was a measure of mutuality between management and its employees in the workshops of firms which have a system of joint labor-management cooperation, the facts from this case study suggest that a close relationship of mutual trust and reliability will not develop between union officials at the shop-floor level and the rank-and-file members whom they should be serving.

IV   Union Officials on the Shop Floor and Union Activity: A Look at the Foundry Workers' Workshops

A   The organization of the *han*

The *han* comprised of the foundry workers had been one of the most active *han* at the time the union was founded. Like the electricians' *han*, it had supplied a good number of leaders to Hitachi Rōso. However, by the time this study was conducted, it had become rather lethargic, its members largely disinterested in the union. It was evaluated by members of the executive committee as a less than satisfactory *han*, and was chided by the leadership for not taking a more serious interest in union affairs. The executive's concern began with the chairman of the *han* committee.

Members of the *han* were responsible for supplying other sections of the factory with cast metal parts. The foundry had always been one of the worst environments in which to work. The ore was smelted at 1200 degrees centigrade; pouring the molten metal into the moulds was dusty work; and the noise of the electric drills and presses constantly assaulted the eardrums. The workers were covered with sweat and grime, relied on ear plugs, and constantly consumed salt while they worked. It was heavy manual labor in the traditional sense, and was known as being the dirtiest work at the Hitachi factory. It was accepted that there would not be much automation in the workshops covered by the *han*. At the time of the survey, the shovelling of the ore into the smelter had been replaced by the use of a reclining magnet attached to a crane. For the most part, however, the foundry had been left behind by the rationalization which was occurring elsewhere at Hitachi. The attitude seemed to be that the foundry could be left to its own devices as long as it did not become too much of a bottleneck causing the factory to become unprofitable.

The foundry's labor force could be said to have had four distinguishing characteristics. First, the foundry had been merged with the raw materials supply depot to form one administrative unit as part of the company's rationalization program. Moreover, the number of employees working in the foundry had been cut from about 800 in 1963 to 160 by 1969. Second, because the work required considerable physical strength, it was performed best by younger employees. However, they disliked the dirty working conditions, and the turnover rate in the foundry was seen as being higher than in the other sections of the Hitachi factory. For example, only three of the ten workers hired in 1960 were still with the *han*'s workshops in 1969. At the time of the survey, the foundry was receiving only one or two new persons annually. Although that may have reflected the general labor shortage among young workers, it appeared that nothing was being done to attract replacements to the foundry. Third, because the demanding nature of foundry work tended to extract a heavy toll from the workers, those who were still there at forty were 'over the hill' and could not be transferred to other sections. They simply accumulated in the foundry section. The result was an inverted age pyramid. Fourth, there were only two persons from the company's industrial arts college to insure that workers would learn basic skills. In the foundry the company tended to rely on workers with previous work experience and to promote the better workers from among the ranks of the temporary work force. In short, the foundry was not seen as being an integral part of the company's operations.

These characteristics meant that interpersonal relations within the foundry were considerably more complex than those found elsewhere in the factory. As is usually the case with heavy manual labor, the work seems to have attracted persons with fairly rough or even violent dispositions. The workers would say in one way or another that they needed a drink to calm their nerves and would always be found outside the work place drinking with their workmates.

The work group was headed by a foreman (*kumichō*). At the beginning of the new year, tradition called for the foreman to invite his workers to his home, give them something to drink, and then march off with them to the factory to begin work for the coming year. This ceremony or ritual tended to draw attention away from several facets of the actual situation. The skilled workers kept all the 'secrets of work' to themselves and disseminated the necessary knowledge to other workers in a manner which required that the semi-feudal relationships of the past be maintained. Only those workers who demonstrated total loyalty to a skilled worker would be taught the more important skills. Loyalty was demonstrated in the first instance by refusing to open oneself up to other skilled workers. Although a number of very close relationships formed between the skilled workers and the workers under their control, many of the production units (*kumi*) in the foundry were characterized by a division between the skilled workers and the other workers who were under their control. This meant that the foundry *han* consisted of union members from a number of *kumi* which in turn consisted of a number of factions and various kinds of petty in-fighting. There was an unspoken tension between the many older workers who had not become foremen and the foremen who were basically the same age but had somehow done better for themselves. Many of the older workers who had not become foremen organized workers around them into their own little factions. For this reason, the sub-sections in the foundry did not come together as cohesive units, and the foremen constantly had to deal with a number of competing factions within their workshops.

The number of operations performed in the foundry was large. In finishing the job, there was the gas cutting, the pressurized finishing, the welding, the tempering and the painting. The difficulty of the work and the working conditions varied markedly from one job to another. It was easy for resentments to form among work groups assigned to different jobs. Rather than the formal organization set up by management, it was the informal task-oriented groups that held the key to understanding the way things worked on the shop floor. Fourth, these very complicated interpersonal relationships meant that young workers did not find the foundry a very pleasant place in which to work. Some of the younger workers felt that there might be a chance to restructure the entire operation once the foremen and the factional bosses retired in another five years or so. At the time of the survey, a number of the younger workers had gotten together to form their own group. In analyzing the operations of the union in the foundry, one had to pay careful attention to the delicate balances of power between (i) the informal factions, task-oriented groups, and young workers' cliques, and (ii) the formal organizational framework centred on the foremen.

B Members of the *han* committee

There were 170 union members in the foundry. The *han* committee consisted of nineteen persons. The committee chairman (a foreman aged 48), the deputy chairman, (a deputy foreman aged 40), and the secretary (aged 25) were the executive officers. Nine committeemen (*han-iin*) (with an average age of about 30), two *hyogiin*, three grievance officers (*kujōshori-iin*) (who were all foremen) and two women and two youth representatives (*seifu-iin*) filled out the *han* committee. Overall, one would have to say that the committee was composed of rather young members of the union. This contrasted with the situation in most other *han* where the union's activities were carried out by the middle-aged and older members of the union, but reflected the fact that in the foundry the authority of many of the older foremen had been compromised by the various factional bosses. A brief introduction to several members of the *han* committee helps to complete the picture.

The chairman of the *han* committee, Mr Tanaka Ichirō, had entered the company in 1940. In his first year he lost sight in one of his eyes owing to an accident while at work. Because he was unable to work on the shop floor, he was transferred to the group responsible for looking after the tools. Following the accident, Tanaka had sought consolation by entering one of the new religions, Seichō no Ei. He later entered the military and came away with the conviction that anything could be done if there was simply the will power to do it. He reentered the company in 1947, and formed the Hitachi Factory Youth Progress Association under the auspices of Seichō no Ie. As one of its activities, he toured agricultural villages putting on theatrical performances. He also organized a number of debates. Since 1950 he had been in charge of the drums which were played each year for the company's foundation day ceremonies. He confided that he was 'happy to have a go at anything,' and was 'fairly well known by most of the section and division chiefs.' He had for some time left union matters to others. Until about four or five years prior to this study, there had been a good number of union leaders in the *han* and it had not been necessary for him to be involved. However, in a relatively short period of time they had all quit or been transferred to other factories. It was at that time Tanaka had thought of serving as the chairman of the *han* committee. Reflecting on the fact that he had drawn some attention to the section by accumulating a fairly satisfactory record as foreman in charge of safety, attendance and pro-ductivity, he felt that there might be something he could contrib-ute to improving the status of the foundry *han* within the union. In a relatively short period of four years, he had served as a *han* committeeman, as a grievances officer and as a councillor. At the time of the study he was serving both as the chairman of the *han* committee and as chairman of the Yamate Factory District Coordinating Committee. He was 48.

One of the councillors, Mr Hirota Kenji, had come to the company in 1951 as a temporary worker. He had been a union activist in the youth section of a union in the nearby Takahagi Mine which had been run by his father. The union was well known as a focal point for activities of the Japan Communist Party and he had been a member of the Party. When the mine closed, he spoke with his brother-in-law who was working for Hitachi and the brother-in-law arranged for him to be put on as a temporary. Because he had written on his resume that he had been a union activist, he was not employed by Hitachi as a regular employee. Nevertheless, it turned out that the head of the personnel section had the head of Hitachi Rōso (a member of the more moderate Japan Socialist Party) looked into the boy's ideological background. In Japan unions were often used in this manner to enforce a kind of thought control. When the youth reapplied, employment was offered to him subject to his withdrawing from the Communist Party and to his promising to keep out of union activities. Through the good offices of Hirota's brother-in-law, it was arranged that the young man would be taken on, with one of the section heads in the foundry as a guarantor. After he had joined the company he was approached by one of the union officials who told him, 'I know all about you and will be keeping an eye on you!' Somewhat frightened, he decided to keep away from union activity. However, six years before this study Hirota's guarantor had retired from the company and he felt he was then free to become involved with the union. So he stood for the position of councillor and was elected. He was involved on the technical side of things as it related to the rough preparation of steel for further processing. A deputy foreman, Tanaka was 44.

One member of the *han* committee, Mr Uchida Saburō, had entered the company as a temporary worker in 1968. That was the first year the Hitachi factory hired high school graduates. After one year at the factory's welding school, he passed the state examinations in welding and was placed in the finishing section of the foundry. Shortly afterwards a number of high school graduates who had come through the company school entered the workshop as welders. Thinking that it would be good to restructure the feudalistic relationships which existed between the bosses and the workers under them, he established a small group of young welders in what was known as 'the welders research study group.' The group met once a month and at first had about fifteen members. From about the fifth meeting, however, the numbers began to fall. He later learned that the other members had been told not to attend by their foremen. For continuing to meet with two others, Uchida got himself on the wrong side of his foreman and was soon transferred to another factory at Totsuka in Kanagawa Prefecture.

It used to be said that anyone transferred elsewhere from the Hitachi factory had to be 'pretty useless.' Accordingly, Uchida received a considerable psychological shock when he was transferred. However, while 'on leave' from the factory, he remained confident in his ability to weld, and he was chosen as one of two from the Totsuka factory to be sent to India for nine months.

Having his skills further confirmed, he became even more resentful of the former foreman who had him 'exiled.' This grew into a resentment against the union which he saw as being too closely aligned with management. After an absence of five years, he was brought back to the foundry at the Hitachi factory. That was one year before this survey was conducted. When he ran for the position of councillor, he had thought most of the councillors were pretty useless. However, he was quite surprised to find himself being put forward as a candidate by all the workers. A bit overwhelmed after having been left 'out in the cold' for so long, the 30-year-old arc welder felt obliged to serve all the members since he had been elected by the others in his workshop.

The representative for women and youth, Mr Sonoda Kazuo, was quite young at 23. He had entered the company in 1965 after graduating from the company's industrial arts college. His dreams of a career had been somewhat shattered when he was assigned to the foundry. Some of his classmates had been fortunate to have been sent to the machinery section where they could wear a necktie and work in a spotless workshop. Instead, he had been banished to a workshop where he had to bathe and put on a completely fresh change of clothes after every shift. At first he had been too embarrassed to leave his building at lunch time for fear of meeting some young women. Also, because there were not many other young fellows working there, he felt the atmosphere was a bit tinged by 'the smell of old men.' In some of the other sections in the factory, the employees talked about skiing together and planned trips; in the foundry the old men could think of doing little else than going out for a drink. Sonoda thought three times of quitting the company. However, although the wages were not particularly great and the working conditions were not the best, he felt he received some recognition or status in society for being employed by Hitachi. Rather than moving to a smaller, less prestigious company, he concluded that his overall life chances would be better served by putting up with the situation at Hitachi. Somewhere along the way he had been invited to a union meeting. At that point he became interested in some of the activities for young workers and women. Involvement in those activities meant he was able to meet young persons from other parts of the factory. Gregarious by nature, he enjoyed the union activities. Having become the deputy head of the women and youth section in the union, Sonoda was seen by some members of the executive as a future leader in Hitachi Rōso.

C   Union activities in the *han*

The *han*'s general meeting was held at noon once a month following the meeting of the Committee of Councillors (*hyōgiinkai*). About 60 percent of the members of the *han* attended. When members of the *han* committee went around trying to stir up interest among those absent, they were told that the absent members were off playing *shōgi* or taking a nap. The chairman of the committee, Mr Tanaka, took the view that members worked hard because they would receive a black mark on their personnel file if they missed work, but that they were happy to leave union matters to others because there was no such disciplinary action if they missed a union meeting. Important matters were decided by general vocal acclaim at the *han*'s general meeting, but in some cases the voting would have gone the other way had all members in the *han* been present to vote as a bloc in a way which would support an otherwise minority view. No funds were collected for the activities of the *han*. It was said that the suggestion box in this *han* was always empty. All the union representatives at this level were said to have been chosen on a rotation basis.

Mr Tanaka believed that his responsibilities as foreman representing management on the front line went hand-in-hand with his duties as chairman of the *han* committee. As a member of the management team he was foreman of the tools shop and foreman of safety. The tools shop consisted of three persons. Their job was to replace damaged tools and to see that the tools to be used by the incoming shift were in good condition and ready to use. The work was relatively light and could be done by a person with a physical handicap or by an older employee. Because the section was not one of the extremely busy sections, the foreman had also been given the responsibility of overseeing safety procedures. This allowed him to walk around the shop floor a good deal. Tanaka saw himself as a kind of lower-level personnel officer responsible for administering personnel policy as it related to safety and hygiene.

In carrying out his duties, Tanaka took it upon himself to see that the safety and hygiene policy was implemented in a way that allowed for the foundry's level of productivity to be improved. His effectiveness in this job could be attested to by the fact that the number of accidents at work had dropped from 30 in 1962 to 8 in 1963, and then to 3 and to 1 in the following years. In 1966 there had been no accidents. Because the number of accidents had fallen to minimal levels, his work had by and large come to consist of workshop tours with a focus on identifying problems before they resulted in an accident. While he was walking about the workshops employees would often tell him about their grievances. He jotted their comments in his notebook and then reported the matters to the section chief. At the time of the study Tanaka was studying to be certified by the Ministry of Labor as a work hygiene administrator. The section chief had advised him to obtain the qualification.

From the preceding discussion it can be seen that one of Tanaka's primary managerial functions came to be the discovery of grievances on the shop floor. It is important to note that the majority of grievances had to do with the work environment. Every day he walked around the workshop as a member of management. The union members would share their grievances with the foreman who was management's person to oversee safety while also being chairman of the *han* committee. He reported directly to the section chief, who then proceeded to have the matters solved by management. In this way, an effort was made to raise the workers' morale and to interest them in attaining higher levels of productivity. The above description illustrates how a large number of enterprise unions actually operate on the shop floor. First, supervisory staff carry out personnel management functions in the name of 'union activity.' Second, union activity and management strategies are well integrated so that basic contradictions do not seem to arise. Tanaka's behavior is typical of union leaders who serve enterprise unions which function as employee organizations.

It goes without saying that the foremen who serve as union functionaries see this arrangement as the natural state of affairs. 'Since becoming chairman of the *han* committee,' Tanaka stated in one interview, 'nothing has changed in my work routine. Because the union also should be involved in issues related to improving safety, there is no conflict of interest and I am able to perform both jobs happily.' Other unionists also saw him as being the appropriate choice because of his involvement in factory safety. He was seen as basically doing the same work in both jobs, and was known to the workers by his frequent meanderings around the shop floor and his willingness to listen to their complaints. Many workers thought it nice that he would also as a result of his union work receive an increment in his salary. The union members did not seem to be conscious of the fact that his work as the union official basically involved him in implementing management's personnel policies rather than looking after their interests. The underlying assumption, of course, was that the union and the company shared the same interests, and improved safety was seen as a means of increasing productivity.

Looking more closely at the consciousness of the foreman himself, we discovered that he was quite fond of saying he would turn his attention to building up the foundry *han*'s position within the union once he had ensured that production levels had been improved in the foundry. He also claimed that he would quit his activities in the union when he came to feel that they interfered with his work as a manager. It was clear that he attached first priority to raising productivity, not to union activity, that he thought of his community primarily in terms of the foundry rather than the factory as a whole, and that he conceived of the union and the company as existing in a symbiotic relationship.

Why did the union members choose the foreman to chair their *han* committee? First, they did not see the union as standing in opposition to the company; they felt that the man in charge of safety would likely be the most appropriate person to also look after their interests. There was also the complicated maze of interpersonal relationships. Those who became too close to one of the senior workers in the foundry were seen as belonging to that person's faction. The foreman in charge of safety did not have a group of men under him and was seen as being somewhat above having those kinds of relationships. The men in the section felt more comfortable in talking to that foreman than to any other foreman. Furthermore, the other foremen would not feel threatened if the workers under their jurisdiction happened to talk with the foreman for safety. Tanaka himself was quite aware of this fact. A third reason the foreman for safety was accepted as the chairman was that he and the section chief were fairly close, having served in the same army platoon during the war. Their houses were in close proximity and it was generally believed that the two men could talk openly about a variety of personal matters. Owing to these ties it was felt that Tanaka would carry more weight with management than would any of the other foremen. From his own perspective as well, Tanaka felt that his understanding of the management system would facilitate his functioning at the head of the union's *han*. It was clear that being a part of management was a definite benefit when it came to carrying out the duties associated with being the head of the han committee. A final consideration was the paperwork which went with the job. It was imperative that the chairman of the *han* committee have a desk. As Hitachi Rōso had become fairly bureaucratized, and its executive had come to rely heavily on the heads of the *han* committees to fill in various forms, the desk of the foreman became an important attribute.

In evaluating the work of the chairman of the *han* committee, it was difficult to find in his activities anything which would single him out as a unionist *per se*. What he did was done largely as a kind of 'hobby' or because he was driven to do so as an 'extracurricular activity.' As chairman of the Yamate Factory Area Association of Unions, he was responsible for organizing seven major activities: a baseball tournament, a softball tournament, the annual fishing party, the indoor games championships, drinks for spring offensive activities, the women and youth dance party, and the activities feedback session. Reflecting the union's orientation towards recreational activities rather than programs to build the union as a workers' organization, the executive donated 70,000 yen to support these seven activities, 10,000 yen for each activity. While there may have been a slight distinction in the minds of employees who participated in union-sponsored recreation as opposed to recreation organized by the company, the two kinds of activities were not seen as being in competition as a means of winning the loyalty of workers to one side or the other; the workers did not mind much who sponsored the activity. In either case, given the fairly structured social relationships which characterize life in small towns like Hitachi City, such activities were seen as an opportunity to get away from work even though the final goal of the sponsoring bodies may have been simply to raise worker motivation and thereby productivity.

There was only one area in which the chairman of the *han* committee could be said to have worked independently of management for the workers in his *han*. That was in pressing for a

special heavy duties allowance, a small amount paid to the foundry workers to offset the fact that they worked in the worst
environment in the dirtiest workshops. When it became apparent
that this would be the one issue on which management would
not make any concessions, Tanaka took the matter directly to
the executive and tried hard to persuade the Committee of Councillors that the matter deserved its careful attention. He even
went so far as to address the committee. He knew it was a
matter which would not be resolved favourably by management
unless it was taken up by the union's leadership, and then not
simply as a grievance within his own *han* but as a matter which
was of concern to the entire union at Hitachi. Although he was
not very optimistic about the chances of winning the allowance
for his men, it was the one instance in which he could be said
to have engaged in union-like activity.

The middle-aged councillor, Hirota Kenji, felt that his job was
primarily to serve as a communications pipeline between the
executive and the shop floor. He was particularly careful about
injecting his own interpretation into his reports to the Committee
of Councillors, as any deviation from what members in his own
han had actually said would later invite criticism that he had
misrepresented those he was appointed to represent. He also
seemed equally careful in reporting back decisions from the committee to the *han*.

His philosophy concerning the role of the union had changed
over time. When he was working in the mines right after the
war, he saw the unions as having an important role to play in a
broader program of social revolution. However, by the time this
study was conducted in the late 1960s he had come to feel that
the union ought to concentrate its energies on trying to improve
the workers' overall standard of living. Although he was familiar
with union rhetoric on serving his fellow workmates, he confided
that he was able to engage in union activity only because the
union gave him some financial compensation. When he had first
become involved in union activity, his overtime had dropped
from 60 hours per month to 18. Because the overtime pay had
been a critical part of his wages and was necessary to make ends
meet at home, he was able to hold his union office only if the
union compensated him for the lost income. In the future he did
not expect to be participating so actively in the union. Although
lower-level union officials such as himself could not be ordered

by the foreman to do overtime, the foreman still considered the willingness of those under his supervision to work overtime when making his personnel evaluations for management. For this reason, Hirota felt it was to his disadvantage to devote time to union activities.

Herein lies a major source of union inactivity at the shop-floor level. Once cooperation with management to raise productivity was accepted as the major premise, it became very difficult for the enterprise union to counter management's view that workers had an obligation to engage in overtime. Management always argued that overtime is necessary for the firm to meet its production targets. Although in principle workers were free to choose whether to engage in overtime, their choice became subject to evaluation when the foreman completed his worker evaluations. For those who wanted to protect their standard of living in the long run there was obviously only one choice. The situation was so structured that one would have been foolish to participate in union activities at the shop-floor level. The idea of honorary positions was clearly something of the past. Those participating in the union required financial guarantees.

The young welder saw his duties as a *han* committeeman as being limited to two activities. One was distributing the union newspaper to members in his work group (*kumi*). The other task was informing persons in his group when the *han* was having a general meeting. Aside from serving as local 'messenger boys,' the committeemen had little else to do as a general rule. Although Uchida was quite cynical in his view of management, he also had considerable reservations about the union. At the time of the spring offensive, when the union leadership was deciding beforehand the strategy it would follow, he observed that the union leaders' wages were secure, regardless of whether they achieved any wage increase for the workers or not: 'It's no skin off their backs whether they obtain a large increase or a small one.' Unhappy with management and the union, he could be said to be the 'doubly alienated' type of employee. He was particularly bitter about management's way of dispatching workers to other locations and about the union's acquiescence in its doing so. The union-management agreement states that the union must approve all transfers. Uchida could afford to be cynical; he was a high school graduate with a welder's certificate who could leave Hitachi any time and easily find another job.

Uchida claimed he was always prepared to quit at a moment's notice and said he would do so immediately were he transferred to a job other than welding.

Other workers were less fortunate in not having the skills or education which would allow them to shift to another employer so easily. They were left having to keep their criticisms to themselves. Indeed, their need to justify their existence at Hitachi probably motivated them to develop a stronger sense of identity with the company over time. Among Uchida's ten classmates who had graduated from high school and become skilled welders, four had already quit working for Hitachi. One even had a big argument with his foreman and quit on the spot. Those who had graduated from the company's industrial arts college found that in the outside world they were regarded only as middle-school graduates. They knew it would be difficult for them to get comparable jobs elsewhere. They were, in a very real sense, 'locked into Hitachi.' For that reason, 'internal graduates' would join the union and see in it their only way of rectifying whatever grievances they might have had. The high school graduates from outside who had any skills would be able to resolve their problems simply by quitting the company. Looking back at Hitachi over the past twenty years, it is interesting to note that the attitude of these high school graduates has not changed.

The representative for women and youth, Sonoda Kazuo, did nothing at the shop-floor level. He sat as the deputy chairman of the Women and Youth Council. Because his job was carried out at the factory level, it was sometimes necessary for him to be absent from his work. This was also why he was not more involved in union activities in his own workshop. Sonda felt guilty about his union commitments, commenting in one discussion that it was a bit unfair to his foreman. He felt particularly bad that his workmates would often do his work for him while he was away on union business. Even when such activity was done outside working hours, he felt uneasy about not being able to do overtime with the other workers. For this reason, he tried as much as possible to avoid being involved in union activities in his own shop. In a shop where the foreman was basically against union activity, ordinary union members quite naturally found it difficult to engage in any activity at all. Although Sonoda's foreman had previously served on the union's executive, he had recently asked Sonoda to consider dropping his union activity, suggesting that he was not very supportive of Sonoda's union activity. Because he was intent on raising the attendance rate, the foreman was not particularly happy about having someone away from the shop area and tended to deny the union representative's requests to be away for union activity. Sonoda recognized that he too would probably take a similar position given the overall emphasis within the firm on labor intensification. The additional increase in everyone else's workload owing to his doing union business seems to have been small by itself, but when seen as being in addition to the marked increases which had already occurred in the workload owing to the company's rationalization drive, it is easy to understand how Sonoda's short absences might have been seen as the final straw. Here again we see an example of the way in which management's single-minded pursuit of higher output levels came to shape the way everything else was done within the factory. It was impossible to engage independently in union activity. The situation was similar in all the *han*, and as the regular production deadline, the twentieth day of each month, approached, the councillors would find it increasingly difficult to leave their work and would often have to ask the union executive to postpone meetings of the Committee of Councillors during that time.

D   Problems on the shop floor and their resolution

The problems associated with overtime, annual leave and the standard times set for various production processes (which were perceived as serious problems in most other *han*) were not perceived as being all that serious by workers in the foundry *han*. Because the work in the foundry involved lots of heavy physical labor, and management was mindful of the fact that excessive fatigue would lead to unnecessary and disruptive accidents, management strove to limit the amount of overtime which was being performed. Accordingly, overtime was kept to an average of about forty hours per month. Many employees wanted more overtime in order to supplement their income, and attendance was higher on days when overtime was scheduled than on normal days without overtime.

As for annual leave, the situation was potentially rather good. Compared with other areas in the factory, it was possible for management to find slack periods and to rotate members onto annual leave without much disruption. However, the chairman of the *han* committee has stigmatized persons taking annual leave as 'bludgers.' As in the electricians' *han*, the foundry workers tended to show a certain reluctance to take their holidays.

As for the standard times, the situation was somewhat less acceptable for some of the workers. Those in the finishing section were given contracted work loads as a group. Because there were a lot of manual operations, it was easy for the group to 'get ahead' in their work and to have a sense of 'being on top of their jobs.' In the technical section, however, contracted work loads were decided on an individual basis and the standard times could be fairly rigorously enforced. The union members in this section felt some unhappiness. Nevertheless, the union itself remained unconcerned with the situation and each employee would, on his own, have to approach the foreman in his own workshop and negotiate his own work load on an individual basis.

V   Four Factors Shaping Union Activity on the Shop Floor

The preceding discussion leads us to conclude that the union was not very successful in organizing shop-floor activities. With the emphasis on higher and higher levels of production during the period of high economic growth in the 1960s, it became nearly impossible in the private sector for enterprise unions of the Hitachi type (i.e., unions which embraced the co-operation with management ideology) to oppose management policies in any way.

There were at least four reasons that this was the case. First was the fact that union members were so busy there was not time for union activity. Second, management took definite steps to wrestle control of the workshop from the union, and to turn the union into a subordinate administrative unit in the service of management's goals. Third, enterprise unions tended to develop organizational structures which parallelled those of management, allowing supervisory staff on the lower rungs of management to constitute the lower echelons of the union hierarchy. Fourth, the union's commitment to co-operation with management in terms of raising productivity made it difficult, if not impossible, for the union to oppose management's plans for rationalization and work load intensification.

Given these factors, the level of union activity came to be measured not by the union's ability and its willingness to stand up to management, but by the extent to which it dealt with the many minute problems of individual workers. The interconnectedness among all the individual problems which gave workers a common element in their existence as members of a working class escaped its attention, which had shifted to counting the number of unionists who would co-operate with the executive as volunteers for its various sections (as identified in Figure 7.2). It evaluated its shop-level officials according to their communicative and administrative functions, their ability to speak out at meetings, their ability to get workers to attend the *han* general meetings, and their ability to command those under them. It evaluated *han* activities in terms of the number who attended the *han* general meetings and participated in the spring offensive activities, the content of their debates, and the willingness of *han* members to paste slogans on the walls. It seemed to be interested in whether everyone was able to function together as a group. Whenever the electricians' *han* was praised by the executive as having the most outstanding union *han*, it was being judged on these kinds of criteria.

The reason for choosing the electricians' *han* and the foundry *han* for the case studies lie precisely in this distinction which the union leadership made between the active and the inactive *han*, the well run and the poorly run *han*. By comparing these two *han*, the aim was to uncover some of the dynamics which characterize the enterprise union in contemporary Japan. Here the four factors mentioned above will be discussed in more detail.

A   The management of the workshop

The first factor to consider is the way management 'rules' the workshop. The first job of management on the shop floor is to raise productivity. To achieve that end, management is concerned with creating a tightly woven group within each workshop and with raising the morale (i.e., the willingness to work) of each employee. This is accomplished through management's various personnel policies. Accordingly, union activities and the behavior of the union's shop-floor officials become a major concern of management.

It is readily apparent that management adopted a different attitude toward union activity in the two *han* which were the subject of this investigation. As a key workshop, the electricians' section was subject to a number of outside influences such as the state of international competition and the labor shortages in the domestic labor market. To accommodate these changes, management sought to raise productivity. In addition to introducing new technology, the obvious move was to improve labor productivity. The steps were simple in terms of altering the labor process: rationalize operations in the workshops, introduce the idea of having work groups each composed of a small tactical elite, rely more on the overtime of a smaller number of employees, set up standard times for the various production processes, and keep a tighter reign on attendance and absenteeism. One dimension of these changes was structural and could be seen in the effort to restructure the social groups involved in production. The other was motivational and focused on the 'spiritual' or 'ideological.' It could be seen in measures to alter the consciousness of each individual worker by inculcating in him the willingness to work harder.

The major strategies were two. One was to bring the foremen clearly into the managerial ranks, making his position as a front line supervisor quite clear. It was then through the foremen that management was able to implement a fairly totalitarian control over everyone in the workshop. It followed that the ability to manipulate other employees in the workshop became a main criterion in the selection of foremen. The second strategy was to positively involve the union in workshop activities in a way which would contribute to higher productivity. In the union a means of regimenting the workforce and a method of dealing with grievances was sought.

As part of its overall plan to 'revolutionize' the shop floor, management instructed section chiefs (*kachō*) to do a number of things to steer union elections in the *han* so that they would result in suitable employees being elected. One was to establish the practice of having foremen consult with the section chief before standing for election to become the chairman of the *han* committee. This was to give the section chief an opportunity to tell foremen not to run for the office when it was not in management's interests. In this manner, management could arrange for the least busy foremen, the assistant foremen and the deputy assistant foremen to take turns in filling the union positions as happened to fit the company's needs. It was also management practice to 'assign' foremen to union positions at the *han* level when the union looked like it was becoming involved in 'political' activity, as occurred with regard to the government's ratification of the Mutual Security Treaty with the United States at the time this study was conducted. Union officials had to have management's sanction in order to engage in union activity. In this way the foremen came to work in the shadow of the section chief, controlling the election of the councillors by instituting this kind of nominating system and having someone from one's own group as the *han* secretary.

Section chiefs were told that union activities were necessary and could be used to administer certain aspects of the company's personnel policy. Accordingly, section chiefs were asked to cooperate in promoting those kinds of union activities which were consistent with management policy. In the electricians' *han*, for example, a number of persons on the *han* committee felt that it was easy to be involved in union activities because the section chief was so 'understanding.' However, the union's agreement with management called for union officials to submit the 'absent from work for union duty form' (*risekitodoke*) for the approval of the section chief (or, as the case may be, the foreman) so that management not only gave permission for union activity, but was also always aware of what the union was doing.

Finally, the section chief was encouraged to take control of the union's spring offensive. It was common for the section chief to sit at the management coordination meetings (*shokusei kaigi*) – which included the section chief, his assistant(s), the planning coordinator and the foremen – to take the initiative in telling the group that a bargain needed to be struck soon with the union in order to maintain stable production schedules.

Because the foundry was seen as a workshop 'on the way out,' it was not constantly being pressured constantly to raise productivity. Management's policy for the foundry was simply to avoid any costly accident and to take whatever steps came to mind to limit 'wear and tear' to either the workers or to the machinery. There was little interest in expending energy to motivate workers. Moreover, the informal leaders were left to their own devices. In fact, the one person who as an idealistic youth had tried to move beyond the pre-modern relationships ran into immediate resistance. Seen as someone who was making 'waves,' he was soon sent to another work location. It was obvious that management was not interested in developing union activities in the foundry workshops, and left the union primarily to engage in activities related to improved safety and hygiene. Reflecting this situation, management was happy to have the safety foreman, with no workers under his control, serve as chairman of the *han* committee. Management did not work to have other foremen do the job in a way which would have united the workers together under a more centralized form of control. As it did not see much room for the union to contribute to improved productivity, management was basically rather cool to the idea of workers in the foundry being involved in union activity. It is not surprising, then, that the foundry's representative for women and youth did not get a very sympathetic ear when he spoke about taking time from work for union activities to his foreman (who had himself been a former member of the union's Executive). Nor is it surprising that one of the councillors felt disadvantaged by having his inability to do overtime reported by his foreman as a negative mark on his work evaluation card.

B Management's complete control of the workshop

In structuring its control over the various workshops, management made a clear distinction betn its core workshops and those which it thought to be peripheral. As shown in Tables 7.3 and 7.4 this distinction was linked to the way in which it treated the union in the two sections described above.

Table 7.3 *A comparison of the structure of two workshops*

Structural areas of concern	Specific areas of concern	The electricians' *han*	The foundry *han*
The hierarchical structure of positions	(1) The basic policy for allocating personnel	given priority as a core section	given little importance as a periphery
	(2) Number of operatives	360 persons (400 in 1965)	160 persons (was 800 in 1965)
	(3) Number of female operatives	50 women	no women

Structural areas of concern	Specific areas of concern	The electricians' *han*	The foundry *han*
	(4) Age profile	pyramidal (large number of young employees thinning out in the middle and upper age groups	many old and young workers, fewest in the middle age groups. Older workers > younger workers > middle-aged workers)
	(5) The turnover rate for young workers	low	high
	(6) Placement of graduates from the company's training school	many placements 45 graduates in the *han*	few placements only 2 graduates in the *han*
	(7) Sense of order in the workshop	reinforced by the alignment of position, skill, seniority and educational achievement	undermined by the fact that position was not always matched by a commensurate level of skill.
	(8) Locus of responsibility for getting the work done	in the production group	in the individual worker
	(9) Number of occupational categories	5	13
The authority structure	(1) Authority of the section chief	strong, a career businessman in the company's elite track of the university graduate	weak, a middle-school graduate in a rather dead-end job
	(2) The foreman's source of authority	support from the section chief	lack of support from the section chief but good ties with the men on the shop floor
	(3) Alignment of authority with designated position	aligned	not aligned
	(4) Informal leaders	not present	present with factional followings
	(5) Relationship between the foreman, his assistants and operatives	clear	ambiguous

Structural areas of concern	Specific areas of concern	The electricians' *han*	The foundry *han*
The communications structure	(1) Formal structure	section chief → foreman → assistants and operatives	poor communications between section chief and deputies and the shop floor, and between foreman and operatives
	(2) Informal structure	absence of cliques which impede good communications	poor communications between section chief and deputies and the shop floor, and between foreman and operatives; informal structure was counter-productive of the formal structure
The structuring of feelings	(1) Workers' faith in the foreman	high	low, discord between foreman and informal leaders
	(2) Cohesiveness of the work group	high	Low
	(3) Informal human relationships	good, work group found to socialize outside of work	poor, workers tended to go drinking only with the persons in their own clique

The electricians' section was characterized by a certain air of stability. The allocation of the workers was given careful thought and management was conscious of the need to make sure that a steady supply of new graduates came to the section each year. One sure measure of the importance which management attached to the section was the extent to which it channelled graduates from the company's educational facilities into the electricians' section. Given management's efforts to keep these young workers with the firm and the established pattern of older workers retiring early and setting up their own company or moving to one of Hitachi's subcontracting firms, the age composition of the workforce took on the shape of a pyramid. As a result, management was able to achieve the ideally patterned career structure for its workforce; education, occupational classification, job position, age and pay were all aligned to provide a fairly predictable career path for those in the electricians' *han*.

In treating the electricians' section as a core workshop area, the company was careful to select a section head who could function with some authority. The section head was always a

Table 7.4 A summary comparison of the two han committees at Hitachi Electric

	The electricians' han					The foundry han		
	Watanabe Yoshihiro	Suzuki Teruhiko	Mabuchi Akio	Hirai Takanobu	Tanaka Ichirō	Hirota Kenji	Uchida Saburō	Sonoda Kazuo
(1) Union office	Chairman of the han committee	Councillor (*Hyōgiin*)	*Han* committeeman (*Han-iin*)	Women and youth representative	Chairman of the han committee	Councillor (*Hyōgiin*)	*Han* committeeman (*Han-iin*)	Women and youth representative
(2) Age	51	28	29	23	48	44	30	23
(3) Number of years employed with Hitachi	33	10	10	6	30	19	12	5
(4) Occupation	coiler	production technician	making electrical wiring	making electrical wiring	foreman in charge of tools and safety	lathe operator welder		making wooden models for clay moulds
(5) Position in the firm	foreman	office worker	*bōshin*		foreman	*boshin*	*boshin*	
(6) Educational background		Hitachi's training school	Hitachi's training school	Hitachi's training school			high school	Hitachi's training school
(7) Previous experience in union activities	much experience as (1) head of the *han* committee (2) *hyōgiin*	much experience as (1) deputy chairman of *hyogiinkai* (2) *hyogiin* (4 terms) (3) chairman of the local factory	nil	some experience as head of the women and youth committee	very little	very little	nil	some experience as deputy head of the women and youth committee

Table 7.4 *continued*

	Watanabe Yoshihiro	The electricians' *han*			The foundry *han*			
		Suzuki Teruhiko	Mabuchi Akio	Hirai Takanobu	Tanaka Ichirō	Hirota Kenji	Uchida Saburō	Sonoda Kazuo
(8) Reasons for being involved in union activities	to raise the productivity of the workers	to improve working conditions (was invited to stand for position by member of Union Executive)	asked to do so by Watanable, the foreman	bitterness at not being accepted into higher level studies at the company's school	to improve the reputation of the foundry	previous experience as a union activist in the mines	because of popular support for his nomination	(1) to improve the atmosphere for human relations at work (2) dissatisfaction with working conditions
(9) Attitudes concerning own role in the union	(1) helping the union executive (2) solidifying views in the workshop (3) looking after the needs of union members in the shop	(1) keeping *han* and rank-and-file mutually informed (2) having a personal input into union affairs	Secretary to the head of the *han* committee		assisting in the implementation of management policy	(1) keeping *han* committee and the rank-and-file mutually informed (2) taking a neutral role in union affairs	nothing in particular	
(10) Relationship to the union	strong identity with the union	strong identity with the union	strong identity with the union	strong identity with the union	no strong feeling for the union	no strong feeling for the union	antagonistic attitude toward the union	strong identity with the union

237

Table 7.4 *continued*

	The electricians' *han*					The foundry *han*		
	Watanabe Yoshihiro	Suzuki Teruhiko	Mabuchi Akio	Hirai Takanobu	Tanaka Ichirō	Hirota Kenji	Uchida Saburō	Sonoda Kazuo
(11) Relationship to management	co-operative	co-operative	co-operative	co-operative	co-operative	co-operative	antagonistic	co-operative
(12) Sense of belonging	dual loyalty	dual loyalty	dual loyalty	dual loyalty	loyalty to management	loyalty to management	loyalty to neither	dual loyalty
(13) Union activities in which person is involved	(1) learning about grievances (2) publicizing the *han* general meeting (3) recruiting people for union office (4) using personnel evaluations to discourage the taking of annual leave	(1) communicating between executive and the *han* (2) little contact with union members	(1) keeping accounts for the *han* (2) miscellaneous duties (3) communicating between Watanabe and union members in the workshop	pasting spring offensive posters around the workshop	(1) learning about grievances (2) solving grievances as a member of management	communicating between the executive and the *han*	distributing the union's newspaper	no activity in the workshop

university graduate with leadership ability. Section chiefs were careful to back up their foremen and to make sure that the lines of authority from the section chief to the foremen to the assistant foremen to the operatives were clearly delineated. This meant that there was little leeway for informal leaders to emerge as long as the employees were kept busy with their work. Accordingly, the authority of the section chief was not subject to challenge the way it was in the foundry. The absence of strong informal groupings which cut across the formal lines of authority meant that communications occurred smoothly as management would have wished. Overall one would have to conclude that the electricians' *han* was characterized by a high degree of cohesion and *espirit de corps*.

A rather stark contrast was cut by the state of affairs in the foundry. The foundry's greatest problem was its age structure. There were many older workers who could challenge the foreman in terms of the skill level. This undermined the foreman's authority considerably. The situation was exacerbated by the fact that appointments had been made which did not reflect the seniority rankings of the workers. Workshop factionalism and the large number of distinct occupational skills required in the foundry tended to promote an approach to work wherein the individual rather than a production team became the basic unit of production. The end result was a rather low level of *espirit de corps*.

Reflecting these problems in the foundry, the lines of authority could not be systematized. A major difficulty was the fact that the work involved heavy physical labor. It was done in accordance with the traditional approaches which had been maintained almost ritualistically by strong-headed workers who were not keen to take advice from somebody in the office with a white collar. Once the decision had been made that the foundry would have low priority in the running of the company, management stopped sending able persons to lead the section and left the running of the foundry in the hands of a middle-school graduate. Of all the section heads in the company, his post had the least prestige. Because the foremen could not expect strong support from the section head, they had to contend by themselves with all the discontented persons who had failed to be promoted to foremen and had turned to forming their own in-groups. Without full authority in the workshop or much influence further up in the company, it is only logical that the foremen would not be very trusted by the men in their subsections.

The ramifications of this situation for communications among workers within the foundry were plain to see. The section was very difficult to mobilize. It was particularly hard on the younger employees who always had to be on guard to avoid being labelled as belonging to one faction or another. The foundry could not put forward a leader who would have widespread support, and morale was very low.

The differences between the two sections in the Hitachi factory were reflected in the state of the union in the two corresponding *han*. First, the union was more active in workshops which were seen to be involved in work that is important to the company. In order for the union to have any influence at all on management, it must be seen to be able to take disputative action, including strikes, against management in those areas which are of crucial importance to the company's overall productivity. The number of workers in the section was also an important variable. Given that the qualitative level of union activity (the sophistication of the union's ideology and the willingness of the workers to engage in disputative action) was roughly similar in the two *han*, the number of members available to participate in union activities was important. There were over twice as many electricians (360) as foundry workers (160). Related to size was a third consideration, the age profile of the union membership in the two *han*. The older membership in the foundry *han* could probably be characterized as having lacked the physical energy which characterized the membership in the electricians' *han*. Fourth, the general level of morale or the sense of *espirit de corps* also determined the nature of union activities. If the members enjoy being with one another at work, they will not mind being thrown together in union activities. In fact, it is likely that the same collective enthusiasm found at work will be applied to the union activities. Because the union's organization parallels that of management, the general morale of the workers as union members and their patterns of communication were shaped considerably by the patterns of communication and the human relationships which existed among them as employees. Fifth, in order to strengthen the workers' consciousness as union members, it is essential that the executive be able to communicate easily and quickly with the rank and file. In Hitachi Rōso, the lines of communication parallelled those of the company. Finally, effective leadership at the shop-floor level can exist only as long as there is effective leadership on the side of management. If authority relations are not clear among management's front line supervisory staff, they will not be any more clearly drawn in the lower reaches of the union's organization.

The overall conclusion is straightforward. The strength of the electricians' *han* reflected management's general nonconcern toward the foundry and the low quality of the leadership which it placed there.

C The production processes and the personality of the operatives

The electricians were engaged in skilled work which required a considerable amount of manual dexterity. The work was not particularly heavy and women could perform most of the tasks. Moreover, it was the type of skill which could be explained in an operations guidebook and fairly easily transmitted from one worker to another in a standard fashion. Accordingly, it was difficult for one worker or a group of workers to monopolize the techniques necessary to perform particular operations. Further, because the work was such that the entire team could take responsibility for the final product, the sense of identity with the work group was strong. The nature of the work and the way the work was organized were reflected in the personalities of the workers. They tended to be open, outgoing, cooperative individuals who had developed a 'modern consciousness.'

The foundry workers were engaged in highly skilled, but dangerous work. A small slip along the way would result in serious injury or even death. The work required a tremendous amount of physical labor, and could not be performed by women. The chances of automating much of the work appeared to be slim. The skills were passed down in a guarded fashion on a one-to-one basis, from the master craftsman to his personal understudy. This led to a number of self-contained and self-interested work groups which did not feel the need to be overly cooperative with other groups in the workshop. The human relationships and personalities associated with the men in the foundry were characterized by a traditional machismo: a certain roughness and stubbornness associated with the 'premodern consciousness.' The men in the foundry would seem to be the stuff of which the classical labor movement was made, and the foundry *han* had been a rather central unit in the Hitachi union right after the war. However, the foundry, its workers and its union activity seem to have 'fallen behind the times' as the factory and the relationships within it came to be 'modernized.' This was clearly reflected in the fact that it had come to be left out of management's programmes for change. Low priority in management's scheme of things was reflected in its decline within the enterprise union.

D   The activity and consciousness of the union's shop-floor officials

In both the electricians' section and in the foundry the section chief (*kachō*) directly involved himself in the selection of union officials at the shop-floor level. However, as Table 7.4 suggests, the results of that involvement were quite different in terms of the officials' sense of identity with the union.

In both *han* leaders were chosen who were roughly the same age, who had worked with Hitachi for about the same length of time, and who occupied the same position in management's hierarchy. This means that each union *han* had roughly the same personnel structure with a definite progression being discerned from the women and youth representatives through the ordinary members of the *han* committee and the councillors to the chairman of the *han* committee.

Despite these similarities, it must also be remembered that the union structure in the two *han* also varied in a way that reflected differences in the personnel structures. The one had factions or cliques defined by occupation, age and competing control structures. It was characterized by counter-productive relationships as informal groupings did not match with the formal organization. These differences were reflected in the sway or pull each *han* committee chairman had over the union members in their respective *han*.

Workers in the foundry were less able to distinguish between union activities and management activities. It seemed natural to them that the person in charge of safety would be best qualified to look after their interests in general, that the amount of paperwork performed by the *han* committee chairman made it necessary that he have a desk, or that he receive higher pay from management for doing this extra work on their behalf.

These differences were further reinforced by differences in the educational background of the employees who formed the membership of the union's two *han*. About three quarters of the union officials in the electricians' *han* had come through the company's training school. This compares with 12.5 percent of all the workers in the *han*. This contrasts with the foundry where only one person had come from the company's training school, two from higher elementary schools before the war and one from an outside high school. The generalization to be made is that *han* which are led by graduates from Hitachi's internal training school seem to be more active than those which do not have many such graduates. It may have been that a fairly tight inner group of such graduates had formed within the union a group which was characterized by high *esprit de corps* born out of the awareness that they each had a fairly bright future at their respective levels in the management of the company.

In this connection, however, it must be noted that in both *han* there were young people who had become involved in union activity precisely because they had been unhappy with the way they had been treated by management as graduates from the company's school. Knowing that their degree from the company's school was not portable and that they would receive even worse treatment in other firms where they would be judged simply as middle school graduates, they felt 'trapped' at Hitachi and turned to union activity as a way out. Nevertheless, the company school had taught them the virtues of the company and the values of loyalty to it; they were not in a position intellectually to engage in the kind of union activity which would have put them at odds with management.

The union officials in the electricians' *han* were quite conscientious about their responsibilities as union officials. That was not so true of the union officials in the foundry. The difference reflected the fact that the former group had had considerable experience in union affairs whereas those from the foundry had not. The former group seemed capable of having two loyalties – one to the union and one to management. Officials in the foundry seemed to have only the one loyalty – to management (although one member of the *han* committee seemed to be antagonistic towards both).

Union officials in the electricians' *han* tended to distinguish clearly between union activity and management activities. On that basis they believed that a cooperative arrangement between labor and management could be developed. The officials in the foundry *han*, on the other hand, seemed unable to distinguish clearly between the goals of the union and those of management. They embraced a form of the 'all-together ideology' (*rōshi ittai shugi*) which makes no distinction between the interests of workers and those of management.

These differences between the officials in the two *han* can be seen in the views of the two chairmen of the *han* committees. In the electricians' *han*, Watanabe's view was that management would push workers to do as much overtime as it possibly can, and that the union must therefore work to impose limitations on the amount of overtime which can be expected of an employee. At the same time, he firmly believed as a foreman that there was a need to raise productivity. In the other *han* Tanaka was fully committed to improving the performance of the foundry within the factory's overall operations. His priorities were clearly with serving management. His view of unionism was such that the question of cooptation or accommodation did not arise, for in his view the union existed to implement the activities of management.

Officials in the electricians' *han* engaged in a minimal amount of union activity in the traditional sense. For example, the women and youth representative in the foundry did nothing in the foundry whereas the representative in the electricians' *han* pasted posters on the wall during the spring wage offensive and led the *han*'s chorus group. Hirai's involvement in these kinds of activities may have reflected the fact that there was a larger number of young employees in his *han*, but at the same time it would also have reflected the fact that the union itself was much more active in his *han*. As for the councillors (*hyōgiin*), Hirota in the foundry did little more than convey messages back and forth, whereas Suzuki took some initiative in coming up with his own ideas and sought to persuade those involved of following one line or another. The chairmen of the *han* committees also contrasted. Watanabe was interested primarily in learning about problems which workers had with regard to their working environment. By handling these kinds of problems, he felt that he would be contributing to higher productivity and to better working conditions. From his point of view, the two went hand-in-hand. There were no special union duties for Tanaka; he simply held the title and went about doing his work as the tool and safety foreman. When he learned of grievances, he reported them to his superiors on the management side and got management to solve the problem. Watanabe, on the other hand, regularly toured the shop floor as the senior union official. When he learned of grievances, he took the matter to the union's executive. He spent extra time explaining the union's affairs to women employees who would otherwise be uninterested. He engaged in a number of activities which were of little direct benefit to management. There were lots of little ways in which the officials in the electricians' *han* behaved as unionists and set themselves off from the rather disinterested stance taken by the union's officials in the foundry.

While mentioning these differences, it is important not to overlook the one overriding similarity. In both *han* the officials tended to give first priority to their role as the front line of management. For example, Watanabe was committed to obtaining a higher *shūgyōritsu* (work attendance rate) in his section, and used his position to discourage workers from taking their annual leave. He also used his authority as foreman to enforce the standard times for production processes and thereby contributed to the intensification of work loads. However, because he had built up a good reputation by doing various other things for the union, he was able to command a following among the men in his *han*. When, as a union leader, he advocated policies which had been laid down by management, unionists could respect his views. From a cynical point of view, it could be said that his position as a union official was sometimes used to cloak his functions as the foreman in carrying out management's policies. The two roles were not as clearly separated as they might appear on the surface.

E   Factors promoting union activity at the shop-floor level

The above discussion suggests that for enterprise unions several factors affect the level of union activity on the shop floor. Most important, perhaps, is management's attitude toward, or policy for, the workshops involved. The union is better able to promote its activities in workshops where management has given priority to improving productivity and is willing to work with the union as a cooperative partner who will help management implement its rationalization programs. Management will allow a certain amount of union activity as a trade-off for its cooperation. In other words, management will not seek to control its employees directly, but will go about doing so indirectly by using the union to implement its policies.

A second consideration concerns the composition of the work group. It is important that the age structure be pyramidal, allowing for a worker's position in the management hierarchy, his occupational skill level, and his seniority to be aligned. Also, the larger the number of union members in the *han* the more active it will be. Finally, clear lines of authority from the section chief to the foremen to the operatives facilitates union activity because counter-productive informal groups are minimized or simply do not exist. Conditions favourable to union activity are more likely to be found in what are known as the factory's core sections. In such sections, the foremen will become the center of the workshop group and will have the authority necessary to hold together the union membership at the shop-floor level.

A third factor is the nature of the work. The union will be more active in shops where the work is semi-skilled and the skilled component can easily be taught to new workers. The union will find it easier to organize activities if the work is fairly light and the working environment is not too harsh. It is more likely that the 'modern' types of employees (in terms of their consciousness), their personality and their behavior will be found in 'modern workshops.' The 'modern' outlook facilitates their organization into the union's activities.

The fourth factor is the extent to which lower level management from among the core workers (i.e., those who have graduated from the company training school) is involved in union activity. The union revolves around these core workers, and others will be viewed somewhat as outsiders. The key element is the ability of shop-floor officials to distinguish clearly between the union and the management as two separate entities while also being aware of their symbiotic relationship and the extent to which the one entity actually functions to support the other.

VI Conclusions

In evaluating the activities of Hitachi Rōso on the shop floor, it is necessary to remember that the enterprise or factory union functions basically as an employee's organization. Accordingly, when we say the electricians' *han* was an active *han*, we are referring primarily to activity which enhances the functioning of management in its drive to raise productivity. The union operates on the basic assumption that there is an imbalance in its power relationship with management, and that it will best serve its members by cooperating with management in raising productivity. The premise is that by doing so it will best be able to press management to respond to the workers' grievances. The result is that the union's functions come largely to be those associated with management's personnel policies. Accordingly, it stands to reason that areas within the factory which are focal points in management's efforts to raise overall productivity at the factory will be the areas where this type of unionism flourishes.

Given the assumptions on which the enterprise union at Hitachi rests, various differences can be seen in the union's activities in various areas of the factory. In this chapter, two areas were chosen for case studies: the electricians' *han* and the foundry *han*. The differences between these two *han* in terms of the union's activities are summarized in Table 7.5. In neither *han* is the union involved in activity to significantly improve the working conditions of its members. Perhaps one could cite the fact that in the foundry there is a special allowance to compensate slightly for the physical energy required and for the dirtier aspects of the work. It is an issue about which the *han* officials can express their views directly to Hitachi Rōso and even to the top power brokers in Hitachi Rōren. Because demands from the workshop come to be reflected in decisions on wage rates, this kind of issue can become the source of shop floor activity in some instances. However, to the extent that an issue is peculiar to the one area of the factory, it is difficult to get workers in the other areas to be concerned about it. In the end, the chairman of the foundry's *han* committee had to address the Committee of Councillors to have the special allowance dealt with as a one-off item.

For these reasons it is easy to see how the union had come to work primarily to raise productivity in line with management's

Table 7.5 *A comparison of activity in the foundry and electricians'* han

Activity	In the electricians' *han*	In the foundry *han*
(1) the *han* general meeting	Once per month meets at noon right after the *hyōgiinkai* meets for about 36 minutes attendance is about 50–60 percent only business is a report from the *hyōgiinkai*	exactly the same as for the electricians' *han*
(2) *Han*-level dues	¥10 per meeting	none
(3) Communications with the union's executive	section visited by secretary and other members of the Hitachi Rōsō executive close links with the executive	no members of the executive from this *han* ties with the executive are weak
(4) Structure of the *han* committee	17 members 14 technical workers 3 office workers	14 members 12 technical workers 2 office workers
(5) Number of union members	360 (including 50 women)	160 (including no women)
(6) Stance on overtime	careful scrutiny to make sure that agreement is observed no effort to renegotiate agreement	because overtime is limited, it is not seen as a problem
(7) Stance on annual leave	not taken up as a problem by union officials at the workshop level	is taken up as a problem by union officials at the workshop level
(8) Stance on standard times for production processes	not taken up as a problem by union officials at the workshop level	not taken up as a problem by union officials at the workshop level
(9) the handling of grievances	no activity on the part of the grievances representative individual grievances dealt with by the head of the *han* committee	no activity on the part of the grievances representative no one to handle individual grievances

	most grievances concerning production conditions were taken up by foremen and chairman of the *han* committee	most grievances about production conditions taken up by chairman of the *han* committee (who is the foreman for factory safety)
	han committee seriously considers grievances	*han* committee does not seriously consider grievances
(10) extent to which union members trust their union officials	considerable	negligible

guidelines rather than to improve working conditions as its first priority. This could be seen in the types of grievances which arose and in the way the grievances were handled. It can also be seen in the extent to which the union was able to hold sway over its members.

In the electricians' *han*, the unionists were not sure what to do when the call came for everyone to join in and support the union in its spring wage offensive. They knew well that the important issues were decided through the system of joint labor-management consultations rather than through collective bargaining. For most unionists the call was nothing more than a request to participate in a meaningless ritual which would not have much effect on the real negotiations. Accordingly, participation was minimal.

Immediately after the war, the foundry's *han* was a key unit in the union movement at Hitachi. At that time it was strongly imbued with a class-based ideology. However, with the defeat of Hitachi Rōso in the big dispute of 1951, the leadership in Hitachi Rōso was replaced by a new leadership which brought in an ideology emphasizing the union's role as an employee organization. Overnight the union's leadership in the foundry's *han* found itself out of step in terms of the direction the union was taking under the new leadership. All of a sudden the pent-up energy and fighting spirit of the workers in the foundry had no outlet. In commenting on the union at Hitachi it is important to note that the present leadership of Hitachi Rōso can trace its roots back to the Mindō group which drew heavily from the electricians' *han* in the years leading up to the big dispute in

1951. Just as there were divisions before 1951, so too are there divisions even twenty years after 1951.

In analyzing the situation of the enterprise union at Hitachi in the late 1960s, careful attention must be paid to the ideological divisions within the union. Obviously, the judgment by the executive that some *han* were very active in union activities while others were not so active was itself based on the extent to which the *han* subscribed to the ideology of those in the executive. Since their ideology called for a cooperative union functioning as an employee's organization, sections of the union with different philosophies (particularly philosophies which saw the relationship with management as antagonistic) were not given much credit for contributing to the union movement. Of course, because those with the cooperative ideology ran the union, their views became the self-fulfilled prophecies. Should Hitachi Rōso again be controlled by those who would have the union function as a class-based organization, it is likely that the electricians' *han* would suddenly be seen as an inactive *han*. However, the likelihood that that would happen was very small in 1969, and is still small today. It is also likely that the situation would be similar in most large enterprise unions in the private sector today.

Basic to the functioning of enterprise unions which seek to be employee organizations is the commitment of management to improving productivity. In such unions, the most active *han* will be those which are seen as being crucial to raising the firm's overall level of productivity and as agreeing to support management programs to raise productivity in their respective workshops.

The situation at Hitachi in the late 1960s clearly revealed the extent to which the balance of power had shifted in management's favor during the period of rapid economic growth. Once the enterprise union accepted the 'bigger pie' as the prime goal and cooperation with management as the means to achieving across-the-board improvements in the standard of living, the basis for workers at the workshop level to protest against the intensification of their workload was eroded. At that point we can say that the workshop had become the 'sacred territory' of management. Had workers been able to resist the inroads of management on the shop floor, it is unlikely that the enterprise union would have retreated as far as it did in most of Japan's large companies in the private sector. The only way for Japan's labor unions to recover is for them to recover on the shop floor. Unless Japan's workshops in the large firms are secured as a place where workers can stand up and speak out, the future for the labor movement in Japan is bleak.

PART THREE

UNIONS ON THE FRINGE AND THE POTENTIAL OF THE ENTERPRISE UNION

8 Unions on the Fringe: The Viability of the Left-Wing Minority Enterprise Unions and the New-Type Unions during the 1970s

In Chapter 3 passing reference was made to unions at the fringe of the labor movement (*henkyōgata kumiai* or *shōsūha kumiai*) (cf. Figure 3.1). It is unfortunate that Japanese unionism has come to be stereotyped in terms of the enterprise union consisting of all employees at a given enterprise or firm. One result has been that minority left-wing enterprise unions and 'new-type unions' are completely overlooked in discussions of Japan's labor unions.

Any forecast about the future requires that at least some consideration be given to possible outcomes. In doing that the possibility of the fringe-type unions making a contribution has never been considered very seriously. In the next four chapters I would like to examine briefly the potential of the fringe-type unions to contribute to the labor movement in Japan.

In this chapter I would like to focus the discussion on two types of unions on the fringe which showed particular vitality during the 1970s. One was the left-wing minority union (*saha shōsūha kumiai*). Although a few such unions were formed when left-wing unionists broke from a dominant conservative right-wing enterprise union, the majority of the left-wing unions consisted of the 'old guard' which had dug in as the 'number one union.' After the schisms in the left-wing industry unions of the 1950s and early 1960s, breakaway unions on the right grew quickly as 'number two unions' and soon became the dominant union at many enterprises. The second type of union on the fringe is 'the new-type union' (*shingata kumiai*). It consists largely of workers in Japan's peripheral labor forces. Membership is based on a characteristic which results in status deprivation. This chapter considers the emergence of these two types of union in the 1970s. The next three chapters then consider in detail the success of some of the left-wing minority enterprise unions as they struggled to survive during that decade.

I Minorities at Work

When reference is made to the fringe of the Japanese labor movement, left-wing number-one unions (and the left-wing counter-reactionary factions, within enterprise unions moving to the right) immediately come to mind. However, also at the fringe are the unions for minorities or disadvantaged groups within the labor force. Many of those workers lie outside the domain of organized labor. They are the employees in Japan's small firms, the temporary employees, the part-timers and the handicapped. Their ranks include many female employees and older workers. Such workers are not necessarily the minority in terms of the percentage composition of the labor force even in a particular firm. For example, employees in firms with less than 100 employees account for nearly 60 percent of Japan's entire labor force. Women account for 40 percent of Japan's labor force.

The distinguishing mark of employees in the above-mentioned categories is that they share a trait or characteristic which results in them being discriminated against. The minority groups consist of those peripheral to the union movement (i.e., those who are not regular male employees in the dominant unions in Japan's large firms). Compared with the core employees whom the enterprise unions serves, non-core employees are subject to very inferior working conditions. They experience discrimination in many forms and are 'put-down' daily by management. The inferiority of their position in the labor force is highlighted by the ease with which they are retrenched by firms intent on maximizing profit or on 'rationalizing' when recession occurs.

Before considering further the position of minorities in the labor force, it is useful first to consider why an understanding of their position is important in any assessment of the future of the labor movement in Japan. During recessions workers are very conscious of the increased likelihood that they will become unemployed or, at the very least, experience a decline in their working conditions. It is at this time that they look to the labor union as the body best positioned to look after their interests. However, the enterprise unions (which are postured around the small group of privileged workers in Japan's large firms) seem uninclined to assist the non-core employees who are most vulnerable in such circumstances. It is not surprising, then, that Japan's labor unions have lost any groundswell of support they might have had among the working population at large, or that the organization rate has declined in recent years from 33 percent in the early 1970s to under 27 percent by the late 1980s. Once the driving force guaranteeing the right to work, the enterprise union showed a distinct disinterest in the third wave of postwar discriminatory firings (*shimei kaiko*) at the end of the 1970s. (Following the red purges in 1949–50 and in 1960, large numbers of employees were reintrenched in shipbuilding and electrical machinery during the recession between 1978 and 1980.)

As the chapters in Part Two reveal, many of the enterprise unions have come to function on behalf of management, often through quality control circles which serve only to find new ways that management might better rationalize the firm's operations. During the recession of 1978–80, in the name of 'joint consultations' unions even helped management lay off workers by preparing lists of employees in the order of their perceived importance to the firm. Not surprisingly the names of the unionists jointly consulted appeared at the very top of such lists. Such an orientation certainly caused the union's *raison d'être* to be questioned. Workers were asking, 'Where is the way ahead for unions which can stand up to management and look after the interests of the worker?' 'What kind of a union can liberate us workers from our bonds at work?'

Older workers in particular faced a contradiction inherent in the enterprise union. Although they may earlier have benefitted from the enterprise union, once 'over the hill' they come to face the prospect of having to work outside its domain. They are the workers the large firms gladly employed as regular employees during the period of rapid expansion and the tightening labor market which produced labor shortages in the late 1960s. By the end of the 1970s, however, they had become a kind of glut which some large firms wished to remove when the increasing pressure of international competition (owing to the emergence of the NICs and to the upward valuation of the yen) seemed to demand further rationalizations. Their departure from the large firms signalled the end of what has come to be called 'Japanese-style industrial relations' – the emphasis on seniority wages and career employment. At that time Hazama (1978) wrote that the dilemma of the middle-aged and older workers (those in their late forties and early fifties) was a fundamental issue which would greatly influence the future of industrial relations in Japan in the 1980s.

In the late 1970s the new type of unions on the fringe provided an alternative for those fighting against the move to the right by the enterprise unions in the large firms. Given the narrow focus of most enterprise unions and the stance taken by the left-wing minority enterprise unions, there was a very large catchment of potential union members – workers who have not been organized but who have a latent need for the benefits which such organizations might be able to offer. This means there is a significance in studying the existence of these 'minorities' and the attempts to unionize them. Present figures on the composition of the labor force suggest that many of the 'minority groups' are increasing in size as more married women return to work and the tertiary sector continues to expand, reflecting larger structural changes in Japan's capitalist economy and in Japanese society itself. Even today the various minorities are largely unrepresented. Had the initial moves to organize those groups been followed by efforts to develop linkages among them, a fairly assertive union movement could have resulted.

The ideology attractive to many in these minority groups would probably go against that favoured by many of Japan's core employees. Employees in Japan's small firms have been imbued with the egalitarian ideals taught in Japan's schools after the war. They are better educated than their predecessors. The same could be said of women and small entrepreneurs in the service sector. However, it is likely that each of the minority groups will seek to develop its own strategies and to fight its own battles. The mainstream in Japan's postwar labor movement has been the single enterprise union. Of course, the enterprise union could in some ways be seen as having been an inevitable outcome of the times. As explained above in Chapter 6, immediately after the war Japan's workers formed single enterprise unions and attempted to form industrial unions with the enterprise groupings as the base. They developed a strong form of industrial unionism which was able to take the initiative against management. Some of the reasons for starting with the single enterprise union were touched upon in Chapter 4. It was an exceptional period when many were starving. Priority was given to incorporating lower level supervisory staff, including section chiefs (*kachō*), in order to raise productivity and somehow obtain a wage with which to buy the bare necessities. It was also the case that paternalistic management practices before the war and the vertically structured organization of labor in Sanpō during the war would have left their imprint. Given the repressive measures used by the establishment to undermine socialistically or industrially inclined unionists, we cannot say that workers were able to choose sufficiently freely or that there was spontaneous support for the enterprise type of unionism which took hold from the 1950s. As the shortcomings of the single enterprise union become more pronouned and better known, it is inevitable that disadvantaged employees will want to form their own unions. As long as that does not occur, it is unlikely that a union movement in the true sense will emerge in Japan. In 1987 the labor movement was able to organize only about 27 percent of Japanese employees, a percentage which had been falling steadily for over ten years. With the establishment of Zenminrōren late in 1989, the 70 percent of Japan's employees who are not organized have even less reason to recognize Japan's enterprise unions as a force working for the good of the large bulk of workers in Japan. On November 21, 1989 Rengō (Nihon Rōdō Kumiai Rengōkai) was formed, mainly by the unions of workers in the large firms. With about 8 million affiliated members, it is the third largest national center in the world, behind the AFL-CIO in the United States and the TUC in Britain. However, its members represent only 17 percent of the 46 million employees in Japan. Representing primarily the interests of male regular employees in Japan's large firms, it is not well positioned to organize female workers, part-timers and many of the workers in Japan's smaller firms. It is ironic that Japan's part-time workers also number about 8 million and could by themselves theoretically form a national center the size of Rengō.

Regardless of whether the new unions fit in with any of the existing theories about unionism, at the end of the 1970s they adapted themselves to the special circumstances of the minority groups which they served. There will be considerable variation in their organizational format, in their ideology and concerns, and in their strategies and slogans. The interest among many workers in having a union to serve their specific needs is perhaps a sign that the union movement entered the 1980s in a state of flux. Japan's labor movement today cannot be understood without a careful analysis of these unions at the fringe of the labor movement. Because the workers they serve represent a large proportion of all workers in Japan the continuing development of such unions will be crucial to any revival the union movement might experience in the years ahead. Employees will be sensitive to the principles followed by unions which have been entrusted with representing and realizing the workers' interests.

Because the new type of unions are on the fringe, categories have not been established for them in the official statistics and we have no clear idea as to how numerous they are. The proportions in Figure 3.1 are simply guesswork. Nevertheless, they represent about ten years' work of 'making the rounds.' During the 1970s the author had the opportunity to visit a good many of the new-type unions, frequently talking with the leadership and the membership, sitting in on various meetings and attending their conventions, and collecting documents created by the unions (reports, agendas, minutes, communiques, memorandums and handouts). While these are the kinds of material that any researcher would collect, it is important to remember that the new-type unions were in their formative stage. Accordingly, much happened on an *ad hoc* basis, and few materials were issued regularly as serials. Rather than a systematic content analysis, the result is a constantly changing collage. In that context the importance of actually participating in the activities of many of those unions is increased. The impressions recorded in the paragraphs that follow were jotted down in March 1979 and are a product of the times. They represent the knowledge accumulated from walking, viewing, listening and feeling. For the reader's convenience I have tried to cite a wide range of collaborative material. However, the validity of the points made will have to be judged against the author's experiences and his ability (or inability) to describe those experiences as objectively and as honestly as possible.

II The Left-Wing Minority Enterprise Unions

As mentioned above in Chapter 3, nearly 12 percent of the unions affiliated with Sōhyō in 1971 coexisted with one or more other unions at the same enterprise. Almost half of the cases dealt with by the Central Labor Relations Commission at that time involved minority unions. Moreover, in those days about 300 new minority unions were being formed each year. In the public sector, nearly all the unions are of the multiple enterprise union type. For example, in the National Railways there were seven unions up until the mid–1980s; at Japan Airlines, four unions; and at the Japan Red Cross Hospital in Tokyo, five unions. Many similar examples can be found in Japan's small and medium-sized firms.

As the government moved ahead with its plans to privatize and to break up the National Railways, it became clear that uncooperative employees would not be employed in the newly formed companies. As employees jostled for position, they left the established unions and formed their own associations. Soon there were over one hundred such bodies. With the six regional rail companies coming into existence on April 1, 1987, these bodies soon sorted themselves into four major groupings: Tetsudō Rōren on the right (affiliated with the Democratic Socialist Party and organizing 68.2 percent of the public rail employees); Kokurō on the left (affiliated with the left-wing in the Japan Socialist Party and the affiliated with the Japan Communist Party and organizing 16.9 percent); Tessan Sōren (affiliated with the right-wing of the Japan Socialist Party, 12.3 percent); and Zendōrō to the left (affiliated with the Japan Communist Party, 0.6 percent) (from *Rōdō Keizai Shinbun* [a newspaper], August 9, 1988). Although the figures have been prepared by Tetsudō Rōren (probably in consultation with management), they are probably fairly reliable. As of late 1988 the government had not supplied any figures on the union situation in the new rail companies.

There is a need in studies of the Japanese labor movement to get away from the notion that schisms will always result in one enterprise union simply replacing another or that the left-wing minority enterprise union which might survive will be unable to have much effect on the affairs of the firm at which it is located.

Enterprise Unionism in Japan

The facts are that minority unions were able to achieve a good deal during the 1970s and 1980s. They managed to have firings and other disciplinary action rescinded, to have discriminatory promotions and wage increases corrected, and even to have the validity of their position fully endorsed by management in several cases. A survey of Japan's major dailies reveals that in each of the past two decades (the 1970s and the 1980s) there were about fifty concrete cases of how minority unions produced such change.

The first successes of the left-wing minority unions can be seen in the early 1960s. One example would be the electric power workers in Zenkyūshū Denryoku Rōso (Zenkyūshū Denryoku Rōdō Kumiai 1979) and in Zenhokkaidō Denryoku Rōso (Kawanishi 1981: 199–201). The railway workers in the Ichihata branch of Shitetsu Sōren provide another example (cf. Shitetsu Chūgokushi Henshū Iinkai 1975). In the 1970s there were the successes of the shipbuilders at the Nagasaki plant of Mitsubishi Shipbuilding (Fujita 1970) and at the Ishikawajima branch of Zenzōsen (Satō 1973), and the victory of the workers at Japan Carbite Company (Nihon Kābaito Kōgyō Rōdō Kumiai 1981). Perhaps the best publicly documented cases would be the events at Kōbunsha (one of Japan's largest, most prestigious publishing companies) (Kōbunsha Tōsō o Kiroku Suru Kai 1977) and the struggle at Zeneraru Sekiyū Seisei (an oil refining company) (Yokoyama and Onogi 1971; Kawanishi 1981, Chapter 3).

During the 1970s a number of minority unions won notable legal cases involving unfair labor practices and various forms of discrimination. The branch of Zenkoku Kinzoku Rōdō Kumiai at the Prince Automobile Factory is but one example. When Prince was absorbed by Nissan around 1960, the left-wing unionists refused to join the conservative Nissan union which was affiliated with Dōmei. After a long period of oppression, the branch obtained a court injunction against Nissan which had discriminated against its members.

The success of one of the branches of Sōhyō's industrial federation in shipbuilding, Zenzōsen, also received wide attention. The factory in question belonged to Sumitomo Heavy Manufacturing. In March 1975 twenty-eight members of the Uraga branch of Zenzōsen filed a petition with the Kanagawa Regional Labor Relations Commission. The Zenzōsen branch argued that management had three years earlier introduced a new wage system which then had been used as the basis for not giving members of the branch any additional wage hikes. The commission ruled that management had been discriminating unfairly against members of the branch in favor of members of the Dōmei-affiliated second union and had been attempting in various ways to undermine the first union. It ordered the company not only to give the twenty-eight employees their proper wage increases, but also to do likewise for the other 200 members of the branch. The Tokyo Metropolitan Labor Relations Commission also ruled that the firm's efforts to force members of the branch to attend meetings for ideological education or to otherwise persuade them to quit the branch constituted unfair labor practices (*Asahi Shimbun*, morning edition, February 5, 1977).

Another example involved Zengakken Rōso. A union of two persons even won an order from a regional labor relations board and from the Central Labor Relations Board. The order effectively stopped the employer discriminating between its two members and members of the majority union. At Gakushū Kenkyūsha (a publisher of educational materials which had grown rapidly), some employees became dissatisfied with the extent to which the enterprise union had come to function on behalf of management as a company union. In 1973 they broke to establish their own union on the left, Gakushū Kenkyūsha Rōdō Kumiai (Zengakken Rōso), only to have thirteen of their group fired. After a long struggle, the Tokyo District Court ruled on April 30, 1982 that twelve of the thirteen should be paid their back wages and that eleven should be reinstated as employees (cf. Sōhyō Sōgi Taisaku Iinkai 1982).

As mentioned below in Chapter 10, Chūgoku Densan (the remnant of Densan which survived in the Chūgoku region) carried on for over thirty years and was able in 1979 to carry out the first strike in Japan against the introduction of nuclear-powered generating plants and effectively counter the national government on one of its central policies. In a mayoral election in one small town where a nuclear generating plant had been planned, the union was able to join with local farmers and fishermen to secure victory for the anti-nuclear candidate. During the campaign seven unionists were officially reprimanded at work. The episode provides an interesting example of how a labor union joined hands with a local citizens' movement to defeat the capitalist forces.

In Kankōrō, the breakaway from Nikkyōso of a left-wing

263

teachers' group in Yokohama (the Yokohama Gakkō Rōdōsha Kumiai) also confirmed that minority unions could become a political force. By the early 1970s Yokohama had earned a reputation as a city with a progressive government. Its mayor was Asukata Ichio, who later became chairman of the Central Committee of the Japan Socialist Party. The Yokohama branch of Nikkyōso had a most respectable organization rate of around 90 percent, and its members were quite smoothly promoted to be principals and deputy principals. However, one portion of the membership felt that the union had become too close to the authorities, with the practice of 'jobs for the boys' [including some women] becoming somewhat institutionalized. Complaining that the union had come to control the membership, as an administrative arm of the education authorities, the unhappy unionists formed the left-wing group in the Yokohama Branch. In 1977 the left-wing teachers formed their own union when Nikkyōso did nothing on behalf of a teacher who was fired for refusing to fill out the student's report cards, believing that the grades were a means of controlling the students (cf. Yokohama Gakkō Rōdōsha Kumiai 1977). Also from Nikkyōso, itself known as a left-wing union, came another break away. The Union of Clerical School Workers (Gakkō Jimu Rōdo Kumiai) was formed by office workers in Nikkyōso. They formed branches in Tokyo, Yokohama, Saitama, Hokkaidō, Hyōgo, Kumamoto and seven other prefectures. The clerical workers had for a long time been a minority group in the teachers' union and had come to feel that their interests were being overlooked by the teachers who controlled Nikkyōso. Viewing the success of other small breakaway unions, these workers finally decided to obtain a solution on their own (Gakkō Jimu Rōdō Kumiai 1975). Similarly, 1500 signalmen and telecommunicators in the powerful Seaman's Union (Kaiin Kumiai) (Japan's largest industrial union with 120,000 members) were motivated to break away and form their own Senpaku Tsūshinshi Rōdō Kumiai (the Union of Communications Technicians in the Shipping Industry).

These developments fostered an important change in the orientation of the left-wing minority enterprise unions. Although the left had always stood for solidarity, believing that solidarity was both the goal of the union movement and its major source of power, those on the left viewed right-wing unionists as opportunists willing to set up competing unions to serve their own narrowly defined interests. They came to see that small unions could be successful even though solidarity had not been achieved. By the late 1970s the labor movement had come to see the minority union not as a weak or dispirited entity destined to lose out completely in its dealings with management, but rather as the only toughened unit able to stand up to management. During the 1970s this outlook came to characterize the thinking of an increasing number of union leaders across the political spectrum. As the move to the right and to conservative enterprise unionism became more pronounced in the early 1970s, left-wing activists divided over strategy. One view called for leftists to break away from the right-wing unions and establish their own unions, even if they were minority unions. The other view was that leftists should remain within the conservative unions and work for reform from within. While left-wing minority unions continued to strengthen their position during the 1970s, the dominance of the right-wing unions meant that those chosing to belong to such unions had to face all kinds of discrimination and oppression at work. Those who adhered to the first viewpoint emphasized their successes. Those who took the second position emphasized the many difficulties facing activists in their left-wing minority factions. Their lot included arbitrary transfers and firings. In many firms only one or two persons continued the battle against management and the full force of the conservative union.

The battle from within had its difficulties. For example, 93 activists were fired by Oki Electric in October 1978. Most of the workers had been members of the Japan Communist Party and the Japan Socialist Party or in other ways associated with the new left. It was a red purge. Had the activists set up their own left-wing union to begin with and then been fired, the dismissal of even one member would have been recognized as an unfair labor practice. In the end, it was only by breaking from the mainstream union and forming their own joint struggle group that they finally obtained satisfaction. On February 27, 1987 the struggle group and the company accepted the court's recommendation that they settle out of court. The conciliation agreement called for 35 of the 71 who had taken the case to court to be reinstated at Oki Electric, for the remaining 36 to be released from employment on their own resignation, and for Oki Electric to pay the struggle group 1.29 billion yen. It was clear that the company had admitted in defeat the error of its ways. The important point is that the crisis and resulting schism in the union at Oki Electric produced a minority left-wing union which would stand up and fight all kinds of dismissals. This reversed the trend of the 1950s and 1960s when all breakaway groups had moved to set up conservative number two unions. Similar histories resulting in new left-wing unions being formed can be found in the schisms which occurred at the Hashihama Shipbuilding Yards and at the Tsurumi Shipbuilding Yard of Nihon Kōkan. At Hashihama the left-wing minority union was formed by eight unionists who had become very dubious of the value of the existing enterprise union's assistance in drawing up a dismissal list for management. The company president had even praised the union for taking the initiative, claiming that it had warned the company of a certain laxness in not paring the workforce. The eight saw this as topsy-turvy unionism and set out to form their own union (*Asahi Shimbun*, morning edition, March 5, 1978).

At the Tsurumi Yards, four unionists set up their own union, arguing that it was shameful to back a union so that it could fire one's own workmates (cf. Kamata 1977: 146–66). Their goal was to establish a union which would not contribute to other workmates losing their jobs. The willingness of the conservative enterprise union to cooperate with management in dismissing employees has become a barometer for measuring the life-chances of existing left-wing minority unions. In the late 1970s eighteen unionists of the left-wing minority unions (branches of Zenzōsen) at the Sanoyasu and Tamashima yards of Sumitomo Shipbuilding were fired; another fifty-four in a Zenzōsen branch met the same fate at Sumitomo Shipbuilding's Uraga yards. Kamata (1980) related these events and the ways in which management and members of the second union came to put extreme pressure on the left-wing unions. In October 1977 Sōhyō was able to gather 10,000 persons from around the country to gather in the premises of Sumitomo's Tamashima factory. It was the first time since the Miike Struggles in 1960 that Sōhyō had become involved in a large 'peoples' struggle' to assist workers at a single plant (*Asahi Shimbun*, morning edition, June 2, 1979). After a struggle of about ten years, management at the Uraga and Tamashima yards acknowledged that the firings constituted an unfair labor practice and agreed out of court to reinstate the employees. These too were important cases. As Japan entered the 1980s, they symbolized the fact that minority unions had hung on for over thirty years and had survived all attempts to remove them from Japan's industrial relations.

III   The Emergence of New Unions in the Peripheral Zone

Several groups of workers bear the consequences of Japan's system of discriminatory labor statuses whenever there is a downturn in the economic fortunes of their employer. Efforts were made to organize these disadvantaged workers into independent labor unions in the late 1970s. In the next few paragraphs examples of such efforts are given for the handicapped, part-timers and temporary employees, workers in firms which go bankrupt, women, and the middle-aged and older worker.

A   The handicapped

It is well known that the handicapped experience various kinds of discriminatory treatment at work. Especially vexing, however, is that they are the first group to be laid off after having overcome tremendous hurdles just to get their jobs. Following the recession in the late 1970s a worker at Saibanetto (a large firm with 1200 employees) complained that 'the company's president made a big fuss about how wonderful the company had been in taking the initiative in hiring some handicapped persons, but then dismissed them first before laying off part-timers and married women as part of a discriminatory ten-month retrenchment program' (Anonymous 1978a). One mother, aged sixty-one, wrote as follows to the *Asahi Journal* at the time her handicapped daughter was fired:

> My daughter is almost thirty. Two days after she returned from a wonderful summer holiday trip she was fired by the firm at which she'd been employed for thirteen years. With an IQ under 50, my daughter is mentally retarded. The letter of dismissal stated the recent recession as the reason. We have somehow feared this every day for thirteen years . . . (Namiki 1979).

267

Every now and then the mass media draws public attention to the plight of the handicapped. However, such articles do not have much influence on management. A labor union willing to look after the interests of the handicapped is needed. Since the ordinary enterprise union will not do that, it stands to reason that many handicapped workers would have a natural inclination to form a new type of union especially suited to looking after their needs. An example of such a union is the independent labor union formed around handicapped employees at the Okubo Bottle Manufacturing Company in Tokyo's Sumida Ward. Among the company's 180 employees, 110 were handicapped. The government's program called for companies which accommodated themselves to its scheme for employing the handicapped to receive lower-interest loans from the office for the Promotion of Employment for the Handicapped and favourable tax treatment. Participation in the program had been one of Okubo Bottle's strategies to gain its preeminent position among bottle manufacturers. However, the company developed a personnel plan which called for workers to be divided into three groups: the ordinary workers, the physically handicapped, and the mentally impaired. Because the firm's enterprise union, which included only the ordinary workers among its members, blithely went along with this, 36 employees in the inspection section decided in 1975 to form their own union which then demanded simply that all employees receive the same bonus. This probably would not have drawn much attention in Japan had not the company president and his son (one of the company's directors) tried to frame the deputy leader of the new union by planting drugs on his motorbike and then dobbing him in to the police. In this case some measure of justice prevailed when police arrested the father and son and then released the unionist (cf. Suzuki 1977; Kuwahara 1981). This kind of story must certainly have been of interest to all handicapped persons desiring to be active in the labor force, and again shows the potential which existed for organizing such workers at the end of the 1970s.

There are also examples of employees at hospitals joining with their physically and mentally handicapped patients to form independent labor unions. In the late 1970s the formation of such unions at a number of health care institutions – including the Midorigaoka Hospital in Shiogama near Sendai, the Shoseiso Hospital in Yokohama, the Fuji Aiikuen Hospice in Tokyo, and the Yuna-gakuen Sanatorium in Okinawa – received much coverage in the media. One motivating factor behind these developments was the desire to improve very bad working conditions. However, the main driving force was the belief that the handicapped and ordinary workers share many things owing to the fact that they live together in the same micro-society. Linked to this was the desire to alter the way in which patients were treated and to provide for the involvement of the union in the management of the hospital. In this broader concern with the social context in which work is done, there was an interesting return to the socially relevant philosophy which seemed to characterize the union movement immediately after the war. Perhaps that reflected a sense of the social responsibility that unions felt when they were in a dominant position *vis-à-vis* management. With management in an increasingly dominant position since the mid–1950s and its subscription to the American-inspired ideology of business unionism and productivity first, unions came to lose their concern for the underdogs in society. The result was a narrow interest only in protecting the wages and working conditions of the aristocracy of labor who were fortunate to be unionized in Japan's elite firms.

Because discrimination in the system of education is an even more basic concern to the handicapped, it is not surprising that moves were also made to form unions in the late 1970s which aimed to strengthen ties between the handicapped and teachers. In Japan discrimination against the handicapped is built into the system of education. The competition to get into the better schools and universities means that the handicapped who lose out are naturally seen as being at the bottom of society's slag heap. Many parents anxious for their normal children to do well in the examination system see the handicapped in their children's class as a burden which will lower the level of teaching and thereby disadvantage their own children when examination time rolls around. Teachers serious about removing this kind of discrimination have organized to fight against facets of the education system which tend to symbolize and to institutionalize such discrimination.

In April 1979 the various locals of the School Office Workers Union and the Yokohama Union of Education Workers launched a campaign against the move to provide special classes for the retarded. In many cases parents of handicapped children wanted their children to be educated with all the other children. Since April 1979 it became policy that students entering primary school would be medically examined. The medical examiner decided the future of children: those deemed to be handicapped were required by law to enter a special school (*yōgo gakkō*). Although the Ministry of Education saw the special schools as being more suited to the needs of handicapped children, most organizations for the handicapped opposed the move. Each of the local unions affiliated with the School Office Workers' Union joined with those organizations to oppose the new policy. They argued that a system of education which emphasized competition, the ranking of children and, ultimately, discrimination went against humanitarian ideals and smacked of fascist control.

B Part-timers and temporary employees

Although part-time employees had increased to large numbers by the end of the 1970s, it was still not clear whether there would be any move radically to change a union movement which had evolved on the basic assumption that it was only for the mainstream career employee. In the spring of 1978 one outcome of Zentei's campaign against the 'productivity program' in the postal services was that Zenkoku Ippan organized about 2000 high school students who had been employed part-time (as *arubaito*) by the Post Office. One report (in the *Asahi Shimbun*, March 5, 1978) concluded that the formation of the union had resulted in a number of small gains for temporary employees, that each individual had received a bonus of ¥34,000, and that a measure of job security had been achieved.

C Workers in bankrupt firms and the unemployed

While unions for part-timers did not suddenly flourish overnight, a number of interesting examples have been reported in the mass media. The union for part-time workers employed by Petori Camera (which hired a large number of middle-aged women) continued to run the firm after it went bankrupt. During the Vietnam War Petori Camera grew quickly by concentrating on the production of cheap cameras which were very popular among American servicemen. However, it fell on hard times once the war ended, and was bankrupt by around 1975. As was common when bankruptcy occurs, all employees were dismissed. However, the union called on its members to stay on at the firm. It occupied the company's offices and began to run the company. Rather than simply sitting around as the victims, the unionists turned the company around. Since the company went bankrupt without paying them their full wages or any retirement pay, the courts tacitly recognized the workers' rights to the assets as their right to survive. The case was settled out of court with the workers coming to own their own company (cf. Kamata 1979: 165–213; Totsuka and Inoue 1982: 515–562).

Some revitalization of the union movement can also be seen in the small-scale sector. Noticeable were the moves among employees of small bankrupt firms to take over what assets remained and to run such businesses. Although most workers who lost their jobs when their employer failed went out and found other work, small numbers remained behind. They hired part-timers when necessary to carry on with production. They utilized hawkers to sell their wares. One report at the end of the 1970s suggested that the number of workers preferring to stay on and work in the same factory under union management was increasing. As concrete examples, in the late 1970s Watanabe Seiko (a manufacturer of dredges), Saitō Tekkō (a manufacturer of paper cutters), Hamada Seiki (a manufacturer of offset printers), Petori Camera, and Paramount Shoemakers all faced bankruptcy. All were on the southern outskirts of Osaka, an area seen as a 'factory scrap heap.' Zenkoku Kinzoku Rōdō Kumiai (a Sōhyō affiliated industrial federation which organized metal workers in small firms) reported to the author that twelve of its branches had taken over the management of their firms. Another Tokyo affiliate organizing longshoremen in small firms, Zenkōwan, similarly reported that ten of its branches had done so.

One might also mention the nine unions formed in Aomori, Miyagi, Hyōgo and other prefectures by unemployed workers. The union movement has traditionally been organized around regular male employees currently employed in large firms in Japan's key industries. Even in the small-scale sector when workers were organized they tended to have a job at some firm. As we will see in the next chapter, there are minority enterprise unions which have opened their membership to former employees – whether they have been retired or fired – but there

271

has always been the link with employment. In the case of the nine unions just mentioned, workers who had been employed formed local unions which superseded affiliation with the firms which had previously employed them. From large and small firms, they sought to develop an organization which could act on their behalf by negotiating with the offices of employment security and the relevant bureaucracies at the prefectural and municipal levels.

D Women workers

The movement to organize the handicapped, part-timers, temporary workers and persons losing their employment as the result of small firms going bankrupt have often revolved around the efforts of women. Rather militant unions demanding an end to gender-based discrimination were organized at Saibaneeto Industries (a manufacturer of integrated circuits), Sutandaado-Vakyuumu (a kerosene distributor), Tokyo Genzōsho (a photographic film manufacturer) and Tachikawa Supuringu (a manufacturer of various kinds of springs). Promoting women's liberation and using the Offices of Inspection under the Labor Standards Bureau (Ministry of Labor) in conjunction with the courts, these unions have paved the way for some very significant changes in the area of wages and retirement. Particularly relevant to the removal of wage discrimination were the cases at the Akita Sōgo Bank, at the Hamamatsu branch of the Daiichi Kangyō Bank, and at Tachikawa Supuringu. The practice of forcing female employees to retire at 25 was discontinued by the Chūgoku Electric Power Authority, and Nissan was compelled to raise the retirement age for women from 55 to 60 to bring it in line with that for male employees.

It has been more difficult for these unions to move against discrimination in promotion and in the allocation of work. The standards by which such decisions are made are often not tangible and the occurrence of discrimination is much more difficult to document in a legal sense than is the case with wages and retirement. Accordingly, it is difficult to take such matters before the courts. There are, nevertheless, a number of interesting cases where the content of the work assigned has been made the focal point in legal hearings. In the late 1970s seven men brought a suit against the Japan Federation of Steel Producers (Nihon Tekkō

Renmei). To face the world's largest steel manufacturers, they acquired the support of fifteen female lawyers (*Asahi Shimbun*, morning edition, February 23, 1978). They angrily protested the way in which they were made to pour tea and take copies for males who entered the firm at the same time but were allowed to take responsibility and do meaningful work in terms of career development. Although the case is still in the courts, it received wide publicity in the media and represented an attack against practices in the most powerful companies in Japan.

There are a number of factors which emplain why female employees are ready to be organized. With higher levels of education, there is among women a growing sense of professionalism and a growing commitment to employment and to an occupation as a meaningful activity in their lives. There is also an increased dependence on the income of female wage-earners in the family at the time of a recession. The women's movement has also had its effects. Until recently women have tended to depend on the courts and on the women's section of their union to wage a defensive battle simply to receive the minimal guarantees laid down in the Labor Standards Law. In the 1970s it became increasingly clear that women were interested in organizations which could take a more positive role in articulating and promoting their interests. Moreover, it is not inconceivable in Japan that such organizations would be unions organized by and for women themselves. Many of the barriers they have faced at work have been put in place by the male-dominated enterprise unions. It may only be by having unions run by women that women will finally be able to negotiate agreements which will more fully accommodate their needs.

In 1973 an all-women's union was formed at Obitani Shitsu (a manufacturer of sheets) in Kaizuka City in Osaka (*Mainichi Shimbun*, morning edition, May 29, 1973). At the time there had been a cooperative enterprise union affiliated with Zensen Dōmei (a major industrial federation affiliated with Dōmei). The enterprise union had negotiated a cooperative agreement with management calling for an extension of the evening shift from 10 p.m. to 10.30 p.m. Two hundred women, representing about 90 percent of the female labor force at Obitani, were angered enough by the agreement that they left the existing union and formed their own union. Similar splits occurred within the male-dominated unions at Midorigaoka Hospital and at the Fuji Aiikuen

Hospice in Tokyo and at Osaka Office Efficiency (a private company which supplied office workers to other firms).

E   Middle-aged and older workers

As they approach compulsory retirement, middle-aged and older employees come face to face with the prospects of unemployment and a marked drop in their wages. While anxiety about employment and income became particularly pronounced after reaching the compulsory retirement age, many workers began to worry about being laid off even earlier. It is not uncommon for firms to pressure older employees to leave whenever they become financially pressed. Part of the resentment felt by older workers comes from their belief that they had a long-term arrangement with the firm whereby they gave their most productive years to the firm for low income in return for a higher income later on when their productivity was not so high.

Although there had been no clear-cut move among these workers to organize themselves previously, in the 1970s Zenkoku Kōreisha Taishokusha no Kai Renrakukaigi (the National Association of Organizations for the Aged and Retirees) and Nihon Chū-Kōnen Dōmei (the Japan Federation for Middle and Old Aged) were formed. One middle-aged couple who worked as supervisors in one of the dormitories for the Tokyo sales outlets of Nissan Sunny formed their own union when the company decided to close the facilities and let all the dormitory supervisors go. After refusing to recognize the two as a union, the company accepted the ruling of the Tokyo Metropolitan Labor Relations Commission that two could constitute a union and it agreed to keep them on, the husband as a security guard and the woman as a cook. As one of the members said, 'What can a small union of two do? That was the challenge! We want to send a message emphasizing the importance of human dignity to those large companies which treat people so shabbily and to society at large' (*Shūkan Asahi*, March 30, 1979). In the demands of this union there was a theme which would be recognized by most older workers.

The two-person union offers another avenue of redress to workers in the large enterprise unions and for the large number of unorganized workers in Japan's smaller firms. Recognizing the potential of this kind of union activity to disrupt the organization of industrial relations in Japan's important industries, officials in the Ministry of Labor and big business have moved to revise those laws which allow for two or more persons to form a union with the right to bargain collectively. Along with certain elements in the newly formed Rengō, they are seeking against legal advice and the protest of many in the labor movement to implement legislation which would reserve the right to bargain for only the largest union at an enterprise.

IV   The Intellectual Thrust of the New-Type Labor Unions

The preceeding section has provided some concrete examples of how workers with peripheral status in the labor force have endeavored to create their own unions after having become disillusioned with the efforts of existing enterprise unions. It is reasonable, therefore, for us to ask whether any generalizations can be made about their intellectual orientation. A careful study of these organizations will perhaps provide some useful material for a systematic study of the sociology of 'organizational solidarity.' To develop such a perspective we must first consider the goals of the new organization: the domain of its demands and the underlying philosophy upon which dissatisfaction with the current way of doing things rests.

1 For a working class culture   The search for a sociology of organizational solidarity leads us to conclude that many of those in the peripheral labor force are seeking a solidarity based on the culture of the working class, an orientation that has been lost as a result of the enterprise union's preoccupation with the material betterment of selected individuals during the period of high economic growth in the 1960s and 1970s. It is an attempt to reestablish that lost orientation as the cornerstone of a revived union movement.

During the period of high economic growth many members of the working class saw their values shift from the spiritual to the materialistic, from the quality of life to quantity in life, from inner development to the outer veneer. Employees became caught in the rush to join the bandwagon to keep up with their neighbors

– the goal became more conspicuous consumption, more colourful or gaudy accessories and decorations, and more faddish fashions. Employees moved away from the traditional culture of the working class which placed emphasis on equality and solidarity among all workers. To the surface came the 'middle-class culture' for which Japan is so well known – a culture which placed a value on the individual's ability to get ahead on his own and the staging of various competitions to determine the winner. The rapid economic expansion was a period when the word 'worker' came to be a label for the down and out, a loser in the economic competition, and nobody wanted to know a loser; the worker's very existence came to be denied by the popular culture which the period created. As one of the members of the number two union which stood against Zeneraru Sekiyū Seisei commented to the author (cf. Kawanishi 1981: 323–429), 'there are no more "workers" (*rōdōsha*) in Japan; everyone has become the "gainfully employed" (*kinrōsha*).' The logic soon became that employees no longer needed labor unions. The unions became *passé* overnight with the new consciousness. The race was 'on' and everyone struggled to join the 'middle class.' Everyone wanted to move from small and medium-sized firms into the large ones or to become entrepreneurs. Many experienced some form of upward social mobility by migrating from the rural areas into the urban sprawl. It was inevitable, perhaps, that the consciousness of the working class would be swept away. However, with that transformation, the basis of the union movement was lost. Without its spiritual gyroscope the union movement could only atrophy. Such was the change wrought by the period of rapid economic growth.

Nevertheless, by the end of the 1970s the 'bubble of prosperity' had burst. The 'culture of competition' produced in many workers only an emptiness, a sense of disillusionment. Once more workers seemed to be searching for meaning in a workers' culture. That is probably the basic reason why workers were reassessing the merits of a 'union for us, the workers.' To go a step further with our analysis, however, we must inquire into the nature of this workers' culture which seemed to show itself but dimly in the various minority labor unions which were then taking the lead in developing an alternative labor movement.

Basic to this new way of thinking was a pride in being a worker. The dominant ideology in a true workers' culture is an insistance on accepting the worker as he is. Those subscribing to such norms do not feel the need to sidle up to management or to behave obsequiously to improve their job evaluations and get ahead. They do not feel the need to elbow their fellow workers and meanly jostle for position on the shop floor. For workers in a large firm to join a minority union and forego the opportunity to enjoy almost automatic promotion, they would have to embrace a fairly powerful set of alternative ideas – an ideology persuasive enough to justify a rather drastic change in their life-styles.

In this regard it may be instructive to consider the situation at Zeneraru Sekiyū Seisei (an oil refining company). In one of Japan 'sunrise industries,' Zeneraru Sekiyū expanded rapidly during the 1960s. The firm could guarantee nearly all members of the union the opportunity to be promoted into the ranks of management. When the second union was formed in 1970, employees shifted from the first union to the second in droves. In doing so, they were trying to adhere to the commonly accepted practice for promotion in many a firm with an enterprise union. The path upwards was clear:

become a leader in the union	be promoted to a → supervisory position	be promoted to a middle → management	become a full-fledged → member of the managerial team
(*kumiai kanbu*)	(*shokusei*)	(*kanrisha*)	(*keieisha*)

Behind the collapse of the first union was the change in the consciousness of the employees which was sweeping Japan at the time – everyone wanted to get ahead and was willing to climb on top of their workmates to do so. As some of the members of the number one union later told us, 'By the time we realized what was happening, those who were leading us had disappeared from the scene.' The leadership had jumped to the second union to ensure that they received favorable career consideration from the firm. Among those who remained in the first union, there was recognition among some of the younger unionists that they 'were the ones who had nonchalantly been left behind.' The young ones who chose to stay behind in the number one union were ostracized from the other employees on the shop floor and were given night shift in a way which required them to work twelve hours continuously, an exposure to shift work that left them exclaiming, 'The sooner I can get out the better! Won't someone help me out of here?' At the same time, however, they held a deep-seated bitterness toward those who had abandoned their workmates to ensure promotion to management's team at the supervisory level. To the extent that these young workers remained in the original union, their chance for promotion or any significant improvement in their wages was nil. It meant that they would spend their entire career as a worker. However, by struggling for their rights they actually sharpened their resolve to live as workers. They saw themselves as having to live on the lower reaches of the factory hierarchy; a bit lonely perhaps, but in that loneliness they found a deeper commitment to the path they had chosen. It was the resolve which brought them victory after an eight-year struggle.

At Chūgoku Densan, described below in Chapter 10, the older workers who stood up to oppose the construction of nuclear power plants have had to live with various forms of disciplinary action. They would have no hope of promotion or even the possibility of having a small electrical goods store upon retirement. However, the decision to oppose the nuclear power plants brought a certain clarity into their lives; an irrevocable decision had been made which left the workers with only one path to follow. At the same time, nevertheless, there was a tremendous sense of relief, the feeling that they 'had finally come to the end of a long dark tunnel' (Hirakawa 1987). Their resolve to stand up for their beliefs came from an inner strength which they had developed through various hardships; it was the source of the union's strength through thirty years as a left-wing minority union which still had a membership of 800.

Workers who lived through their firm's bankruptcy probably shared this same resolve. For various reasons, many employees accepted the invitation to 'resign on their own' and to take their chances with a new job. During the period of high economic growth there seemed to be a plethora of jobs, and the risks involved in taking that course of action would not have appeared to have been so great. However, having once left the 'sinking ship,' would things actually be so easy? The other view was that there would be more personal satisfaction in staying with what was left of the bankrupt firm, taking over its operations, and then creating a new work environment based upon the workers' culture. One part-time worker stated, 'The pay is not very good, but at least I know where I stand. To have gone off to another firm which could later go bankrupt would only leave me in the same situation. Although I'm not eating as well as I once was, I've become more resourceful and am making out all right' (*Asahi Shimbun*, morning edition, December 27, 1977).

In all of this there was an optimism, a sense of 'getting along' that is not evident among those who had opted for the 'economically rational' course of action. In the resolve of the workers to stay on after being fired when Oki Denki carried out its red purge we can again see the emergence of this working class culture. However, to feel at home in that culture one must be willing to live at a level commensurate with one's income. Here an attachment to working-class culture is important. One must be able to free oneself from the false consciousness being promoted by the ideologies of consumerism and the mirage that was 'middle-class society.' To feel at home in a workers' culture, workers needed to have some notion of 'the worker's life-style.'

2 For a worker's life-style A second component for organizational solidarity is a realistic concept of the worker's life-style. During the period of rapid economic growth, many workers sought to obtain unlimited materialistic gains. One of the workers from one of the many bankrupt firms on the southern outskirts of Osaka described the motivation of workers during that period in the following manner: 'Those of us who worked in the small neighborhood factories had a kind of inferiority complex. We tried to compensate for our inferiority by improving our materialistic façade, by giving ourselves a superficial veneer which would somehow cover over our inferior status at work. We sought to buy a better standard of living with money.' We could perhaps say that those who have accepted the invitation 'to retire voluntarily' or to join the number two union were still under the spell of that money. Most were motivated by a desire to maintain at whatever cost the comfortable middle-class life-style toward which they had been striving. For them, a retirement handout and the possibility of a new job symbolized the hope that they would surely succeed in their quest.

The comments of a worker at Saseho Heavy Industries points to similar conclusions. When the firm went bankrupt in the mid–1970s, the government passed legislation to assist it. The outcome meant that many workers were retrenched and that those who remained had to put up with large wage cuts and long hours. The mass media likened the inhuman conditions to those which characterized the early years of the industrial revolution in nine-teenth-century England. Several found the going too hard and committed suicide. One of the activists in the union commented to this researcher in the following manner:

> 'I will not choose death in these circumstances. I will bite my
> lip and carry on. . . . I have something to eat. Those that
> committed suicide did not do so because they were starving.
> They did so because they lost hope when they could no longer
> maintain the standard of living to which they'd become
> accustomed during the period of high economic growth.'

Along similar lines a woman writing to the *Asahi Shimbun* described her husband's decision to commit suicide because he was finding it more difficult since retiring from his second job to maintain the standard of living to which his family had become accustomed. His widow, who had felt the devastating effects of his unemployment on relationships within their family, made the following observations:

> When our grandchildren came to visit we were no longer
> able to buy ice cream and chocolate the way we used to do.
> No longer could we give them a huge birthday celebration
> or some kind of present to congratulate them on entering a
> new school. It was inevitable [under those circumstances] that
> they would feel less inclined to spend time with their
> grandparents. For our daughters as well, we became less than
> the ideal set of parents. (*Asahi Shimbun*, morning edition,
> April 5, 1978).

The wife's story catches the essence of the transformation to the materialistic orientation which occurred during the period of rapid economic growth. Rather than the natural emotional empa-thy that used to bind families together, family members have come to be judged in terms of their utilitarian value in narrow economic terms. Her thoughts are those of an empty heart.

The key to the success of minority unions and the new type of unions described above lies in the alternative they offer to the materialism which grew out of Japan's spectacular economic growth. They presented what seemed to be a new idea as to what the life-style of the ordinary worker could be. The new orientation can be seen in the eight behaviorial principles of the minority union at Zeneraru Sekiyu. One of the principles is that workers live frugally. The workers in some of the bankrupt firms in Osaka also gave that top priority in their everyday lives. Although they had a salary which had been set across the board at 50,000 yen for everyone, and even though that had not been paid for three years, leaving them unable to buy their food, they nevertheless had been able to live off the leaves of horse radishes which others had discarded and were therefore able to carry on with their program of self-management. For these workers, a meaningful life was not based on the accumulation of material goods, but, as one unionist from the branch at Tanaka Manufacturing put it, 'on the sense of comradeship and inter-dependence which came out of their common struggle against capital and was symbolized by their very sense of independence' (cf. Kamata 1977: 7–64).

In the early 1970s the struggle at Sanrizuka began when the government pushed ahead with its plans to build the airport at Narita. For many that struggle became the focus of the farmers' movement (*nōmin undō*). At the same time the struggle to control the bankrupt companies on the southern outskirts of Osaka represented the focal point for the labor movement. Maeda Toshihiko, long-time leader of the tenant farmers in Kyushu and editor of his own journal, *Hyōmantei Tsūshin* (Humanity Communications), came to Chiba lead the struggle at Sanrizuka. He felt that the workers' struggle in Osaka and the farmers' struggle at Narita had something in common, and exclaimed that

The worker and the farmer are not fighting for material gain. They are fighting for their dignity as human beings. Both have fought to improve their material lot in the past, but now is a time for steeling our determination rather than for making new demands (told directly to the author at the time. Also in an issue of *Rōdō Jōhō* at about the same time.)

3 For independence and self-autonomy A third facet of organizational solidarity is the emphasis on independence and self-autonomy. Compared to the rather conservative approach of the ordinary Japanese worker who tends to entrust his career and his livelihood to the firm that employs him, the thinking and behavior of workers who took over the bankrupt firms in Osaka represented a new independence. One of the workers had worked for twenty years, believing that things would improve greatly once his firm got a bit bigger. After holding on for a long time, without enough income to send his children to high school, the company went bankrupt. The company president had swindled funds from the firm. The worker's hopes and his poor wages are the lot of many who toil in Japan's small firms. With bankruptcy, however, his life changed completely. Ten members of his family and the family of a close workmate formed their own union. They occupied the factory and took over production on their own. From being dependent on the company for their livelihood, they have become the company in their own right and now work independently for themselves.

This same outcome can be seen in the direction being pursued by the couple who, when dismissed by Nissan Sunny, formed their own union as a branch of Unyu Ippan Rōso. In their own unions, women too have found a new sense of freedom and dignity. No matter how conscientious the male leadership may be in a male-dominated union, there is still the desire of many women to be less dependent on the magnamity of the large firm and to be less dependent on the willingness of the large male-dominated enterprise union to 'look after' their interests. No matter how well intended male leaders might be, it was felt, in the final analysis, that women would have to look after the interests of women. The handicapped workers who formed their own union in the inspection section of Okubo Bottling also had the same orientation, insisting that 'through struggle they would show the management at Okubo their value and their skills.'

The unionists with this sort of orientation refer to their interpersonal relationships as being based on 'the notion of autonomy' and on the unspoken agreement that mates would not double-cross each other. They were also guided by the commitment to an egalitarianism which shifted workers' efforts away from competition with their workmates. Although they were completely subsumed within a work environment controlled by management's supervisory staff and by the majority number two union, the workers in the minority enterprise unions did not capitulate to management's divisive tactics. An inner strength derived from the ideology that workers should never double-cross their mates seemed to carry them through their trials and tribulations. At Zeneraru Sekiyū one of the unionists argued that by internalizing the values associated with this ideological viewpoint, young workers were able to stand up to management and say, 'We won't be pushed around by the likes of you. How can we believe the line given us by someone who has stabbed us in the back?' (as quoted in Kawanishi 1981: 371).

In short, workers in the two types of unions on the fringe have been trying to change the social order at work, replacing a very hierarchical and competitive structure with an approach which is much more egalitarian. From their point of view, the social order at work has been structured largely by management in its own interests. It has been a divisive order which has discriminated between those with different educational backgrounds, between office and factory workers, between males and females, and between regular employees and temporary employees. Furthermore, they would argue, these differentiations of labor status are used to compel employees to work harder, for the extent to which each employee works hard has come to be judged according to the extent to which they compete with others. It is this ethos, which has contributed to the long hours of work employees experience and to their inability to use the paid holiday leave which has accrued to them, that the new type of unions and the minority enterprise unions are trying to change.

For example, after winning a bitter fight drawn out over seven years, Kōbunsha Rōso (the labor union of Kōbunsha employees) amalgamated with Kisha Rōso (the labor union of correspondences who were non-regular employees) and with Rinji Rōdōsha Rōso (the labor union of temporary workers). Together they were able to push successfully for a unified system which called for all employees to be treated similarly regardless of employment status (cf. Kōbunsha Tōsō o Kiroku Suru Kai 1977). At Petori Camera, where 180 workers had continued production on their own with about 50 part-timers, everyone contributed to the workers' savings scheme and those who received unemployment benefits pooled those funds as well. Although the unemployment benefits would have varied considerably from one person to another, the pooled resources were distributed according to a plan drawn up by all the unionists at a plenary session.

Part-time workers belonging to the branch of Zenkoku Kinzoku at Motoyama Manufacturing pooled their wages, and the union developed a system whereby each member could apply for whatever amount they needed to survive for the month (cf. Zenkinzoku Motoyama Tōsō no Kiroku Henshū Iinkai 1974). Here again we can see the tremendous sense of solidarity which grew out of the struggle of a number one union to survive. Motoyama was a metal manufacturer in Sendai employing about 1000 persons. Motoyama had grown rapidly during the 1960s, emerging as a major producer. Although management had kept a lid on unionism, firing immediately anyone who seemed likely to organize the employees, a number of young workers finally succeeded in establishing a militant union in 1968. In 1971 management assisted the formation of a second union. The following year it hired a famous gang as guards and had the mobile police units brought in to assist in locking out the 226 employees in the number one union. The company ignored court orders and the directives of the local Labor Relations Commission. Sōhyō assisted in organizing a demonstration of 10,000 persons in front of the company gate. To survive, the unionists took part-time jobs and pooled their earnings for the union to redistribute as democratically as possible. The dispute continues.

The idea of management assessing the performance of employees and then differentiating among them in terms of their pay went against the egalitarian principles of these unions. The number one union at Chisso Corporation in Minamata came up with the idea of pooling the amount which was paid to employees as a result of such assessments. The families of the unionists then got together and spent a week discussing how the lumped monies ought to be redistributed. At the Ichikawa Tutoring Academy the teachers' union struggled against the personnel assessments, arguing that the rationale for having a union was lost if it came around to accepting the assessment system. There are numerous examples of small unions which have organized around the principle of equality in some shape or form.

4 For solidarity　The fourth feature associated with the culture developed by workers in unions on the fringe would be the emphasis on solidarity. Those in the ordinary enterprise unions no longer refer to 'solidarity' as a guiding principle. However, those in the minority unions continued to aim for that ideal. A major assumption was that victory will be won only by the combined support of all workers. Victory was seen as occurring when there is a critical mass, and in the final analysis it might be only a small voice that would give a union the necessary critical mass. Each person's contribution, however small by itself, is crucial when combined with that of others in order to achieve that critical mass. In the past, the notion of solidarity was invoked mainly when unionists were trying to get a union to donate money to another union locked in a hard struggle with management.

In the late 1970s the notion of 'solidarity' came to be given a fair amount of attention as a concept binding together workers in the same union in local and regional struggles. A good example of local workers' struggle can be taken from the activities organized by Zenkoku Kinzoku's regional for the workers mentioned above on the southern edge of Osaka. Workers throughout the country were impressed to learn how that regional had created such a strong sense of solidarity among workers in unions at twenty-one small firms. While maintaining their own autonomy the unions had forged together to form a very strong bond in their fight against management which went bankrupt and/or fired workers.

Although the union movement had always been strong in this area, the solidarity of these unions was particularly important in carrying the workers along after the oil shocks in the mid–1970s. The slogans read 'FEAR NOT EVEN A SINGLE WORKER!' and 'ONE WORKER FOR ALL AND ALL WORKERS FOR ONE!' Those in the minority groups were quick to criticize the idea of working for 'the greatest good for the greatest number.' Such slogans symbolized an approach which always left them out. If one of the organized firms went bankrupt and began to lay people off, workers at the other factories would mobilize themselves to lend support. They would negotiate with management in their own firm and pressure it to give work to the troubled firm, or to hire laid-off workers on a part-time basis. Most importantly, the regional organization of Zenkoku Kinzoku would provide various kinds of support and see that collective bargaining occurred on a local basis, thereby bringing the weight of the entire organization to bear on the problem.

Beginning with their victory in the 863-day struggle at Hosokawa Steel, the local maintained its momentum by supporting its branch at Tanaka Machinery early in 1979. When Tanaka Machinery claimed it was going bankrupt, workers in the other unions in the area rushed to support the workers at Tanaka. They got together rice, *tatami* mats, bedding and money. Some middle-aged women workers in a nearby factory rushed in to make meals every day for 200 persons, claiming, 'I'll be there if only to wash a single dish!' At 8.30 each evening, about 150 workers would gather after having finished their own work. They would vigorously debate how best to help their mates at Tanaka Machinery. Because no barriers had been built which would divide workers in one firm from those at other firms, this kind of solidarity which is basic to the labor movement was possible.

By the late 1970s examples of this sort could also be found in the Tokyo area. For example, a call for 'class solidarity, class dialogue and class action' appeared in the policy proposal at the Fifteenth Regular Convention of Sōhyō Zenkoku Ippan Rōso's South Tokyo branch which met in February 1978. The branch consisted of unions at about 300 enterprises in the area. Another example would be the local struggle waged in support of the workers at Okubo Bottles. About sixty joined the movement in support of the Okubo workers, and they distributed some 300,000 handbills around the area. Considerable support was generated among workers and residents in Sumida Ward, an area with a high concentration of small factories. Demonstrators moved from one alley to another, receiving applause from those looking out the windows of one factory or apartment complex after another. Onlookers would shout, 'Good on ya mate, we know what you're up against!' In one year over two million yen was raised. Through their local organization the unions had stirred the souls of the local residents.

There are also examples of the workers reaching out beyond the confines of their own and developing ties with local residents in general. Among local residents (who faced their own problems every day) there was a feeling that most enterprise unions were rather conservative and oriented toward maintaining the establishment. Many local residents found it difficult to identify with such unions. For thirty years since the war the political situation had been analyzed in terms of two conflicting forces: progressive labor unions and conservative farmers and fishermen. However, that simple dichotomy no longer seemed appropriate in the Japan of the 1970s, for the unions too had come to be associated with conservatism and the maintenance of the establishment. The union had come to be regarded as a stranger in its own land.

It took the unions on the fringe to present many Japanese with an alternative. Based on a good deal of reflection, they were trying to devise ways of overcoming the atrophy from within – a process which resulted from the barrier lying between Japan's workers and the enterprise unions, on the one hand, and the local residents and the ordinary population on the other. One example of a bridge between labor and the average citizen can be found in the move against the generation of nuclear power which was led by the minority labor union at the Chūgoku Electric Power Authority. In their efforts to generate a grass-roots movement, the union developed ties with some of the agricultural and fishing communities. At first they were unsuccessful as they continued to be held with suspicion by the more conservative elements in those communities. However, once the strike had begun and the union-ists began to bear the brunt of all kinds of disciplinary action and the locals became more aware of the price the unionists were paying for their commitment to the cause, several persons in the fishing communities came to have a change of heart. They became more critical of the authority and they began to offer support to the unionists. This new solidarity prompted the slogan 'Come to the sea and return to the land' (Hirakawa 1987: 4). When the unionists decided to camp outside the offices of the authority in protest against the disciplinary action, next to the union's flag was the banner of the fisherman's cooperative, and sitting next to the unionists were the fishermen. This was the first time in the history of the labor movement in Japan that this kind of solidarity with fishermen and farmers had been achieved. During the 1970s there were similar forms of solidarity between the workers in number one unions, fishermen and local residents in the three major cases of pollution which were taken to court: the Minamata case in Kyushu (against the Chisso Corporation); Niigata's Minamata case (against Shōwa Denkō); and the Yokkaichi case (against Ishihara Industries). In all three cases, the victims of pollution won significant judgments in their favor. The fight against the resumption of land for the Tokyo International Airport also brought attention to the interest which unions on the fringe had in broader notions of solidarity.

V Conclusions

As the preceeding discussion suggests, the two kinds of unions discussed above have developed an ideology based upon (i) a commitment to the worker, (ii) some notion of working-class culture, (iii) a commitment to the autonomy and independence of the labor movement, and (iv) the active promotion of working-class solidarity. During the late 1970s those unions were laying the foundations for their future cohesiveness. In doing so, they were building a comprehensive foundation for a return to the independence which characterized the union movement immediately after the war.

The ideology which emerged was quite comprehensive, providing unionists with (a) a vision of how their human relationships should be organized, one with another, (b) an approach to how their consumption and daily life ought to be organized, (c) a set of activities in which unions ought to be involved, and (d) a sense of identity. Taken together, these orientations provide workers with a comprehensive view of the world – a view which came to form the core of their workers' culture. It would seem clear that the new type of union which emerged in the late 1970s and the left-wing minority enterprise unions were conceived as a means of creating that kind of culture.

The notion of a 'workers' culture' (*rōdōsha bunka*) can perhaps be better grasped by considering briefly the concept which stands in opposition: 'the culture of the employee' (*jūgyōin bunka*). In societies which are structured around the logic of capitalism under the guidance of dominant managerial groups which run the business firms, members of society are guided by the culture of the employee. In its classical form, that culture is shaped by the logic of capitalism which appears to the employee as work rules and the other directives formulated on a daily basis by management. In addition, employees pick up the informal culture of the enterprise when they are inculcated with the work customs and traditions which have been developed over time on the shop floor. On top of that is the ideology and style of the social enterprises which create the 'Toyota Man' or the 'Matsushita Man.'

In saying this we must recognize that the culture of the employee is not simply forced onto the employee. Employees take it upon themselves to mould their thinking and their behavior to the expectations of management. At the same time, we need to recognize the power relationship which exists between the employee and management. The latter seeks to use its power to push the employee toward achieving the goals of the firm. The control which results manifests itself most clearly in the work rules. Although the rules leave room for the employee to take his own initiative is certain areas, the important point is that the extent of his discretion is still fairly limited to areas which will help maximize the firm's profits. Should he go beyond his authority, he will be sanctioned in one of a number of ways or even asked to resign. It is within the confines of the needs of the enterprise, as defined by management, that the culture of the employee exists.

The 'culture of the worker' refers to the culture which emerges more or less spontaneously out of the life-style and everyday needs of the worker. But what are the needs of the worker? Whereas the culture of the employee arises out of the needs of management and does not create an orientation in the workers which goes beyond those needs, the culture of the worker incorporates reference to needs which go beyond those needs which can be met simply by serving a particular firm. It is oriented toward maximizing the benefits enjoyed by all workers engaged in productive economic activity. In that orientation there is the assumption that the capitalist modes of production set the interests of management and those of labor against each other. Accordingly, the concept of the 'culture of the workers' indicates a commitment to the collectivistic values which puts faith in the independence of the worker, in comradeship among workers, and in government or decision-making by the workers.

The success or failure of these unions in fostering such a culture of the workers will in no small measure be reflected in the direction the labor movement takes in the future. There is little doubt that the unions currently on the fringe of the Japanese union movement have presented workers in Japan with an alternative approach to unionism and an alternative way of viewing working life. For that reason they compete with the large conservative enterprise unions which are seen as being the mainstream of the union movement in contemporary Japan. Whether they gain more of a following or not will have to be left to the future. To explore the notion of the workers' culture and the potential of unions on the fringe to contribute to its revival among the working population in Japan, the next three chapters examine the findings from several of the author's case studies on the left-wing minority enterprise union.

9 The Position of the Minority Enterprise Unions

I Introduction

The situation of the minority enterprise union is not very well understood. Most research on the enterprise union in Japan has focused on unions at firms where there is only one union. Although the situation of the majority union at enterprises with more than one union may be similar to that of the single enterprise union, the situation experienced by the minority union has been somewhat different, and deserves careful analysis before any final generalizations can be made about Japan's enterprise unions. As the discussion in Chapter 3 suggested, at a large number of firms two or more unions compete. This is also confirmed by other studies. One by Nikkeiren shows that a fair number of its member firms had two or more unions (Table 9.1).

Table 9.1 *Percentage of firms affiliated with Nikkeiren which have single and multiple unions*

Number of unions	Number of firms affiliated with Nikkeiren	Percentage
No union	283	21.1
1 union	856	63.8
2 unions	157	11.7
3 unions	24	1.8
4 unions	11	0.8
5 or more unions	11	0.8
TOTAL	1342	100.0

Although the position of the minority unions may initially have been in doubt, by the mid–1970s it was clear that a large number of minority unions had stabilized their positions and would likely continue to coexist at the same firm with another enterprise union. Nevertheless, little was known about the minority enterprise unions.

Because no systematic study had been made of such unions, I decided in 1975 to survey them. This chapter reports on the findings from that survey. The second step was to engage in some case studies. The following two chapters report on two case studies carried out in the Hiroshima area.

II The Survey as an Approach to the Minority Enterprise Unions

In November and December 1975 and in August 1976 a survey was sent to 575 unions at firms where two enterprise unions coexisted. The sample was compiled as a result of discussions with a number of industrial federations which had been introduced by the leadership in Dōmei (7 federations) and Sōhyō (8 federations). Surveys were distributed and collected both by the industrial federation and by myself. Forty-seven of the 211 Sōhyō-affiliated unions contacted (22.3 percent) returned the survey; only 7 of the 364 Dōmei-affiliated unions (4.6 percent) did so.

While the use of the mail questionnaire was one reason for the low response rate, there was also the fact that many of the unions being approached were in the midst of an all-out struggle with the other competing union at their respective enterprise. Compared with enterprise unions fully in control of the situation at their own firms, the unions in competition with another union would have been very reluctant to answer questions which probe their affairs too deeply. The situation is such that only through careful case studies will we be able to grasp adequately how the left-wing minority enterprise unions function. There remain a number of areas where written questionnaires will not result in the data necessary for such detailed analysis.

Considering that no previous survey had been done along these lines and that it is unlikely that the response rate would improve in the near future, it is useful to evaluate the meagre results which were returned. Because the returned surveys had been completed by the union's general secretaries (*shokichō*), it could be said that the findings represent the formal position of the unions surveyed. Developing further the discussion in the preceding chapter, the analysis in this chapter focuses on 39 left-wing

minority unions affiliated with Sōhyō-linked industrial federations. Although some of the administrative costs were borne by
Chiba University and some research funds had been received
from the Ministry of Education, a good deal of the cost was
covered by myself. Accordingly, the more costly interviews
(which would have provided much better data) could not be
arranged.

Table 9.2 accounts for the 211 Sōhyō-affiliated unions to which
surveys were sent. The seven unions in Dōmei's industrial federations which had replied were all majority unions, averaging a
membership of 1075 persons and a unionization rate of 85.7
percent. Of the 47 unions in Sōhyō's industrial federations which
responded, 46 could be called 'number one unions' (*bunretsu
saha kumiai*) (left-wing unions remaining after a schism). Thirty
nine of those were minority unions and seven were majority
unions. The analysis in this chapter will focus on the 39 minority
unions; the seven left-wing majority enterprise unions will be
referred to only occasionally for comparative purposes. This
chapter provides only a basic summary of the findings from the
above-mentioned survey; the more detailed analysis has been
provided elsewhere (Kawanishi 1976b, 1977).

III Union Schisms and the Minority Enterprise Union

Ninety percent of the unions responding to the survey coexisted
with another union which had been formed when a single enterprise union had split. The remaining 10 percent of the respondents coexisted with a union which had been formed in response
to an initiative taken by management when it had learned that
a left-wing union was going to be formed. In other words, these
unions lived in competition with another union which had been
formed to displace it. Each union leader responding to the survey
felt that a single enterprise union at each firm was the desirable
goal.

In all cases management's intervention in the union's affairs
had been a key element accounting for there being two enterprise
unions at the same firm. For this reason, interpersonal relations
among employees were colored by a strongly emotional element.

Table 9.2 *The sample of forty-six left-wing enterprise unions*

Industrial federation	Number of affiliated unions	Number of affiliated unions in firms with two or more unions	Number of surveys distributed	Number of surveys returned	Number of coexisting unions with a leftist orientation	Number of minority unions with a leftist orientation	Number of majority unions with a leftist orientation
1 All Japan Federation of Metal Workers (Zenkoku Kinzoku)	1300	130	80	18	18	15	3
2 Allied Chemical Workers (Kagaku Dōmei)	130	35	35	10	10	9	1
3 Private Railway Workers (Shitetsu Sōren)	243	20	20	7	7	4	3
4 Paper and Pulp Workers (Kamipa Rōren)	116	8	7	2	2	2	0
5 Chemical Workers Federation (Gōka Rōren)	128	25	25	5	4*	4	0
6 All Japan Federation of Shipbuilders (Zen-zōsen)	35	11	11	2	2	2	0

Table 9.2 *continued*

Industrial federation	Number of affiliated unions	Number of affiliated unions in firms with two or more unions	Number of surveys distributed	Number of surveys returned	Number of coexisting unions with a leftist orientation	Number of minority unions with a leftist orientation	Number of majority unions with a leftist orientation
7 All Japan Union of General Workers (Zenkoku Ippan)	not clear	not clear	30	2	2	2	0
8 All Japan Federation of Electric Power Workers (Zendenryoku)	3	3	3	1	1	1	0
TOTAL	1955	232	211	47	46	39	7

*One of the unions affiliated with Gōka Rōren was the conservative number two union at a firm where the number one union was affiliated with Kagaku Dōmei. As it was not a leftist union, it was excluded from the study which is focused on left-wing minority enterprise unions.

Although many of the unionists may have had very different views as to how their firm's industrial relations should be run, it was the political realities of the in-fighting – the cross-cutting deceptions and loyalties – that took the emotional toll.

This general interpretation may be further substantiated by reference to the fact that 88.6 percent of the unions responding to this survey in late 1975 were in enterprises where two enterprise unions coexisted in the same firm; the remaining 11.4 percent were in firms where three or four enterprise unions coexisted. This means that the competition and the political realities and sense of hierarchy were explicit. This differs from the situation in Britain, for example, where one survey showed for 1972 that employees at 23 percent of all British firms in the private sector were divided among six or more unions organized along occupational lines (Clark *et al.* 1972: 70; cited in Hazama 1974: 161). In nearly all cases, the unions surveyed in Japan were opposed by unions that had arisen from the splintering-off of a right-wing group from what had been a single union. In two cases, however, it had been the left-wing group which had moved to form the competing union.

In about half of the cases the creation of a second union had occurred while the original union was having a dispute with management. The data in Table 9.3 provide some further information on the unions surveyed. The pattern which emerges is consistent with the commonly accepted view that right-wing unions tend to affiliate with the more conservative national centre, Dōmei, and to symbolize the pressure which Dōmei-affiliated unions have been placing on the Sōhyō-affiliated unions since the late 1950s. Nevertheless, it may be surprising that only half of all coexisting conservative unions (which stand in opposition to the surveyed unions) are affiliated with Dōmei; about one third have no affiliation and can therefore be regarded as being 'company unions' (*kaisha kumiai*). It is also interesting to note the absence of a correlation between firm size and the affiliation of those unions.

Moreover, only half of the schisms occurred at a time when there was a dispute with management. That half of the Dōmei-affiliated and 'independent' unions were formed when there was no dispute may indicate that some preparation had gone into the union's formation in such circumstances. This interpretation is consistent with the idea that those forming such unions colluded

Table 9.3 *Some characteristics of the right-wing unions standing in opposition to the forty-six left-wing unions surveyed*

National center with which opposition union is affiliated	Total number of left-wing unions with opposition unions	Breakdown of unions by position vis-à-vis the opposition union		Breakdown of unions by the size of the firm (number of employees)			Situation at time second union was formed	
		Minority status	Majority status	1–499	500–999	1000+	dispute in progress	no dispute formed
Dōmei	47.8 (22)	43.6 (17)	71.4 (5)	50.4 (8)	55.6 (5)	42.9 (9)	47.6 (10)	48.0 (12)
No affiliation	34.8 (16)	35.9 (14)	28.6 (2)	43.8 (7)	44.4 (4)	23.8 (5)	38.1 (8)	32.0 (8)
Dōmei and no affiliation (2 or more unions in opposition)	6.5 (3)	7.7 (3)	0	6.3 (1)	0	14.3 (3)	0	12.0 (3)
Sōhyō	6.5 (3)	7.7 (3)	0	0	0	14.3 (3)	9.5 (2)	4.0 (1)
Chūritsu Rōren	4.3 (2)	5.1 (2)	0	0	0	4.8 (1)	4.8 (1)	4.0 (1)
TOTAL	100.0 (46)	100.0 (39)	100.0 (7)	100.0 (16)	100.0 (9)	100.0 (21)	100.0 (21)	100.0 (25)

with management to achieve mutually acceptable ends. Once the goals were agreed upon, there would have been little reason for the two parties to wait for a dispute to occur before implementing their agreement. This does not mean that management and man-agement-oriented unionists were indifferent to the opportunities which disputes between management and leftist-led unions might have presented.

The fact that this pattern may be different from that which characterized the formation of second unions in the 1950s deserves some mention. By the 1960s the notion of unfair labor practices had become well established. Accordingly, large firms concerned with their reputation did not want to be openly accused of stooping to such tactics. Instead, they would consult with unionists in Dōmei and develop over some years an environ-ment conducive to the formation of a number two union which could immediately affiliate with one of Dōmei's industrial feder-ations. Managements in smaller and medium-sized firms, how-ever, did not feel that they could afford such niceties, and often were quick to jump in 'boots and all.' They were much more blatant in pushing for number two unions and in working for the total capitulation of the number one union.

A closer look at the responses to the survey suggests that the splintering of an enterprise union cannot be understood simply in terms of conservative number two unions rising to challenge radical number one unions. The phenomenon is much more complex. First, only a third of the 39 minority unions surveyed became minority unions upon the formation of the second union. The average organization rate of the second union upon forma-tion was only 37.4 percent. In other words, the split was effected by a minority of workers in most cases. However, once the second unions were established, the first unions experienced further attrition and within a year or two found themselves being the minority unions. The process of attrition reflected both the involvement of management and certain difficulties in the original left-wing unions themselves. If the splits were inevitable for the left-wing unions, so too was it inevitable that the left-wing unions which survived would soon become the minority unions. It should be noted that the left-wing majority unions which fought on were not in major firms. Their average organization rate of 62.8 per-cent was generated by an average membership of only 269 per-sons.

Second, schisms 'within the left' also occur. For example, Table 9.3 includes two cases where a schism had occurred within a union affiliated with one of Sōhyō's industrial federations in the chemical industry (Kagaku Dōmei) and the resulting second union affiliated with another of Sōhyō's industrial federations covering the same industry (Gōka Rōren). Another case from the same table involved a number one union from Gōka Rōren which coexisted with the number two union affiliated to Zenkoku Ippan. Two other cases involved a breakaway from enterprise unions affiliated with Sōhyō's industrial federation for metal workers (Zenkoku Kinzoku) and the creation of second enterprise unions which affiliated with Denki Rōren, an industrial federation for electrical machinery workers belonging to yet another national centre, Chūritsu Rōren.

Table 9.4 shows that nearly two thirds of the splits occurred between 1965 and 1975, with nearly a third occurring between 1970 and 1975. Only a little over one third had occurred before 1965. It was the period of high economic growth – a time not only of changing values, but also of heightened differentiation among workers – which produced the schisms. Of course, as a period in which arrangements were altered in preparation for the period of high growth, the 1950s also produced many schisms; however, by the 1970s those divisions had been resolved with the number one union being completely dismantled.

Table 9.4 *The length of time left-wing unions had coexisted since schism*

Time at which schism occurred	Left-wing minority unions		Left-wing majority unions		Right-wing majority unions	
1971–5	30.8	(12)	42.9	(3)	0	
1965–70	35.9	(14)	28.6	(2)	87.5	(7)
before 1965	33.3	(13)	28.6	(2)	12.5	(1)
TOTAL	100.0	(39)	100.0	(7)	100.0	(8)

Table 9.5 suggests that leftist unions are particularly vulnerable to schisms in their early years. A third of the unions in this survey experienced their split within five years of having been formed. It should be noted, however, that a long history as an enterprise's only union does not preclude a challenge; nearly twenty percent of the unions experienced their splits after they

had been around for twenty years or more. Complacency and other problems associated with organizational aging seem to have been very real.

Table 9.5 *Distribution of left-wing unions by the number of years between the original union's formation and the formation of the second union*

Years following the union's formation until the split occurred	Percentage of left-wing unions		Percentage of right-wing unions	
–5	32.7	(15)	25.0	(2)
6–9	13.0	(6)	0	
10–14	13.0	(6)	37.5	(3)
15–19	17.4	(8)	12.5	(1)
20–24	8.7	(4)	12.5	(1)
25+	10.9	(5)	0	
Not clear	4.3	(2)	12.5	(1)
TOTAL	100.0	(46)	100.0	(8)
X	11.5		13.7	

The first skirmishes with management occurred right after the initial schism appeared. When asked about the reasons why the schisms occurred, all of the unions responding to the survey pointed to the key role of definite policies taken by management to produce such a split. An affiliate of Zenkoku Kinzoku claimed that management began to move against it just when its membership was expanding and it had become able to engage in political activity. Management did so by introducing 'job-based' wage differentials (*shokumukyū*) to divide the labor force.

Another affiliate of the same federation stated that management sought to sap the workers' fighting spirit by restricting the workers' rights and strengthening managerial controls over the labor force at the supervisory level. An affiliate of Kagaku Dōmei replied that management set out to split it after failing in its attempts to coopt the union.

Any serious analysis of the sources of conflict is confused by accusations and counter-accusations. The researcher is soon overwhelmed by the complexity of the various interpersonal relationships. Table 9.6 summarizes responses concerning the event which immediately precipitated the split. Simple reference to a basic difference in views concerning the orientation of the union was the most common answer. Even when the response was more concrete in terms of specific differences over specific issues, the issues themselves reflected basic differences in philosophy as to the direction the union movement should take. In particular, disagreement revolved around the extent to which unions should push management in shifting resources from the management to the workers.

Table 9.6 *Distribution of left-wing unions by the reason why the initial schism occurred*

Cause of split	Left-wing minority unions	Left-wing majority unions	All left-wing unions coexisting with one or more other unions
1 Disagreement over union policy	43.6 (17)	28.6 (2)	41.3 (19)
2 Disagreement over the union's wage struggle	17.9 (7)	42.9 (3)	21.8 (10)
3 Disagreement over the union's anti-rationalization struggle	20.5 (8)	14.3 (1)	19.6 (9)
4 Disagreement over the union's struggle to revise its agreement with management	2.6 (1)	0	2.2 (1)
5 Disagreement at the time of the union's elections	5.1 (2)	14.3 (1)	6.5 (3)
6 Firing of union official	2.6 (1)	0	2.2 (1)
7 Disagreement over affiliation with higher level union	5.1 (2)	0	4.3 (2)
8 Disagreement about support for a political party	2.6 (1)	0	2.2 (1)
TOTAL	100.0 (39)	100.0 (7)	100.0 (46)

Although we do not have figures on 'casualty rates' for minority unions, the distribution suggests that at least some minority unions will continue to exist indefinitely. Table 9.7 also shows that the membership of the left-wing minority unions was small, the average being only 113 persons. The average unionization rate among their firm's employees was a meager 9.5 percent;

although nearly 30 percent of the unions were able to maintain an organization rate over 30 percent, 60 percent of the unions had fewer than 100 members. While the left-wing majority unions existed only in the smaller firms, nearly half of the left-wing minority unions existed at firms with over 1000 employees. This finding runs counter to the commonly held view that the minority unions will be found only in Japan's smaller enterprises. In this regard, it is interesting to note that the organization rate did not seem to effect the activities of the 39 minority unions, whereas firm size did.

Table 9.7 *Some characteristics of the left-wing minority unions*

A Size of the union	
Less than 100 members	59.5
100–199 members	21.6
200 or more members	13.5
Unclear	5.4
TOTAL (N=39)	100.0

B Unionization rate at firm where union is located	
Less than 11 percent	37.8
11–30 percent	27.0
31–49 percent	27.0
Unclear	8.1
TOTAL (N=39)	100.0

C Size of the firm at which union exists	
Less than 500	
0–499 employees	29.7
500–999 employees	24.4
1000+ employees	45.9
Unclear	0.0
TOTAL (N=39)	100.0

A comparison of the age of the membership in the 39 left-wing minority unions and the 8 right-wing number two majority unions (including one affiliated with Gōka Rōren and the other seven with the Dōmei federations) indicates that the average age of the membership was similar (35.1 and 32.7 years respectively). As for years employed at the firm, the average for the 39 left-wing unions was 14.9 years while that for 8 right-wing unions was 13.8 years.

These findings go against the commonly held view that the minority unions consist only of hard core radicals who have aged over time and are about to be faded out of the company. It is generally held that all new employees would be encouraged by the firm to join the conservative union if they expected promotion and other benefits during their employment in the firm. According to that view, few of the new employees join the left-wing minority union. If this were correct, the average age of unionists in the left-wing unions should be considerably above that of those in the more conservative unions. However, it would seem that a small portion of the younger employees are joining the minority unions. An even more likely explanation, however, is that those who joined or stayed with the left-wing union after the schism were mostly young workers. The result is that by the time of the survey (8.5 years, on the average, after the schism occurred) the average age of the members of the left-wing union was finally somewhat on par with that of the membership of the dominant conservative union.

The average number of officials in the 39 left-wing minority unions was 8.8 persons, above the figure of 7.3 persons for the 7 left-wing majority unions. However, most of the officials in the 39 minority unions served as honorary officers. The average number of paid officials was only 0.4 persons. Further, it is interesting to observe that 64.1 percent of the union officials were blue-collar and 35.9 percent were white-collar. This compares with 66.2 and 33.8 percent for all 46 left-wing unions (Table 9.8). This too contrasts with the strong image given by the frequent references to 'the workers' spirit in the minority unions' (*shōsūha kumiai no rōdōsha tamashi*). Although the returns were not complete for the right-wing unions, the tabulations yielded an average age of 34.6 years for officials in the 46 left-wing unions and 34.5 years for those in the right-wing unions. As might be expected there are other clear differences in the socio-economic background and in their political preferences of leadership in the two types of union (Table 9.8).

The number of 'intellectuals' in the minority unions is surprisingly large. It is also interesting to note that only 17.5 percent of the union officials in the minority unions belonged to the

Table 9.8 *Some characteristics of the leadership in the left-wing and right-wing unions*

Background characteristics	In the 46 left-wing unions	In the 8 right-wing unions
A Education		
middle school (prewar primary)	46.1 (333)	16.0 (12)
senior high school (prewar middle)	45.4 (328)	54.7 (41)
teritiary (prewar higher)	8.6 (62)	29.3 (22)
	100.0 (723)	100.0 (75)
B Occupation		
blue-collar	66.2 (210)	41.9 (26)
white-collar	33.8 (107)	58.1 (36)
	100.0 (317)	100.0 (62)
C Position		
managerial/supervisory	12.3 (39)	38.7 (24)
not managerial or supervisory	87.7 (278)	61.3 (38)
	100.0 (317)	100.0 (62)
D Party membership		
Japan Communist Party	11.8 (33)	0
Japan Socialist Party	19.3 (54)	0
Democratic Socialist Party	0	33.3 (15)
No affiliation	68.9 (193)	66.7 (30)
	100.0 (280)	100.0 (45)

Note: The figures in the parentheses represent the actual number of union officials for whom information was supplied.

Japan Socialist Party and only 10.9 percent belonged to the Japan Communist Party. Half belonged to no party at all, perhaps giving the lie to the stereotype that the left-wing unions are led by communists. The suggestion is that the *raison d'être* for the minority unions lies not in a push for some brand of political unionism, but in the individual beliefs of the members and in some aspect of the situation at each particular firm which motivated a certain number of employees to go ahead with their own brand of unionism.

IV Industrial Relations in a State of Co-existence

When the union movement is divided at a particular firm, the firm's industrial relations come to reflect the power relations between three actors: management, the left-wing union (*bunretsu saha kumiai*) and the right-wing union (*bunretsu uha kumiai*). A general framework for analyzing such situations is provided in Figure 9.1. Basic to our understanding of this phenomenon is the way management discriminates between the unions. The survey revealed that leaders of the left-wing unions perceived that their unions and their members were treated more harshly than were the conservative unions and their members. This perception was more commonly held by the 39 minority left-wing unions than by the 7 majority left-wing unions (Table 9.9). Of the seven items where over half of the minority unions felt discrimination occurred, three concerned the ability of the union to function as an interest maximizing organization: collective bargaining, management consultations and the collective agreement. Four areas involved discrimination directly against individuals: wage levels, promotion, job assignments and work evaluations. Discrimination against individual members reflects perhaps the fact that excessive pressure on the union itself can result in accusations of unfair or illegal labor practices, whereas such allegations are more difficult to substantiate when the target is an individual. It is also likely that management will treat individuals differently in an attempt to lure less committed employees away from the left-wing union. The management's tactic is clearly to demonstrate that the left-wing union has less bargaining power and that their members have a less promising future within the firm. When it came to the collective bargaining sessions (item 1 in Table 9.9), holding fewer bargaining sessions, making less time available when bargaining sessions are scheduled, holding the sessions away from the company's head offices, and not bargaining during normal hours of work were mentioned as examples of discriminatory treatment. The position and number of persons sent to represent management and the attitude of the representatives were also mentioned as examples of discriminatory treatment. The position and number of persons sent to represent management and the attitude of the representatives were also mentioned. Finally, many of the left-wing unions felt they were

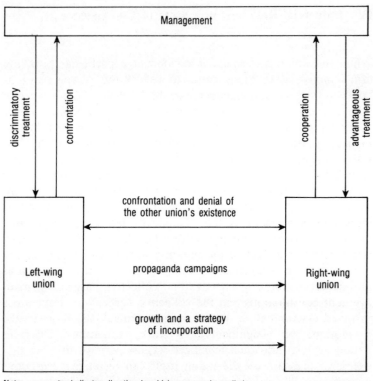

Figure 9.1 *Industrial relations in enterprises with two unions*

dealt with only after negotiations with the right-wing union had been concluded. One seventh of the 39 left-wing minority unions complained that management would not deduct union dues directly from their member's pay packets. A similar proportion saw the conservative union receiving office space from the firm while they received either no space at all or markedly inferior accommodation. In short, management seems to have used various strategies to indicate its disdain for, or obliviousness to, the minority union's existence.

The same is also true regarding the treatment meted out to individuals belonging to the first union. In addition to discrimination in terms of promotion, pay rises and the overall work evaluations handed down by the personnel department, job assignments were used to give individuals in the left-wing unions

Table 9.9 *The percentage of left-wing unions which feel discriminated against in specific areas*

Area of discrimination	Percentage of left-wing unions	Percentage of left-wing minority unions
(1) In collective bargaining	67.4	66.7
(2) In joint consultations with management	60.9	64.1
(3) In concluding the contract with management	58.7	61.5
(4) In the total amount of wage increments	4.3	2.6
(5) In setting wage scales	10.9	12.8
(6) In the way wage increments are distributed individually among employees	45.7	51.3
(7) In the total amount of bonuses	4.3	2.6
(8) In the way bonuses are distributed	36.9	43.6
(9) In having the 'check-off' system	15.2	15.4
(10) In having the company supply an office for union activities	15.2	15.4
(11) In obtaining miscellaneous funds for the union's use from the company	13.0	12.8
(12) In promotions	67.4	71.8
(13) In personnel assignments	60.9	61.5
(14) In personnel evaluation	71.7	69.2
(15) In access to company housing and the company dormitory	23.9	28.2
(16) In housing allowances	15.2	15.4
(17) In the use of company facilities	21.7	23.1
TOTAL number of unions responding	100.00	100.0
N	(39)	(7)

uninteresting or non-challenging work, if any at all. Their access to company housing or space in the company's dormitories, their opportunity to use various company facilities, and their chances of qualifying for housing support schemes were greatly restricted in many firms. Again, the general approach taken by the firm was simply to indicate in various ways the non-importance of such individuals to the firm. This kind of treatment was cited as the greatest hardship faced by members of the left-wing union.

Enterprise Unionism in Japan

In most cases there was little the union could do to respond other than fostering through the notion of worker solidarity a psychological commitment in the worker to 'tough it out.' Where possible, the union's leadership would point to gains they had made by opposing management rather than by cooperating with it. If they were lucky, they would be able to press management openly to desist from such discriminatory behavior, thereby raising the status of the minority union in the eyes of its membership. Of course, this is what the struggle between management and the left-wing union in Figure 9.1 is all about.

The figures in Table 9.10 suggest clearly that the left-wing unions were less effective following the split. Nevertheless, Table 9.11 indicates a number of areas in which the minority left-wing unions seemed to have been particularly effective despite discrimination and a drop in their effectiveness relative to what it was before the split: wage struggles, campaigns to improve industrial hygiene and safety, and the application of pressure to protect the rights of individual members.

Table 9.10 *Union schisms and the union's effectiveness (unit: percentages)*

Answer	The 39 left-wing minority unions	The left-wing majority unions	All left-wing unions
(1) The union has not been effective at all since the split	12.8 (5)	42.8 (3)	17.4 (8)
(2) The union continues to be somewhat effective at times, but is not as effective as it was before the split	61.5 (24)	28.6 (2)	56.5 (26)
(3) There are times when the union is more effective than it was before the split	23.1 (9)	0	19.6 (9)
(4) The union is much more effective than it was before the split	2.6 (1)	0	2.2 (1)
(5) Don't know		28.6 (2)	4.3 (2)
TOTAL	100.0 (39)	100.0 (7)	100.0 (46)

Notes: (1) The above answers are to the following question: 'It is often said that the union movement will not produce much unless it can get its act together and face the enterprise with a single union at each firm. [Reflecting on the experience of your union,] How do you feel about this proposition?'
(2) The figures in the parentheses indicate the number of unions.

308

Table 9.11 *Areas in which the effectiveness of the minority union improved the most*

Area	Left-wing minority unions	Left-wing majority unions	All left-wing unions
(1) In the spring wage offensive	33.3	71.4	39.1
(2) In the struggle for bonuses and various allowances	7.7	14.3	8.7
(3) In the area of safety and hygiene	23.1	14.3	21.7
(4) In the area of fringe benefits	0.0	0.0	0.0
(5) In terms of the rights of union members	17.9	0.0	15.2
(6) In the fight against rationalization	5.1	0.0	4.3
(7) In the struggle against pollution	0.0	0.0	0.0
(8) In terms of the protection of workers in subcontracting firms	0.0	0.0	0.0
(9) In terms of maintaining contact with other unions and with worker's outside the firm	10.3	0.0	8.7
(10) In terms of ties with various citizens' groups or movements	0.0	0.0	0.0
(11) No answer	2.6	0.0	2.2
TOTAL	100.0	100.0	100.0
N	(39)	(7)	(46)

Note: Unions were asked to indicate the three areas in which the union's activities improved the most. This table shows the distribution of the single most improved area only.

By belonging to industrial federations, some of the minority unions might have been able to push for a kind of 'spill-over effect' and to obtain going rates in the industry whereas those which were affiliated with Dōmei or were even non-affiliated company unions seem to have had some difficulty in doing that. The left-wing minority unions also took the initiative in promoting industrial safety and hygiene. Finally, the members of the minority left-wing union always felt the brunt of discrimination. It perhaps was inevitable, then, that such unions would treat the issue of their members' rights as individuals seriously. Also, since many of the issues concerning the rights of individuals as unionists can easily be fought in the courts, many unions have successfully resorted to litigation.

For these reasons we can conclude that the minority left-wing unions were by the late 1970s doing better than most observers reckoned. Nevertheless, however surprising their performance may have been, they were still not strong enough to protect fully their membership from all forms of discrimination. Nor were they able to win significant concessions from management. Their strategy was one which sought to minimize discrimination, to obtain clarification of their rights in the courts, and to otherwise sidestep the efforts of management to undermine their activities. The left-wing minority union had to take its power relationships with management as a given and to work for improvements in areas where its relationship with management would not have become an insurmountable obstacle.

One such area would have been its relationship with the conservative union at the same firm (Table 9.12). However, only one of the 39 left-wing minority unions had established a formal procedure for communicating with its more conservative counterpart, and even that was not publicly acknowledged. The three columns on the right-hand side of the table suggest that relations between the two unions at the same enterprise may have been somewhat fixed at or shortly after the time the schism occurred, and that those relations did not change much as the events and emotions surrounding the schism receded into the past. A look behind the figures in columns A and B revealed that nearly half (44.8 percent) of the respondents cited their counterpart's refusal as the reason for not having such a mechanism in place; 31.1 percent claimed the two unions could not get along; and 24.8 percent simply said they could not work with the right-wing organization they did not seriously regard as a labour union. All of the left-wing unions actively wooed members of the conservative unions. They tended to include such unionists as a target group in their education programs in the hope that a reorientation might occur within the conservative union. The most important means of reaching members of the other union was a regular newspaper and handouts. Thirty percent of the unions published either a daily or a weekly newspaper; 85 percent used simple copy machines or mimeograph machines in order to issue an up-to-date news publication at frequent intervals. Ninety percent claimed that they distributed the paper to members of the conservative union, and 70 percent stated that the paper was edited primarily with that readership in mind. Only slightly over 20 percent replied that the paper was prepared primarily for their own members. The aim of most left-wing minority unions was clearly to expand their membership or to alter the environment in which they existed. As a contrast, the left-wing majority unions published with their own membership in mind and with the aim of maintaining their membership levels and improving the degree to which members were integrated into the organization.

Table 9.12 *The number of left-wing unions having various kinds of association with right-wing unions in the same firm*

Type of association	A Left-wing minority union	B Left-wing majority unions	Years since union split		
			C −5 years	D −6 years	E 11 or more years
(1) Formal mechanizm for inter-union communications	1	0	→ 0	1	0
(2) Private discussions between leaders in the respective unions	17	2	→ 4	6	9
(3) Social exchange between members of the respective unions	27	5	→10	11	11
(4) No communications as unions are in competitive relationships in the workshop	10	1	→ 1	2	8
TOTAL types of contact	55	8			
Number of unions	39	7			

Notes: (1) Unions were able to nominate each category independently, and some unions had several types of association.

The overall impression is that the educational or propaganda activity of the minority unions has gradually come to bear fruit. The result is an increasingly fluid situation on the shop floor in firms where left-wing minority unions are waging a struggle against more conservative majority enterprise unions. This conclusion is verified by the findings in Table 9.13. Seventy percent of the 39 minority unions felt that social exchange between their own members and members of the right-wing unions had been improved; 30 percent felt that such activities served ultimately to improve the climate so that the two unions could join forces in some activities in order to increase the pressure on management at the shop level. In this manner many minority unions felt they were able to influence their firm's industrial relations on the shop-floor. Forty three percent of the 39 minority unions claimed that, as a result of such activity, they were able to find officials in the conservative majority unions who had a sympathetic ear for their message and for their positive or sincere attitude.

Table 9.13: *Coverage of Union Membership*

| | Percentage of Left-Wing Unions Including Persons With Various Employment Statuses | |
	the 39 left-wing minority unions	the 7 left-wing majority unions
persons who have been fired	79.5	28.6
retired employees	43.6	14.3
temporary employees	69.2	28.6
workers employed by subcontractors	43.6	0.0

The right-hand portion of Table 9.12 suggests that such interchange increases over time: 28 of the unions which had coexisted over ten years had such exchange whereas only 15 of the unions coexisting less than six years had such contact.

V. A Vision for Change in the Activities of the Left-Wing Minority Enterprise Unions

In most cases, the potential of the enterprise union is delimited by its catchment: regular employees at the single firm. This in turn means that its goals will be defined in terms of those employees, and that room for activity aimed at strengthening class-based solidarity is quite limited. However, as Table 9.13 shows, the left-wing minority unions tended to have their doors open to (i) workers who had been fired and were no longer employees of the firm, (ii) temporary employees, (iii) retirees, and even (iv) those who were employed by subcontractors. Only a quarter of the minority unions refused to accept members from all four of those categories. Here, the difference with the left-wing majority unions should be noted. The minority unions obviously see these other categories of workers as an open target in their efforts to increase membership. However, careful attention needs to be paid to the basic ideological difference this strategy fosters. As opposed to the ideology of simply enlarging the pie – an approach which emphasizes more across the board for a small elite of core workers, the ideologies of the minority left-wing unions emphasized a working class solidarity which would encompass both core and non-core employees. There is then, in the left-wing minority union the possibility of breaking out of the closed organizational confines of the enterprise union.

Most large enterprise unions have become bureaucratic organizations not open to new ideas or to feedback in general from their members. The much smaller left-wing minority unions have experimented with several forms of 'direct democracy' in an effort to overcome the problems associated with impersonalized organization. Only 20 percent operated with a system of elected representatives who make the decisions (Table 9.14). Eighty percent allowed for all members to participate, although the experience of the left-wing majority unions (which are larger in size) suggests that direct democracy is possible only within small organizations. Forty three percent of the unions allowed any member to address the executive committee: one union even allowed ordinary members to attend and to vote at meetings of the executive committee (cf. Table 9.15). Given that the average size of the minority unions is 113 persons, it is obvious that a special effort had been made to involve ordinary members in the affairs of the union at the decision-making level. Again, there may be something to learn from these unions about ways to check the move toward centralization and bureaucratization in Japan's ordinary enterprise unions.

Since the single enterprise union often enjoys a situation in

Table 9.14 *Percentage distribution of left-wing unions by their style of decision making*

Style of decision-making	The 39 left-wing minority union	The 7 left-wing majority unions
Participation of all members (*zen-in-sanka*)	82.1	57.1
Participation only of representatives (*daigiin*)	17.9	42.9
TOTAL	100.0	100.0

Table 9.15 *Percentage distribution of left-wing unions by the extent to which the rank and file can participation in the deliberations of the executive committee*

Extent of participation	the 39 left-wing minority unions	the 7 left-wing majority unions
cannot attend executive committee meetings	25.6	28.6
can observe executive committee meetings without the right to debate	25.6	14.3
members have the right to observe and to debate but not the right to vote	46.2	42.9
members have the right to observe, to debate and to vote	2.6	0.0
Not clear	0.0	14.3
TOTAL	100.0	100.0

which all employees automatically affiliate with it, it is commonly argued by observers of the labor movement that such unions become slack in promoting activities which are in the true interests of their members. Once a union shop is formed there is no longer a need for the union to consider carefully its *raison d'être*, to prove itself to the membership, or to compete for the loyalty and support of its employees. However, because the left-wing minority union daily faces the struggle to survive, and because their members have the easy choice of belonging to the other union, it tends not only to be more responsive to its members needs but also to be more likely to have a motivated membership than is the large single enterprise union. Several concrete illustrations of this point may be provided.

First, the shop-floor unit of the minority union often takes the initiative in organizing shop-floor activities without waiting for the executive to develop its own action program. Five of the six left-wing minority unions with 200 or more members have workshops which published their own newspapers. Among them four had more than ten workshops which published their kown newspapers. Among them four had more than ten workshops which published their own newspapers. In four of the unions at least one workshop published a daily newspaper. In 90 percent of all 39 left-wing minority unions the workshop unit was able to negotiable directly with management on a number of issues such as the work environment, shortening hours of work and the size of work teams. Issues which were of vital importance to employees in all workshops accounted for about 60 percent of the problems dealt with by the union on the shop floor. The respondents to the survey indicated their belief that the spontaneousness with which the shop-floor unit dealt with such issues served to win support even among members of the right-wing union.

Second, many of the left-wing minority unions are willing to speak out at the executive level on behalf of the individual. It has been a common complaint against the large single enterprise union that the individual member gets lost among the institutionalized consultations between labor and management. Individuals who confront management and make waves on their own behalf are seen as disturbing the status quo. Peace and 'consensual' order have become the goals of the union leadership in many large enterprise unions. Not making waves has become part of the union's commitment to cooperate with management. That attitude is seen by many employees as placing a damper on the spontaneous involvement of members in the activities of their own union. However, nearly half (47.2 percent) of the 39 left-wing minority unions allowed individuals to speak out and negotiate directly with supervisory staff on their own behalf. Although the leadership in 27 percent of the 39 unions did report that they were not sure how to evaluate such behavior, the majority seemed to approve of individuals taking the initiative on their own behalf (Table 9.16). To permit and even to encourage such initiative is one way minority unions hope to enhance the ability and willingness of their members, who are positioned here and there throughout the firm, to fight against the inroads of management on the shop floor.

Table 9.16 *Views of the union leadership on individual negotiations with management on the shop floor*

Evaluation	the 39 left-wing minority unions	the 7 left-wing majority unions	the 8 right-wing unions
undesirable	8	0	8
desirable	21	1	0
other	0	0	0
don't know	10	6	0

Minority unions must also grapple financially. Because they do not reap economies of scale, their members have to bear a fairly heavy *per capita* burden in terms of their dues. Nearly two-thirds of the unions had to raise their dues or subscription rates following the formation of the other union. Dues rose about threefold on the average, and the per member fee was already 88,000 yen per annum at the end of 1975. Given this situation, it is not surprising that officials in the minority unions provided for their own lunches. After schisms occurred, most full-time officials experienced a drop in their income and all officials found they could no longer depend on the various allowances usually provided to union officials; the union officials in the left-wing minority unions felt economic restraints in one form or another. Despite these various kinds of problems many remained with the minority union and found in it an outlet for their own individualism. The end result appears not to have been lower morale, but to have been a greater willingness of individuals to dedicate themselves to the union. Of course, union members cannot be expected to pick up the tab whenever they participate in outside activities and the minority unions still find half of their budget going for *per diem* allowances so that the members will participate.

Most observers are aware of the ease with which single enterprise unions fall into the trap of cooperating with management, ending up with a shop floor fully controlled by management. The left-wing minority unions seem to have avoided that danger by adopting an ideology on the assumption that management and labor have different interests. Their ideological stance makes them wary of cooperative arrangements and places them in direct opposition to management on certain key issues. One fourth of the 39 left-wing minority unions refused to conclude collective bargaining agreements with management. Rather than viewing such agreement as being to their advantage, the unions seemed to feel more comfortable negotiating working conditions as the need arose and developing tactics appropriate at the time of negotiations. As the findings in Table 9.17 reveal, most of the unions subscribed to an ideology which embodied the notion of class conflict and the idea of political involvement. While this ideological orientation would seem to limit the extent to which these unions could develop close cooperative ties either with management or with the conservative union at the same firm, one would have to conclude that such an ideology was essential to the survival and well-being of the left-wing minority union which was seeking to present itself as a viable alternative to the dominant conservative enterprise union which was bent on cooperating with management at all costs.

Table 9.17 *Number of unions which adopt each of seven ideological orientations basic to labor-management relations*

Type of antagonism	the 39 left-wing minority unions	the 7 left-wing majority unions
(1) class antagonism	32	7
(2) socialistic ideology	29	6
(3) Marxist-Leninist ideology	19	3
(4) sympathy to reformist views	31	5
(5) sympathy to the idea that unions should be involved in politics	38	6
(6) support for Japan's reformist parties	29	5
(7) sentiments in support of anti-pollution movements	18	3

VI A Prognosis for the Minority Enterprise Unions in the 1980s

In considering the future of the minority enterprise unions, one must not overlook the strong commitment they have to developing a unified movement at the plant level. It is obvious that they would not be for any reunification which was simply a capitulation to and absorption into the conservative unions. Until there is a willingness among the majority unions to negotiate with the minority unions, the latter will opt for a continuation of the status quo. The results in Table 9.18 and 9.19 show, however, that left-wing minority unions continue to attach importance to attaining the ideal of having one union for all employees at the one firm. However, the push from the small left-wing unions was for unification *and* solidarity (*tōitsu to danketsu*). This meant that they would seek to change the conservative unions by example, by a continued campaign promoting propaganda and joint struggle on the shop floor, and by taking the initiative in bringing about reunification. In this sense they were true believers. How such reunification would take place in concrete terms was unclear.

The final resolution will depend heavily on the ability of the minority unions to hold their own or even to increase their membership. By the mid–1970s 38.5 percent of the left-wing minority unions were seeing a drop in membership, but a few had experienced increased membership, and 51.3 percent were maintaining existing levels (Table 9.20). However, there was

Table 9.18 *The views of left-wing unions on the existence of several unions within the firm at the time of the survey*

Evaluation of the existence of several unions	the 39 left-wing minority unions	the 7 left-wing majority unions	the 8 right-wing unions
the status quo is fine	2	0	2
not the best of worlds, but is inevitable	15	2	6
a situation which needs to be remedied	22	5	0

Table 9.19 *Assessments of the multiple-union situation by left-wing enterprise unions*

Assessment	the 39 left-wing minority unions	the 7 left-wing majority unions	the 8 right-wing unions
desirable and should remain the same	1	0	0
undesirable, but inevitable	4	0	5
both unions of our enterprise should explore ways to unite	34	7	3
both unions at our enterprise should unite immediately	0	0	0

optimism for the future: 38.5 percent anticipated increases and only 23.1 percent expected some decline. About half of the unions that had lost members replied that the decline had resulted from the large number retiring at the age of 55; about a fourth attributed the decline to a drop in the number of new employees entering the union. Sixty percent of the 12 left-wing unions which anticipated a further decline in their membership to result from retirement saw retirement as a problem for the future. The low number of young entrants was also a source of serious concern. This sombre outlook contrasted with the more sanguine expectations of the right-wing unions, more of whom anticipated a declining membership. To be sure, there was also some optimism. First is the position of the minority left-wing unions *vis-à-vis* the conservative unions with which they compete. As Table 9.20 indicates, their right-wing competitors may also have experienced declines in this context, the overall appeal of the left-wing minority union's high level of activity must be given its due. They seem to have been successful in creating the image that they look after all workers while the right-wing unions simply stood by inactively. Legal victories in the courts where unfair labor practices are concerned, favourable labor market conditions, and management's single-minded pursuit of further rationalization were also mentioned as factors which provided an environment further facilitating the growth of the minority unions. Many of the left-wing minority unions also mentioned a waning of the emotional hostility toward them. With the passage of time, many of the personalities who had directly been involved in the schism had retired. Moreover, the view of those completing the survey was that a number of changes in the national economy would also favour the minority unions. Recessionary conditions and further attempts to rationalize were seen as developments which would put further pressure on employees in the conservative unions. The minority unions were confident that they had developed a reputation for having championed the workers' interests in these regards.

Table 9.20 *Trends in union membership*

Trend	the 39 left-wing minority unions	the 7 left-wing majority unions	the 8 right-wing unions
A *Present trends*			
increasing membership	4	0	1
decreasing membership	15	4	4
stable membership	20	3	3
don't know	0	0	0
B *Anticipated future trends*			
increasing membership	14	3	4
decreasing membership	9	3	0
stable membership	11	0	3
don't know	5	1	1

Using my work on the minority unions as a starting point, Komatsu (1978) examined 55 such unions in the Mitaka, Ichikawa and Hachioji area in June 1977. His major findings were six. First, the minority unions had been able to maintain their commitment to the basic union principle of being an organization for the masses which remains independent from management. Second, the minority unions placed great emphasis on activities on the shop floor. Third, the minority unions engaged in activities to realize a wide variety of workers' demands, not just those for higher wages. Fourth, the minority unions demonstrated a commitment to industrial democracy. Fifth, the minority unions functioned to place a check on management profits and other activities done in the name of the enterprise. Six, the minority unions sought to foster a wide sense of solidarity with workers outside the enterprise. In all of these areas, he concluded, the left-wing minority unions were far in advance of the conservative majority unions.

Mine (1980) also uses my research as a starting point for his study. Looking carefully at five minority unions, he provides further evidence of the success of the minority union in terms of its many activities. He too emphasizes its adherence to the basic union principles of union democracy and advocacy against management during the period of rapid economic growth which saw the emergence and institutionalization of the conservative enterprise union. Finally, he provides evidence that the minority union has gained the respect and trust of many union members. The major difference between his conclusions and mine would be in the extent to which we emphasize differences in the functioning of the minority union and the single enterprise union.

These other studies corroborate the findings presented above in the last two chapters. They clearly suggest that the minority union must be seen as better living up to the ideals traditionally embodied in the union movement. It now remains for researchers to examine four areas more carefully. The first concerns the likelihood that these unions will continue to survive into the future. The second concerns the tangible fruits born by their efforts. The third would be the extent to which minority unions will be able to regain their status as majority unions. Assuming that these unions continue to exist, and there is every sign that they will, the fourth area for research regards the ways in which their organization and structure will adapt to the challenges of the late 1980s, the 1990s and beyond.

I have tried to consider these areas in this part of the book. Chapters 8 and 9 have considered the fourth area, though they also touch upon the first. Chapter 10 will throw some light on the first area, and Chapter 11 should give us some ideas about the potential of minority unions to contribute substantially to the workers' well-being. Chapter 11 will also give us reason to doubt propositions that the future of the conservative single enterprise unions is preordained. However history unfolds, the evidence in the next two chapters should suggest that there is more to the Japanese labor movement than the single enterprise union which has until now received so much attention in the writings about work and industrial relations in Japan.

10 The Road to Survival: Some Lessons from a Minority Union in the Electric Power Industry

This chapter considers some data collected in the late 1960s concerning the extent to which Japanese unions could continue to function as a class-based movement. The aim was to focus on the survival of Japan's minority unions as class-based organizations in looking for clues as to the future of the enterprise union. The continuing survival of the left-wing minority union will show that there is nothing inevitable about the enterprise union as it is commonly conceived. The analysis focuses on some minority unions which have survived for extended periods of time in the electric power industry. For a more detailed account of the analysis presented in this chapter, the reader is referred to the seven chapters provided elsewhere by Kawanishi (1981: 169–322).

Although a good deal has been written about the factors which have made it impossible for enterprise unions to exist as class-based organizations, little time has been spent by researchers probing the factors or conditions which might facilitate the further development of left-wing minority unions. The left-wing minority unions have for some time been subject to various forms of pressure which have been generated by management and many of the conservative, management-oriented number two unions associated with Dōmei.

For a long time those in the union movement believed that the number one unions could not stand up to the combined onslaught of management and the number two union. Moreover, the union movement had long developed around an ideology which emphasised unity and solidarity. For example, at the Fourth General Meeting of the World Federation of Trade Unions in 1948, the aims of having one enterprise union at each firm, one industrial union in each industry, and one national center in each country was clearly stated. By committing themselves to the principles of unity and solidarity, Japan's left-wing unions left themselves somewhat open to the initiatives of management and the number two unions. The strategy of the conservative forces called for 'division and then unity.' Having divided the number one union by forcing a schism, the internal democratic processes of decision-making were circumvented; however, once the number two union has been established and had developed a majority position, the call for unity was issued to the left-wing minority union. Leaders of the conservative union movement spear-headed Dōmei's push to form an alternative labor movement bent on cooperation with management in the 1960s and 1970s. In the 1980s they further took the initiative by calling for the reunification of the labor movement in the private sector, isolating Sōhyō and the left-wing unions in the public sector. Those moves culminated in the formation of Zenmin Rōren in November 1987.

Given this situation leaders in the left-wing union movement have long taken a fatalistic view of their own situation. However, it is interesting to note that a good number of left-wing minority unions have continued to exist despite predictions to the contrary. That such unions have continued to lead a viable existence for quite extended periods of time, leads us to look for some clues to their success. By uncovering some of the factors accounting for the success of the left-wing minority union and the legitimation of a working class culture along the lines described above in Chapter 8, some grounds for optimism may be found, and the way ahead opened some for a union movement oriented to serving the needs of Japan's many workers. To develop our analysis in this manner, the case study approach was again utilized.

This chapter begins by introducing briefly the union which formed the basis of the case study. It is a union with many older workers who have, despite experiencing various hardships as members of a minority union, held steadfastly to their principles through the years. The discussion then turns to consider the union's external affairs, including its relations with management and the conservative union in terms of the interaction shown above in Figure 9.1. The analysis focuses on how the minority union was able to survive and to enhance its position by adapting its policies to influence the surrounding environment. Attention is then shifted to a consideration of how the union has developed internal policies aimed at strengthening their members' sense of identification with the union and at heightening their motivation and morale as participants in a class-based labor movement.

I The Case Study

The discussion in this chapter concerns the union which was born out of the Chūgoku Regional Organization of Densan when it disbanded. Once number two enterprise unions had been formed in each of the regions in which electric power was produced, Denrōren (which was later to be the Dōmei-affiliated federation in the industry), was quickly formed as their umbrella organization. Densan was dissolved in March 1956. In some regions (Hokkaidō, Kantō and Hokuriku) Densan's regional organizations merged with those of the number two enterprise unions. In other regions (Tōhoku, Chūbu, Kansai, Shikoku and Kyūshū), Densan's regional organization simply dissolved and its members made individual decisions to join the Denrōren affiliate where they worked. However, the Chūgoku Regional Organization (which centered on the region around Hiroshima) refused to disband after the schism in 1953. It established itself as a union in its own right and carried on even when it became the minority union in 1955. Because it continues as a healthy minority union even in the late 1980s, this study of its activities in the early 1970s still has a particular significance for our understanding of the labor movement in contemporary Japan.

The successor of Densan's Chūgoku Regional Organization, this left-wing minority union was called 'Densan Chūgoku' (hereafter, DC). By the early 1970s it organized just over 10 percent of unionists in the industry (Table 10.1). Figure 10.1 shows the organizational structure of DC. Although Densan was dissolved in March 1956, many of the personal ties within Densan remained. It is not surprising, therefore, that some of them regrouped. In Kyushu the Densan branch dissolved itself in July 1958 and was absorbed into the Denrō union. However, when some of the 'old guard' criticized the new leadership at the union's annual convention the following year, they were made to resubmit their membership applications, again pledging allegiance to Denrō. The old guard saw this as harassment and an infringement on their freedom of speech. Arguing that the Denrō union had gone against basic principles of a free trade union movement, they left the union in August 1959 and formed their own union. In 1962 it joined with several other unions to form the All Japan Federation of Electrical Power Unions

Table 10.1 *Trends in the membership of Densan Chūgoku and the Denrō affiliate: 1953–88*

Year	A Number of unionists in Densan	B Number of unionists in Denrō	C Total number of unionists	D Percent of unionists in Densan $\frac{A}{C} \times 100$
1953	11,988	500	12,488	96.0
1954	7277	4800	12,077	60.3
1955	6056	6073	12,129	49.9
1956	4072	7866	11,938	34.1
1957	2543	9419	11,962	21.3
1958	2217	9628	11,845	18.7
1959	1896	9950	11,846	16.0
1960	1657	10,114	11,771	14.1
1961	1556	9901	11,457	13.6
1962	2033	9387	11,420	21.7
1963	1833	9463	11,296	16.2
1964	1775	9361	11,136	15.9
1965	1676	9235	10,911	15.4
1966	1558	9633	11,191	13.9
1967	1477	9617	11,094	13.3
1968	1400	9595	10,995	12.7
1969	1306	9284	10,590	12.3
1970	1189	9548	10,737	11.1
1971	1114	9492	10,606	10.5
1972	1045	9581	10,626	9.8
1973	1013	9646	10,659	9.5
1974	982	9560	10,542	9.3
1975	967	9596	10,563	9.2
1976	927	9538	10,465	8.9
1977	882	9609	10,491	8.4
1978	795	9606	10,401	7.6
1979	714	9558	10,272	7.0
1980	672	9668	10,340	6.5
1981	647	9907	10,554	6.1
1982	625	10,140	10,765	5.8
1983	583	10,292	10,875	5.4
1984	530	10,148	10,678	5.0
1985	472	10,278	10,750	4.4
1986	410	9807	10,217	4.0
1987	357	9852	10,209	3.5
1988	317	9887	10,204	3.1

Note: These figures are for July each year, and were compiled by the author from the reports made each year to DC's annual convention.

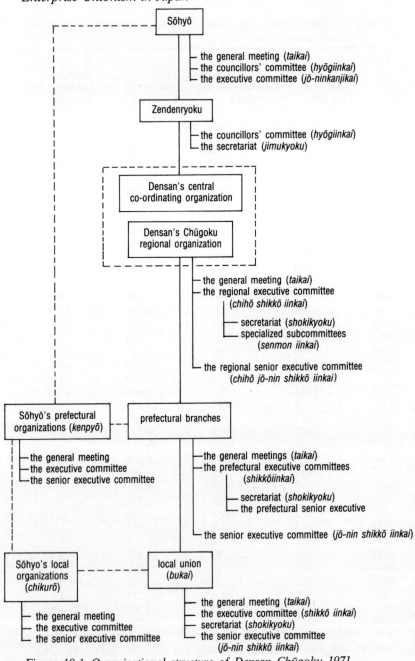

Figure 10.1 *Organizational structure of Densan Chūgoku 1971*

(Zendenryoku) which became affiliated with Sōhyō. DC played a central role in the establishment Zendenryoku. The industrial federation had one member on Sōhyō's Councillors Committee (*hyōgiinkai*) in 1975. Table 10.2 lists the unions belonging to Zendenryoku in 1971.

Table 10.2 *The affiliated membership of Zendenryoku: 1970*

Affiliated union	Year in which union was founded	Number of union members	Number of councillors on Zendenryoku's councillors' committee	Number of union officials in Zendenryoku
Nihon Denki Sangyō Rōdō Kumiai (Densan)	1946	1,200	3	3
Zenkyūshū Denryoku Rōdō Kumiai (Zenkyūden)	1959	3,000	7	4
Zenhokkaidō Denryoku Rōdō Kumiai (Zenhokuden)	1968	250	2	1
Zenkyūshū Kenshin Shūkinnin Rōdō Kumiai (Kenshūrō)	1961	600	2	1

At the time the research for this chapter was conducted in 1970 and 1971, the membership of the DC was 1200 persons. As Tables 10.3 and 10.4 show, the membership of DC would seem to have been considerably older than that of the Denrō affiliate (the number two union). Although data was not available from Denrō, it is safe to assume that nearly all employees not in DC would belong to the Denrō affiliate. It is interesting to note that 77.2 percent of the members of DC had been employed by the Chūgoku Electric Power Company for over twenty years (as opposed to only 42.8 percent of all employees). This means that the majority of workers had experienced the 1952 Densan dispute and the aftermath which led to the schism and to the formation of the second union. By broad occupational category, skilled workers accounted for 75.5 percent of DC's members (as opposed to 60 percent of all employees). Another 20.4 percent were office workers (as compared with 40 percent of all employees). The remaining 4.1 percent consisted of unskilled maintenance workers.

Table 10.3 *The percentage age distribution for the Densan Chūgoku membership and for the employees of the Chūgoku Electric Power Company*

Age group	DC membership	Employees of the Chūgoku Electric Power Company
–20	0.5	2.4
21–25	1.8	9.1
26–30	4.4	8.4
31–35	5.2	9.4
36–40	18.0	17.4
41–45	32.3	25.6
46–50	22.8	15.7
51–	15.0	11.6
Total	100.0	100.0
N	941	10,750

Notes: (1) The figures for the DC membership were compiled by the author from the information provided on the cover sheet on a survey form administered by DC in August 1971. Of the approximately 10,000 questionnaires returned, 941 had provided information on their age.
(2) The data on all employees was obtained from the personnel section chief in an interview conducted on 26 August 1971.

Table 10.4 *The percentage distribution of DC unionists and all employees by years of employment at the Chūgoku Electric Power Company*

Length of employment	DC membership	All employees of the Chūgoku Electric Power Company
–4	1.6	10.2
5–10	8.1	9.9
11–15	6.9	11.8
16–20	6.3	25.3
21–25	46.9	26.8
26–30	21.3	12.2
31–35	8.4	3.5
36–	0.6	0.3
Total	100.0	100.0
N	320	10,750

Notes: (1) The figures for the DC membership were compiled by the author from the information provided on the cover sheet on a survey form administered by DC in August 1971. Of the approximately 1000 questionnaires returned, 320 had provided information on the length of their employment at the power authority.
(2) The data on all employees was obtained from the personnel section chief in an interview conducted on 26 August 1971.

In the electric power industry it is common for skilled workers to be promoted to office jobs. The figures presented immediately above show that there are more operatives among the DC membership than among the Denrō union's membership even though DC's members are, on the average, much older. The data suggests that the members of DC seem to 'get stuck' in their jobs as skilled workers. Because the membership of DC is much older than that of the Denrō union, one would expect more of their members to have received promotion to office jobs given the importance generally attached to seniority in making such promotions. However, the reverse holds. In other words, union membership seems to be reflected in career patterns.

The union pays salaries to nine full-time officials and one part-time official. The number seems large as a percentage of the membership and their remuneration accounts for 52.7 percent of the union's budget. Seven of the nine full-time officials experienced the schism; they have worked as union officials for an average of 12.4 years. The head of DC had been an official for 25 years; his deputy, for 21 years. Among the officials there is considerable experience and expertise in union affairs.

II   Strategies for DC's External Affairs

A   Developing the union's role as a class organ

DC has worked hard to establish its reputation as an organization working on behalf of the working class. Several policy orientations underline its commitment to the working class. Four in particular deserve special mention.

1 The principle of equality   Above all else DC has consistently insisted that it be treated on par with the Denrō union in its negotiations with management. In terms of collective bargaining, it has forced management to negotiate simultaneously with it and the Denrō union and to deal with the same issues, although each union may be bargained with in a different location. DC has also called for management's two negotiating teams to be composed so that they represent nearly equal status and authority in terms of their negotiating profile. In terms of seniority, the second, third and fifth ranking persons were to represent management in its negotiations with DC; the first, fourth and sixth would form the negotiating team which met with the Denrō union.

The working conditions for members of DC and for those of the Denrō union were the same. Equal treatment extended to the concessions management made for the union: both unions received an office, members of both unions were permitted to engage in union activities during work hours, officials in both unions enjoyed the same privileges *vis-à-vis* this company, and both unions received dues from their membership through a check-off arrangement. In its joint consultations with management DC was very conscious of the fact that it had only a limited number of officials. It sought unsuccessfully to establish an arrangement whereby labor and management would send the same numbers to the joint consultative sessions. Nevertheless, the final arrangement was that management send no more than twice the number that participated from DC. Moreover, the head of DC would not attend a consultative session unless his counterpart in management – the power company's vice-president responsible for personnel affairs – also attended.

DC placed tremendous emphasis on the 'principle of equality' (*taitō gensoku*). When negotiations occurred on working conditions, it was common for management to reach agreement with the Denrō union first, and then to arrive at the same agreement with DC a few days later. One undesirable outcome of that arrangement for DC was that it contributed to the general perception among young employees that working conditions were set by the Denrō union and management, and that the members of DC, who were not really able to exercise their rights as unionist to bargain and to strike, simply received a 'spill-over' or 'flow-on' owing to the bargaining power of the other union. For that reason DC made a conscious decision to sometimes be the first union to settle with management. Of course, that involved a calculated risk, for it was always possible that the Denrō union would later obtain a better settlement.

In 1969, DC was able to use that strategy to improve its image. By taking the initiative to settle first with management in the struggle for better bonuses and improved travel allowances, it found that the leadership of the Denrō union came under pressure from its membership which wanted to know how it was that the employees in DC already knew when their bonuses would be paid whereas employees in Denro were still 'up in the air'. Although the leadership of DC was fully aware that management would welcome its initiative, taking advantage where possible to play the one union off against the other one, it saw certain benefits for itself as an exercise in public relations which would give the union a higher profile. In terms of appearing to implement the principle of equal treatment, that was an important accomplishment given the overall difficulties which DC faced as the minority union.

2 A socialist perspective Another important principle was the union's commitment to improving not only the working conditions of the regular employees who belonged to DC and Denrō, but also those of temporary employees and of the peripheral labour force employed by the industry's subcontractors. Its commitment to socialist principles could also be seen in its repeated call for the 'socialization of the electric power industry' (*denkijigyō shakaika*). DC's position called for union participation in management decisions as the first step toward socializing the industry. By taking the initiative in managing the industry, it was argued, the union could open the way for electricity consumers to be involved. The ultimate goal was an industry run by a tripartite board consisting of representatives from management, the union and consumers. The union was committed to the reformist parties and to the idea of having the industry rationalized under a socialist government. In line with that emphasis, the union maintained a serious interest in the political situation, and devoted about 15 percent of the space in its newspaper to explaining its ideological concerns in that regard. There was about one major article on this topic in two out of every three issues of the newspaper.

The focus of its campaign to democratize the industry was on limiting the extent to which management made a profit. In 1971 its main contention was with management's plans to reduce the number of power generating stations in the region by two thirds from 36 to 12 in order to provide electricity to rural or remote areas. Although fifty employees (including fifteen of its own members) living in rural areas supported management's plan and were to be transferred to one of the city offices, DC opposed the plan because it would increase the profits of the Chūgoku Electricity Authority at the expense of people living in the region's underpopulated areas. The campaign against the plan lasted for six months.

It involved the distribution of handbills in rural areas and house-to-house canvassing. DC worked to have local assemblies pass resolutions against the proposal. DC engaged in six negotiating sessions and launched one strike. Its stance contrasted sharply with that of the Denrō union which wholeheartedly supported the rationalizations as a means of obtaining higher wages for its members.

The principle of making class-based demands could also be seen in DC's position on working conditions, especially regarding wages. DC always worked through Zendenryoku and stayed within the framework of the joint struggle committee for the spring offensive. It has never broken ranks by independently arranging settlement to its own advantage at the expense of the other union it was working with. Rather than pushing for the ability-to-pay principle adopted by Denrō, an approach based on some notion of what the national or local economy could bear, DC aimed at settlements within the confines of (i) the lowest acceptable minimum which would be in line with the national minimum set by the joint struggle committee and (ii) an upper figure determined by household expenditure surveys among their members which indicated accurately the living costs actually borne by the families of its members.

3 Standing up to management A third way in which the DC leadership responded to its situation could be seen in its readiness to deal quickly with changes in the environment which affected its relations with management. Its responsiveness was reflected in the frequency of its negotiations with management. In 1970 alone it was in touch with management on a daily basis. Interaction in small committees occurred 89 times; in formal collective bargaining, 30 times; and in joint consultative sessions, 4 times.

Much of the contact between the union and management consisted of the deputy head (*fukuiinchō*) of DC meeting with the authority's section chief in charge of personnel management (*rōmu kachō*). Their meetings were fairly informal and covered a broad range of issues. The small committees often involved several officials from each side who came together to discuss in concrete terms the issues which would be dealt with in the bargaining and joint consultative sessions. Excluding minor contact which occurred on a daily basis, DC was negotiating with management nearly once every three days. In this regard it is important to note that DC was taking the initiative in most of these situations. The consultative sessions are mentioned in this context because DC considered them to be another form of collective bargaining.

DC's general opposition to management could also be seen in 1969 when it conducted a seven-month campaign against 47 points in management's rationalization plan. Whereas the Denrō union simply accepted the plan as it was, DC engaged in successive rounds of negotiation with management. Although it reached full agreement with management on only three points and management went ahead without accommodating the union's views on eleven points, DC did manage to win significant concessions. Adjustments were made with regard to 24 of the 47 concerns. Another three points were made the subject of continuing negotiations. Three were left for management to consider and four were left for further deliberations in the future.

The willingness of DC to stand up to management is also visible in the type of agreement it has negotiated with management. Compared with the agreement reached by the Denrō union, that of DC attaches much more weight to maintaining the union's vested interests, to underlining points of difference with management, and to protecting the rights of unionists as individual employees.

4 Including the periphery A fourth area in which DC's policy toward the outside world set it apart from the Denrō union was its relations with workers on the periphery. DC has steadfastly stood against the idea of enterprise egoism and solidarity which would benefit only a select aristocracy within the labor force. It was critical of unions which organized only employees at a single enterprise. DC pushed hard to abolish non-regular employment, and its demands in this regard were always reiterated when the collective bargaining agreement with management was being negotiated. However, it was never successful in obtaining management's agreement to a contract which would allow non-regular employees to join the union. The contract was always with a union which organized only regular employees (though excluding, of course, regular employees who handled confidential matters for management – such as those in the personnel section, those in security-related jobs and the telephone operators). Nevertheless, with regard to working conditions, DC always submitted demands for temporary employees with its demands for its own members.

The demands on behalf of the temporary employees were carefully based on the same guidelines which were used in formulating demands for the regular employees. Again, DC's general weakness in bargaining meant that such demands went largely unheeded, and the result has been widening differentials between regular employees and those casually employed. Nevertheless, its ideological stance did not go unnoticed by employees, and DC engaged in a number of activities aimed at facilitating or promoting the removal of the two-tiered system of employment.

In the early 1970s, some time before the notion of equal opportunity received widespread publicity, management's agreement with the Denrō union called for no women to be hired as regular employees. Women were to be employed only as office workers in non-career positions with the expectation that they would 'retire' at age 25. DC claimed this was unconstitutional, and attacked this kind of sex discrimination in nearly every issue of its newspaper. Again the Denrō union showed itself to be uninterested in an important human rights issue. Although DC was unable to win significant concessions from management, it nevertheless raised this issue at all levels at which it negotiated with management. One of the DC members even took it upon himself to write a private memorandum to the head of the Denrō union indignantly asking why his union took such a backward stance on that particular issue. Although women did not belong to DC because of their employment status, the union was able to persuade a number of the female employees to take their case to court. The minority union backed the women completely, and its position was further elevated by the general support it received in the mass media. It was later vindicated in 1978 when the courts ruled in favor of the women and the discriminatory employment system for women was abandoned by the company.

With regard to the peripheral labor force, DC's strong ties with unions of workers in subcontracting and related firms in the electric power industry should be mentioned. The power authority had developed an arrangement whereby most of the operations were subcontracted to smaller firms with employees of the authority working primarily in supervisory roles. The result was a sharp delineation between employees of the electric power authority and employees of the subcontractors. Densan took a stand against this hierarchical arrangement and sought to develop ties with employees in the peripheral sector. Accordingly, many of those underprivileged workers came to have a strong sense of identity with DC and its goals.

DC's adherence to the four policies just outlined has meant that it never fit in with the approach to industrial relations developed by Denrō and the management. The result had been considerable antagonism and conflict along the lines depicted above in Figure 9.1. Table 10.5 provides information on how the DC leadership evaluated its effectiveness in negotiating with management. The leadership was asked to evaluate the outcome of each of its negotiations as being 'successful,' 'acceptable' or 'unacceptable.' Although 30–40 percent of the issues were resolved 'successfully,' it must be noted that a favourable outcome was achieved largely in terms of the least important issues. The second category of 'acceptably resolved issues' included settlements with which DC could live although its view was that a different arrangement would have been more satisfactory. This category included many important issues such as wage rates, the provision of various allowances and other matters commonly covered in the collective bargaining agreement. The third category included issues on which management went ahead without the acquiescence of the minority union. Management negotiated with the Denrō union for its cooperation and then simply ignored the opposition of DC on a number

Table 10.5 *An evaluation of the effectiveness of DC's negotiations with management: a percentage distribution of outcomes in 1969, 1970 and 1971*

Outcome of negotiations with management	1969	1970	1971
1 successful	43.3	32.2	40.8
2 unsuccessful, but DC to accommodate	30.0	45.1	40.8
3 completely unsuccessful, with management going ahead on its own	26.7	22.7	18.4
All issues negotiated	100.0	100.0	100.0

Note: I was able to gain access to the union's 'Diary of Daily Activities' for the three years 1969–71. To my knowledge this is the only time a researcher has had access to a union diary. The original table with the raw tabulations contained information on roughly 10,000 issues in each of the years. Unfortunately, this table was too large to be published and this represents only the most condensed version. In preparing this for publication an effort was made to find the original table. However, having been constructed nearly twenty years ago, I was unable to find it among the many boxes of materials which have accumulated over the years.

of important issues, most of which involved changes to promote rationalization.

The second and third categories represented issues on which DC was largely or totally unable to influence the outcome. In each of the years for which information is available, the issues on which DC 'lost out' were the important ones. Moreover, they represented 60–70 percent of the issues dealt with. At the same time, its Denrō counterpart was able to say that it reached agreement on all the important issues. In this regard, then, the two unions cut a sharp contrast.

B   Strategies for survival

Despite its poor record in winning concessions from management on the most significant issues, DC continued to follow its 'class-based approach.' Its leadership continued to believe that such an approach would eventually highlight and exacerbate the potential contradictions and latent tensions existing between the policies of the Denrō union and those of management. There were two premises which fundamentally underpinned their views.

1 The best defense   To survive the minority union must always be quick to take the initiative. It must have the ability to fight tenaciously but intelligently. The 'iron law' of minority unions is that 'a good offense is the best defense.' The biggest threat to a minority union is repression and its failure to create a situation in which management will demonstrably bend over backwards to 'let sleeping dogs lie' rather than do anything which might be construed as taunting it with obviously repressive measures.

To avoid having its existence ignored and a situation developing in which all aspects of industrial relations in the power industry are determined exclusively by management and the Denrō union, DC continually had to make its existence publicly known. However, the constant tension created by such an approach serves only to steel the determination of both management and the majority union to destroy the minority union. There is often a kind of spiralling escalation. The result, however, is that the union's ideological orientation becomes an important source of self-identity for its members. Should DC have tried to adopt a more cooperative approach in dealing with management, it might well have lost its *raison d'être*. Moreover, should the Denrō union have decided to take a militant stance against management, its position would have been so compromised that it would immediately have lost its status as the dominant union.

It is no mean accomplishment for a minority union to survive such an escalation in hostilities. It must constantly be on guard to avoid being out manoeuvred. It is not simply a matter of fighting the number two union or management. The minority union must be especially alert for the coordinated attack of management and the conservative union. The tension produced by always being on edge has resulted in many a minority union seizing the opportunity to merge with the majority union 'in the name of solidarity and unity.' By 1970 DC had developed a certain toughness which could be seen in its outwardly aggressive stance toward management and the Denrō affiliate, and in its ability to stay on the offensive even when it was making little headway on concrete issues. Perhaps this toughness was one expression of the unionists' sense of *esprit de corps*.

2 *Solidarity* Particularly important in any minority union's struggle to survive is its ability to retain the commitment of its membership. For this reason as well, DC sought to maintain a high level of mobilization and a strong sense of crisis. Central to mobilizing its membership was the effort to provide members with a sense of destiny or mission and the effort to strengthen its organizational mission and the effort to strengthen organizational effectiveness.

Although most unions in Japan were caught off-balance by management's concerted offensive which accompanied the introduction of new technologies in the late 1950s and were able to respond only by coming around to help administer management's personnel policies during the period of rapid economic growth in the 1960s, DC was able to survive without sacrificing its commitment to the principles of the union movement in Japan immediately after the war. This accomplishment was the result of DC adhering to a policy of escalation, intensifying the sense of conflict in the industry's industrial relations, and instilling a sense of crisis in the minds of its members. Seen only in terms of improving each member's material standard of living, Densan and its remnant, DC, might be criticized for failing to respond adequately to the opportunities provided by rapid growth and by the emphasis placed on rationalizing activity. From that perspective, DC was out of step with the times. However, in its relations with management and the Denrō affiliate it was able to keep alive a broader perspective which emphasised the value of social equality and highlighted management's policies which contributed to greater inequality. In pursuing an antagonistic policy which emphasized points of difference with management, DC was able to articulate an alternative philosophy which had an attraction for those employees which constituted its membership. In doing so, its aim was to impart the impression that it was a union concerned about the welfare of its workers as responsible citizens within the broader confines of Japanese society.

C   Trends in DC's external affairs in the early 1970s

Trenchant adherence to a class-based ideology and action program was obviously one reason for DC's failure to make much progress in negotiations with management. In the late 1960s this presented DC's leadership with a serious dilemma. A growing number of members were becoming disillusioned with its ideology and critical of its inability to win significant concessions from management. They clamoured for a more conciliatory approach which would open the way for a more effective relationship with management. The crisis had to be dealt with head-on; failure to do so would mean that the strategy which had hitherto kept DC afloat would suddenly sink in the 1970s. Accordingly, DC had to come up with other ways of implementing its ideology. The resultant redirection in its activities could be seen in three areas.

1 Accepting management initiatives   One visible change could be seen in DC's willingness to compromise in a number of areas where it had previously adhered rather rigidly to its class-based ideology. This could be seen when compiling the data for Table 10.5. Over time it became more willing to accommodate itself to management initiatives. To give the impression that it had at least some influence while also avoiding open defeat DC's leadership began to accept management's policies but highlighted very minor changes for which it sought to claim credit.

Management was quick to respond to this change. Although its reliance on 'power politics' had resulted in a certain amount of attrition from DC to the Denrō union in the early years following the schism, it had come to realize that DC's membership had levelled off and had not declined further during the 1960s. Rather than inviting further attrition, its efforts to force further change upon DC had in some cases served only to produce an aggressive backlash from the DC membership. Moreover, as it had become the most profitable of the nine regional power authorities, management was increasingly confident that DC's existence could be dealt more effectively as an internal matter out of the public limelight.

Nearly the entire leadership of DC belonged to the Japan Socialist Party. About 100 of its members were extreme leftist activists who belonged to the Maoist faction. Another twenty were members of the Japan Communist Party, even further to the left. Given that situation, management saw in the more moderate leadership of DC a further means of controlling the radical leftist elements which it employed. In response to the changes initiated by the DC leadership, management's new policy in the early 1970s was essentially one of containment. It was like rounding up a minority and confining it to a reservation in a manner similar to the way Indians had been treated in America for many decades. Within certain parameters DC was given some leeway to influence the way in which work was organized. The end result was recognition of DC's right to exist. The new strategy called for management to avoid unnecessary confrontation with DC. Rather than active destruction it was premised on the idea that by simply waiting DC's membership would age, resulting in a natural decline in its membership as members come to face compulsory retirement.

This reorientation of DC and management resulted in some decline in the level of hostility, and it appeared that DC would have an easier time, at least in the short run. However, the increased willingness of the DC leadership to accept management's initiatives was interpreted by many as an admission of defeat or even as a kind of 'selling out' or 'cooptation.' There was thus the very real danger that this fundamental shift in the union's orientation would lead to its long-term downfall for the reasons given above. Its ideological identity was seriously compromised. However, DC entered the 1970s hoping to secure an autonomous base for moving out into surrounding territory occupied by Denrō on behalf of management. In the end this strategy and DC's open 'flaunting of the truce' led to renewed friction with management.

2 The propaganda offensive DC wandered off its 'reservation' when it undertook to develop a propaganda program aimed at the members of Denrō. The propaganda campaign rested on three assumptions. First was that many of Denrō's members could be 're-educated' so that they would recognize the appropriateness of an approach to unionism which was radically different to that being promoted by their union. Second was that a 're-educated' membership would itself reorient the Denrō union in the right direction. Third was that an invigorated Denrō membership would be more willing to fight concertedly for better working conditions. In concrete terms, DC sought to shift resources from a rather ineffective confrontation with management to wooing support from within Denrō. Strikes came to be conceived less in terms of their effect on management and more in terms of their educational value for members of Denro. Four examples of how this new policy was implemented are given below.

The written word gave DC a very conspicuous presence. Although DC had only 1200 members in 1970, its monthly four-page tabloid, *Densan Chūgoku*, had a circulation of 3000. It printed 1000–6000 copies of its special issues. The publication was obviously edited with the secondary readership – employees belonging to Denrō – in mind. The publication was always widely distributed throughout the offices and workshops so that every member of Denrō would have an opportunity to read it.

Another propaganda activity drawing attention to the views of the DC leadership was the campaign during *shunto* (the spring wage offensive). Because the offensive is a prolonged operation focusing on an issue of primary concern to the members of both unions (i.e., higher wages), the offensive provides a natural basis for joint-struggles. Denrō's inclination to ignore any DC initiative, including its call for a joint struggle prior to 1971, eventually gave way to jointly sponsored activity during the spring wage offensive in 1971. Left to its own devices, DC had usually launched its own offensive each February, choosing an early start to maximize the propaganda effect *vis-à-vis* the Denrō membership. The Denrō union usually launched its activities two months later in the second week of April. Denrō would usually reach a quick settlement which had been derived from that obtained by its counterpart in the Tokyo area. DC would then criticize the settlement and continue with its demands until the early part of May. In 1971, however, for the first time since its establishment, all the unions affiliated with Denrō, including the Denrō affiliate at the Chūgoku Electric Power Authority, were still negotiating with management in May. DC took advantage of the situation by intensifying its propaganda which called for a joint struggle on the shop floor. The outcome was that the Denrō affiliate broke a bit with the national leadership of Denrō and cooperated in five waves of strikes with DC. This seemed to open the way for a stronger sense of common purpose. The DC leadership hoped that a change in the orientation of its Denrō counterpart would be brought about, and that Denrō's very first dispute with management would alter the consciousness of its membership. The DC leadership was not so naive as to believe employees would on that basis alone shift their membership from the Denrō affiliate to DC. To have done so would immediately mark an employee for life: no promotions and no further salary rises based on career advancement. For an employee with a family to support much more was needed. However, the move still won for DC support among non-members. For example, one survey among Denrō members in Yamaguchi Prefecture in 1978 revealed that 95 percent felt it was good that DC existed (findings reported in an issue of *Densan Chūgoku* around that time).

A third area in which DC seemed to have been making headway was industrial safety. In the electric power industry, most accidents are serious and potentially fatal. In its propaganda, DC took the position that individual employees have the right on their own cognizance to refuse work or even to strike when they felt they had been given excessively dangerous work which put their lives in jeopardy. Denrō's leadership tended to argue that management's authority took priority over the individual's own judgment, and that only the union could decide when a member would refuse to work. And even then it was accepted that Denrō's leadership itself would not go against management on such issues. DC, however, had developed a fairly detailed outline of the conditions under which work was considered dangerous. It is interesting to note that there were no instances where management had reprimanded or withheld wages because a member of DC had refused to work. When a serious accident did occur, DC was quick to take action regardless of the union or firm with which the employee was affiliated. When a death occurred, a flag of mourning was immediately raised by DC workers in each work location. Collective bargaining was initiated to pinpoint responsibility for the accident. This approach helped to consolidate the perception that management and Denrō were less interested in safety than were the workers. The aim was to create the impression that DC could be trusted to look after the interests of employees whereas the Denrō affiliate and management would not. One of its successful slogans was, 'It's Densan Chūgoku which will look after your life!'

A fourth area highlighted in DC's propaganda concerned the rights of unionists. Its message was that Denrō should first move to protect its members' rights as unionists. It argued that union officials ought to make the rounds of the workshops, talking to members and listening to their grievances. It pushed the Denrō affiliate to reiterate constantly its right to broadcast union information to workers on the job. DC was very quick to point out instances where management tried to interfere in union affairs by putting pressure on foremen and their assistants. It was able to point to numerous examples where DC had obtained letters of apology from management or had pressured management to take disciplinary action against its own personnel when they have engaged in such practices. DC fought tirelessly for employees who had been fired. In the early 1970s a member of Denrō was fired for refusing to accept a disadvantageous transfer. The refusal was seen by management as contravening the conditions of employment. The Denrō union accepted that as management's prerogative. However, a member of DC working on the same floor spoke out on behalf of the Denrō unionist, only to be suspended from work for one month. (Such a suspension is a disciplinary measure just short of firing. For more details on this case, see Kawanishi 1981: 264–5). This obviously added to the impression that DC cared for the welfare of all employees and was willing to stand up and be counted when it came to matters concerning safety.

In this regard it should be noted that the rules or conditions of employment (*shūgyō kisoku*) are laid down in writing at every Japanese firm. Any infringement of the work rules leads to some kind of disciplinary action. Great importance is attached to the duty of employees to follow precisely the directives of management. Though never spelt out in full detail, management's discretion is extensive. Conditions of employment are often said to be a firm's independent constitution, and they are often seen as overriding the employee's rights as laid down in the Constitution of Japan. It is very difficult for employees to go to court over the conditions of employment which they accept when they take up employment with a firm. The current situation in part reflects the present imbalance of power between labor and management. It also reflects the conservative nature of the judiciary, especially at the higher levels where it is said that Supreme Court judges are given their decisions by the Prime Minister. For this reason, the willingness of DC to take up these issues must be given its due.

DC worked hard to live up to its slogan 'stick up for the worker by sticking to management like a bad smell.' While such propaganda can be dismissed simply as the duty of a minority union, or even as being counterproductive, it was an effective means of eliciting a positive response from among the members of Denrō. Evidence for this can be found in the amicable relationships which the members of DC were able to maintain with members of Denrō in the workshop. Despite the deep animosity between the leadership of the two unions, DC's record on sticking up for the rights of its members seems to have left a deep impression on the members of Denrō. DC's impact on the Denrō membership was further heightened by the failure of the Denrō affiliate to take any supportive action and by the general approval it gave to management's policies on such matters. Another evidence of this amity was the general receptivity of Denrō's members to the posters and handouts distributed by DC in the workshops. Denrō members could even be found to distribute DC's publications in workshops where there were no DC members. In the early 1970s members from the Denrō union often made anonymous contributions to DC. Realising that DC was stretched financially, at least some of Denrō's members must have felt that they benefitted from DC's existence. Although they were not prepared to join DC and thereby give up their chances for promotion, they did feel sympathy with its cause. There was also the large number of phone calls which came into DC's office from members of Denrō complaining about management or working conditions. Finally, Denrō members tacitly supported DC-sponsored strikes by finding excuses for declining work which was not being done by the DC unionists. Although the number of employees who actually shifted their union membership from Denrō to DC was small, there was a fair number who wrote to the office saying 'my body is with Denrō, but my heart is with Densan Chūgoku!'

3 Outflanking Denrō and the management No matter how hard DC might have tried, its overall effectiveness remained circumscribed by its minority status. It simply did not have the power to extract significant concessions from management on significant issues. Nor did it seem likely that it would be able over the short run to alter significantly the path Denrō was following. Accordingly, to bolster its position at the bargaining table and to improve its status in the eyes of the Denrō employees, it sought to raise its profile by 'externalizing' its industrial relations. The plan was to 'outflank' management and the majority union by developing a program of activities outside the firm.

The most obvious step in that direction was improved ties with Sōhyō. At the time it was able to shift attention from its minority status within the firm to the fact that it was at the national level affiliated with Sōhyō. At that time Sōhyō was the majority national labor center (with 4.3 million affiliated unionists in 1970), whereas Denrō was affiliated with Dōmei, the minority national centre (with only 2.1 million members). This strategy served to legitimate DC in the eyes of many employees. It would have been suicidal for a minority union which was struggling just to exist in a privately owned public utility to engage in a politically oriented strike. To have done so would have opened the door for legally recognized disciplinary action under the labor relations legislation for public enterprises. The disciplinary action against striking railway workers in the Japan National Railways was legend. Nevertheless, DC faithfully supported the political action of Sōhyō because of the benefits just mentioned.

Another goal was to strengthen Zendenryoku. This was called DC's 'multiple union strategy' (*fukusū kumiairon*). By bringing these together with Zendenryoku, DC had hoped to regenerate industrial unionism in the electric power industry. For example, its support for the newly formed minority union in Hokkaido is particularly worth mentioning. In 1969 it sent twenty organizers to assist the new union with its membership drive and a fund-raising campaign which brought the new union one million yen. Each of the volunteers used two weeks' holiday leave to make the trip. DC entered the 1970s knowing there were left-wing minority unions at three of the nation's nine regional electric power authorities. Although it was unsuccessful in promoting the formation of such unions at the other six authorities, the initial success of this strategy improved the confidence of the DC leadership. The fact that many of labor's vested rights continue to be recognized in the three electric power authorities where Zendenryoku branches organized resistance to management has not gone unnoticed. It is particularly significant that the rights which Hokkaido's electric power workers lost while the Denrō affiliate was their sole representative were regained when Zendenryoku's branch was established.

DC's biggest achievement was in continuing to exist and to function as an independent union after Densan was disbanded. At the time Densan disbanded, there were two views among activists at the local level. One was to fight on as a minority union; the other was to work from within the Denrō union. In the end, DC proved viable while the activists who had entered the Denrō affiliate soon found themselves neutralized, isolated from decision-making positions and unable to affect the policies pursued by their union officials. Those who remained with DC were vindicated in arguing that unity and numbers for the sake of numbers would not generate a strong union movement unless there was a carefully reasoned philosophy behind it. They hoped that DC would in the end win on principle even though it would temporarily become a minority union. In pushing for its own brand of multiple unionism, the DC leadership believed that DC was the guardian of the correct philosophy and that the majority Denrō unions would eventually come to grief as long as there were minority unions which pursued the proper objectives in their dealings with the various power companies.

While recognizing the problems inherent in DC's external policies, one would have to say that its general reorientation and the subsequent propaganda campaign in the 1960s had been fairly effective in broadening its base of support. As a result DC's existence is ensured at least for the near future. DC (and the Densan leadership before it) had been criticized both by its own members and by others for being too rigid in its adherence to a narrowly focused ideology. Developments in the 1960s showed, however, that it could be much more flexible than most people thought. This flexibility and the willingness of the DC leadership to adjust its strategies accounted for the reinvigoration of DC as a minority union in the late 1960s and early 1970s.

To survive, minority unions must be flexible. DC demonstrated such flexibility at several critical points during its life. Some time earlier Nakayama Ichirō, a member of the Central Labor

Relations Commission which often handled cases involving Densan, once stated that Densan was a very intelligent union, 'coldly self-interested in its calculations' (Rōdō Sōgi Jittai Chōsa 1957: 23). He was, no doubt, referring to this ability of the Densan leadership to command their union in a flexible manner. (It is important to note that the Chūgoku branch had been instrumental in the affairs of Densan, supplying many of its leaders and taking on responsibility for the affairs of Densan, including an important legal case after its executive disbanded in 1956. What Nakayama had said about the Densan leadership in the late 1950s would certainly have applied to the DC leadership over a decade later.)

III The Internal Affairs of Densan Chūgoku

In order to maintain the loyalty of its membership, DC's successful adaptation to the external situation had to be accompanied by policies which would create in its organizational structure an openness to its members. However, a careful analysis of DC in the mid–1960s shows that communications between the leadership and the rank-and-file were hierarchical, that the leadership was bureaucratic and authoritarian, that the education programs for its members were underdeveloped, and that it was only moderately able to provide the types of mutual aid usually supplied by unions to their members. Accordingly, in trying to account for the high motivation of its membership, we might hypothesize that other factors are important. For example, attention might be given to DC's sensitivity to the aspirations and values of its members.

A Satisfying aspirations of the members

By staying with DC, employees sacrificed their material well-being. It would be difficult to conclude that the union helped its members satisfy their material aspirations. Far from satisfied with the situation in which they found themselves, many members directed their resentment toward their union and toward management. They were displeased with management for discriminating against them (i.e., for treating members of the Denrō union more favourably), and felt that they received differential treatment in three areas.

1 Wages The salary system was structured so that there would be a base wage (*kijunnai chingin*) plus an additional amount (*kijungai chingin*). The former consisted of a job component (*kihonkyū* or *shokumukyū*) (75.3 percent of average total monthly earnings in 1971), a skill allowance (*shikaku teate* or *shokunōkyū*) (5.8 percent) and a family allowance (*setai teate*) (10.1 percent). Although the third component depended on size of the employee's family and was objectively set, the first two were determined within an evaluation system which simply formalized the arbitrary assessments of personnel handed down by management. In other words, management had direct control over 81 percent of the employee's monthly earnings.

In 1966 the skill allowance (*shikaku teate*) was introduced. Feeling that the changes in job pay had been somewhat watered down owing to the opposition of DC, the skill allowance was seen by management as another means of establishing order in the Electric Power Authority. The secondary array of job classifications shown in Table 10.6 was developed. For all intents and purposes the allowances served as a means of reintroducing the prewar system of job statuses with a new name.

Although the amount seemed small, even in 1971, the fact was that its relative importance in the wage system was increasing with time. Members of DC who felt they were discriminated against were particularly upset by the fact that management would never spell out the criteria for promotion, for awarding those in one category more than those in another or for assigning employees to different categories. Because decisions rested on very subjective evaluations, the DC unionists felt particularly vulnerable. In 1971, 72.7 percent of the total automatic across-the-board increment and 22.1 percent of the total negotiated wage increase were to be distributed as skill allowances. The members of DC who were surveyed for this research complained bitterly about discrimination in the pay system, offering an endless number of concrete examples from their own experience. Sixty-three percent of DC's members said their wives were also working in order to make ends meet. Although similar figures

Table 10.6 *The payment of the skill allowance*

Office workers	Skill category and level Technical staff	Medical personnel	Fixed maximum number of employees	Amount of the allowance (in yen)
A Administrative officer	A Technician	A Medical personnel		
class 1	class 1	class 1	209	18,100
class 2	class 2	class 2	454	14,400
class 3	class 3	class 3	689	11,200
B Administrative assistant	B Technical assistant			
class 1	class 1	class 4	1125	9,100
class 2	class 2	class 5	2586	7,300
C Clerk	C Technical operator			
class 1	class 1	class 6	2593	6,100
class 2	class 2	class 7	1668	4,900
class 3	class 3	class 8	919	4,200
class 4	class 4	class 9	46	3,700
D Clerk's assistant	D Operator's assistant	—	—	3,600
E Office worker	E Technical worker	—	—	3,200
F Probation employee	F Probation employee	B Probation employee		2,400

do not exist for members of Denrō, the percentage would be higher for employees belonging to DC than that for the average employee.

2 Promotion   DC members were dissatisfied with their prospects for promotion. Twenty were assistant administrative officers (*shunin*), the lowest supervisory position, but none held higher positions. None of DC's members had been promoted to managerial posts. However, the age structure of its membership suggested there ought to have been many members suitably qualified. If one keeps in mind the fact that about 20 percent of employees in these kinds of large firms have some kind of title and that the Chūgoku Electric Power Authority employed about 10,000 persons, one would have expected there to be about 200 members of DC in such positions had the age structure been the same.

These figures show dramatically the extent to which DC's members were closed out when it came to promotion. It is interesting to note, however, that DC's members seemed willing to accept this situation as an inevitable outcome of being affiliated with DC and its anti-management ideological stance.

3 Worker evaluations In relation to the wage system and promotion, employees were particularly unhappy about the way they were evaluated for their on-the-job performance. The evaluations resulted in a grade from A (top) to E (bottom) being awarded to each employee. Most members of DC received the grade 'C.' As only 10 percent of all employees received D's or E's, the unionists in DC felt they were actually being given the lowest grade.

If DC had been able to do something about its members' dissatisfaction with these kinds of discrimination, it would have gone a long way toward channelling or releasing a good deal of its members' pent-up hostility toward management. However, since it was unable to do so, it entered the 1970s having to live with the fact that a certain amount of the frustration was being directed at its own inefficacy. The frustration with DC expressed itself in several ways. One was in the rather hysterical demand that DC launch an all-out struggle to remove such discrimination. As such dissatisfaction fed on itself, the latent anxiety of the members came to the surface. Tired and overworked without deserved promotions, some of the older and experienced members would write in the union paper confessing their conversion to another set of values more in line with those advocated by the Denrō union. Some even called for the DC leadership to reach an accord with the Denrō affiliate so that DC could be absorbed within it. There were also the outright defections. As Table 10.7 shows, DC was losing members even in the late 1960s and early 1970s. Although the members' dissatisfaction with the union's inability to eliminate the discrimination was obvious, and even accounted for a number of persons leaving the organization each year, the number of defections was surprisingly small considering the situation and the depth of the members' feelings. The average number of defectors was only 1.4 times the number of members who retired each year. That represented an attrition rate of only 4 or 5 percent per year. The only remaining explanation for DC's success is its sensitivity to the value orientations of its membership.

Table 10.7 *Changes in the DC membership: 1966–88 (unit: persons)*

Year	A Number joining or returning to DC	B Number of members quitting DC	C Number of members leaving due to retirement	D B + C	E A − D	F Membership of DC
1966	50	104	54	158	−108	1,558
1967	50	79	53	132	−82	1,477
1968	14	53	44	97	−83	1,400
1969	28	74	38	112	−84	1,306
1970	9	74	43	117	−108	1,189
1971	9	34	43	77	−68	1,114
1972	12	34	47	81	−69	1,045
*1973	22	14	40	54	−32	1,013
*1974	24	18	37	55	−31	982
*1975	27	15	27	42	−15	967
1976	12	24	28	52	−40	927
1977	6	19	32	51	−45	882
1978	2	51	38	89	−87	795
1979	3	21	63	84	−81	714
1980	7	7	42	49	−42	672
*1981	9	2	32	34	−25	647
*1982	6	5	23	28	−22	625
*1983	5	4	43	47	−42	583
1984	2	4	51	55	−53	530
*1985	6	1	63	64	−58	472
1986	2	4	60	64	−62	410
1987	1	5	49	54	−53	357
1988	1	5	36	41	−40	317
Totals	307	651	986	1,637	−1,330	
Yearly average	13.3	28.3	42.9	71.2	−57.8	
Yearly average during the period of this study (1966–71)	26.7	69.7	45.8	115.5	−88.8	

Notes 1 No records were kept on the situation before 1966.

2 The figures in columns E and F are not always in accord with each other. The small discrepancy indicates the difficulty which even DC had in keeping track of its members.

3 The years marked with an astrick are those in which the number of employees joining DC was greater than the number quitting.

4 With regard to column A, the union figures do not allow those joining DC for the first time and those returning to DC from Denrō to be separated.

5 The figures are for the year ending in July, and were taken from reports presented to the annual convention each year.

B Responding to the values of the membership

The word 'value orientation' is used in this essay to refer to the workers' basic orientation (*genri no ishiki*). Mita (1966: 93) described this orientation as 'the orientation which one has to provide consistency to his behavior by reference to an internalized moral system and set of principles.' This author interviewed a large number of DC unionists and came away with the impressions given below. (For more detail and the identities of those interviewed the reader is referred to Kawanishi 1981: Part Two). The interviews suggested that the members of DC had five basic value orientations. Each is described briefly.

1 Commitment to socialism   DC inherited an ideology which emphasized the inevitability of economic collapse in the capitalist world and the revolution of the impoverished. The inevitability of change resulted in a passive stance – a waiting for the revolution-producing conditions to emerge. DC's policies were premised on a belief in the inevitability of a socialist revolution. For the old guard such a revolution was guaranteed by a kind of iron law. Most of DC's members had joined Densan at a time when this brand of ascetic socialism was quite prevalent. They had a philosophical outlook which cultivated a willingness to wait. This contrasted with the impatience for change which seemed to characterize the outlook of the younger generation.

2 A pride in Densan   Most members of DC were aware of Densan's role in the postwar labor movement and took a special pride in continuing the Densan tradition. With DC's transition to minority status, its hard-core members came to feel they had been given the special mission of keeping alive the fighting spirit that was Densan's. They referred to themselves as 'the high-minded individuals who dared assume the heavy responsibility of carrying the burden of Densan's honor and glory.'

3 Spreading the word   Most members felt an abiding commitment to raise the consciousness of the employees who had joined the Denrō affiliate.

4 Comrades DC members possessed a strong sense of loyalty toward fellow unionists. They were imbued by the union with a strong disdain for anyone who compromised or otherwise betrayed another member. They were repeatedly told how the central figures in the move to establish the Denrō affiliate had later joined management and sold out the union movement. By constantly repeating this message, the union had been able to attach a strong feeling of guilt to any thought of leaving DC. The principle of loyalty thereby functioned to limit attrition.

5 Solidarity with Sōhyō By the end of the 1960s Sōhyō's prominence as the leader of the Japanese labor movement had begun to wane. This led to a strengthening of DC's commitment to Sōhyō. The collapse of Sōhyō would mean that members of DC could no longer claim to be affiliated with majority unionism in Japan. A marked movement to right-wing unionism, no matter how symbolic it might be, would serve only to undermine the the very basis on which the argument for multiple unionism and the belief in the inevitably of revolution rested. For this reason the DC leadership even more readily accepted the Sōhyō line. The Sōhyō line called for opposition to management, the achievement of socialism, support to the peace movement (meaning no rearmament, no military alliances, disarmament, no nuclear weapons, and no nuclear power plants), and an emphasis on regionalism in the union movement. This contrasted with Dōmei's call for cooperation with management, its recognition for West European socialism (recognizing capitalist modes of production, its support for negotiated security (the mutual security treaty with the USA, the peaceful use of nuclear energy, and only partial disarmament), and its promotion of an American-style business unionism based on industrial federations.

The reason for DC's ability to maintain its membership at a stable level once the initial schism had occurred and the number two union had stabilized itself must be found in the fact that its members had internalized the five values explained just above. If that prognosis is correct, and if, further, we can generalize from the experience of DC, the internalization of those values can be accepted as another key increment contributing to the success of Japan's radical minority unions.

C   The internalization of left-wing values

1 Living up to expectations   By subscribing to the five values just mentioned, members of DC were able to maintain a necessary measure of optimism in the face of depressing odds. Their optimism was linked to expectations they entertained for their fellow unionists. First, on the level of the individual unionist there was the security which came from sharing the belief that they would not be betrayed by their mates. Second, on the external level was the expectation that Sōhyō, Zendenryoku and the other regional affiliates of Zendenryoku (all descendants of Densan) would continue to carry forward the mission that was Densan's. In all of DC's activities there was a reference to this hope that by remaining true to the Densan ideals DC would eventually pave the way for a new era of industrial unionism. In all of DC's activities there was a reference to this hope that by remaining true to Densan's ideals DC would eventually pave the way for a new era of industrial unionism.

Finally, there were the expectations which some members of management and some members of the older union held her head toward the DC unionists. Many of the Denrō unionists felt that DC was in its principles more of a labor union than was the Denrō affiliate. At the same time, moreover, Denrō's members recognized that they had deserted DC for a higher material standard of living. In succumbing to the 'charm of the yen,' many of those employees came to feel morally inferior to those in DC who had accepted lower incomes, had learned to live on the short end of various discriminating practices, and had remained loyal to a legitimate union movement. Feeling they were envied by members of the other union, many unionists in DC felt a certain pride which worked to reinforce in them a sense of moral superiority.

Among management as well there were those who privately admired the DC unionists. University graduates, they had been members of Densan and mainstream activities until the dispute of 1952. However, able to read the writing on the wall, they withdrew from union activity and were eventually able to gain promotion to their current positions. Had many of DC's capable leaders also turned their backs on union activity they too would have achieved a similar status within the power authority. Instead, however, they had accepted honest poverty and remained true to their ideals. Many managers empathized with the DC leaders whom they left behind to man the trenches. In their sympathy with the cause of such dedicated union leaders, they were willing to 'hold back' on implementing repressive measures against the union. Knowledge that some managers felt this way served to reinforce the belief of the DC leaders that they had 'done the right thing'.

2 Defiance A second contributing factor was the general aura of defiance toward Denrō which was engendered in many of DC's activities. This was one manifestation of the sense of moral superiority which members of DC held toward the leadership in Denrō. There was a sharp distinction between those who were ideologically correct (i.e., the members of DC) and the 'heretics' (those who led Denrō). Even if the Denrō affiliate was able to increase its influence by procedures legally acceptable in a court of law, it could never attain a moral supremacy over DC. Basic to the moral framework in which DC members put themselves above many of those belonging to the Denrō union were the notions of '*sei*' (what is proper or righteous) and '*ja*' (what is wrong or improper). Those in DC had behaved properly or correctly; those in Denrō had not.

3 Precedence in tradition and custom The DC membership followed established practice. It seemed reluctant to disturb set patterns for doing things or to stray from established tradition. This orientation manifested itself in two ways. Once a certain behavior has been practiced for so long and a positive value is attached to it, a kind of 'clean-record mentality' or 'record-breaking endurance mentality' seems to emerge. Not having given in so far and with retirement coming into view, there was a certain psychology according to which the unionists felt spurred on to acquire an unblemished record in the union movement. Many men who had not been particularly active in DC's activities nevertheless were quite adamant in rejecting the temptation to cross over. In other words, once they had resigned themselves to the fact that they were stuck on the promotion ladder without the prospect of ever receiving top wages, most DC unionists were able to adjust to the material standard of living which could be achieved even with the discrimination. As Mita (1966: 66–7) once observed, much 'heroic behavior' can be understood as an attempt to avoid the sense of dislocation which comes in breaking with the established norms or expectations which have been internalized in one's own regime.

Another source of the members' commitment to tradition was their emotional attachment to DC in a manner not dissimilar to the special feeling one has for one's home town. In their own minds is a kind of romanticized vision of the past, memories of Densan's golden age when the union dominated management. Many of the unionists who had experienced the freedom of those days had great difficulty adjusting to the regimentation which a reinvigorated management brought in following Densan's defeat at the end of 1952. The more management sought to control their work the more these unionists idealized the past, thereby further strengthening them in their resolve against management. In other words, many of the older members who had been with Densan before 1952 stayed with Densan because they could not adapt to the new environment at work.

4 Human relations The human relationships which members developed in DC tended to please the members and to give them a certain inner peace with themselves. The industry experienced a tremendous amount of rationalization during the 1960s. Not only was new technology introduced, personnel policies were structured to make work as competitive as possible for those who wanted promotion. For many, human relationships became a means to an end. The very pronounced loneliness at the top meant those who made it to the top lost the joy of being with their work mates. Because DC unionists were precluded from promotion, they were better able to focus on the quality of their interpersonal relationships. Accordingly, their sense of community and solidarity with other members of DC was much stronger than was the case for most Denrō unionists. For the same reason, DC unionists also received a certain satisfaction from having the time necessary to being more socially aware. By the early 1970s management had come to treat employees in DC with kid gloves, fearful of creating a row or giving the employees a pretext for an open dispute. However, it was said that they would make all kinds of unreasonable demands on Denrō's members. Always mindful of the need to flatter their superiors, the Densan employee felt a certain pride in being able to command management's respect. 'Rather than changing to Denrō and then being at someone's beck and call,' they would say, 'it was better to stay in DC and feel comfortable in standing up to management.'

5 Assimilation in the outside world By belonging to a number of related groups it is often the case that a person's loyalty to the organization of primary affiliation is strengthened. In the case that a person's loyalty to the organization of primary affiliation is strengthened. In the case of DC members one outside group with which they often had close ties was the local Sōhyō chapter, Chikurō (cf. Figure 10.1). One could even say that DC members played a central role in the life of Chikurō. Their own subgroup (*bunkai*) supplied a good number of the officials in Chikurō. Twenty-five DC members were elected to local government bodies at the village, city and prefectural level owing to the support given Chikurō. In 1970 DC stood an additional seventeen candidates in the unified local elections. Sixteen were elected. That record is a tribute to the solid reputation for fulfilling 'its responsibility' to supply leadership for the local labor movement. It also served to keep DC members within the fold. Because the path to getting ahead at work was blocked within the power authority, a number of DC members sought an outlet for their 'political' ambitions in local politics. Given the broad base of support which Chikurō could mobilize, it was clearly to their advantage to stay in DC. Denrō unionists sought a career within the company; DC unionists looked for it outside in the political arena.

Reflecting this political orientation, another association in which DC members were active was the Japan Socialist Party which 75.6 percent of DC members supported in 1970. Another 6.9 percent supported one of the other political parties. The involvement in politics was much higher than that found in most enterprise unions. In this way, then, certain of the DC unionists were able to realize their political aspirations and this was satisfying for many of them. The end result was a greater commitment to DC and a lower rate of attrition than would otherwise have been the case. Not surprisingly, therefore, a good number of DC's new members joined DC and a political party simultaneously.

D Staying put

As the DC member's consciousness was heightened, so too was his commitment to stick with DC strengthened. For this reason, it was said, 'DC behaved conservatively with a radical ideology.' This is illustrated by the fact that as the average age of its membership rose the vitality of DC seemed to slip a little, and it later failed to display its earlier ability to respond to the structural changes being initiated by management. Nevertheless, rather than saying that the DC membership had become increasingly conservative, it would be more accurate to say that it was adhering more rigidly to its basic orientation. The many years spent fighting the system gave them an inner strength or even keel. Many of the DC members had learned how to stand alone. Their sense of spiritual oneness with their mates has provided a basis for holding fast in the face of organizational pressures and against the temptation of material rewards. DC has drawn on that strength.

IV Some Generalizations about the Future of Enterprise Unionism and the Minority Union

In this chapter a case study was introduced to illustrate some of the conditions which allow a minority enterprise union adhering to a class based ideology to exist over a long period of time. It was argued that three basic conditions were met. First, the minority union held to its commitment to be a class-based organization and consistently pursued a confrontationalist line with the management. Second, the union was able to develop a balanced set of programs which allowed it to be in equilibrium and to function in a stable manner. Third, DC allowed its members to pursue on an individual basis outside of DC and the work environment strong philosophical commitments to certain values. While these elements seem clearly to have worked for the other unions in Zendenryoku as well, to what extent can generalizations be drawn for the Japanese trade union movement as a whole?

To answer that question a functional perspective is useful. Unions behaving as class-based organizations have some advantage *vis-à-vis* the conservative union when two or more enterprise unions exist at the same firm. There are times when the class-oriented union and the management-oriented union work to complement each other. In other words, the absence of either would be detrimental to workers belonging to the other union. In most instances the enterprise union is a contradiction. It proclaims a socialistic idealism which underlines its commitment, in principle, to functioning as a class-based organization. In reality, however, it works as an employee organization oriented to implementing management's personnel policies. The result is that considerable time and energy are expended on internally-oriented activities to maintain its organizational integrity, and few resources are left over for externally-oriented activities. Enterprise unions which include all of the employees at a single enterprise face the difficult problem of unifying and integrating a disparate group of individuals who have different interests and commitments. The idealism on which the union movement was founded is left to the individual to work out for himself, and the union becomes bogged down in the everyday routine of administering management's personnel policies. Those who argue that enterprise unionism is inevitably business unionism are pointing to this phenomenon.

When multiple unions exist, the freedom of individuals to join the union of their choice is guaranteed. Each union can put out its own ideological flag. DC can proclaim its egalitarian class orientation and the Denrō affiliate can seek to attract employees with its productivity-based approach. The idealistic employees are able to affiliate with DC, while the more materialistically-oriented employees can find their place in the Denrō affiliate. In this fashion, each of the enterprise unions is better able to reflect the interests of its membership and can function relatively smoothly without worrying about dissident members. In the case of DC, once the 'better life-style faction' had left, those who remained could proceed in their own manner, seeking their own objectives without feeling the need to be constantly looking over their shoulder. Moreover, DC was not having to struggle along without the working conditions of its members being guaranteed.

Because DC has, in consistently adhering to its principle of equality, been able to guarantee for its members minimal working conditions, DC unionists were able to engage in whatever activities met their fancy without worrying greatly about the consequences in terms of vicious reprisals from management or the other union. The same is also true for the Denrō union. Accordingly, this arrangement functions latently to produce a division of labor, with each union taking responsibility for pressuring management in its own areas of concern. With each union attacking management from a different angle, the two-union approach provides enterprise unions with an interesting strategy which might well enhance their overall ability to function. From this perspective, consideration of the minority union and the coexistence of multiple enterprise unions at the same firm as a viable option begins to make sense theoretically. From this perspective the experience of the two unions at the Chūgoku Electric Power Authority might serve as a model for an enterprise union-based labor movement. One very important consideration allows us to draw this conclusion. In Japan the growth of the single enterprise union (with only one union at each firm) was made possible by the rather closed nature of the labor market and the unwillingness of employees to move from one firm to another. However, around 1970 there seems to have been an increase in the inter-firm mobility of workers in the tertiary sector and in small firms. As mobility among firms increases with a corresponding drop in the extent to which employees feel their fate is tied to a particular enterprise, the usefulness of the single enterprise union will decline and the extent to which the workers' needs can be served by industry-wide or regionally-based unions will increase.

Even so, the marriage of radical minority enterprise unions and conservative enterprise unions will face an uphill struggle. Only in very unusual circumstances will multiple enterprise unions come to coexist with stable working arrangements between them. The reason is that in the future it is likely that management will increasingly adopt personnel policies which distinguish between core and non-core employees as labor mobility increases. Moreover, core employees will increasingly welcome managerial policies which discriminate against non-core employees. As their elitist consciousness becomes stronger, core employees will increasingly turn to the enterprise union as a means of maximizing their own self interest. On the other hand, the non-core employee will not expect to stay with the firm. He will have much less commitment to the firm, and will identify more with some sort of horizontally structured union. Accordingly, it is conceivable that within one firm two enterprise unions will exist – one as a union for key employees and one for non-core employees. We can call these the 'core employees' union' (*kikan kumiai*) and the 'peripheral employees' union' (*henkyō kumiai*). The former would be a union only of a single firm's employees, whereas the latter would be an enterprise branch union with a more broadly based industrial union.

The case study presented in this chapter suggests that such a scenario is not beyond the realm of possibility. The members of DC were, for the most part, employees who had come to constitute the marginal fringe of the power authority's permanent labor force. Moreover, DC has maintained rather close ties with the authority's temporary employees (*rinjikoteki jūgyōin*) and other unions organizing employees in the subcontractors and other related firms in the same industry. It is, therefore, the non-core union (*kikan kumiai*) or peripheral union (*henkyō kumiai*) which organizes the secondary labor force as shown in Figure 10.2. The Denrō affiliate will continue as a union interested only in the core employees. At the same time, one could also say that Zendenryoku is the core union in the industry while each of the Denrō affiliates is a peripheral union in the following sense. DC unionists have a low level of commitment to the firm but a strong commitment to the industry; the Denrō unionist has a strong commitment to the particular power authority which employs him but a weak sense of identity with the industry. In other words, the former type of employee will change firms often but will usually stay in the industry; when the latter type leaves his employer, he will usually leave the industry. The possibility of two or more enterprise unions coexisting at the same firm cannot be overlooked.

V An Afternote

When this study was conducted in 1970–6 DC had a membership of about 1200 but was losing a net total of about 100 persons per year. Had that kind of attrition rate continued, the union would have disappeared by the early 1980s. However, its active involvement with and fight against (i) industrial accidents and (ii) the installation of nuclear power plants attracted a number of younger employees. By the early 1980s the number of new members had surpassed the number leaving for the Denrō union,

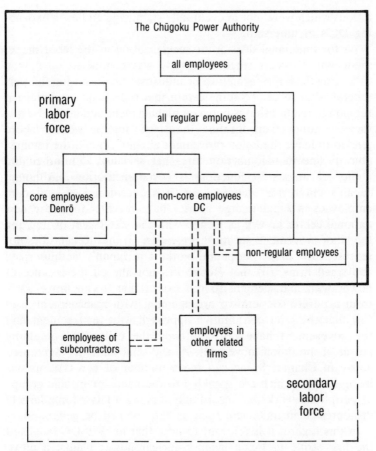

The Chūgoku Power Authority

all employees

primary
labor
force

all regular employees

core employees
Denrō

non-core employees
DC

non-regular employees

employees of
subcontractors

employees in
other related
firms

secondary
labor
force

Figure 10.2 *The two labor forces in the electric power industry*

although DC continued to experience a slight net decline owing
to the number of members being retired at the compulsory
retirement age. Most important, however, DC has been able to
increase the number of young employees in its ranks. In 1988
the union's secretary was aged 27. Earlier in the 1980s its paper
Densan Chūgoku, January 10, 1981) featured a discussion among
seven members in their twenties, telling how they had felt a new
sense of confidence as workers following their decision to shift
from the Denrō union to DC. The study presented in this chapter
focused on interviews with the older members and on the con-

ditions which were met in eventually stabilizing and even expanding DC's membership.

As for functional division or specialization in the labor movement, the 18 years since this study was conducted have seen little growth in the formation of industrial unionism for the peripheral labor force. To some extent that reflects how unbalanced the power relationship is between management and labor. Nevertheless, rather than forming industrial unions, workers have tended to leave the union movement altogether, and the remarkable decline in unionization rates has seriously diminished the ability of unions to function as social institutions. Although Japan's enterprise unions – which are centered around core employees in Japan's large firms – have recently formed a new national center known as Rengō with the stated aim of unifying the labor movement, we must remember (i) that Rengō does not represent the many peripheral workers in Japan's medium-sized and small firms, (ii) that Rengō has not altered the balance of power with management to the extent that it can move away from a purely cooperative arrangement with management, and (iii) that the joint consultative approach with management and the government have not improved the collective bargaining power of the union movement. At the same time, as mentioned above in Chapter 8, we can see a number of new-type unions being formed which are speaking to the needs of specific groups of peripheral workers. Accordingly, among a labor force largely disinterested in unionism, such an interest can be generated.

In this regard, it is relevant to note that in 1979 DC launched the first strike in Japan against nuclear power plants, a move which drew much attention. It had three reasons for launching the strike. First, it pointed to its social responsibility to guarantee the safety of the people. Second, it claimed its policy was sensitive to the anti-nuclear sentiment which is particularly strong in Hiroshima. Third, it underlined its commitment as a minority union to confronting management on such issues. Since 1979 it has annually organized a strike against nuclear power plants, and similar strikes have come to be organized in other parts of the country. Although Denrō's cooperation with management has ensured that the nuclear plants were built, DC continues to oppose the policy of using nuclear energy to generate electricity. Following the nuclear accident at Chernobyl the anti-nuclear movement organized mainly around housewives became much more active. DC provides a kind of center where such activities could be coordinated. DC has developed ties with various citizens' groups against nuclear power and has played an active role in the anti-nuclear movement on a national scale. In April 1983 the Shikoku Electrical Workers Union, with 910 members, affiliated with Zendenryoku.

11 From the Minority to the Majority: The Push for Majority Status by One Union at a Private Railway Company

I Introduction

The general image of the minority enterprise union is that it struggles to survive. It is generally seen as a mixture of idealistic no-hopers and aging radicals. Most would be surprised to learn that some minority unions have successfully fought a determined battle to win back members and have regained their position as majority unions. The long-term viability of the minority enterprise union can be appraised by how successfully they manage their affairs at three critical stages in the process of 'coming back.' First, can it meet the minimal requirements to survive as a minority union? Because it is very easy for a union to continue on the downhill slide into oblivion, special care needs to be taken at this early stage. Second, once it has stabilized its situation, can it set significant goals and achieve them? Third, can it mount programs that will transform it from a minority union into a majority union?

The ways in which Densan's only remaining union met the first criterion were discussed in the preceding chapter. However, it has not made much headway in raising its organization rate. Elsewhere I have examined the matter of setting and achieving goals through a case study of the union at Zeneraru Sekiyū (Kawanishi 1989). This chapter returns to the same Hiroshima area to consider another minority union which has been successful in reestablishing itself as the majority union, the number one union at Hiroshima Dentetsu. In 1954 the union at Hiroshima Dentetsu (the Hiroshima Railways Company) split. A second union was formed, and by 1959 the membership of the number one union had fallen to 200, accounting for only 10 percent of the employees at Hiroshima Dentetsu. However, rather than experiencing a slow death, the union made a come-back, and in 1980 it once more represented the majority of the employees at Hiroshima Dentetsu. In this chapter I will briefly provide some information on the union being studied and then an overview of its development as a minority union before looking at its transition from a minority union to a majority union.

It should be clear that examples of such enterprise unions are rare. But they do exist and most examples can be found among the unions affiliated with Shitetsu Sōren (cf. Nihon Shitetsu Rōdō Kumiai Sōrengōkai 1966), Tanrō, Shimbun Rōren (cf. Hōchi San Tansō Kyōtō Iinkai 1976; Tokyo Shimbun Rōdō Kumiai 1977), Zenkoku Kinzoku, Zenkoku Ippan and Zenzōsen (cf. Zenzōsen Kikai Rōdō Kumiai 1974). The interest here is in examining one of the affiliates of Shitetsu Sōren to see if any 'lessons' might be gleaned for other minority unions. To date no careful study has been made of this process of rehabilitation apart from my own earlier work which forms the basis for this chapter. The case study was jointly carried out from May 1983 until September 1984 by this author and Professor Matsudo Takehiko (at Nara University). At the time the study was facilitated by the good offices of Mr Uchiyama Mitsuo who was head of Sōhyō's Disputative Strategies Policy Committee.

II The Case Study at Hiroshima Dentetsu

A The Shitetsu Sōren branch

Shitetsu Sōren, the Sōhyō affiliated industrial federation for workers in the private railways, has nine regional organizations. Only two – in Hokkaidō and in Chūgoku – are unions in their own right. The other seven are loose confederations. The Chūgoku Regional Organization of Shitetsu Sōren was formed in 1952. It consists of eighteen locals which had a total membership of 6000 persons in 1983. In the same year seven other enterprise unions having semi-affiliated status represented an additional 2000 members.

Shitetsu Sōren has had much useful experience with schisms and minority unions. Among its 227 affiliated enterprise unions, 27 had experienced schisms prior to 1983. Nine of those had been able to reestablish themselves as majority unions. Three of its minority unions had achieved a position on par with that of the number two union. Twenty-three majority unions had already successfully fought back against number two unions, reabsorbing members from the rival union when it disbanded.

In the Chūgoku Regional Organization, eight of the eighteen locals compete with second unions. Of the eight, four have been successful in regaining majority status. In assessing Shitetsu Sōren's success in reestablishing number one unions as the majority unions, attention must be given to Shitetsu Sōren's many activities as an industrial federation. It has in many ways functioned as an industrial union. This fact should be kept in mind as we discuss the developments at Hiroshima Dentetsu.

As an industrial federation, Shitetsu Sōren provides members with four important services. One of the federation's functions is to assist in the formulation of demands for unions in the industry. It plays a leadership role in organizing industry-wide disputative activity. This primarily involved the annual publication of standards for the industry with regard to wage rates. It would use the wage rates achieved by its more successful member unions as a basis for formulating industry-wide demands. The aim was to create a spill-over effect. Of course, it was able to facilitate the exchange of various kinds of information among its affiliated enterprise unions. The federation was also involved in formulating strategies to combat the attempts of management and other employees to create schisms and number two unions. Apart from providing advice on how to deal with the ordinary day-to-day problems faced by unions that have split, Shitetsu Sōren also arranged for the leaders of such unions to gather for an annual general meetings. The exchange of information at such sessions was invaluable to those leaders.

A second function of the federation is to provide a leadership role in determining working conditions in the industry. In 1984 it organized 92 percent of all employees in private railways and in tramways, and 86 percent of the employees working for bus companies owned by the private railways. It could thus have an influence which the industrial organization for the number two unions – Kōtsū Rōren (an affiliate of Dōmei at the time of the study) – could not challenge.

The third task Shitetsu Sōren set for itself was the provision of assistance and support to local branches and enterprise unions engaged in confrontation with management. It could take up collections on behalf of workers who might have been without wages while on strike. Because it represented 260,000 members, a contribution of just ¥100 per member became a sizeable amount. It was also able to mobilize its members in various other ways to support affiliates having disputes with management. In this regard it could be said that Shitetsu Sōren looked after its constituency and had a good reputation among those in the labor movement for having done so.

Its fourth major concern has been to heighten the sense of solidarity which members share in their everyday lives. By doing so it was able to give members of a minority enterprise union the pride of belonging to the largest industrial federation. On this point one recalls the manner in which members of Densan Chūgoku felt a similar pride when they thought of themselves as being affiliated with the largest national center, Sōhyō. This instilled in each of Shitetsu Sōren's members a deeply ingrained sense of superiority towards those employees who joined the number two unions.

Shitetsu Sōren's Chūgoku Regional Organization (Shitetsu Chūgoku) was structured so that members of its affiliated organizations joined the organization as individuals. This meant that members paid their dues directly to the Regional Organization. The amount was 2 percent of their base wage (*kihonkyū*). At the time of this study that represented an average monthly subscription of about ¥4000 per member. The Regional Organization retained 32 percent of its receipts and redistributed 68 percent to its branch organizations. This approach allowed many of the more mundane activities of the smaller branches to be adequately subsidized. For example, when the federation held meetings in Hiroshima, it was possible for even the smallest affiliates to send their representatives. Because the regional organization was established as a unit union and could provide funds for all delegates, it could freely take the initiative in organizing meetings when its leaders deemed necessary. This was particularly important when organizing disputative activities, as it would have been almost impossible for each of the affiliates to establish sufficient strike funds on their own. It was also able to organize group negotiations for six branches and their managements at six of the larger firms in Hiroshima Prefecture. The ability of Shitetsu Sōren to take the initiative in setting a fairly high standard or going rate at the large firms assisted many of the smaller unions which benefitted from the spillover effect.

In trying to explain the success of the minority unions which were able to reestablish themselves as majority unions in the region's private railways, the overall role played by Shitetsu Sōren's Chūgoku Regional Organization needs to be remembered.

B Management at Hiroshima Dentetsu

The company employed 2400 persons in 1983. It was one of the local medium-sized railroad companies which are so common in Japan. The firm was engaged in five main lines of business: the old tram lines in Hiroshima, the rail line from Hiroshima to Miyajima, city buses inside Hiroshima, inter-city buses, and tourist buses. It was also involved in real estate. The rail line and tramway divisions, as well as its real estate activities, made money and covered the losses which were generated by the buses. Nevertheless, the company was able to generate a profit of 270 million yen in 1982.

Very few of the regional rail companies were making much money, but Hiroshima Dentetsu was one of the exceptions. After perpetually running at a loss, it succeeded in generating profits from the late 1970s onwards. It was common that regional rail companies would profit from their rail lines and perhaps the city bus lines. But they would always accumulate huge losses on the inter-city lines which connected the large cities with the more sparsely populated centers in the rural areas. In the case of Hiroshima Dentetsu, however, the strong performance of the rail and tramway divisions in the early 1980s resulted in the company running at a profit. As mentioned below, this favorable up-turn in performance was one of the necessary conditions which allowed for the Shitetsu Sōren branch at Hiroshima Dentetsu to reestablish itself as the dominant union.

Although there were no outstanding or dominant individuals among the shareholders, about 60 percent of Hiroshima Dentetsu's shares were owned by individuals. Just over 10 percent of the shares were held by banks; 8 percent by insurance companies; and about 20 percent by other types of companies. The large percentage of individual stock holders made Hiroshima Dentetsu somewhat different from other local railway companies. Also

conspicuous was the absence of large financial concerns with a
strong presence in national politics as was the case with a number
of other regional firms such as Kokusai Kōgyō and Fukushima
Transportation which came to be known for their close ties with
the Liberal Democratic Party and politicians such as Tanaka
Kakuei. In this respect Hiroshima Dentetsu was slightly different
from many of the other local railway companies.

C Trends in the organization rate

Some figures on the membership of the union in August 1983
are given in Table 11.1. At that time there were 2414 employees:
1286 belonged to the Chūgoku Regional Organization of Shitetsu
Sōren (through the branch at Hiroshima Dentetsu); 1014
belonged to the enterprise union affiliated with Denrō (the
Dōmei-linked industrial federation in the same industry). The
Branch at Hiroshima Dentetsu organized 55.6 percent of the
employees at Hiroshima Dentetsu at that time. (The figure had
risen further to 57.4 percent by 1986.) The table shows that the
union drew its membership largely from the divisions of the
company which had the largest number of employees, the rail
and motor vehicle divisions. Within the motor transport division,
the first section ran the intra-city buses and the second section
ran the inter-city buses. We can thus conclude from the table
that the branch at Hiroshima Dentetsu was particularly strong
among employees in the most profitable sections of the company.
This gave it a certain status which was reflected in the complexity
of the firm's industrial relations.

Although the table does not give the occupational breakdowns,
they too need to be considered. The branch was particularly
successful in organizing some key occupational groups such as
the bus drivers, the train engineers, and the conductors on both
trains and buses. In the division of personnel affairs, for example,
the organization rate of 67.2 percent reflected the branch's ability
to organize 42 of the 62 persons in the welfare benefits section
(who were largely employed to run the company's cafeterias).
In the division of general affairs, where the branch's organization
rate was only 40 percent, it had been successful in organizing 9
of the 16 employees in the records office and most of those in
the printing office.

The concentration of its membership in certain key sections

Table 11.1 *The unionization rate of the Hiroshima Dentetsu branch by division and section: August 1983*

Administrative division	Number of employees	Employees eligible to join a union	Unionists in the Hiroshima Dentetsu branch of Shitetsu Sōren	Unionists in the affiliate of Denrō	Number of employees not joining a union	Percentage composition of branch membership	Branch's unionization rate
Secretariat	6	3	0	3		0	0
President's office	2	3				0	0
General affairs division	44	32	13	19	1	1.0	40.6
Personnel affairs division	78	64	43	20		3.3	67.2
Railways division	541	541	422	119		32.8	78.0
Transportation section	388	388	333	55		25.9	85.8
Administration section	5	5	1	4		0.1	20.1
Carriage section	71	71	40	31		3.1	56.3
Mechanical section	77	77	48	29		3.7	62.3
Motor vehicle division	1185	1182	683	497	2	53.1	57.8
First motor vehicle section	459	459	364	95		28.3	79.3
Second motor vehicle section	708	705	317	388		24.7	45.0
Administration section	18	18	2	14	2	0.2	11.1
Motor vehicle maintenance division	167	167	41	126		3.2	24.6
Maintenance section	90	90	26	64		2.0	28.9
The Gion factory	77	77	15	62		1.2	19.5
Tourist division, tourist section	115	115	22	93		1.7	19.1
Coordination division	9	9	2	6	1	0.2	22.2
Real estate division	24	24	0	24		0	0
Management information center	7	5	1	4		0.1	20.0

Table 11.1 *continued*

Administrative division	Number of employees	Employees eligible to join a union	Unionists in the Hiroshima branch of Shitetsu Sōren	Unionists in the affiliate of Denrō	Number of employees not joining a union	Percentage composition of branch membership	Branch's unionization rate
Other	236	169	59	103	7	4.6	34.9
Personnel officers	30	30	2	28		0.2	6.7
Seconded personnel	33	33	2	31		0.2	6.1
Persons on leave without pay	6	5	2	3		0.2	40.0
Division deputies	17	0					
Section chiefs	49	0					
Union officials	12	12	7	5		0.5	58.3
Specialist employees	89	89	46	36	7	3.6	51.7
Totals	2414	2311	1286	1014	11	100.0	55.6

Source: The above was compiled by figures taken from materials published by management and by the branch. Both parties have accepted this table as an accurate record of the situation.

371

and occupations meant that the branch had considerably more influence than its overall organization rate of 55.6 percent would seem to indicate. Even though less than 60 percent of the employees belonged to the branch, it was able to show its superiority by openly pushing for the collapse of the number two union and calling for members of that union to return to the fold of the number one union. Nevertheless, in terms of its ability to wage a strike (which is one of a union's ultimate weapons) there were a few sections of the company in which the branch was weak and underrepresented: the inter-city bus section (where its organization rate was only 45.0 percent), the motor vehicle repair shops (24.6 percent), and the tourist bus section (19.1 percent). It needed to raise its organization rates in those sections before it could truly be said to have a free hand.

D   A longitudinal look at the organization rate

Table 11.2 shows changes in the organization rate of the branch in each of the firm's divisions over time. Data with the breakdowns for each division has been available only since 1968. The branch's strengths were already evident in 1968. The first column shows for 1968 that the branch organized 55 percent in the first motor vehicle section. Its presence was much more problematic in the railways division (36 percent), the second motor vehicle section (27 percent) and in the tourist division (37 percent). During the 1970s the branch continued to recruit members from the railways division and the second motor vehicles section, while it was much less effective in the tourist division. Table 11.3 shows changes in the percentage composition of the branch's membership by division over time. It can be seen that the motor vehicle division supplied the branch with 64.1 percent of its members in 1968 (when that division was overwhelmingly the most important division in the branch's affairs). By 1983 members had been recruited from other divisions and the relative importance of the motor vehicle division had declined somewhat. During that period the percentage of the membership supplied by the railways division increased from 19.5 percent to 32.9 percent. Table 11.4 provides a breakdown of the branch's membership by occupational category. While the organization rate seemed to increase in all categories (except in the category for employees engaged in supplying employee services, a category in which the organization rate had always been high), increases in the organization rate were particularly noticeable for those in administrative positions (the category which consisted mainly of the firm's lower-level management). Among those in managerial or administrative positions, the rate increased from a mere 6.2 percent to 65.3 percent. The movement in this category, including the jump upwards in 1975 and the sustained growth thereafter, shows clearly the decline of the Denrō affiliate.

The three tables suggest several generalizations. First, in the earlier years, the branch relied heavily on its ability to recruit members from the first motor vehicle section. Success there perhaps allowed for it to increase its organization in similar areas such as the second motor vehicle section and the railways division. Second, during that early period of reestablishing itself, the branch had come to be heavily oriented toward the bus drivers and toward the engineers and conductors on the trains. It had, in the words of its own union leadership, become a 'drivers' union'. As it neared majority status, it shifted its orientation in order to represent better the interests of employees in all divisions of Hiroshima Dentetsu. The battle with the number two union was won by the movement of junior management personnel into the branch. Third, the amalgamation of interests was accompanied by a surfacing of certain conflicts of interest between employees in different divisions, different occupations and different age groups. Most of these differences reflected the differential treatment accorded to the employees in different career modes. The branch's success as a majority union will depend on its ability to bridge such cleavages and to manage conflicts arising out of those kinds of differences.

III A Periodization of the Union's History

Building on the general information presented above, we can begin to explain how the branch revitalized itself. Figure 11.1 shows graphically the data on the membership and organization rates for the two unions at Hiroshima Dentetsu. The figure helps us to identify a number of distinct periods in the history of the two unions. Obviously, a union's membership will reflect the

Table 11.2 *Changes in the unionization rate of the Hiroshima Dentetsu branch by division: 1968–83 (%)*

Administrative division	1968	1969	1970	1971	1972	1973	1974	1975	1976	1977	1978	1979	1980	1981	1982	1983
General affairs division	5	8	8	21	15	24	24	23	30	32	40	39	40	38	38	42
Personnel affairs division	55	53	56	58	57	64	64	61	63	63	64	65	67	69	68	68
Railways division	36	38	36	32	35	38	41	42	45	47	59	70	70	73	75	78
Motor vehicle division	37	35	34	38	39	41	43	44	50	50	50	51	50	56	57	58
First motor vehicle section	(51)	(50)	(51)	(59)	(60)	(58)	(62)	(63)	(77)	(78)	(78)	(77)	(78)	(79)	(80)	(79)
Second motor vehicle section	(27)	(25)	(24)	(23)	(31)	(31)	(30)	(30)	(31)	(31)	(31)	(32)	(33)	(42)	(43)	(45)
Motor vehicle maintenance division	11	12	13	11	12	15	16	14	14	18	22	23	24	25	25	25
Tourist division, tourist section	37	39	32	33	20	37	29	37	31	22	21	21	20	31	29	18
Coordination division						20	29	20	0	0	0	11	11	13	11	25
Management information center						0	0	0	0	0	0	0	0	0	17	20
Other	20	15	11	14	17	11	16	13	13	14	13	13	18	15	20	16
Totals	32.6	32.1	30.9	33.4	35.5	36.7	38.2	38.8	42.6	43.3	46.3	49.2	50.1	54.8	55.6	56.0
Number of unionists	1,018	966	877	873	836	842	864	865	930	923	968	1,012	1,017	1,146	1,201	1,232

Notes: (1) 'Other' includes persons attached to the personnel section, those on outside business, those in certain sections in various divisions, those on leave from work, the assistant division managers, section heads, and those working full time for the union.

(2) These figures include those employed in special contracted jobs (as '*tokubetsu no shokutaku*').

Source: This table was compiled from the yearly records kept by the personnel office of Hiroshima Dentetsu.

Table 11.3 *Changes in the percentage composition of union membership in the Hiroshima Dentetsu branch of the Chūgoku regional organization of Shitetsu Sōren by division: 1968–83 (%)*

Division	1968	1969	1970	1971	1972	1973	1974	1975	1976	1977	1978	1979	1980	1981	1982	1983
General affairs division	0.2	0.3	0.3	0.5	0.6	1.0	0.9	0.8	1.0	1.0	1.2	1.2	1.2	1.0	1.0	1.0
Personnel affairs division	5.2	5.2	5.8	5.3	5.3	5.4	4.7	4.3	4.1	3.7	3.4	3.9	3.9	3.4	3.4	
Railways division	19.5	20.8	21.1	23.1	24.2	24.9	24.7	24.3	23.9	24.3	28.9	32.9	33.5	32.0	31.2	32.9
Motor vehicle division	64.1	61.6	61.2	64.4	62.6	60.0	61.5	62.5	64.8	64.1	59.4	56.0	54.8	57.2	54.4	53.5
First motor vehicle section	(37.9)	(37.0)	(36.9)	(36.5)	(33.9)	(33.8)	(35.9)	(37.6)	(42.2)	(41.8)	(38.5)	(35.8)	(33.8)	(31.6)	(29.4)	(28.4)
Second motor vehicle section	(25.9)	(24.4)	(24.2)	(25.1)	(26.1)	(26.7)	(25.6)	(25.0)	(22.6)	(22.3)	(20.9)	(20.3)	(20.9)	(25.4)	(24.9)	(25.0)
Motor vehicle maintenance division	4.9	5.3	5.6	2.6	2.8	3.3	3.4	2.8	2.7	3.5	3.9	3.9	3.8	3.3	3.2	3.2
Tourist division, tourist section	5.0	5.8	5.0	3.0	2.9	3.6	2.7	3.0	2.0	1.4	1.4	1.3	1.1	1.3	1.5	1.5
Coordination division		0	0			0.1	0.1	0.1	0	0	0	0.1	0.1	0.1	0.1	0.2
Management information center		0	0			0	0	0	0	0	0	0	0	0	0.1	0.1
Other	1.0	1.0	0.9	1.1	1.8	1.1	1.3	1.7	1.4	1.6	1.3	1.2	1.6	1.1	1.4	0.9
Totals	99.9	100.0	99.9	100.0	100.2	100.1	100.0	99.9	100.1	100.0	99.8	100.0	100.0	99.9	100.2	100.0
Number of unionists	1,018	966	877	873	836	842	864	865	930	923	968	1,012	1,017	1,146	*(1,250)	*(1,274)

Notes: (1) indicates totals in which special contracted workers are included.
(2) The empty boxes indicate divisions for which there were no totals available. If there was information on a division and the number of unionists was zero, then '0' is entered to indicate the fact.

Source: This table was compiled by the author from the yearly records kept by the Personnel Office of Hiroshima Dentetsu.

Table 11.4 *Changes in the organization rate in the Hiroshima Dentetsu branch by job type: 1968–83* (%)

Occupational activity sector (*bumon*)	1968	1969	1970	1971	1972	1973	1974	1975	1976	1977	1978	1979	1980	1981	1982	1983
Driving	40.7	40.1	38.8	41.6	42.6	45.2	46.7	48.8	51.3	51.3	54.7	56.3	56.7	59.6	59.8	60.1
Factory work	15.5	12.3	12.5	11.3	11.9	19.9	21.9	21.3	23.9	25.5	27.8	30.2	32.8	37.5	40.1	40.8
Administration	6.2	7.1	6.8	13.4	15.5	18.0	18.7	20.1	33.9	37.1	41.9	51.4	51.2	64.4	66.1	65.3
Provision of welfare services	65.4	63.3	65.4	58.2	57.1	68.2	67.6	64.5	65.0	64.9	64.2	64.8	67.8	69.8	68.3	68.8
Other office work	0	0	0	0	0	2.1	4.0	2.0	0	0	0	0	2.7	2.8	5.4	8.1
Other	20.0	15.2	11.0	14.5	16.7	11.4	16.4	13.3	12.7	13.5	12.5	13.0	17.8	15.5	37.9	35.8
All union members	32.6	32.1	30.9	33.4	35.5	36.7	38.2	38.8	42.6	43.3	46.3	49.2	50.1	54.8	55.6	56.0

Source: This table was compiled from the yearly sets of material kept by the personnel office of Hiroshima Dentetsu.

type of strategy it pursues at any given time. Important was the ability of the branch to shift its strategy as its fortunes changed.

The Shitetsu Sōren branch was first formed in 1946. It experienced its schism in 1954. Following the formation of the second union, its numbers dropped drastically for about five years. Although its numbers began to level out and then slightly increase from about 1960, membership in the number two union continued to climb until the middle of the 1960s. The organization rate of the number two union, however, began to decline from 1960. The membership of the number one union proceeded upwards until the late 1960s when it experienced a decline along with the number two union in the early 1970s. It then increased again, surpassing the figure for the number two union in 1980. Since then the branch has been the majority union. We can thus say that the first breakthrough occurred in the early 1960s and that the final turning point occurred in the early 1980s.

It may be useful to analyze the comeback of the branch by dividing its twenty-year struggle into several stages. Figure 11.1 highlights the key periods. The two decades between the first and final turning point can be divided into a number of stages, the years during which the unionization rate was in the tens, in the twenties, in the thirties, and then in the forties before reaching 50 percent, the point at which the branch again became the majority union. While this division might seem artificial, we will see that the transition from each 10-percent band to the next involved some key events. For example, during the second period, two important disputes seemed to contribute to the branch's recovery. One concerned the division of streets into areas for cars and areas for trams. The other concerned changes in the suburban workshops. The branch's success in these two disputes allowed it to increase its membership to over 20 percent. In moving the organization rate up into the 30-percent band, a positive boost was received from the successful campaign to retrieve for workers some measure of input into the formulation of work schedules through joint consultations and the struggle against the job-and-status-based wage system (*shokkai shokumu-kyū seido*). As the branch's organization rate surged past 40 percent, the movement against the company's rationalization programs and the 'fight to maintain the tramways' gained the branch further support among the company's employees. Once it reached the 40 percent level, the decline of the number two

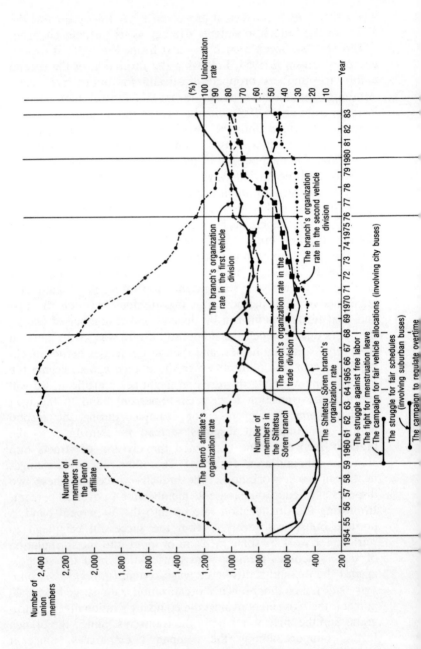

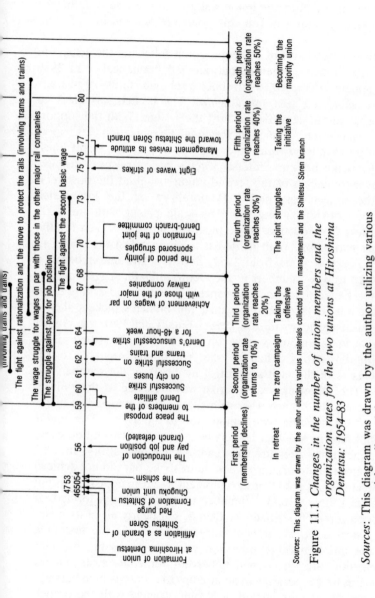

Sources: This diagram was drawn by the author utilizing various materials collected from management and the Shitetsu Sōren branch

Figure 11.1 *Changes in the number of union members and the organization rates for the two unions at Hiroshima Dentetsu: 1954–83*

Sources: This diagram was drawn by the author utilizing various materials collected from management and the Shitetsu Sōren branch.

union seemed inevitable. *Esprit de corps* among the members of the branch was high and the activity level of the number two union left a good deal to be desired. Having firmly taken the initiative, the number one union was able to exercise an influence far beyond its numbers (on this point see Kawanishi 1977 and 1981).

With the formation of a second union following the schism in 1954, the branch's organization rate fell dramatically. In 1956 management attempted to introduce a job-and-status-based wage system (*shokkai shokumukyū seido*). The branch was quick to launch an all-out campaign against the system. With the support of Shitetsu Sōren's Chūgoku Regional Organization, 1000 persons were mobilized from other regions to join the picket lines, and the strike became Shitetsu Sōren's largest postwar dispute. However, members of the second union assaulted the picketers, and the branch lost badly. Demoralized by the loss which occurred notwithstanding the large-scale picket with the 1000 supporters from outside, more members left the branch for the number two union. With its defeat the branch lost the ability to strike. For two years from 1959, however, the union began a campaign to woo members of the Denrō affiliate, suggesting that they too benefitted from the branch's activities and asking them at least not to take action against the branch's pickets should the branch again organize a strike. Finally, in 1961 the branch felt able in the motor vehicle division to launch its first strike since its devastating defeat in 1956. The branch was able to win the strike with the tacit support of members in the number two union. The following year a strike was launched in the railway division and the branch was again successful in persuading members of the number two union not to interfere. The major accomplishment was that leaders in the number two union came under increasing pressure to organize their own strike. In 1963 the Denrō affiliate organized a 48-hour strike but did not achieve its objectives. As a further development a schism appeared within the Denrō affiliate and a 'number three union' was formed. It was soon forced to disband by Denrō, but nearly all of its members returned to the branch. Interestingly it was the first time that the question of reunification was raised. As the branch's unionization rate approached 30 percent in the late 1960s, Denrō became more cooperative in an attempt to retain its membership. For example, it participated in a joint struggle with the branch to obtain wages on par with those paid by the large firms in the industry. Although that strategy was pursued until 1973, the Denrō affiliate continued to lose members and was finally obliged to adopt a more independent line from the mid–1970s in order to justify its own existence. Once the branch was able to break the 40 percent barrier with a series of strikes in 1975, even management began to explore ways of developing a working relationship with the branch.

In the paragraphs below, the decline and recovery of the number one union at Hiroshima Dentetsu is discussed in terms of the periods which have been identified in Figure 11.1. In particular, attention will be given to the factors which helped the branch recover its position in the firm.

IV The Anatomy of Discrimination: An Interpretation of the Period of Decline, 1954–9

Any analysis of the success registered by the Shitetsu Sōren branch at Hiroshima Dentetsu must begin with a careful look at the reasons for its sudden decline during the late 1950s. My view is that the core of the problem was the ingrained discrimination which management had introduced to distinguish between members of the two unions. Figure 11.2 indicates a number of areas in which discrimination occurred and their interconnectedness. It is common at any Japanese firm with two unions that members of the number one union are discriminated against from the time the number two union is created. However, the situation went to the extreme at Hiroshima Dentetsu.

The work situation for many employees is the bus or train; often they are the only employee at their place of work. At most there are only two persons: a driver or engineer and a conductor. Accordingly, there is a certain sense of isolation on the job. One must be prepared to carry on by oneself under whatever circumstances present themselves. At certain times the roads are very crowded; at others they are not. Sometimes it rains; sometimes it does not. The chemistry of any given group of passengers is unique. But the composition of the group changes at the next stop. In short, the working conditions vary immensely over short

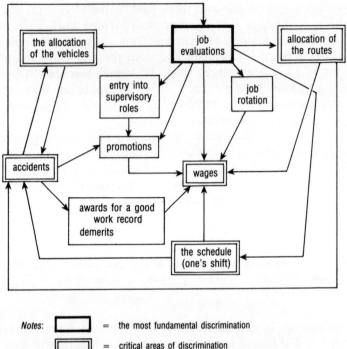

Notes:

☐	=	the most fundamental discrimination
☐	=	critical areas of discrimination
☐	=	other areas where discrimination occurs
⟶	=	the direction of the flow-on from one area to another

Figure 11.2 *The structure of discrimination: the interrelatedness of discrimination at various levels*

periods of time. In most instances a rather skilled person is required just to operate the equipment. In addition, however, the operator must constantly be making judgments about the changing environment. Compared with many other jobs, a good amount of self-confidence and the psychological predisposition of 'the lone wolf' are required. Many of the drivers and engineers feel strongly that they do a job that only they and a few others can do. Management's view, of course, is that the drivers and engineers can be replaced if the need arises. With older employees management tends to feel that whatever an older driver can do a younger one can do better, and that older workers who have difficulty accepting that basic fact can be fired. For management, it's as simple as that.

These are jobs which allow for a large gap between the objective reality of the task required and the subjective assessment of what is required. There is plenty of room for misunderstandings and disagreements not only between workers and management but also among the workers themselves. There is a competitiveness among the drivers based on the inflated pride they have in their own ability. The competition often results in one driver typing to 'put other drivers down.' This was a situation management could easily exploit. It was easy to find drivers who would complain about other drivers, and obviously the evaluation of such complaints would be a most subjective matter. Out of this hazy situation drivers soon got one message fairly clearly: to avoid unfavorable ramifications and to survive at work, join the number two union. Here we might comment on several forms of discrimination.

1 The allocation of vehicles There was always competition over who would drive the new vehicles. Even among the older vehicles, there was an interest in who would drive the ones in better condition and who would be left with the 'jalopies.' In the late 1950s the system was that each of the main drivers would be allocated a vehicle which then became his property to drive and to look after. The person in charge of allocating the vehicles belonged to the number two union. From my interviews I gained the strong impression that it was a real joy for a driver to get a new vehicle. The vehicle one drove determined one's working conditions; the state of the brakes, the clutch and the steering very much determined the ease with which a vehicle could be driven. A vehicle's mechanical condition affected the probability that it would be in an accident. Knowledge of that fact was reflected in the stress employees felt when driving the older vehicles. No wonder that they would exclaim, 'A new vehicle is more beautiful than a young wife!' Members of the number two union got the new vehicles; those belonging to the number one union got stuck with the dilapidated onces. The decision as to allocation of vehicles was almost entirely in the hands of the allocation foreman.

2 The allocation of the routes Hiroshima Dentetsu had bus routes which extended into the suburbs around Hiroshima, and longer ones which reached out to the underpopulated mountainous regions in Yamaguchi, Shimane, Tottori and Okayama Prefectures. Nearly all the long-distance drivers on the rural routes lived in agricultural areas near their routes, spending half their time on the land and half their time driving for Hiroshima Dentetsu. However, the right to decide where employees would work rested solely with management and such decisions reflected the whims of managers in the personnel affairs division. It was common for management to assign 'unruly' employees to inconvenient routes in order to keep them in line. Employees who belonged to the number one union were sent one after another 'to the ends of the earth.' Members of the number one union who lived in the remote areas of Yamaguchi Prefecture would be assigned to routes in the remote areas of Shimane Prefecture. If they were given some indication that the route would be permanent, they would uproot their family and buy another house in the vicinity of the new route only to be shifted again to another remote location. There were cases of workers who could not endure the situation and felt compelled to quit. In 1959 one thousand persons were employed on the routes outside Hiroshima, and the number who belonged to the first union fell to 33. The company had offices at sixty different locations, and the union soon found itself with absolutely no presence at many of the places of work.

3 Work schedules   There were two types of schedules, the ordinary schedule and the special schedule. The ordinary schedule called for eight hours of work which were divided between the time spent actually working and the time allowed for lunch and tea breaks. The working time was further divided between periods on the road driving and periods of waiting. The work schedules were different for every route, and no two drivers would have the same schedule. Accordingly, the amount of 'loose time' a driver had would vary from one schedule to another. In other words, this part of the working conditions would vary according to the amount of congestion on the roads, the particular area through which the route passed, and the time of day. The amount of 'loose time' (the time drivers had to rest between periods of intense concentration while they drove) depended on the schedule they received and how it was put together. In addition, there were decisions as to who would take the next route when several drivers finished their assigned route at the same time. There were also decisions about manning the first departures and the last departures each day. The drivers knew which schedules were easy and which were trying. The schedules were drawn up by the supervisors in the office where all the employees were members of the second union. Given the near impossibility of devising schedules which ensured a perfectly equal work load for everyone, it was easy for the supervisors to take advantage of the situation and arrange for members of the number one union always to have the worst schedules singly and in combination.

Drivers on the ordinary schedule were organized into two shifts: a morning shift from six in the morning until two in the afternoon and an afternoon shift from one in the afternoon until nine at night. Drivers were rotated from one shift to the other every week. A special schedule, however, called for the number of buses leaving early in the morning and/or returning late in the evenings to be increased. The increased amount of driving was covered by having the drivers do two or three hours of overtime. The overtime could be assigned in a number of ways. One arrangement might call for a driver to do a normal shift from six in the morning until two in the afternoon, and then to do overtime from four until six in the evening. In that case the driver would spend another four hours at work and have two hours of overtime. Rather than spending the thirty minutes or so to drive home and relax with a drink, drivers found it easiest to stay in the office and pass the time smoking and chatting with their workmates. For the drivers, that was the most acceptable arrangement. The second most popular overtime combination was to drive during the morning rush and then to return for the afternoon shift at one. However, members of the number one union would never be given either of these combinations. In fact, many were given no overtime at all.

As in other industries, the employees at Hiroshima Dentetsu needed the overtime to make ends meet at home. The wages were insufficient. On the routes which took drivers outside the city, there were schedules which had overtime built into them. School charters often involved day trips within school hours from one local stop to another. But there were also four-day trips to Tokyo. With the overnight allowance and lodgings paid in addition to the overtime, a driver on one such trip in 1983 would have been able to gross an extra ¥30,000 or ¥40,000. Those in the number one union were again excluded from the most lucrative arrangements. While I was unable to obtain figures for the late 1950s, to appreciate the meaning of having that extra amount even in 1983 we need to refer to regular salaries being earned in the same year. At Hiroshima Dentetsu twenty-year olds were receiving a pre-tax monthly salary of about ¥100,000; thirty-year olds, ¥150,000; forty-year olds, ¥200,000; and employees in their mid-fifties just before retirement, ¥250,000. A driver aged 50 and making ¥230,000 per month at the most would have been hard pressed financially with house repayments and one or two children in high school or even university. Only by doing over-time could his family survive financially, and even then it was likely that his wife would also be working. Even younger workers have debts to repay to the cooperative for loans to buy a stereo or a car. Some workers in their late twenties were relying on overtime to repay loans up to ¥30,000 per month. Drivers earned about ¥1500 before tax per hour of overtime with the 25 percent penalty rate. Two hours of overtime would gross them ¥3000.

4 Disciplinary action following accidents In the transportation industry traffic accidents are unavoidable. They also result in complications and are the one thing that any driver wants to avoid. Whenever an accident happens, the driver is left waiting for a company superior to hand down a judgment on the extent of the driver's responsibility. In the case of Hiroshima Dentetsu, the person who decided the fate of the driver was the head of the accidents section, again someone who belonged to the Denrō affiliate. We can imagine how easy it was for him to make subjective judgments which consistently disadvantaged drivers who belonged to the Shitetsu Sōren branch. Did an accident occur because the victim dashed out too suddenly? Or was there just enough time to have avoided the tragedy had the driver been a bit more intent on the road in front of him? When the body of a bus was scratched, could the problem be rectified with a few strokes of a paint brush or would it require a complete repainting costing several thousand dollars? Once the head of the accidents section had made his evaluation, the decision was recorded on the driver's personnel file. The file was referred to when making decisions on pay rises, promotion and even the assignment of vehicles. Once a driver was found responsible for an accident, the amount of his annual wage increase is cut and much later this affects the calculations for the employee's retirement pay. More-over, he was disqualified from management's safe driving award.

For drivers who did not have an accident for a set period of time, management would arrange a holiday for the driver and his entire family. Obviously as their safe driving record accumulated and they began to plan for such a trip with the family, the disqualification was immediately felt in material terms by the whole family.

5 Career transition   Another area in which it was easy for management to discriminate against members of the first union when drivers wanted to make the transition from driving to more was skilled work in one of the maintenance or repair shops. Such job changes were controlled by an examination system. The examination was made to appear very objective, but in fact there was considerable room for subjective evaluation. Further, because the assessment was not made public and was done by one of the members of the personnel section and a unionist from Denrō, there was little a member of the branch could do when told he had not passed the examination. Another commonly sought after job change was from conductor to driver. Again, an examination system was in place, but it functioned in a similar manner.

6 The wage base   Figure 11.3 shows the categories used in the wage system which was introduced following the establishment of the number two union in the mid-1950s. The job-and-proficiency wage base (*gōhō kihonkyū*) was derived from a wages table. The wages table provided for increases in two ways. One was by moving occupationally to positions of higher authority. There were about eleven occupational categories (*shokkyū*). The other was by performing the same job at higher levels of proficiency. There were forty grades of proficiency (*shokkai*). The top wage was reached by moving up in both directions. The higher levels of authority of course meant that one became part of the lower echelons of management as a foreman, supervisor, or station master. However, promotion in either direction in the wages table depended largely on the subjective decisions of management. It was clear here as well that members of the first union were greatly disadvantaged.

The various forms of discrimination are summarized in Table 11.5. It was clear that the Hiroshima Dentetsu branch of Shitetsu Sōren would have to protect its members from such discriminatory treatment if it was to retain its members and attract others from the Denrō affiliate.

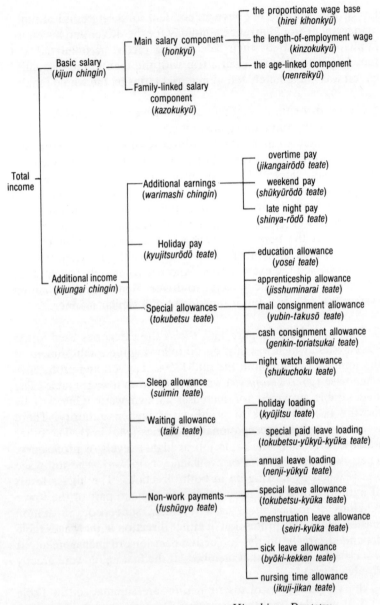

Figure 11.3 *The wage payment system at Hiroshima Dentetsu*

Table 11.5 *Summary of various types of discrimination practiced in the vehicle division against employees belonging to the Hiroshima Dentetsu branch of the Chūgoku regional organization of Shitetsu Sōren*

Type of discrimination	Focus of discrimination	Consequences of discrimination
1 Allocation of vehicles	the office worker in charge of vehicle assignments has complete discretion	new vehicles to the members of the Denrō affiliate old vehicles to the branch members
2 Routes	changing the routes which drivers cover	using assignments to fill vacancies as a warning to employees not to join the branch
3 Work schedules	(1) work schedules (normal schedule + overtime) (2) extra-ordinary schedules (normal schedule incorporating overtime)	most desired schedules given to members of Denrō most undesirable schedules to members of the branch
4 Accidents and related discipline	(1) arbitrariness in allocating responsibility (2) arbitrariness in deciding the degree of culpability	Branch members given unfavor-personnel records, meaning slower promotion, delayed wage increments, etc.
5 Career progression	normal progression: conductor→driver/motorman ↓ mechanic office worker→foreman/supervisor ↓	examination system which can discriminate against branch members
6 Promotion	promotion to lower levels of management	examination system which can discriminate against branch members
7 Wage system	job-based wage component	(1) allocation of job content by subjective process leading to undesirable competition among employees (2) *chōseikyū*

V The Fight Against Discrimination: 1959–64

Once its position had been stabilized, the branch at Hiroshima Dentetsu was ready to move against the discriminatory treatment its members were receiving. This signalled the transition into the second period. In most cases a number one union's struggle against discrimination focuses on the removal of differential treatment and the demand for equal treatment of employees in both unions. However, the strategy developed at Hiroshima Dentetsu differed in at least one important way. One of the leaders of the branch explained it in the following manner:

Management's policy of discriminating between members of the two unions can be a double-edged sword. Such a policy can obviously be used to bring considerable pressure to bear on our branch. However, at the same time the very use of such a policy also serves to indicate how severely pressed management must also feel. It is based on the divisive ploy of buying off or coopting a small number of employees. This is a good way to split a number one union, but when the number two union comes to embrace a large number of the employees the policy can come back to haunt management because it is unable to buy off large numbers of employees. There will be members of the second union who realize that they are not among the select few, and soon there will be a sense of disparity between the rank-and-file and the elite unionists. This does not happen in the number one union even though the overall treatment of its members may be unfavorable. I feel sorry for the workers who went from our branch to the number two union thinking they would be well treated by management and be guaranteed a good livelihood. In fact, all many get is leftover rice. There are not a few who went over to the number two union and are now very disappointed since they were still getting zero marks on their personnel evaluation sheets. It is easy to drive a wedge into that group of unionists. When they come to realize that management's discriminatory use of the carrot and the stick is essentially an inhuman approach benefitting the average employee very little, the conditions are there for some kind of joint struggle.

Based on this kind of thinking, the branch's leadership decided to fight for the removal of discriminatory treatment. Rather than focusing on the significance of membership in a particular union as the basis for their protest, they latched on to the idea that such treatment in the end distinguished between a small elite and the large number of ordinary employees. In fighting to remove the arbitrariness with which management made personnel decisions, the branch was able to strike a chord with employees in the number two union. It is not often that we find a minority union with that kind of flexibility in its thinking. Many take the road to martyrdom, righteously boasting with pride about being 'true to the cause.' They carry on, fueled by a smoldering sense of resentment, determined to survive any form of discrimination while steadfastly refusing to make any concessions to the 'enemy.' The minority union at Hiroshima Dentetsu, however, had a different quality. The organizers seemed to have cultivated an image of being a bunch of 'stoic scoundrels.' There was a tone of maturity, a careful calculation of the long term, a sense that the leadership was coolly working to a ten- or twenty-year plan. The leadership realized that management had pushed ahead with its policies of discrimination. It also recognized that its minority status with a unionization rate of only ten percent or so would in the short run not allow it to make much headway by focusing its energies on the small grievances of specific individuals in each shop. To have done so would only have focused attention on its weakness.

With that realization as the starting point, the leadership sought to develop its own counter-offensive. In July 1958 the leadership of the branch described the strategy that had been adopted as follows:

> 'We decided not to resort to the tactic of organizing shop floor demonstrations or strikes aimed at getting the company to stop specific discriminatory practices. To have done so would probably have resulted in a string of isolated defeats, one after the other. Instead, we took a long-term view, communicating to management our commitment to non-discrimination in general. The goal was to impress upon management our determination to go the distance. If we were not successful this year we would be there again next year and the year after that until the matter was satisfactorily

resolved. Along with the determination to stand up to management, emphasis was placed on educational activities which were designed to raise the consciousness of members of the number two union.'

This long-term struggle was called the 'Zero Struggle' and helped to shift the attention of the rank-and-file from the day-to-day battles to the overall campaign. In the eyes of the union's leaders, this turned out to be an important means of maintaining a high level of morale among their unionists and must be credited as one factor accounting for their ability to draw back those who had joined the number two union.

With that orientation the union focused on two types of discrimination during the early 1960s. One had to do with the way in which vehicles were assigned. The other had to do with the procedures for transferring employees. It is instructive to consider each briefly.

A The struggle over vehicle assignments

As mentioned in the preceding section, affairs at the workshop level came to be taken over completely by management and discriminatory treatment could be seen in a number of areas. The union collapsed and employees were left to get ahead by sidling up to management in an obsequious or subservient manner. In the city bus division management had devised a number of schemes for getting employees to compete among themselves. One was a competition urging drivers to conserve fuel. Management put up a table showing the rankings of the drivers, awarding them with the title used in the Japanese sport of *sumo* wrestling. The winner would be the '*Yokozuna*' (Grand Champion); those almost up to his standard, '*Ozeki*' (Junior Champions); and so on down through the ranks. Those rankings would later be translated onto each employee's personnel records. The bus conductors were organized into a ticket selling competition and given similar rankings so that they would push themselves up and down the aisles on crowded buses to sell more tickets. At about the same time a system of body searches was in place. Because the drivers and the conductors dealt with money, they were frisked by one of the supervisors after their shift whenever they returned an amount of money below what was expected. It was a time when management could request workers to strip to the waist for such inspections. Here too, it should be pointed out, not all workers were required to be checked in this way. Management arbitrarily exercised its right to humiliate workers in this way, and seemed to single out members of the first union for this kind of search.

There was also the clean bus competition. A supervisor would put on a white glove and run his hand around the outside of the buses, one glove to a bus. The gloves would then be arranged from the cleanest one to the dirtiest one. Those responsible for the buses would on that basis be given their *sumo* rankings. Here too employees began to respond in a subservient way, complying with whatever management imposed in the name of improving bus services. It was soon common practice for drivers and conductors to spend their lunch breaks and other time off, including time before and after their officially paid shift, cleaning their buses. Some even wiped off the undercarriage of their buses to ensure that they would pass the 'glove inspection.'

Of course this kind of competition provided the company with unpaid labor. The Shitetsu Sōren branch at Hiroshima Dentetsu was determined to do something about this kind of exploitation. At first its members refused to do such unpaid work, and soon engaged in a struggle against management. However, by taking this line there was the danger that the branch would only open up the gap between itself and the membership of the Denrō affiliate. Members of the second union were not working for free because they liked to do so. They did so because they knew that their willingness to do such work would be reflected in the personnel files and later affect their chances for promotion. They believed that they could not afford to 'make trouble' at work if they were to support their families and to get on in the world. To ridicule their behavior would only result in their turning on members of the branch. To avoid that happening, the branch developed a struggle in which members of the second union could also participate.

The branch sensed an uneasiness among members of the second union who felt unable to speak out about the impositions which resulted in the unpaid work. The issue was debated for some time within the branch as some of its members saw the unpaid work done by members of the number two union as precluding any cooperation. The strategy which was finally adopted distinguished between the leadership of the number two union and its rank-and-file. It thus arranged for hours of unpaid labor to be systematically recorded for about forty days. The results were posted and showed clearly to members of both unions that employees were on average doing one unpaid hour of work a day. In other words, the average employee was doing three or four thousand yen worth of free work for the company each month. That was an amount equal to 15–20 percent of the average monthly salary. The branch used that data as the basis for demanding overtime pay from management. In the end it was the branch's threat to report the matter to the Labor Standards Office of the Ministry of Labor that forced management to back down. In the end management agreed to pay overtime to all its employees for such work and discontinued the clean bus competition and other practices which encouraged employees to compete outside their normal hours of work. In this manner, then, with an organization rate of only 10 percent the branch was able to institutionalize the principle of human rights in the work place and also to develop the idea that members of both unions had some common interests. For the branch the result was a membership much more confident in its leadership.

With that success behind it, the branch was then ready to focus its efforts on the discriminatory system of vehicle allocation. The city bus section had about 100 vehicles at its disposal. The branch followed the approach it had adopted for dealing with unpaid labor. It kept a careful record of who received the new vehicles and posted the results. When the results became known, there was a great outcry. It became obvious to all that employees affiliated with the branch had almost no chance of receiving a new vehicle. However, it also became very clear that some members of the Denrō affiliate were receiving a new vehicle nearly every year while many other members of Denrō were overlooked year after year. The arbitrary assignment of vehicles upset many of the workers in both unions. The branch was again able to find an issue which would unite many of the members of the Denrō affiliate in a common cause with its own members. It publicly demanded that the company set down some principles by which it would allocate vehicles and soon afterwards launched its vehicle allocation struggle. Management rejected the demands, arguing that the buses were the property of the company and could be allocated at management's discretion. In other words, the use of the company's own property should not be a matter of concern to the union. The union's position was that the condition of a driver's bus directly affected his work environment and was an important part of his working conditions which were an issue for collective bargaining. The struggle lasted two years. The branch took the initiative by drawing up its own list of principles for allocating the vehicles and then launched several waves of strikes. Although the branch was still very much the minority union, it was able to gain the support of many of the Denrō unionists and thereby had a considerable impact on management. In 1960 management finally adopted the branch's proposals. The agreement is summarized in Table 11.6.

The principles called for drivers to be classified into three groups. The first consisted of those who had been driving for over three and a half years since being promoted from conductor to driver. The second group consisted of those who had been driving for over three and a half years since entering the firm as a driver. The third group consisted of those who had been driving for over three and a half years since having received a new vehicle. The drivers in each group were to be divided first according to the number of years they had been driving since getting their licence and then further subdivided by age. The important point is that objective criteria were chosen which would limit management's ability to make arbitrary decisions. In this way the branch gained a reputation among the Denrō unionists for being objective and fair. When members of the branch's executive toured the work stations to announce the agreement, they were received like heroes by members of both unions. This victory confirmed that a minority union could carry out a successful campaign against management and gain the support of members of the majority union by dealing with issues which were of vital importance to employees in both unions.

B   The struggle to establish principles for transfers

Having developed its initial momentum, the branch turned its attention to the situation of those working on the inter-city buses. Around 1960 its rate of unionization among the 1000 employees in the inter-city bus division had dropped to 3.3 percent. The leadership puzzled over its unpopularity among the workers in that division of the company's operations. A good deal of

Table 11.6 *The 1960 agreement on principles for vehicle allocation (regarding one-man buses)*

Item	Principles	Other considerations
Selection of the drivers	(1) must have spent at least 1.5 years in present position in the company (2) must be chosen according to length of time employed by the company (3) age will be the secondary criterion after (2)	
Assignment of new vehicle	(1) Employees would first be ranked according to the time driving since last receiving a new vehicle (2) Employees with the same ranking according to (1) would be further ranked by the number of years employed at Hiroshima Dentetsu	(1) until everyone in a particular group has received a new bus no one in another group will receive a new bus (2) no one will receive a new bus within five years of having received a new bus (3) a driver's ranking will be dropped if in the last year – he is fined for a traffic violation (dropped to bottom) – he has had five accidents each costing the company over ¥30,000 (dropped two ranks) – he has had an accident which is a traffic violation under 4.2. (dropped one rank) – he has been away from driving (i.e., doing a desk job) over 30 days (over 90 days if owing to employer's needs) (dropped four ranks)
Allocation of old vehicles	(1) The more recent models to be allocated according to the length of time a driver has been driving a one-man vehicle (2) The secondary criteria are to be the same as for new vehicles	Principles (1) and (3) above are to apply

Note: This table is for the company's one-man buses. Similar tables can be drawn for the two-man buses and for the charter buses.

discussion and debate led to the conclusion that the most serious grievances in that division related to the problem of arbitrary transfers. Many of the drivers of the inter-city buses came from farming communities where they spent their spare time working the land. They drove daily with the fear that management might transfer them to another route in some faraway location. That would invariably separate them from their family and cause hardships for those left behind to tend the family farm. By tackling this issue, the Branch leadership reckoned they would attract considerable support from among the employees in that division. In 1960 they served their demands on management. The negotiations took five years and several strikes. Again, the result was an agreement to implement a set of principles prepared by the branch and seen as being fair and objective by the employees of both unions.

Basic to the principles for transfer was the distinction between transfers which were initiated by the employee himself and those which were initiated by the company. In the case of employees requesting transfers, the company was to post the names of those who had applied for transfer. When positions became available at the desired location, they were to be filled in the order of application. If two persons applied at the same time, preference was to be given to the person who had first been employed by the company. After that preference was given by age. In the case of company initiated transfers, the company had a free hand in transferring employees who had been with the company for less than eight months. Among all other employees, single employees were to be transferred before married employees. Again, the two seniority principles were applied in ranking single employees. After the single employees came those already living apart from their families and then those living with wives and/ or children. Special consideration given to persons with special circumstances such as children in school or persons ill at home. The safest group were those aged over 45: they could not be required to move for any reason. (That is not to say that the firm could not ask employees to move and obtain their assent by offering them promotion or better working conditions.)

In evaluating the success of the branch, weight must again be given to the establishment of objective criteria – criteria which severely limited the scope for managerial discretion. Again the branch found an issue of great concern to members of the Denrō affiliate. Having launched the first strike with only 33 members (from among 1000 employees), the branch soon found itself with 55 members. The second wave of strikes resulted in further defections from the Denrō affiliate and the branch soon found itself with over 100 members. Although management steadfastly refused to consider the issue at any bargaining session, the tide had begun to turn. Clearly making headway, the union decided to launch a third wave of strikes. The night before the third wave was to begin, management asked the branch leadership to come to the bargaining table. The final agreement is given in Table 11.7.

Table 11.7 *The 1967 agreement on principles for transferring employees*

I   Transfers initiated by the employee

   A   Principles for transfer selection
     (1) Applicants for transfers are to be ranked according to the date of their application.
     (2) Applicants applying on the same day will be further ranked according to length of employment with the firm.
     (3) Age will be used as the third criterion should further ranking be necessary.

   B   Additional guarantees
     (1) If the application has been made so that an employee may be reunited with his spouse, the period of waiting since application shall be treated as double the actual period.
     (2) Applicants with top priority will not necessary be transferred in that order during the winter months (from November 1 to the following March 31) to areas where there are heavy snow falls. They will, however, be transferred according to priority after March 31 of the following year.
     (3) When someone who has been on some kind of leave comes back and applies for a transfer to the location he was in before his leave, he shall be given top priority.
     (4) Drivers responsible for the health of someone else will not, when given their transfer, be requested to take the routes with the most time outside normal hours or the routes which have the longest shifts.
     (5) Drivers with a family member in the hospital for over 10 days will be given top priority.
     (6) The company will post the names and details of all applicants for transfers.

   C   Addendum
     (1) Employees transferred from other sections to the inter-city bus division will be treated as new employees in terms of seniority.

(2) When one applies for a transfer and then cancels the application, their next application will be placed at the end of the queue.

II Transfers initiated by Hiroshima Dentetsu

    A Principles for implementing transfers

        (1) Employees will be grouped according to the time they entered the firm. Employees in the group with the least seniority will be transferred first. Within each group, transfers will be made in the order of the following groups:

            (a) single employees (and then by age) (from the youngest),

            (b) married persons living by themselves (and then by age),

            (c) persons with families (and then by age), and

            (d) persons with families and children attending school (and then by age).

        (2) Within each seniority group, the last persons to be transferred will be

            (a) those who are where they requested to be, are living with their family and who have been there for over five years,

            (b) those who are within ten years of the retirement age, and

            (c) those who have already been transferred to a location they did not want.

    B Additional guarantees

        (1) Special consideration will be given to persons who have in their families persons who are attending school or are receiving treatment for illness or in the hospital for over thirty days.

    C Notes

        (1) These principles are not to be applied to persons who have been in the company for less than 8 months.

III Costs involved in transfers

    A The company will transfer the employees belongings in a company truck or pay the costs of having the belongings transported by other means.

    B The following shall be paid to cover costs involved in preparing for the move (*shitakuryō*):

        (1) all of the costs when transfer is initiated by company,

        (2) 30 percent of the costs when move is initiated by employee and he has been employed by the company over two years,

        (3) 10 percent of the costs when move is initiated by employee and he has been employed by the company less than two years, and

      (4) all of the costs for the first transfer of any employee after entering the company.

  C Separate housing allowance
      (1) Paid when the transfer is initiated by the company.

  D Family allowance
      (1) Transport is paid by the company when the transfer is initiated by the company.

IV Special leave

  A When accompanied by his family, the employee will be given the necessary time off to complete the move.

  B Bachelors and those living by themselves will be given one day off.

In both campaigns against management, simple issues of fundamental importance to all employees had been carefully selected. The branch carefully developed an approach which cultivated the sympathy of unionists belonging to the Denrō affiliate. With the flow of members back from the second union, the branch developed a momentum which was to carry it into the next stage of its recovery.

VI The Counter-Offensive over Work and the Wage Systems: 1964–8

Following the initiatives taken in the two bus divisions, the branch decided to turn its attention to the rail divisions. Having pushed its organization rate from ten to twenty percent during the early 1960s, it moved on to the question of company-wide wage policy and to serving employees in the company's key divisions. Again the emphasis was on the establishment of acceptable procedures which management would be bound to follow. Again the attention given to the development of objective and fair guidelines won the branch leadership the respect and trust of those in the Denrō affiliate. The development of the branch's activities during this period can be seen in several specific campaigns.

A   The struggle over the work schedule

In the train division work was assigned with consideration being given to the number of hours worked, to the intensity of the work and to the level of productivity. Accordingly, control of the work schedule had a huge significance for the branch. Whoever controlled the work schedule controlled the work environment. The branch set its sights on attaining a say in how the schedule was put together.

In the early 1960s automobiles began to appear on the roads in large numbers. In the cities they would cross over into the path of the trams and cause delays. However, when a tram returned late to the depot, the operator would often find himself having to start off immediately on another round without having time for a break. The problem was that the company had established unrealistically tight schedules. The branch easily demonstrated how unreasonable the schedules were simply by 'working to the rule.' In doing so, it followed strictly the guidelines laid down by the Ministry of Transportation: keeping the speed under 15 kilometres per hour when following within 100 metres of another tram, or reducing speed to a prescribed level when going around a curve or when intersecting with another track. The branch then requested that management revise the schedules and launched its 'Correct Scheduling Campaign.'

It also launched its 'Full Rest Break Campaign' which sought to guarantee drivers a minimum of ten minutes' rest whenever their street car reached the depot over ten minutes late. The branch emphasized the importance of the company's social responsibility to the public, arguing that the company could not be providing a high standard of safety if it were forcing its drivers to work when extremely fatigued. With the buses, a particularly gung-ho driver can swing his bus around a parked one and move to the head of the queue. When a tram stops, however, those behind it are also required to stop, and the short delay of one tram can cause the others to back up 'like a string of beads.' Accordingly, even with a few employees participating a small union can soon cause considerable disruption. Initially the company responded by trying to replace those from the branch who refused to move until they had taken their break with members of the number two union. However, the Denrō unionists also felt the strain of working without proper breaks and were very reluctant to step in on a regular basis. The result was a *de facto* victory; the practice of taking a break soon became standard practice.

The branch then pushed the company to have reserve drivers on hand to fill in at such times. Rather than asking members of the Denrō affiliate to give up their rest period to make up for time lost owing to traffic jams and other delays, it argued, the company ought to have reserve drivers waiting to take over. The demand was not to hire extra employees; it was for a more reasonable workload for the operators and the opportunity for many to earn overtime according to a set schedule. Again the branch had been successful in identifying an issue of prime importance to workers in both unions.

B   The rotation of the bus routes

The introduction of the principles for allocating vehicles had led to a great improvement in the working conditions of the bus drivers. However, it did not immediately result in the complete removal of all discrimination. Management still distinguished among the drivers in the assignment of various routes. To remove this discrimination as well, the branch devised a plan to rotate the routes among all the drivers. The plan called for each vehicle to be fixed to a certain route and for the drivers to rotate the routes. The outcome would be that each driver would have to drive each bus and each route, and that there would then be no discrimination among the workers in those regards.

In pressuring for changes to the schedules and other matters affecting the working conditions of the drivers and operators, the branch gradually developed its expertise in matters related to the collective bargaining agreement. It was thus able to locate those areas where improvements could best be made. For example, although the collective agreement called for eight-and-a-half-hour days, the branch ensured that the real work day came to be 7 hours 39 minutes, an improvement of nearly one hour. Although the collective agreement called for a 25-minute lunch break, the branch was able to negotiate for an extended break of 40 minutes. The agreement called for drivers to drive a maximum of 5 hours 50 minutes, but in reality the maximum fell to 4 hours 55 minutes. Although most of the collective bargaining agreements had been negotiated with the Denrō affiliate, the branch was able to win improvements in the actual working conditions of employees by asking management to accede to changes on the shop floor which went beyond the agreement. While these examples point to the dangers of judging working conditions only from an examination of the collective bargaining agreement, they also clearly illustrate the directness with which the branch sought to better the working conditions of all employees.

C The struggle against occupational and job-based wage categories

As mentioned above, wages at Hiroshima Dentetsu were mark-edly affected by the evaluations of those in the personnel affairs section. In this area the branch also sought to introduce accept-able guidelines and waged a thirteen-year struggle to realize that goal. Three changes were particularly important. The first was the move to limit the discretion of the personnel affairs section in ranking employees. The union pushed for a change from five classifications (A-E) to three (A-C). It then insisted that the proportion of employees in groups A, B and C be 10 percent, 80 percent and 10 percent respectively. It later pushed to have the ratios changed to 5 percent, 90 percent and 5 percent. The result was a severe limitation on the number who were singled out as superior or inferior employees. Those in the third category were clearly those who had minimal work loads or who had performed in a clearly negligent fashion. By limiting manage-ment's ability to make invideous distinctions, the branch helped to dampen the atmosphere which promoted excessive competi-tion among employees in the same occupational groupings.

The second change involved the introduction of a mechanism to ensure automatic wage increments. Previously an employee's wages would not rise significantly unless they were promoted upwards from one occupational category (*shokkyū*) to another. Four principles were to be followed under the new system. First, employees who had been employed for twelve years, the last five in the same occupational category, and who had risen to the top of the proficiency ladder would be promoted to the next higher occupational category. Second, employees who had been working for the company for nineteen years, the last ten in the job category (*shokkyū*), and who had cleared the second proficiency level would automatically be promoted two occupational categories. Third, each year 30 percent of those who had fulfilled either the first or second set of time criteria but who had not received an appropriate increment in their proficiency level (in other words, those who had received very low work assessments from the personnel affairs section) and were within the 30th level would be promoted. Fourth, employees who were in one of the first two occupational groupings (i.e., in the most poorly paid occupational categories or *shokkyū*) would automatically be promoted after being employed for nine years in the company and for five years in the same job. The branch fought a long struggle here too, with repeated strikes again part of the process. The final result was further restriction of management prerogatives. Management could still promote workers into its own ranks, but employees were guaranteed some amount of promotion regardless of how management evaluated them provided they met the conditions stipulated in the preceding paragraph. This achievement removed from the work place the need for excessive competition and the betrayal of workmates in order to be promoted to the lower level supervisory positions.

The third change came in terms of the weighting given different criteria in the overall distribution of wage income. The branch pushed successfully for the introduction of age and length of employment as wage criteria, each to account for the distribution of 13 percent of the wage package. The importance of one's position on the job-and-proficiency wage table in determining the main salary was reduced from 70 percent to 30 percent. Again, scope for managerial discretion was diminished and the importance of objective criteria strengthened.

The overall effect of these kinds of reforms was that the work place became a much more pleasant environment in which to work. Of course, the branch was again seen as developing programs with which members of the Denrō affiliate could identify and the organization rate rose to 30 percent as other workers dropped out of Denrō and affiliated with the branch.

VII   Joint Struggles and the Campaign to Protect the Trams: 1968–76

During the late 1960s and early 1970s, trams disappeared from one city after another – from Sapporo to Tokyo, Kyoto and Kobe. Trams were seen both as the source and the victim of urban traffic congestion. As the trams found it increasingly difficult to follow set schedules, passengers looked to other means of transportation. Throughout the country tram companies began to record serious deficits.

Hiroshima was no exception. In 1965 the management of Hiroshima Dentetsu announced its plan to rationalize the trams. The catch phrase for rationalization was, 'Let's make everyone's work on the tramways more enjoyable!' In concrete terms it meant having the last trams run from 10.00 p.m. instead of 11.00 p.m. It meant running the trams less frequently. For the workers it meant shorter hours of work and the deintensification of work loads. The Denrō affiliate welcomed the proposals and many of the members of the branch also seemed to accept them with approval. At this early stage management made no statement suggesting that the tramways might be abandoned altogether.

The branch decided simply to wait and see. There was a deeply ingrained suspicion of management and disbelief that the company would be going out of its way to make things easier for the workers. For two or three years the branch was unable to reach any decision at its general meetings. The leadership came under heavy fire from the membership for not going along with the times, shorter work weeks and improved working conditions. The branch leadership tried its best in negotiations with management to uncover the company's intentions, but there was the constant worry that its indecisiveness would alienate it from its membership. As it gradually became clear that the trams would be abandoned in Sapporo, Tokyo and Kyoto, the branch leadership finally concluded that management wanted to introduce the 'reforms' in order to further diminish the attractiveness of the trams to their customers. The increased deficits would then be seen as 'forcing' the firm to cancel the services altogether.

Any move to terminate the tramways would obviously result in some employees losing their jobs. The branch leadership did not believe that the company could absorb the 1000 or so

employees in the tramways division by transferring them elsewhere within the company. It thus decided that the trams should
be maintained at all costs so its members would continue to be
employed. Operators of buses could probably find employment
in other companies driving buses, trucks or taxis, but there was
no place for those on the trams to go if they were retrenched.
The branch issued the following statement:

> Those of us working in the transportation industry have a
> mission in society. That mission is to strive to serve the
> community with better rail service. That means providing
> safe, prompt, comfortable and effective transport to the
> public at a reasonable price. We should strive to please
> passengers to the utmost. Since we live in a capitalist society
> in which firms are tied to making a profit, the bottom line
> is: can we make the trams once again profitable? To bring
> our customers back onto the trams is the way to generate a
> profit for the company and to protect our jobs and
> employment. (From interviews with the Branch Executive,
> July 13, 1983)

The branch adopted the above statement after a number of years
of debate. Management's response was to emphasize the need
to scrap the trams because they were losing money. On the other
hand, the branch began to devise ways to improve operations
and maintain the viability of the trams within the company's
overall operations. The obvious step was to restore the old tram
schedules to the pre-rationalization period so that trams would
run more frequently. This meant running them until 11 p.m. But
the branch went further in suggesting ways to step up the pace
of work. It proposed giving up the rest period it had fought for
when trams were delayed by traffic. It offered to do whatever
was possible to see that the trams ran on time. It also proposed
ways to improve the service for passengers, such as redesigning
the stops so that passengers could easily transfer from one tram
to another. With the longer stop areas, it suggested, two tram
cars could be coupled to increase the number of passengers able
to be transported, a step which actually intensified the work load
of the single driver. A number of the branch's own members
saw this as a reversal. They accused the branch of backing down
on its commitment to improve their working conditions. The

main reason it took so long for the branch to announce a policy was the need to resolve differences of opinion among its own members. This issue was debated repeatedly in as open a manner possible, and the leadership took pains to avoid the appearance of imposing its will on the membership. The result was full support when the final policy was decided and announced.

Once the branch had committed itself to saving the trams, the Branch began to develop various strategies. For example, it called for signals which would sense when a tram approached and give it the right-of-way. This improved greatly their ability to navigate the more congested intersections. However, the most important factor was the political campaign to obtain legal restrictions prohibiting cars from driving on the tramtracks. In 1971 the Prefectural Safety Committee issued orders to that effect. The committee's ruling had been the result of concerted lobbying amongst politicians at many levels of government from the local ward councils upwards. Once this objective had been attained, the way was open for the company to purchase very inexpensively the trams being retired in Sapporo, Tokyo and Kyoto. The decision to leave the 'imported' trams just as they were gave the company a tourist attraction. Thus today in Hiroshima one can ride the Arashiyama or the Mount Hieizan trams from Kyoto just as they were in the past.

It was obvious that the success in improving the productivity of the employees in the tramways division was in large measure the direct result of the branch's program to mobilize the labor force. There was, to be sure, considerable debate about whether the program was really the sort of thing that a union ought to be supporting, let alone initiating. In addition to the doubts held by some of the members of the executive committee, the branch also invited criticism from other unions in the area. However, in the end the view which predominated was that 'if there are a hundred proposals from management to rationalize, there must also be one hundred ways of responding.' The bottom line was that a very innovative response would be required in the face of what seemed to be the inevitability of management's rationalization. To have done otherwise would have been to compromise the interests of the one thousand employees in the tramways division, as well as the 4000 family members who depended on them as breadwinners. A clear distinction had been made between protecting the jobs of the workers and assisting Hiroshima Dentetsu. Looking back some 15–20 years later, one can say that it was the correct strategy which saved the trams 'just in the nick of time.'

When management finally abandoned its plans to disband the trams and accepted an agreement which clearly established the future of the trams in May 1978, something unexpected occurred. The head of the Sendamachi depot, which was responsible for 150 employees and was the largest of the company's fifteen tram depots, suddenly decided to join the branch. Several of the unionists I interviewed related the incident as follows:

'The Depot Head, Mr Kawakami, came into our Branch Office. He came over to the Head of the Executive, Mr Obara, and asked, "If I join your union that will just about tidy things up at my depot, don't you think?"'

'To which Mr Obara replied, "The majority of workers will decide in their own good time. However, the company won't be happy to learn that a member of management, a non-unionist such as yourself has joined the Branch!"'

' "Well," came back the retort, "it's an open shop and that means I'm free to join the branch if I wish to. That management gets upset is to be expected. Although the existence of two unions has meant a fair bit of confusion in the running of things, management has done little to resolve the situation. I feel some anger about that. I am just about to retire. I began to work for this company in 1938. I've spent my life working in rail transport. So, at the end of my career with this company it seems that the one thing I can do for it is to see that we normalize the union situation in the depot for which I am responsible. Give me my membership card!" '

'At that Obara began to yield. "Okay, Okay. I wish you luck. We will be happy for all the members you can get us in your depot!"'

'Kawakami continued, "I came to work here at the age of sixteen. I've been with the trams ever since. I like them; they're like my children. After all that time I finally got promoted to Head of the Sendamachi depot. Then I heard about plans to close down the trams. I decided then that if they did that I would quit the company. As Depot Head I had to represent management in a number of collective bargaining sessions. However, I soon found that the company's position was simply that the trams were losing money and that the tracks should be ripped out. That contrasted with the position of the branch which was doing everything possible to keep the trams running. Among the non-unionists there is a good number who were inspired by the branch's position and who began working to keep the trams. To see the hopes of those people realized, it is important, I feel, to find a way of bringing the two unions together. In order to get the Denrō unionists to join the branch I wish to work with you."

' "I am very happy to hear that," Obara replied. "It is as through an army has come to our assistance. Let's work together!" '

'The two men then vigorously shook hands. Having witnessed that exchange the rest of us were quite moved. We shortly afterwards had a meeting and that was the first time that we were fully confident of unifying the union movement at Hiroshima Dentetsu.'

At the time the branch had 145 members from the tramways division; the Denrō affiliate had 110 members. When Kawakami joined the branch, a number of supervisory staff under him did likewise. At the time of this research in 1984, the branch had 252 members whereas the Denrō affiliate had fallen to 34. The success of the branch in the tramways division had ramifications elsewhere. In April and May 1979 a large number of workers in the railway division joined the branch, and by 1984 there were 91 branch members and 14 in Denrō. The tide had turned.

VIII   Some Generalizations

Having surveyed the developments which accompanied the transformation of the Shitetsu Sōren branch from minority status to majority status, a number of themes reoccur. It seems to me that these point to the essence of a strong union and may be used to develop a framework for designing a successful union.

Below five characteristics accounting for the branch's success are briefly outlined.

A The emphasis on equality

First was the branch's ability to inject some notion of egalitarianism into the way relationships among the company's employees would be structured. This is significant given that management had gone to such lengths to develop a discriminatory policy of personnel administration. Generally speaking, when a split occurs in the labor movement at a particular firm it is common for management to openly support the conservative number two union. That this was especially the case at Hiroshima Dentetsu reflects the type of work involved. The men who drove the buses and operated the trains and trams were an independent lot. They worked by themselves (or at most with a conductor); where they went their 'palace' went with them. Moreover, the place of work was not only the machinery but the ever-changing conditions in which the machinery was operated. The weather, the traffic, the chemistry among the passengers: these shaped the work environment and were always changing. The process could not easily be automated. The workers took pride in what they considered to be skilled work, work which required them constantly to be making fine judgements to ensure the safety and well-being of the hundreds of passengers they carried each day. These workers were able to enjoy a degree of job satisfaction which was unknown to most factory workers. The employees were obviously aware that this satisfaction came from an entire way of life which depended upon their 'sovereignty' being recognized.

The operators of the trains and buses believed that very few other persons could do their work. Management, however, saw them as replaceable. The operators clearly resented management types who denigrated their work. The work allowed for considerable differences of opinion in assessing its difficulty and the performance of those doing the work. It was easy for competition to be stimulated among the operators themselves and for animosity to arise between the operators and the management. Given this work environment, management was able to take advantage of divisions in the union. They heightened competition among the workers and then denigrated those who fell behind in the competition. Denigration took the form of various discriminatory practices. Those who complained were told to join the number two union. By doing so, workers found their status improved in subtle ways, and this was no doubt of psychological importance to many of them.

In this manner, the values of management came to pervade the various work locations. Those values took concrete form in numerous discriminatory practices. The branch therefore began its recovery by concentrating on the practices which directly affected a large number of employees in the number two union. Moreover, it did so by removing the arbitrariness of management and injecting a measure of objectivity into the decision-making procedures which most directly affected the working conditions of employees. Length of employment and age were highly visible criteria; they were also individual attributes which management could not change but which, at the same time, provided each individual with the assurance that they would in time be upwardly mobile within the firm. The implementation of these criteria resulted in an alternative set of values being brought into the work place. From the perspective of the branch, the emphasis on invidious forms of competition was replaced with an emphasis on equality. By winning the struggles to remove discrimination in the allocation of vehicles and in the transfer of personnel, the branch was able not only to restrict the arbitrariness of management, but also to negate any material benefit which might have flowed to employees who chose to join the second union rather than the branch. It also meant that employees could stand up at their work stations with a measure of pride. Before those changes were introduced, employees who wanted to get ahead had to ingratiate themselves with management. Twice a year during the appropriate seasons, subordinates had to take presents to their superiors. Over time, rumour had it, gifts of tobacco and rice wine no longer had much influence; a washing machine or a refrigerator was needed to be promoted to be foreman. There was even the term 'bathhouse foreman' to refer to those who had been promoted to foreman for having gone to the section chief's house to stoke the fire for his family's bath every night for some extended period.

Many workers openly avowed that they would be quite happy to do a fair day's work if only they could be promoted according to some seniority principle rather than for doing favors for management. The new system allowed the workers to stand up to management and to have some confidence in their own opinions. No longer could they be punished in material terms for having a view at odds with some manager. The new atmosphere at work proved attractive to many of those who had joined the number two union. This was the significance of the branch's anti-discrimination campaigns.

In reflecting on these achievements, the American system of seniority comes to mind. American unions developed a set of practices to limit the discretion of management in terms of lay-offs, promotion and reemployment. It is interesting to note, however, that the branch at Hiroshima Dentetsu did not have American practices in mind when it waged its campaigns. Rather, with their backs to the wall as a minority union, the leadership of the branch relied on their own natural instincts as workers to develop policies for workers. Perhaps there is something universal in the situation at work that makes such practices as seniority acceptable to workers on both sides of the Pacific Ocean.

B The promotion of workers' self-management

In the struggle to retain the trams we can see the second important element in the branch's overall orientation: the emphasis on union initiatives in 'taking care of business.' It is commonly accepted that managers should manage and that unions should take a defensive role in looking after the interests of workers. However, by taking the initiative in saving the trams and making them a profitable operation, the branch showed that management was not fulfilling its responsibilities. The branch seized the opportunity to inject a measure of entrepreneurial creativity into the operations of the firm. Clearly, its experiment in workers' self-management (*rōdōsha jishu kanri*) was successful. From a situation in which management could define what it meant to be a driver (i.e., as an exchangeable type of labor), the campaign to save the trams ended up putting the branch in a position where labor could define what it meant to be a manager. The symbolic significance of that shift should not be underestimated. Following the success of the branch in saving the trams, management's attitude toward the branch changed completely. They realized that the branch might again be required to take the lead in certain areas. Certainly the leadership of the branch contrasted with that of the Denrō affiliate which was willing to lead its members subserviently down the road to disaster if so ordered by management.

For the workers, the campaign became a means of psychological liberation. They had a new air of confidence – a belief that they could run things themselves, a sense that they, rather than management, knew how to run things. The extra work load seemed small compared to the joy which came from being 'one's own master,' for there had been something degrading in having to follow blindly the orders of an incompetent management. In those circumstances it was natural that members of the Denrō affiliate would increasingly identify their interests with the policies of the branch.

C   The joint-struggle approach

A third factor in the branch's comeback was its ability to develop campaigns which gained the support of all employees, including those in the Denrō affiliate. Their success was reflected in terms of membership growth as mentioned above. Here a few comments might be made on the branch's policy toward employees in lower managerial positions.

From the time of the Mitsui Miike struggles onwards it became a practice of left-wing unions to exclude lower management from their ranks. This is one reason number-one unions gradually declined while the number two unions were able to expand their influence and maintain their membership. This point was made in Ōta Kaoru's account of the Miike Struggle (in Kawanishi 1986). It is important to note the differences which characterized the orientation of the branch. Fairly early the branch settled on a policy for lower level management which came to be known as the 'Three Principles.'

First was the notion that lower level managers are essentially workers, and that in performing low level managerial functions they are unable to communicate their views very effectively to high-level management. They were seen as a group of workers who became 'caught in between.' For that reason the branch was happy to incorporate their demands into its struggle with management. For example, lower level managers were interested in obtaining higher wages, in reducing hours of work, and in having the compulsory retirement age extended. These issues

413

clearly fell within the domain of the union's interests. Second, because the transportation industry is basically involved in providing the public with a service, the union should work to enhance the ability of workers in lower level managerial positions to perform functions which improve that service. Third, the branch took a very firm stance against any person with managerial authority who (a) discriminated against women workers or against members of the *mikaihō buraku*, (b) engaged in unfair labor practices, or (c) misused managerial prerogatives. The branch communicated its position to lower level managers, making it clear that they would cooperate with those who did not oppose the branch in these matters. Given agreement on these matters of principle, the branch assured lower level managers that there would be no disruption to their work. The overall approach was to win over lower level management and then to limit their authority by strengthening branch organization at the shop level. Around 1979 and 1980 a large number of lower level managers joined the branch, but that movement must be understood within the broader framework of the union's philosophy and action regarding such personnel. Its approach was consistent throughout the various disputes discussed above in this chapter.

D Improving discipline among the workers

A fourth element in the branch's success was its willingness to improve discipline among its members. Prior to the dissolution of the Japan National Railways in April 1988 there was a concerted campaign in the media and in government circles to criticize members of Kokurō (Union of National Railway Engineers) for being poorly disciplined (e.g., for eating and drinking on the job, for bathing while on duty, for falsifying claims for various allowances, for taking phony trips, and for featherbedding in general). Kokuro became engaged in an unsuccessful struggle against privatization. Hyōdo (1982) and Takagi (1984) clearly show that many of the charges against the members of Kokurō and the other unions in the National Railways were false, part of a vicious political campaign to manipulate public opinion. Management failed to honor commitments clearly stipulated in its collective bargaining agreements with the unions. In short, management resorted to various unfair labor practices to crush the militant Kokurō. Nevertheless, the union's control over its membership was considerably relaxed following its success with the anti-productivity campaign in 1971, and the breakdown of discipline within the union did in part make the union an easy target for the criticism levied against it once the government had decided to move ahead with privatization.

To be strong and healthy, a union must discipline its own members. Otherwise, the job of maintaining order among the labor force will, by default, be assumed by management. The union will then find its influence on the shop floor seriously eroded. A major source of union's power *vis-à-vis* management is its ability to discipline (i.e., mobilize) the firm's employees in a way that management cannot. In considering the success of the Shitetsu Sōren branch at Hiroshima Dentetsu, attention must be paid to this facet of the union's activities.

This was touched upon when discussing the branch's decision to increase the workload in order to save the trams. Another example is the route rotation system which the branch compelled management to establish. Because the rotations were decided some time in advance and workers could know several months ahead of time when they were going to have a difficult route to drive, some drivers would decide to take their paid leave at just that time. The branch thus had to take the initiative in encouraging workers to show some self-discipline in that regard.

Another example is the assignment of overtime. Although management decided who would work overtime, the branch was able to arrange for the allocations to be decided upon by the workers. The practice at the depot level was for the drivers to apply for overtime and then allocate it to those who had previously had the least overtime (provided they wanted it). However, some drivers would apply for overtime, and then on the scheduled day decide that they didn't want to come in. The workers handled this by penalizing workers who applied for overtime and then did not come in. They would be placed at the bottom of the overtime list for some time.

A third example concerns the problem of employees who had borrowed more money than they could repay. This was known as the 'sarakin mondai,' and the union took several steps to protect itself from that problem. Not only did it pressure management to refuse to display advertisements for credit finance in its trams, trains and buses, it also would not allow employees with such financial problems to join the union.

Another example is the branch's strict adherence to 'brown bag lunching' (*tebentōshugi*). The branch steadfastly refused to pay allowances to members involved in union activities. This practice contrasts, for example, with the situation at the Hitachi union described above in Chapter 7. The union leaders worked the morning shift along with other activists, finishing at 2 p.m. in the afternoon. On most days, the leadership and its supporters would remain until the evening working on union business. This meant that they were unable to do much overtime and therefore had considerably less monthly income. However, despite foregoing several hundreds of dollars a month in income, the leadership did not receive any compensation at all from the union. Nearly all unions pay their leaders' expenses when attending the various regional gatherings held to coordinate activities, but the expenses of the branch's representatives attending these meetings were not covered. It must have been difficult sitting at such meetings while the other representatives quietly took their small allowance out of an envelope prepared for such events. Even today when it has become increasingly difficult to find young employees willing to sacrifice the time needed to take part in the union programs, the branch continues to function on the principle of voluntarism in all its activities. By doing so, it can maintain the notion that unions are there to serve their members, rather than a small number of select officials with ingrained self-interests to protect.

In line with its overall policies of financial restraint, the branch was zealous in promoting subscriptions to various kinds of cooperatives. Within Hiroshima Prefecture, it was known for having the highest percentage of members (568 persons) take out car insurance from the workers' insurance cooperative. It had the second highest percentage of members (120) who took out group life and accident insurance policies with the insurance cooperative. For fire insurance it was fifth highest (with 119 subscribers). The promotion of this kind of financial management was in line with its philosophy of workers standing together with their own resources to protect themselves rather than depending on management. In this manner, then, the union has been able to promote the idea of worker solidarity in the everyday lives of its members.

In discussing the emphasis on union discipline, the above examples highlight the importance which the branch attached to financial independence. As of 1986 the branch had accumulated a strike fund of about 40 million yen, a union building fund of

160 million yen and a fund of individual members' emergency holdings equivalent to 350 million yen. Its total assets were about 550 million yen. This was equivalent to two months' salary for each employee. The significance of that achievement is twofold. First, as a strike fund it means that the union had the resources to hold out for two months. That provides a lot of bargaining power and confidence when the union comes up against management. Although some of the members have in the past felt that union subscriptions were too high, the leadership has been quick to defend its approach by pointing out the benefits which have flowed from its careful financial management. However, the second consequence is even more interesting. In 1986 management's total assets were only about 900 million yen, about 1.7 times that of the union. Should management again make the kinds of mistakes which pushed the trams into the red in the late 1960s, the union would be able to protect its members jobs by buying out the company and running the trams as a kind of union cooperative. This too points to the importance of self-discipline in managing the union's financial affairs.

E The system of labor-management bargaining

Finally, attention should be directed to the system of labor-management bargaining. The branch's executive has worked hard to develop a system of labor-management bargaining (*rōshi kōshō seido*) which gives priority to collective bargaining (*dantai kōshō*). Like other firms in Japan, Hiroshima Dentetsu has had a system of joint labor-management consultations (*rōshi kyōgi seido*). However, there are a number of features which lead me to use the term 'labor-management bargaining' to describe consultations at Hiroshima Dentetsu. Four features stand out.

First, when referring to 'joint consultations' in many large firms it is common for matters pertaining to the overall direction of management planning to be explained to union leaders (*setsumei jikō*) and for matters pertaining to rationalization or raising productivity to be discussed with union leaders and submitted to them for their scrutiny (*shimon jikō*). As the discussion of Hitachi in Chapter 7 suggested, matters related to working conditions were generally downplayed and left for collective bargaining. Over time the importance attached to labor-management relations has gradually declined. At Hiroshima Dentetsu, however, the branch went along with the joint consultations format, but ensured that all matters pertaining to working conditions would also be part of those consultations and decided on jointly by management and union officials (*kyōgi jikō*). By having matters in all three categories decided on jointly, the branch was able to give the 'consultations' the strong flavor of a collective bargaining session.

Second, the joint consultation sessions were seen as a preliminary to collective bargaining. Issues which were not settled in those sessions were taken to collective bargaining. In other words, the branch was careful not to let consultations diminish the importance of the bargaining table. Accordingly, joint consultations may be seen primarily as a means of clearing the table for more effective collective bargaining rather than as a mechanism with its own domain of authority.

Third, decisions made in joint consultative sessions had the same effect as those made through collective bargaining. They were integrated into the collective bargaining agreement. This again meant that the sessions must be seen as being an integral part of the bargaining process.

Fourth, failure to agree on a matter in joint consultations did not by default give management the right to go ahead on its own. That had not always been the case. In the early 1960s management often consulted only with the Denrō affiliate and then went ahead without a word to the branch. But since 1965 it has not gone ahead without a green light from the branch. If management had a new proposal on which agreement was not reached with the branch, the proposal would not have been implemented. It would be put on the shelf and not taken down again until management could revise the plan to make it more acceptable to the union. In 1965 the company wanted to introduce one-man buses on the route to Hijiyama. It took five years of repeated revisions before the branch would accept the plan. Management had learned that it would have to be patient and work with the branch in order to successfully implement its plan.

Once the organization rate of the branch was over 30 percent, 'the writing was on the wall.' At the same time, the branch seems to have taken a fairly flexible attitude in its dealings with management. For example, it was quick to recognize that rationalization was necessary for the company to survive. Accordingly, it did not oppose rationalization in principle. In indicating its flexibility, however, the branch also asked that management work together with it. It carefully checked each proposal to improve their overall effect on levels of employment, working conditions and the rights of employees at work. By taking a tough, but responsible stance in its dealings with management, it was able to institutionalize an approach which might well be labelled a 'system of labor-management bargaining'.

IX Conclusions

Above I have described the stages through which the Shitetsu Sōren branch at Hiroshima Dentetsu progressed in coming back from minority status as a left-wing union to regain majority status. To summarize, the elements which made that comeback possible were (i) commitment to fair and objective egalitarianism, (ii) care to develop programs which could be supported by all employees, including those in lower managerial positions, (iii) preserving the union's independence by disciplining its membership, especially with regard to financial matters, and (iv) developing its collective bargaining muscle and maintaining its ability to strike. These were the fundamentals which allowed the branch to succeed. Of course, they are only the basic prerequisites for success. A closer analysis would also show the importance of specific individual efforts. However, the story of the individuals involved will have to be left to another occasion.

Before generalizing from this case study, a number of points need to be kept in mind. In addition to the personalities of those involved, there is the industry itself. The transport industry differs from manufacturing in many ways. What applies to employees working in their 'moving palaces' may not apply to workers brought together on the shop floor of a factory. A third set of peculiarities can be found in a number of factors specific to the firm studied. Finally, we must recognize that in becoming a majority union the branch too will change. Certain contradictions inherent in the branch will surface in a way which they had not when the branch was a small minority union.

However, despite all the particularistic elements which delineate the experience at Hiroshima Dentetsu as a unique history, the thirty years' struggle of the Shitetsu Sōren branch has a special significance. To understand that significance we need to consider briefly the development of Japanese capitalism and its industrial relations over the past hundred years. The superb research of Hazama (1963, 1964 and 1978) indicates that the history of Japanese-style management is the history of management control. Propagating the notion of '*wa*' (harmony), Japan's managers sought to bring all workers in a single workshop under one umbrella, then those in an entire work area, then everyone in the entire factory or division, and then, finally, all employees of the enterprise were brought into some kind of company community. Management consistently despised workers who took disruptive action. The best strategy for controlling employees has been the organization of all employees into a single union which could be used as an administrative arm of management.

It is ironic, therefore, that the enterprise union has also shown itself capable of strongly resisting management. No doubt this reflects the notion of labor-management relations as a relationship structured around some basic contradictions. However, whenever strong unions have appeared, management immediately adopted its reserve policy – to split the union. Accordingly, the history of tough enterprise unions is almost always accompanied by the history of schisms as management facilitates the development of a second union and works to isolate the militant number one union. It is in this regard that management refuses to respect the legitimacy of unions to organize its employees. Whenever its own interests are not promoted, management will freely strike out against unions. This attitude, then, has been a major factor preventing the development of industrial democracy in Japan.

In this context, knowing that even a few minority unions have successfully rebounded offers some hope to those concerned with industrial democracy. The first condition for industrial democracy is a power balance which results in the principle of equality between management and labor's representatives being accepted (or at least enforced). The experience of Hiroshima Dentetsu provides us with some useful ideas on balancing power relations between labor and management and on how industrial democracy might be developed against formidable odds. It also challenges researchers engaged in case studies to see beyond the special characteristics of their particular study. It is in the larger flow of history that the otherwise particularistic situation begins to take on a more universal significance.

PART FOUR

THE FUTURE OF THE ENTERPRISE UNION

12 The Future of the Labor Movement in Japan

A number of important changes at the end of the 1980s will have far-reaching consequences for the trade union movement in Japan. With the consolidation of the public sector unions into Rengō in November 1989, observers must now reassess the prospects for the enterprise union both in terms of the new national centres and in respect of the interaction between unions for core employees and those for workers in the peripheral sector. This chapter looks first at the national centres, and then at the enterprise unions for the peripheral and core labor forces.

I The Establishment of the New Rengō

The union movement in postwar Japan has been characterized by periods of unification and periods of schism. On November 20, 1987 Zenminrōren (the old Rengō) was formed by private sector unions from the four national centres (Sōhyō, Dōmei, Shinsanbetsu and Chūritsu Rōren). Two years later on November 21, 1989 public sector unions joined to form the new Rengō. The new national centre consisted of 74 industrial federations and four other pro-Rengō organizations. Its 8 million members accounted for about two thirds of Japan's unionists. Its political connections were with the right wing of the Japan Socialist Party and with the Democratic Socialist Party. The formation of the new Rengō has ushered in a new era for the labor movement in Japan; the new Rengō is generally seen as providing the pivotal point around which the union movement will rally at the beginning of the twenty-first century. For this reason it is necessary to begin any appraisal of Japan's labor movement by examining carefully the likely role which the new Rengō will play.

While recognizing the influence of the national center, one must be careful not to exaggerate its importance. On the one hand, Rengō is now the third largest national center after the AFL-CIO in the United States and the TUC in England. (The fourth would be the DGB in West Germany.) As the chairman of Rengō stated in the *Asahi Shimbun* (November 17, 1989: 16) shortly after the affiliation of the public sector unions, the increased bargaining power of the new Rengō *vis-à-vis* management and the government should leave the labor movement with a more pronounced influence on social policy, especially in the areas of employment and social welfare. At the same time, the new Rengō does not represent more than two thirds of organized labor. Nor will its formation lead to a sudden increase in unionization rates. Moreover, Rengō itself has its own contradictions. Several facets of Rengō's more problematic side might be briefly mentioned.

A The new divisions

The process by which Rengō was born also gave birth to new schisms and a new sense of floundering and confusion in the labor movement. The union movement now has three national centers, and a large number of unionists (about 20 percent) are affiliated with none of the three. At the same time that Rengō was formed, Zenrōren was formed by 29 industrial federations and 41 regional organizations. According to figures from the *Asahi Shimbun* (December 27, 1989: 16), Zenrōren embraces 1.4 million unionists (11 percent of all unionists) and is aligned with the Japan Communist Party. Zenrōren thus stands in opposition to the new Rengō. Also formed on December 9, 1989 was Zenrōkyō, a national center aligned with the left wing of the Japan Socialist Party, with the new left, and with independent left-wingers. Its 55 affiliated organizations and 22 regional bodies account for another 500 thousand unionists (about 4 percent of all unionists).

The process leading to the formation of Rengō was characterized by the competition of each new center to acquire as many members as possible. One outcome was the appearance of schisms at the enterprise, industry and regional levels. This competition is continuing, and the struggle for members has produced a certain amount of chaos in the union movement. Fierce debates on whether to affiliate with Rengō were waged in many organizations around the country. Schisms occurred in most of the public sector federations belonging to Kankōrō and in some of the private sector unions. The 'Story of the Three Main Houses of Sōhyō' provides symbolic examples. The unions affiliated with Kankōrō (the Federation of Central and Local Government Employees) all split. The mainstream from Nikkyōso and Jichirō affiliated with Rengō, and the anti-mainstream faction entered Zenrōren. In the case of Kokurō, the anti-mainstream faction with joined with Rengō while the mainstream faction affiliated with Zenrōkyō. In the private sector similar divisions were seen in Gōka Rōren, Zenkoku Ippan, Sekiyū Rōren and Zenkoku Kinzoku.

Rengō and Zenrōren are competing at the regional level as well. In some cases a Zenrōren regional body was formed out of a split in the Sōhyō organization at that level. In other cases Zenrōren simply moved to set up its own independent regional organization. The main point is that there were a number of areas in which the local Sōhyō organization did not integrate smoothly into the Rengō fold. The *Asahi Shimbun* (November 21, 1989: 4) reported such difficulties in Kyoto, Nagasaki, Shizuoka, Chiba, Hokkaido, Aichi, Tokyo and Fukuoka. As the Sōhyō regional organizations were dismantled, the factions choose between the three national centers in each prefecture and the greater municipal area.

B Rengō's restricted membership base

Although the new Rengō boasts that its 8 million members account for the vast majority of Japan's organized labor, one must remember that Rengō accounts for only 17.5 percent of all employees in Japan. It cannot in any way be seen as representing Japan's entire labor force. It is a national center representing primarily permanent male employees in Japan's large firms. There is little likelihood that it will expand to include non-regular workers, especially females, in Japan's small firms where the vast majority of the Japanese labor force is employed.

C Rengō's organizational structure and ideological orientation

As was shown above in Chapter 3 with regard to the steel, automobile and electric goods industries, and in Chapter 6 with regard to the electric power industry, the industrial federations which formed Rengō consist largely of the enterprise unions which organize Japan's core labor force (i.e., regular male workers in the large firms). These unions tend to adopt a cooperative approach to industrial relations, an approach which has greatly reduced their bargaining power *vis-à-vis* management. Chapter 4 argued that the history of industrial relations in postwar Japan is, in part, the history of how management has overwhelmed the union movement and how unions with a cooperative ideology have come to the fore. Rengō is a national center for unions of the cooperative type which basically serve as organizations of core employees. Accordingly, the ascendency of Rengō must be seen in terms of the particular historical context in which a particular form of unionism has come to be entrenched as the mainstream. The notion of industrial democracy is based on the idea of equality between labor and management. Because the current mainstream unions have not been able to assert their equality with management given their emphasis on cooperation at all costs, one would have to argue that the formation of Rengō has taken the union movement in Japan one step further away from realising the goal of industrial democracy.

D Economic nationalism and the entrenchment of Japanese-style industrial relations

As I have written elsewhere (Kawanishi 1982c: 31–3), the unions affiliated with Rengō tend to attach a positive value to Japanese-style industrial relations. In doing so, they tend to be uncritical of Japan's rapid economic growth. Rather, they compliment themselves on their contribution to Japan's successful economic development. They seem to be unconcerned with the various social and economic contradictions which accompanied that development: high levels of pollution, widening income differentials between the haves and the have nots, the slowness with which social infrastructure such as housing, sewage and roads have been provided, the lack of democracy within the firm, inadequate social welfare and the excessive competition which characterizes Japan's system of education. Furthermore, the unions affiliated with Rengō take credit for their members' higher wages and the expansion of employment opportunities, but it is commonly recognized that those goals have been achieved simply by the expansion of Japan's economic pie and the labor shortage which have resulted from factors exogenous to Japan's industrial relations.

Given this emphasis on economic growth, it is important that one notice the emphasis on national economic goals following the oil crisis in the 1970s. Productivity-oriented unions were quick to call for wage restraint and to accept employment adjustment in order to maintain the productivity of their employing organizations. They showed much less interest in protecting the ordinary worker's standard of living. Accordingly, we can expect in the future that these unions will tend to give priority to maintaining the competitiveness of the Japanese economy in the face of growing international economic friction. The emphasis is likely to be on promoting the cause of economic nationalism and on protecting the national economy rather than on raising the standard of working conditions of ordinary Japanese workers. It is unlikely that the unionism supported by Rengō will provide many alternatives to Japan's politically conservative government or to Japanese capitalism. It is unlikely that this kind of unionism will foster the critical open debate which is necessary if many of the social contradictions in Japan are to be resolved. On this point Nakano Takanobu wrote in the *Asahi Shimbun* (November 22, 1989: 1) that 'Rengō attaches importance to the notions of "participation and cooperation" in its stance against management and the government, but there is a worry that Rengō will end up as little more than a huge organization to look after the workers in only the most general manner unless it is able to back up its pronouncements with some form of power and strict adherence to a set of principles.'

E   Rengō and the grass-roots

The union movement has in the postwar period taken the lead in many areas other than industrial relations. It is expected that the emergence of Rengō will serve to limit the broader concern with social issues which characterized many of Sōhyō's activities. This can be seen, for example, in Rengō's stance on the Mutual Security Treaty with the United States. It is unlikely that it will contribute much to the peace movement of citizens interested in promoting armed neutrality or to those opposing Japan's involvement in military alliances and America's military bases in Japan.

The movement against nuclear weapons, which had relied on

Sōhyō as a major supporter in the past, will not be expecting much from Rengō. The old Dōmei unions in automobiles and shipbuilding now play a key role in Rengō. They tend to be in favor of having a munitions industry, and it is unlikely that the new national center will want to engage in any discussions which might 'rock the boat.' Other key actors in Rengō reinforcing this 'hands-off attitude' with regard to nuclear weapons are the unions at the large electrical equipment manufacturers. The electric power industry workers previously affiliated with Dōmei and now within Rengō will be in favor of nuclear power plants and will prevent Rengō from taking a stance against the building of more such plants.

Mention should also be made of the steel workers (previously in Sōhyō), the chemical workers (previously in Sōhyō and in Dōmei) and the electric power workers (previously in Dōmei) who have an interest in polluting industries. They will counter any suggestion that Rengō take a clear stance either against pollution or for the environment. We can thus see the union movement distancing itself from the most typical of Japan's postwar citizens' movements – the peace movements, the anti-pollution movements and the anti-nuclear movements. Not only will Rengō be non-cooperative, it may even be antagonistic toward these kinds of grass-roots movements. However, in losing touch with those movements the union movement will itself lose an important source of support among the people.

While Rengō has these various contradictions which it must overcome, we cannot conclude therefore that the other national centers will be stepping in to 'pick up the slack.' Although Zenrōren and Zenrōkyō may have the sympathy of ordinary Japanese and those in the grass-roots movements in terms of their policy orientation, their membership is limited in size and they could not be said to be particularly influential socially. There will also be ordinary Japanese who are wary that Zenrōren is too directly under the influence of the Japan Communist Party. The future of the labor movement in Japan will very much be shaped by how the three national centers develop, and by how they interact in the future.

In Chapter 3 a pie diagram was used to show the relationship of the union movement to the structure of the labor force. The structure of the labor market is now reflected in the new national centers. It is obvious that Rengō has come to embrace mainly the core employee, whereas Zenrōren and Zenrōkyō have membership drawn largely from the peripheral labor force. In this regard, it is interesting to note that most of Japan's unorganized workers are in the peripheral labor market, a fact which may well determine the future direction in which each national centre develops.

This volume has argued that two types of unions coexist in contemporary Japan. One is the orthodox enterprise union for core employees (*chūsūgata rōdō kumiai*). The other is the fringe-type union for workers in the peripheral labor force (*henkyōgata rōdō kumiai*). While it is impossible to predict the future, we may gain some idea of the likely changes to occur in the Japanese labor movement by considering the challenges facing each of these two types of unionism. In the remaining portion of this chapter each is considered separately.

II The Fringe-Type Union

The immediate concern of most fringe-type unions is how to increase their membership. Because workers in the peripheral labor force far outnumber employees in the core labor force, the growth potential for this type of union is enormous. It is even possible that this type of union might one day become the majority type. To move in that direction, however, the fringe-type unions will have to alter society-wide perceptions, as well as the perceptions of their own members. Current sterotypes tend to pigeon-hole them as perpetual minority unions. In the political arena, one can see the psychological effects on the opposition party which have resulted from being in opposition for so long. Can they really assume power? Can they really function as a majority party? Is not their predestined role only to be the social critic in the background, to serve as a kind of social conscience which is necessary every now and then as long as it does not get in the way of the everyday functioning of the economy?

Over the past decade and a half I have been researching the conditions under which the minority enterprise union might become the majority enterprise union. I have conducted a number of case studies primarily in the transportation industry. It has been my belief that a close examination of those minority unions which have successfully stood up to management might uncover some applicable lessons for the labor movement as a whole. It is my conviction that the union movement in Japan is currently in deep trouble, and that a new approach is required if the union movement is to be something more than an administrative arm of management which is organized to mobilize a small number of core employees – an aristocracy of labor which benefits itself at the expense of the majority of the labor force. The experience of the unions I have been studying in the transportation industry suggests that generalizations might be made in three areas where the minority unions have been successful in terms of matching practice to theory: the distribution of income, the role given to labor in production, and the use of the joint struggle.

A   Egalitarianism and the insistence on reasonable wage differentials

One of the first tasks facing the new-type unions is the instigation of a more egalitarian ethos within the firm. The ethos which develops within a firm, sometimes called 'corporate culture' (although that term often suggests that the culture is created by management), determines and reflects the norms that maintain the social order at the place of work. Unions which aid and abet discriminatory work practices may over the short run gain a following as long as that discrimination can be connected with increased productivity and a higher standard of living for their members. However, as happens when schisms occur, management is quick to use 'productivity criteria' as a means of inflicting discriminatory treatment on those who disagree with its policies. Such discrimination was discussed in concrete terms in Chapter 11. As it becomes systematized and institutionalized, such discriminatory practices will spread to all aspects of a firm's personnel administration: the wage system, promotions, skill qualification procedures, shift assignments, discipline, job rotation, transfers, and hiring. Discrimination in these areas tends to heighten the sense of competition among employees. To the extent that they are on a salary system, they are willing to work long hours in order to 'keep up with the next fellow.' While this may result in short-term gains in productivity, it also increases the arbitrary discretion and authority of management, and goes against common notions of industrial democracy. The end result often is a gloomy workplace, a dispirited union which mechanically administers personnel policy, and an alienated labor force. Unions which acquiesce in that state of affairs are not able to gain the trust and support of their members. For this reason, priority must be given in the union movement to the removal of all forms of discrimination and inequality designed only to promote invidious competition among employees.

The removal of discrimination does not stop with the equal treatment of the members of number one and number two unions. It includes the removal of discrimination based on gender, ethnicity, age and educational background. To the extent that all aspects of personnel policy, including promotion, can be tied to objective criteria like seniority, the advantages which flow from joining a number two union (as opposed to a number one union) become marginal. The result is an atmosphere in which workers can be themselves. Having to be an 'X Company man' removes their individuality; it makes them artificial, someone other than who they are. Many workers want only to get along with their workmates and to do a good job. As long as they can be rewarded by seniority-based promotions, they are happy to work hard. They will respect and trust a union which can provide them with that kind of work environment.

Some readers may well ask, 'What about the bludgers? Is not a system which allows them to progress at the same rate as those who work hard the worst kind of egalitarianism?' Many workers would ask the same question. And that was the doubt which management worked on when it sought to privatize the power industry by breaking it up into regionally based enterprises. The *Densangata* wage system described in Chapter 6 attached importance to age and to family size. However, once management had the necessary margin to differentiate among employees, it presented the *Densangata* wage system both to its employees and to the public as the 'worst kind of egalitarianism.' It goes without saying that this was the same strategy adopted by the Japanese government in dividing and privatizing the national railways a quarter century later.

Perhaps that history shows how fragile the concept of 'fair wages for fair work' is. In any case, after several decades of economic growth the situation in Japan today is quite different from that in the late 1940s. It is also different from that in the 1970s. Accordingly, one of the challenges facing the new unions today is the need for a new wage system, one which will capture the imagination of the ordinary worker and be seen at the place of work as a fair arrangement, rewarding people according to effort, but not in a way that maintains the invidious competition which has characterized so many places of work in contemporary Japan. The design of a new wage system is linked to another concern, the work ethic.

B   The work ethic

A second task for the new-type unions is to take the lead in developing the work ethic and in helping workers to live up to their full potential, especially in terms of demonstrating a useful creativity. To the extent that the union can show the way ahead, as it did with the trams in Hiroshima, it will be able to win the trust and support of the majority of employees.

Concrete experience suggests that unions will not be able to control the situation at work unless they can also control the way in which work is defined. Two events which have highlighted this fact are the Mitsui Miike Struggles in 1960 and the break-up of the national railways in 1987. Each of the unions involved was said to be the strongest in Japan at the time the dispute started. However, management and the government were able to mobilize the mass media to paint a negative picture of the unions which clearly made them responsible for the inability of management to discipline its labor force. It was then easy for the union to be perceived as the source of all conceivable evils at work. In the transport industry the conservative majority unions have often talked about the need to discipline their members in order to fulfill their social mission. According to their logic, the Constitution guarantees the public the right to a reasonably cultured or civilized way of life. With that comes the right to expect the best and most convenient transportation. Those working in the transportation sector have a civic duty to provide the public with reliable service. In Japan it is often said that public transportation is the feet of the people. To disrupt those services is likened to cutting off the feet of the people. It has been an effective metaphor. Given the public acceptance of those perceptions, it was easy for management to let losses accrue and then to isolate the left-wing unions by publicly blaming them for the operations being in the red.

Somewhere amongst the jargon and ideological slogans it is important to see the nexus which links the union's commitment to improving working conditions to the notion of service in what is an important public utility. Nor is that kind of thinking limited to the public sector. The notion of service is an important ingredient in the ideologies of many private firms.

In saying that, however, it is important to realize that economic rationality and the pursuit of profit may also at times contradict a company's publicly stated commitment to service. The Shitetsu Sōren branch at Hiroshima Dentetsu provides a good example of how a union was able to take the initiative. To protect the jobs of union members and to win back their place of work, the union initiated a campaign of work intensification. By taking the lead in a movement which put the trams back in the black, the union was able to legitimate its position. In doing that, the union was in effect saying that it had a social responsibility to maintain services which management sought to discontinue. In emphasizing the importance of safety, reliable scheduling, comfort, convenience and economical fares, the union was underlining its acceptance of social responsibility. By linking in with grass-roots organizations, it was in many ways better able to tell what was socially acceptable than management.

To maintain the tram service for the people, it obviously had to provide a service which was profitable. This is not to say that work intensification occurred without any debate. There was a myriad of views. Some unionists saw in work intensification something which went against the general philosophy of the union movement itself, or at least against a movement which was about improving the working conditions of the membership. In the end it boiled down to two conclusions. First, if there are a hundred ways to rationalize a company's operations, then too there must be a hundred ways for a union to respond to selfishly motivated rationalizations. In the case of the tramway workers in Hiroshima, work intensification was perhaps the only chance the Shitetsu Sōren union had of rescuing the situation. Second, in 'saving the trams for the people,' the Shitetsu Sōren union was able to 'connect' at the grassroots level. By doing so, it discovered that management did not have a monopoly on what it meant to 'serve the people' or to 'fulfil one's social responsibility.' The union was able to develop a campaign which was not narrowly defined in terms of protecting the interests of its company. It was a campaign which incorporated not only the interests of its own members but also those of the other union's members. The key was in having been a campaign which attracted widespread support. The most significant product of the campaign was the new orientation of the workers, who came to see the Shitetsu Sōren union as the true leader of the work force.

C   Solidarity

To survive, the minority union needs to find an intellectual basis for pushing ahead with the notion of joint struggles. The sooner it can shift its attention from the need to compete in an unproductive manner with members of the conservative majority union or to confront supervisory staffs, the sooner the union can concentrate its energies on constructive policies and on the development of policies which will attract wide support from a good cross-section of employees.

To develop successfully a sense of solidarity on the shop floor, a delicate balance is required between (a) the commitment to the principles and philosophy of the fringe-type union and (b) the ability to empathize with members of the conservative union. In the past, committed unionists have often lashed out at members of the conservative union, labelling them 'scabs' or 'management lackeys.' However, many members of the second union joined it out of fear, not out of a commitment to its ideals. When such accusations are thrown at them, they tend to retreat into the only refuge they know, the second union. In the long-run they come away with an even stronger distaste for the minority union, and the chances for a joint struggle are thereby diminished accordingly. The solution is first to consider key areas where members of the other union feel their interests are not looked after. The union can then develop programs which will lend support to those unionists while also articulating further the union's position in those key areas. In this manner a sense of common destiny and solidarity can be folstered.

The other main group of workers who have interests in common with members of the minority union are the supervisory staff. In nearly all of the major disputes in the postwar period, unions have failed to incorporate those workers in its campaigns. They have labelled supervisory staff either as 'the enemy' or as 'the spearhead of management.' In doing so they have invariably alienated this important group of workers. To incorporate supervisory staff in union campaigns, four principles might be observed. The first is to view the supervisor as a work mate who had been placed in an awkward position. As the last link in the chain of command which communicates management's demands to the labor force, supervisors are often not able to press their demands on management. For that reason, they often appreciate the efforts made by unions on their behalf with regard to various working conditions such as the extension of the retirement age, the shortening of hours of work, and better wages. Because their job often involves efforts to improve services to the public, the second principle is to cooperate with supervisors wherever possible. The third principle is to withdraw that cooperation from supervisors who attempt to implement discriminatory practices on the basis of ethnicity, gender or union affiliation. However, before withdrawing cooperation, efforts should be withheld only from the most recalcitrant supervisors. The aim is to create as few enemies as possible while winning as many friends as possible. In the past Japan's unions have not paid enough attention to the importance of developing broadly based joint struggles which would build rather than undermine the sense of worker solidarity.

The three areas examined above are interlinked. If the Japanese labor movement is to see a new era of unionism, those linkages will need to receive careful attention. The first step in that direction is for unions which have experience in these areas to exchange their views.

III Enterprise Unions for Core Employees

Enterprise unions for core employees will be undermined by their tendency to be bureaucratized in the service of managerial goals. As an expression of business unionism, this type of union seems to have difficulty in providing for the open participation of its rank-and-file. In this regard, Ogawa Noboru (1981) has argued that the leadership of Japan's business-oriented enterprise unions will not attach much value to spontaneous contributions from their memberships. Rather, it will place priority on establishing a working relationship with management and with the government in order to promote productivity within the confines of a capitalist enterprise system. It will demand for its members only that surplus which exists after the needs of the enterprise as a profit-making operation are met. From this perspective, the enterprise union becomes a kind of craft union which functions as a labor supply organization subcontracting its labor to management.

Seen from this perspective, the enterprise union for core employees can be said to have three distinguishing characteristics. First, it is established as a kind of interest group which is committed to maintaining the economic, political and social system as it currently exists. The concern of these unions with social issues such as discrimination will be negligible. Second, as an organization which subcontracts to supply various supervisory and administrative services to the enterprise, this type of enterprise union promotes an arrangement whereby participation in management decision-making is confined to a few selected union leaders, but not allowed for the ordinary union member. Third, its bargaining power is linked directly to the number of employees it embraces. Membership size is an index of its ability to serve as a communications network, just as the number of viewers determines advertising revenue for a television station. The sense of solidarity or commitment among its members is of secondary importance in its relations with management.

In general, this type of union receives various benefits in exchange for the willingness of its leadership to discipline the membership in ways which increase the firm's economic competitiveness. Ogawa argues that the benefits which a union leadership receives from the firm for its supervisory services can then be understood as a resource which the union leadership can parcel out to its membership. Members of the union will evaluate their leaders according to the benefits which trickle down in the form of improved working conditions. The benefits will depend upon (i) the market value of the management skills which the union leadership demonstrates when supervising the membership as employees, and (ii) the ability of the leadership to alter through negotiation the perception of the value which ought to be attached to their supervisory skills. Solidarity and the union's bargaining strength are much less important. In fact, the more pronounced these qualities are, the less successful the leadership will be in giving the appearance that it is able to supervise its members at work.

Having a view of the union as a body which has value precisely because it can efficiently supervise a valuable labor force, Koike (1981) argues that members of the peripheral labor force (those in small firms, women, part-timers, temporary employees, etc.) are not in a position to form a viable union movement. Koike argues that union members will not participate or join the union unless it supplies them with some service valued at or above the cost of belonging to the union. At places where there is no internal labor market, he argues, it will be very difficult to get the workers together unless a high level of skill is involved. At such places, small numbers of workers will be unable to maintain full-time union staff that can supply them with worthwhile union services. Even if there is a large number of workers in the peripheral labor force, in Koike's view the possibilities of workers organizing themselves outside the internalized labor market are extremely limited. He also claims that in all countries the upper limit for the organization rate is about thirty percent, and that organized workers everywhere are concentrated mainly in the large enterprises.

The findings of the research presented in this volume contradict Koike's assertions. They show that small unions among workers on the fringe can be viable. This is not the same as saying they will be the dominant unions in the future, but the evidence does point to the need to consider seriously the potential for a dual labor movement in Japan. There is also some evidence to suggest that America's business unions have in their very size undermined their own bargaining power, and that the decline of the American union movement may in part be linked to this weakness (Shimada 1982). The lesson is that unions which grow large for the sake of size may appear to be quiet healthy on the outside while they atrophy on the inside because they are unable to provide opportunities for the active participation of their membership.

In Japan the notion of business or economic unionism is often linked to notions of the firm as a community of individuals having the same fate in life. As Koike (1982) has argued, the essence of the internal labor market is that employees who leave lose, while those who stay profit in proportion to the length of time they remain. The establishment of the internal labor market results in the economic well-being of the employee being linked to well-being of the firm which employs him. If the firm does well, the employee will soon be promoted. If it does not, he will have to wait some time to improve his lot. If the firm totters, unemployment might be the result. To avoid that eventuality, employees work all out to ensure that their firm is profitable. Koike shows how easy it is for employees to develop a competitive consciousness in which they see their entire future as being tied to the success or failure of their company in it competition with other firms in the same industry. This is the basis for the outlook which equates the enterprise with a community which is tied together by a shared fate. When the enterprise union is based on a philosophy linked to notions of business unionism, it is easy for workers to forget about the similarities they share with other workers occupying similar positions in the social system as a result of the work they do. It is easy for them to get caught up in an endless struggle to compete with other workers simply because they are at another enterprise and they feel the need to make sure their own enterprise comes out on top.

In considering the future of the enterprise union for core employees, we need to consider how workers embroiled in this kind of competition can foster the spirit of industrial democracy or become agents for social change. In a capitalist system such as the one found in Japan, management is committed to competition in order to make a profit. Management at a specific firm will seek to mold labor into a competitive team which will carry the company banner into battle. It will seek to mobilize its labor force and to institutionalize the sense of team spirit in order to achieve its goals of profit maximization. A labor movement which is committed to the development of internal labor markets in line with the principles of business unionism will naturally gravitate toward an enterprise-based approach to organization which will serve to protect only the interests of the small number of core regular employees who come to form an aristocracy of labor. Accordingly, this approach to unionism will always result in management having the initiative in industrial relations. As long as management sets the agenda and the enterprise union adopts the goals of management as it is own goals, it will be unable as an equal partner to work with management on behalf of its members. It will from the beginning be working on the assumption that some of the workers' interests should be sacrificed whenever necessary to maintain the firm's competitive edge. It is tied to a philosophy which can serve the workers only after first serving the interests of management.

As long as business-led unionism is the dominant form of unionism, it is unlikely that the worker can be thought of as a principal actor in shaping society and its institutions. Moreover, by having workers take a passive stance in organizing their place of work, union leaders are hardly assisting their members to develop the skills necessary to play a significant role in shaping their society. Those skills are not implanted as an instinct which is activated once power is won or responsibility otherwise thrust upon a person. The skills have to be learned, and can only be learned through a long process of socialization and practice in one's everyday life. This is the area where the enterprise union is most seriously compromised. Although business unionism may work as a guiding philosophy in the United States where the union movement is organized around industrial federations, when it is adopted in Japan by enterprise unions it is likely to result only in cooperation between management and a few core employees at the large firms – a cooperation which will foster the sense of the firm as a community of elite workers sharing the same fate. The ultimate outcome is heightened competition among workers which ultimately manifests itself ideologically as some notion emphasizing the importance of working for the 'national interest.'

This form of unionism is represented by the new national center, Rengō. Rengō is basically an organization of core employees in large private enterprises in Japan's key industries. The philosophical basis for this group of unions is derived from the United States rather than from the social democracy models found in Western Europe. As I have written elsewhere (1982: 33–5), Zenminrōren added to the basic economic orientation of business unionism the notions of national interest and the fate-sharing enterprise community. Rengō's challenge will be to overcome this narrow parochialism. Failure to meet the challenge will frustrate its efforts to develop into a more broadly based democratic labor movement.

All movements have their contradictions. Although Rengō has

started with a problematic philosophy emphasizing cooperation with management at all costs, as long as it recognizes the contradiction and patiently strives to resolve the problems built into that contradiction, it will continue to evolve. One interesting development to watch carefully is the incorporation of Sōhyō's Kankōrō into Rengō at the end of 1989. It is certainly possible that the new Rengō will reflect some of Kankōrō's orientation. The new Rengō will adjust to Kankōrō's presence and will no longer have the same orientation as the old Rengō or its predecessor, Zenminrōkyō. It is also likely that some of the larger fringe-type unions will also affiliate with the new Rengō, also resulting in further adjustments. At the same time, there are the smaller national centers which have been formed in opposition to the new Rengō: Zenrōren (affiliated with the Japan Communist Party) and Zenrōkyō (affiliated with the left wing of the Japan Socialist Party, the new left, and a number of independent forces). The relations between the three national centers will also affect the direction the Japanese labor movement takes as Japan prepares to enter the twenty-first century. At the same time, the two types of unions – one for core employees and one for the peripheral labor force – will continue to coexist. Each will be forced by its own internal contradictions to evolve, and there is ample room for the two to interact in some areas. Those interested in the empirical study of the union movement in Japan will be challenged to record and interpret these changes as the labor movement evolves into the next century.

Notes

Chapter 1   Introduction

1   The Jinbun Kagaku Iinkai (the Human Sciences Coordinating Committee) was established shortly after the war as a means of coordinating research on Japanese society by scholars working in a number
of distinct disciplines in the humanities (such as philosophy, law,
anthropology, ethnology, and folklore studies) and in the social
sciences (such as economics, sociology, and political science).

2   In 1950 the Jinbun Kagaku Iinkai was reorganized and became the
Nihon Jinbun Kagaku Kai (Japan Association of the Human
Sciences). Over the years it sponsored a number of studies, including
the surveys at Hitachi Mines and Hitachi Manufacturing (published
in 1955), at Toyota (published in 1963) and at Sakuma Dam (published in 1958). As the disciplines seemed to move in the direction
of further specialization, the Association was again reformulated and
became known as the 'Kyūgakkai Rengōkai' (the Consortium of the
Nine Disciplinary Associations).

3   The Shakai Seisaku Gakkai (The Association for the Study of Social
Policy) was formed in 1897, primarily by economists and legal scholars. It has the honor of being Japan's oldest academic association.

Chapter 3   Towards a New Theory of the Enterprise Union

1   After the division of the Japan National Railways with privatization
in April 1987, in each of the resulting railway companies three of
the six unions amalgamated.

2   The dismissed workers formed their own protest organization. After
so many years of struggle, the company finally gave in and some
form of accommodation was reached. The author was personally
involved in assisting these workers to organize and has chosen this
example because he is familiar with it.

3   The dismissed workers formed their own protest organization and
took the matter to court. Nine years later on February 27, 1987 both

441

sides accepted the mediation plan of the court. The plan called for 35 of the 71 workers to be reinstated and for the company to pay restitution totalling 1.29 billion yen to the reinstated employees (cf. Nakayama Morio: 1987). Again, the author was personally involved in assisting these workers and was able to learn of the situation from 'first-hand experience'.

4 The points discussed here are explained in much more detail below in chapter seven.

5 This system of classification is explained in Chapter 7.

6 The work-time coefficient (*shūgyōritsu*) was calculated as follows:

The actual number of minutes each employee spent working

The number of minutes each worker was formally employed by the firm.

The numerator was equal to the denominator minus any time not at work owing to the use of annual leave, going to the toilet, taking coffee or tea breaks, union activity and any other leave (as for illness). If no leave was taken at all, the coefficient would be 1.0, and that was considered the ideal by management. Workshops were made to compete to achieve a ratio as close to 1.0 as possible.

Chapter 6   The Establishment of the Enterprise Union

1 It should be noted, however, that the above was a policy statement. To this author's knowledge, workers in subcontracting firms and related businesses did not, in fact, join Densan.

2 Yoshida Kazukichi later commented on these aspects (as recorded in Tokyo Denryoku Rōdō Kumiai 1976: 411–12).

3 This quote is from the declaration which was prepared for the launching of Kanpai Rōso. It appears in the historical materials in Rōdō Shō (1949: 404).

References

Abegglen, James C. (1958), *The Japanese Factory: Aspects of Social Organization*, Glencoe, Ill.: Free Press.

Anonymous (1978a), 'Kanagawa Saibanetto Kōgyō: Kubikiri Funsai de Kumiai kessei' (Kanagawa Saibanetto Manufacturing: A New Union is Born Out of Dispute Over Firings,' *Rōdō Jōhō* (no. 20: 1 May), p. 3.

Ayusawa, Iwao (1966), *A History of Labor in Modern Japan*, Honolulu: East-West Center Press.

Chūō Rōdō Iinkai (Central Labor Relations Commission) (annual), *Rōdō Iinkai Nenpō* (The Annual Report of the Central Labor Relations Commission), Tokyo: Chūō Rōdō Iinkai.

Clark, R. O., Fatchett, D. J. and Roberts, B. C. (1972), *Workers' Participation in Management in Britain*, London: Heinemann.

Dore, Ronald P. (1973), *British Factory-Japanese Factory*, London: George Allen & Unwin.

Fujita, Wakao (1955), *Daini Kumiai* (The Number Two Union), Tokyo: Nihon Hyōronsha.

— (1959), *Kumiai to Sutoraiki* (Strikes and the Unions), Tokyo: Tokyo Daigaku Shuppankai.

— (1961), *Nihon Rōdō Kyōyaku Ron* (Theories About the Labor Contract in Japan), Tokyo: Tokyo Daigaku Shuppankai.

— (1968a), *Rōdō Kumiai Undō no Tenkan* (The Turning Point for the Labor Unions), Tokyo: Nihon Hyōronsha.

— (1968b), *Daini Kumiai* (The Number Two Union), new edition, Tokyo: Nihon Hyōronsha.

— (1970), *Shinsayoku Rōdō Undō Jūnen – Mitsubishi Nagasaki Zōsen Shaken no Tōsō* (Ten years of the New Left's Labor Movement: The Struggle at Mitsubishi-Nagasaki Shipbuilding), Tokyo: San-ichi Shobō.

Fujita, Wakao and Shiota, Shōbei (1963), *Sengo Nihon no Rōdō Sōgi* (Labor Disputes in Postwar Japan), two volumes, Tokyo: Ochanomizu Shobō.

Gakkō Jimu Rōdō Kumiai (Union of School Office Workers) (1975), *Gakkō Jimu Rōdōsha* (Office Workers at Schools), Tokyo: Gendai Shokan.

Hazama, Hiroshi (1963), *Nihonteki Keiei no Keifu* (The Origins of Japanese-Style Management), Tokyo: Nihon Nōritsu Kyōkai.

— (1964), *Nihon Rōmu Kanri Shi Kenkyū* (Research on the History of Personnel Management in Japan), Tokyo: Daiyamondosha.

443

— (1974), *Igirisu no Shakai to Rōshikankei* (Society and Industrial Relations in Great Britain), Tokyo: Nihon Rōdō Kyōkai.

— (1978), *Nihon ni Okeru Rōshi Kyōchō no Teiryū* (Behind Labor-Management Cooperation in Japan), Tokyo: Waseda Daigaku Shuppankai.

— (1979), *Keiei Fukushishugi no Susume* (For Management Welfarism), Tokyo: Tōyō Keizai Shinpōsha.

— (1981), *Nihon no Shiyōsha Dantai to Rōshi Kankei* (Japan's Employer Organizations and Industrial Relations), Tokyo: Nihon Rōdō Kyōkai.

Hirai, Yōichi (1979), 'Mitsui Miike Tankō no Shokuba Tōsō' (The Mitsui Miike Struggles in the Mines), *Shakai Seisaku Gakkai Nenpō* (The Annual of the Association for the Study of Social Policy), vol. 23, Tokyo: Ochanomizu Shobō, pp. 153–81.

Hirakawa, Tadashi (1987), *Hangenpatsu Nikki* (Diary of the Fight Against Nuclear Power), as reprinted in *Rōdō Jōhō*, no. 24, p. 4.

Hōchi San Tansō Kyōtō Kaigi (The Joint Industrial Union Struggle Committee at Hōchi), ed. (1976), *Hayaku Takaku Shōri o* (For a Quick Smashing Victory), Tokyo: Rōdō Junpōsha.

Hōsei Daigaku Kokusai Kōryū Senta, ed. (1979), *Dantai Kōshō to Sangyō Minshusei* (Collective Bargaining and the System of Industrial Democracy), Tokyo: Bokutakusha.

Hyōdō, Tsutomu (1981), 'Kokutetsu no Rōdō Undō' (The Labor Movement in the National Railways), in *Tenkanki ni Okeru Rōshi Kankei no Jittai* (Industrial Relations at a Turning Point), edited by Rōshi Kankei Chōsa Kai (The Industrial Relations Study Group), Tokyo: Tokyo Daigaku Shuppankai, pp. 337–514.

— (1982), *Kokutetsu Rōshi Kankei to Kokutetsu Kaikaku no Mondaiten* (Industrial Relations and Restructuring in the National Railways), the Second Special Issue of *Keizai Hyōron* on Labor Issues, Tokyo: Nihon Hyōronsha, September.

— (1983), *Gendai no Rōdō Undō* (The Labor Movement Today), Tokyo: Tokyo Daigaku Shuppankai.

Inagami, Takishi (1982), *Rōshi Kankei no Shakaigaku* (The Sociology of Industrial Relations), Tokyo: Tokyo Daigaku Shuppankai.

Ishikawa, Akihiro (1975), *Shakai Hendō to Rōdōsha Ishiki* (Social Change and the Workers' Consciousness), Tokyo: Nihon Rōdō Kyōkai.

Ishikawa, Tadanobu (1986), *Tōshiba Fuunroku* (A Record of Life at Tōshiba), Tokyo: Tōyō Keizai Shinpōsha.

Kamata, Satoshi (1973), *Jidōsha Zetsubō Kōjō* (The Automobile Factory with No Hope), Tokyo: Gendaishi Shuppankai. Published in English as *Japan in the Passing Lane*, translated by Akimoto Tatsuru, Sydney: Counterpoint – Unwin Paperbacks, 1984.

— (1977), *Shokuba ni Tatakai no Toride o* (Having a Fort for the Struggle on the Shop Floor), Tokyo: Gogatsusha.

— (1979), *Shitsugyō* (Unemployment), Tokyo: Chikuma Shobō.

— (1980), *Rōdō Genba* (The Work Place), Tokyo: Iwanami Shoten.

Katayama, Tokuji (1946), *Densan Suto Jissoki* (A Record of the Actual Events in the Densan Strike), Tokyo: Kōgyō Shimbunsha.

Kawanishi, Hirosuke (1972), 'Kigyōnai Shōsūha Kumiai no Sonzoku Jōken' (Conditions for the Survival of the Minority Enterprise Union), *Nihon Rōdō Kyōkai Zasshi*, no. 162: September, pp. 24–40.

— (1974), 'Senzenki Kigyōbetsukumiai no Kinō no Kenkyū – Tokyo Dentō Kaisha Jūgyōin Kumiai no Jirei: Taishō 14 nen-Shōwa 15 nen' (Research on the Functions of the Enterprise Union in Prewar Japan – The Case of the Employees' Union at the Tokyo Electric Company: 1925–1940), *Shakai Kagaku Ronshu* (Journal of Tokyo Kyōiku Daigaku's Bungakubu), no. 21: March, pp. 1–83.

— (1976a), 'Kigyōnai Fukusū Kumiai to Shōsūha Kumiai' (Multiple Enterprise Unions and Minority Unionism), *Nihon Rōdō Kyōkai Zasshi*, no. 212: November, pp. 10–23.

— (1976b), 'Fukusū Kumiai Heizonka no Kumiai Kankei no Jittai – Bunretsu Sahakumiai to Bunretsu Uhakumiai no Hikaku o Tsūjite' (The Situation Where Multiple Enterprise Unions Coexist: A Comparison of Left-Wing and Right-Wing Multiple Unions), *Kenkyū Hōkoku* (Chiba Daigaku Kyōyōbu), no. A–9, pp. 167–208.

— (1977), *Shōsūha Rōdōkumiai Undō Ron* (A Theory of Enterprise Unionism with Minority Unions), Tokyo: Kaien Shobō.

— (1978), 'Sengo Rōdō Undō no Shōgen (I): Ogawa Teruo Shi (Densan Daiyondai Iinchō) Kikitori Kiroku' (Testimony from the Postwar Labor Movement I: Mr Ogawa Teruo – Fourth Committee Chairman of Densan – Record of an Interview), *Kenkyū Hōkoku* (Chiba Daigaku Kyoyobu), no. A–11, pp. 241–75.

— (1979a), 'Shōsūha Rōdō Undō no Mezasu Mono' (The Aims of the Minority Unions), in *Kigyō to Rōdō* (Labor and the Enterprise), a special issue of *Jurisuto*, no. 14: month, published by Yūhikaku, pp. 245–52.

— (1979b), 'Densan Jūgatsu Tōsō to Densangata Chingin no Keisei' (Densan's October Struggle and the Formation of the Densan Wage System), *Gekkan Rōdō Mondai*, no. 268: December, pp. 108–19.

— (1981), *Kigyōbetsu Kumiai no Jittai* (An Analysis of the Enterprise Union), Tokyo: Nihon Hyōronsha.

— (1982a), 'Densan 27-nen Sōgiron' (Some Theories about the 1952 Densan Dispute), in *Sengo Rōdō Kumiai Undōshi Ron*, edited by Shimizu Shinzō, Tokyo: Nihon Hyōronsha, pp. 407–44.

— (1982b), 'Sengo Rōdō Undō no Shōgen (IV): Ōyama Seiki Shi (Densan Daisandai Iinchō) Kikitori Kiroku' (Testimony from the

Postwar Labor Movement V: (Mr Ōyama Seiki – Third Committee Chairman of Densan – Record of an Interview), *Kenkyū Hōkoku* (Chiba Daigaku Kyōyōbu), no. A–15, pp. 417–34.

— (1982c), 'Rōdō Kumiai "Saisei" no Kiban' (The Basis for a Rebirth of the Labor Union), in *Sengo Rōdō Kumiai Undōshi Ron* (Theories of the History of the Union Movement in postwar Japan) edited by Shimizu Shinzō, Tokyo: Nihon Hyōronsha, pp. 27–67.

— (1983), 'Sengo Rōdō Undō no Shōgen (V): Densan Reddo Paaji Kikitori Kiroku' (A Recorded Interview on the Red Purge), *Kenkyū Hōkoku*, Chiba: Chiba Daigaku Kyōyōbu, no. A–16, part 1: December, pp. 257–95.

— (1984), 'Sengo Rōdō Undō no Shōgen (VII): Densan Reddo Paaji (1950–1954): Fujikawa Gitarō Shi (Tōji Densan Kantō Chihō Honbu Fukuiinchō) Kikitori Kiroku' (Personal Statements on the Postwar Labor Movement (VII) – The Story of the Red Purges (1950–1954): Mr Fujikawa Gitarō: Former Vice-Chairman of the Kantō Regional Office of Densan – Record of an Interview), *Kenkyū Hōkoku* (Chiba Daigaku Kyōyōbu), no. A–17, part 1, pp. 179–264.

— (1985), 'Sengo Rōdō Undō no Shōgen (VII): Sasaki Ryōsaku Shi (Tōji Densankyo Chūō Kyōdō Tōsō Inkai Fukuiinchō) Kikitori Kiroku' (Testimony from the Postwar Labor Movement VIII: Mr Sasaki Ryōsaku – Former Vice-Chairman of the Central Joint Struggle Committee of Densankyo – Record of an interview), *Kenkyū Hōkoku* (Chiba Daigaku Kyōyōbu), no. A–18, part 1, pp. 101–52.

— (1986), *Sengo Nihon no Sōgi to Ningen* (Labor Disputes and the Human Element in Postwar Japan), Tokyo: Nihon Hyōronsha.

— (1989), *Kigyōbetsu Kumiai no Riron* (A Theory of the Enterprise Union), Tokyo: Nihon Hyōronsha.

— (1990), *Shōsūha Rōdō Kumiai Undō Ron* (A Theory of Enterprise Unionism with Minority Unions), revised edition, Tokyo: Nihon Hyōronsha.

Kayama, Shigetaka and Ohara, Yasuyuki (1976), *Kumiai Bunretsu to Tatakau* (Fighting Schisms in the Union), Tokyo: Rōdō Kyōiku Senta.

Kenmochi, Kazumi (1979), *Soshite Shitsugyōsha ga Nokotta* (So the Unemployed Are Left), Tokyo: Tabata Shoten.

Kōbunsha Tōsō o Kiroku Suru Kai (The Group to Record the Struggle at Kōbunsha) (1977), *Kōbunsha Sōgi Dan: Shuppan Teikoku no Buraiha = 'Outlawtachi' 2414 Nichi no Kiroku* (The Struggle Group at Kōbunsha Publishing: The 'Outlaws' of the Imperial State of Publishers – A Record of the 2414 Days), Tokyo: Shakai Hyōronsha.

Koike, Kazuo (1977), *Shokuba no Rōdō Kumiai to Sanka* (Unions and Participation on the Shop Floor), Tokyo: Tōyō Keizai Shinpōsha.

— (1981), 'Howaitokaraaka Shita Kumiai Moderu' (The Model of the

White Collarized Union), *Nihon Rōdō Kyōkai Zasshi*, no. 271: October, pp. 2–11.

— (1982), 'QC Saakuru Katsudō wo Sasaeru Jōken' (Conditions Supporting Activities in Quality Control Circles), a special issue of *Keizai Hyōron* on 'Nihonteki Rōshi Kankei no Hikari to Kage' (The Success and Failure of Japanese-Style Industrial Relations), May, pp. 66–79.

Komatsu, Ryūji (1971), *Kigyōbetsukumiai no Seisei* (The Formation of the Enterprise Union), Tokyo: Ochanomizu Shobō.

— (1978), 'Kigyōnai Shōsūkumiai no Dōkō to Mondaiten: Rōdō Kumiai no Genten o Toikakerumono' (Trends with the Minority Union and Some Issues they Raise: Towards a Questioning of the Basis for the Labor Movement), *Nihon Rōdō Kyōkai Zasshi*, no. 233: March, pp. 2–14.

Kōshiro, Kazutoshi (1978), *Tenkanki no Chingin Kōshō* (Wage Negotiations at a Turning Point), Tokyo: Tōyō Keizai Shinpōsha.

— (1980), 'The Economic Impact of Labor Disputes in the Public Sector', in *The Labor Market in Japan: Selected Readings*, edited by Nishikawa Shunsaku and translated by Ross Mouer, Tokyo: University of Tokyo Press, pp. 236–54.

— (1982), *Nihon no Rōshi Kankei* (Japan's Industrial Relations), Tokyo: Yūhikaku.

Kōyama, Seiki (1981), *Densan Tōsō Shiki* (A Personal Account of the Densan Struggle), Tokyo: Ronsōsha.

Kumazawa, Makoto (1978), 'Igirisu no Rōdō Undō to Rōdōsha no Sekai' (English Labor Unions and the World of the Workers), in *Kiki no naka no Rōdō Undō*, edited by Rōdōsha Gakushu Kyōkai, Tokyo: Unitashobō.

— (1983), *Minshushugi wa Kōjō no Monzen de Tachi Sukumu* (A Democracy Unable to Get Inside the Factory Gates), Tokyo: Tabata Shoten.

Kuwahara, Tōru (1981), *Shōgaisha Sabetsu Kōjō de Mataraku* (Working in the Factory of Discrimination Against the Handicapped), Tokyo: Jihi Shuppan.

Masumi, Junnosuke (1985), *Genzai Seiji* (Contemporary Politics), Tokyo: Tokyo Daigaku Shuppankai.

Masuyama, Tasuke (1970), 'Daiichi Yomiuri Sōgishi' (The History of the First Yomiuri Dispute), in *Sanbetsu Kaigi* (Sanbetsu Kaigi), edited by Rōdō Undōshi Kenkyūkai (Association for the Study of the History of the Labor Movement), Tokyo: Rōdō Junpōsha, pp. 9–56.

— (1976), *Yomiuri Sōgi 1945/1946* (The Yomiuri Dispute in 1945 and 1946), Tokyo: Aki Shobō.

— (1978), *Sanbetsu Kaigi Jūgatsu Tōsō* (The October Campaign of Sanbetsu Kaigi), Tokyo: Gogatsusha.

Matsumoto, Seicho (1960), *Nihon no Kuroi Kiri* (Japan's Dark Mist), Tokyo: Bungai Shunjū Sha.

Matsushima, Shizuo (1962), *Nihonteki Rōmu Kanri no Tokushitsu to Hensen* (Personnel Management in Japan: Its Special Features and their Transformation), Tokyo: Daiyamondosha.

Matsuzaki, Tadashi (1982), *Nihon Tekkō Sangyō Bunseki* (An Analysis of the Steel Industry in Japan) Tokyo: Nihon Hyōronsha.

Mine, Manabu (1980), *Daiichi Kumiai* (The Number One Union), Tokyo: Ochanomizu Shobō.

Mita, Munesuke (1966), *Kachi Ishiki no Riron* (The Theory of Value Orientations), Tokyo: Kōbundō.

Mitsufuji, Tadashi (1965), *Rōshikyōgisei to Keiei Sanka* (The System of Joint Labor-Management Consultations and Workers' Participation in Management), Tokyo: Nihon Rōdō Kyōkai.

Nakayama, Ichirō (1974), *Rōshi Kankei no Keizai Shakaigaku* (The Socio-Economics of Industrial Relations), Tokyo: Nihon Rōdō Kyōkai. Also available in English as the second half of Nakayama (1975).

— (1975), *Industrialization and Labor-Management Relations in Japan*, translated by Ross Mouer, Tokyo: The Japan Institute of Labor.

Nakayama, Morio (1987), *Kigyō Shakai no Tobira wo Hirake* (Open the Door to the Enterprise Society!), Tokyo: Rōdō Junpōsha.

Namiki, Yasuko (1979), 'Kirisuterareta Musume' (My Discarded Daughter), *Asahi Janaru*, September 23, p. 107.

Nihon Denki Sangyō Rōdō Kumiai Kyōgikai (1946), 'Kyūyo Iinkai Tōshinsho' (Report of the Committee on Wages), a document produced within the union, dated June 2.

Nihon Kabāito Kōgyō Rōdō Kumiai (the Labor Union at Japan Carbite Manufacturing) (1981), *Sake wa Nondemo Kaiko wa Nomanu* (Even Drinking Won't Wash Down a Firing), Tokyo: San-ichi Shobō.

Nihon Shitetsu Rōdō Kumiai Sōrengōkai (The Japan Federation of Private Railway Unions), ed. (1966), *Gōrika to Soshiki Bunretsu* (Rationalization and Organizational Schisms), Tokyo: Rōdō Junpōsha.

Niino, Kazunori (1979), 'Oki Denki Shimei Kaiko no Tsugi wa Nanika' (What Comes Next After The Oki Denki Direct Firings), *Gekkan Rōdō Mondai*, no. 262: June, pp. 78–83.

Nikkeiren (1952), 'Densan Sōgi ni Taisuru Warera no Kenkai' (Our Views on the Densan Dispute), Nikkeiren, October 28.

Numata, Inejirō and Sasaki, Hiroshi (1972), *Kaiin Sōgi to Kaiin Kumiai* (The Seamen's Dispute and the Seamen's Union), Tokyo: Rōdō Junpōsha.

OECD (Organization for Economic Cooperation and Development) (1973), *Manpower Policies in Japan*, Paris: OECD.

References

OECD (1977), *The Development of Industrial Relations in Japan: Some Implications of the Japanese Experience*, Paris: OECD.

Ogawa, Noburo (1981), *Rōdō Kumiai no Shisō* (The Intellectual Orientation of Labor Unions), Tokyo: Hihon Hyōronsha.

Ōkōchi, Kazuo (1952), *Reimeiki no Nihon Rōdō Undō* (The Beginnings of the Japanese Labor Movement), Tokyo: Iwanami Shoten.

— (1954), *Nihon Rōdō Kumiairon* (A Theory of Japanese Labor Unions), Tokyo: Yūhikaku.

— (1955), *Sengo Nihon no Rōdō Undō* (The Labor Movement in Postwar Japan), Tokyo: Iwanami Shoten.

— (1956a), 'Kumiai Undō no "Hansei" to Kumiai Kenkyū no "Hansei" ' (Rethinking the Labor Movement and Rethinking Research on the Labor Movement), in *Sengo Nihon no Rōdō Kumiai*, edited by Shakai Seisaku Gakkai (The Association for the Study of Social Policy), Tokyo: Yūhikaku, pp. 1–8.

— (1956b), *Rōdō Kumiai Undō no Saishuppatsu* (The New Take-Off of the Labor Union Movement), Tokyo: Nihon Hyōronsha.

— (1961), *Nihon no Keiei to Rōdō (2)* (Japanese Management and Labor: II), Tokyo: Yūhikaku.

— (1963), 'Nihonteki Rōshi Kankei no Genkei' (The Origins of Japanese-style Industrial Relations), in *Shakai Kagaku no Kihon Mondai* (Basic Issues in Social Science), edited by Tokyo Daigaku Shakai Kagaku Kenkyūjo (The Social Science Research Institute of Tokyo University), Tokyo: Ochanomizu Shobō, pp. 543–56.

— (1970a), *Kurai Tanima no Rōdō Undō* (The Labor Movement in Dark Times), Tokyo: Iwanami Shoten.

— (1970b), *Shakai Seisaku Yonjūnen* (My Forty Years with Social Policy), Tokyo: Tokyo Daigaku Shuppankai.

— (1972), *Rōshi Kankei Ron no Shiteki Hatten* (The Historical Development of Theories of Industrial Relations), Tokyo: Yūhikaku.

Ōkōchi, Kazuo, ed. (1954), *Nihon Rōdō Kumiai Ron* (Theories of Labor Unions in Japan), Tokyo: Yūhikaku.

— (1956), *Rōdō Kumiai no Seisei to Soshiki* (The Formation and Organization of Labor Unions), Tokyo: Tokyo Daigaku Shuppankai.

Ōkōchi, Kazuo and Matsuo, Hiroshi (1969), *Nihon Rōdō Kumiai Monogatari – Sengo I* (The Story of Japan's Unions: The Postwar Period I), Tokyo: Chikuma Shoten.

— (1973), *Nihon Rōdō Kumiai Monogatari – Sengo II* (The Story of Japan's Unions: The Postwar Period II), Tokyo: Chikuma Shoten.

Ōkōchi, Kazuo and Shirai, Taishirō (1957), 'Densan Rōsō no Keisei to Bunkai' (The Formation and Breakup of Densan), in *Densan Sōgi* (The Densan Dispute), edited by Rōdō Sōgi Chōsakai (The Labor Disputes Survey Group), Tokyo: Chūō Kōronsha, Chapter 2, pp. 25–147.

Enterprise Unionism in Japan

Ōkōchi, Kazuo, Ujihara, Shōjirō, and Fujita, Wakao (1959), *Rōdō Kumiai no Kōzō to Kinō* (The Structure and Functions of Labor Unions), Tokyo: Tokyo Daigaku Shuppankai.

Ōta, Kaoru (1957), *Shuntō no Shūen* (The End of Shuntō), Tokyo: Chūō Keizaisha.

Ouchi, William G. (1981), *Theory Z: How American Business Can Meet the Japanese Challenge*, New York: Avon Books.

Reischauer, Edwin (1979), *Za Japanizu* (The Japanese), translated by Kunihiro Masao, Tokyo: Bungei Shunjūsha.

Rōdō Shō (Ministry of Labor) (1945–52), *Shiryō Rōdō Undōshi* (Historical Source Materials on the Labor Movement), Tokyo: Rōmu Gyōsei Kenkyūsho.

— (annual), *Rōdō Kumiai Kihon Chōsa Tōkei* (Statistics from the Basic Survey of Labor Unions), Tokyo: Ōkurashō Insatsukyoku.

Rōdō Shō (Ministry of Labor), ed. (1973), *Shogaikoku no Rōshi Kyōgisei* (System of Joint Labor-Management Consultations in Several Overseas Countries), Tokyo: Nihon Rōdō Kyōkai.

Rōdō Sōgi Jittai Chōsakai (The Labor Disputes Survey Group), ed. (1957), *Densan Sōgi* (The Densan Dispute), Tokyo: Chūō Kōronsha.

Rōshi Kankei Chōsakai (The Industrial Relations Study Group), ed. (1981), 'Tenkanki ni Okeru Rōshi Kankei no Jittai' (Industrial Relations at a Turning Point), Tokyo: Tokyo Daigaku Shuppankai.

Saga, Ichirō (1983), *Nissan Sōgi* (The Nissan Dispute), Tokyo: Gogatsusha.

Saitō, Shigeo (1974), *Waga Naki Ato ni Kōzui wa Kitare* (The Deluge After My Death), Tokyo: Gendaishi Shuppankai.

Sakamoto, Teiichirō (1979), *Kaisō: Densan Shōshi* (Reflections on the Short History of Densan), Sendai: Densan Tōhakushi Kankō Kai.

Satō Hajime (1976), *Shimoyama Jikin Zenkenkyū* (The Research on the Shimoyama Incident), Tokyo: Jiji Tsūshinsha.

Satō, Yoshio (1973), *Atarimae no Rōdō Kumiai e* (Toward a Labor Union in Its Own Right), Tokyo: Aki Shobō.

Shimada, Haruo (1982), 'Kyūtenkan suru Beikoku no Rōshi Kankei' (The Rapidly Changing Face of Industrial Relations in the United States), *Ekonomisuto*, no. 2449: March 9, pp. 10–15.

Shimizu, Shinzō (1963), 'Mitsui Miike Sōgi' (The Mitsui Miike Dispute), in *Sengo Nihon no Rōdō Sōgi*, edited by Fujita and Shiota (1963), pp. 479–584.

— (1978), 'Sengoshi no naka no Rōdō Kumiai' (Labor Unions in the Postwar History of Japan), *Keizai Hyōron*, vol. 33, no. 10: October, pp. 47–64.

Shimizu, Shinzō, ed. (1982), *Sengo Rōdō Kumiai Undōshi Ron* (Theories of the History of the Union Movement in Postwar Japan), Tokyo: Nihon Hyōronsha.

450

References

Shirai, Taishirō (1979), *Kigyōbetsu Kumiai* (The Enterprise Union), Tokyo: Chūō Kōronsha.

— (1980), *Roshi Kankei Ron* (Theories of Industrial Relations), Tokyo: Nihon Rōdō Kyōkai.

Shitetsu Chūgokushi Henshū Iinkai (The Editing Committee for the History of the Private Railroads in the Chūgoku Region), ed. (1975), *Shitetsu Chūgoku 23 Nen no Ayumi* (Twenty Three years of the Private Railways in the Chugoku Region), Tokyo: Rōdō Kyōiku Senta.

Sōhyō Sōgi Taisaku Iinkai (The Dispute Strategy Committee of Sōhyō), ed., *Sōgi Taisaku Jōhō* (Information on Strategies for Disputes) (An in-house publication of Sōhyō), no. 3: July 5.

Sōhyō Soshiki Dyoku (Sōhyō: The Bureau for Organization) (1982), *Sōgi Taisaku Jōhō* (Information on How Strikes are Dealt With), No. 3: July 5.

Sugimoto, Yoshio and Mouer, Ross (1982), *Nihonjin wa 'Nihonteki' ka* (How 'Japanese' are the Japanese?), Tokyo: Tōyō Keizai Shinpōsha.

Sumiya, Mikio (1950), 'Rōdōryoku ni Okeru Hōkenteki naru Mono: Hannō-Hankō ni tsuite' (Feudalistic Elements in the Labor Force: Some Comments on Being Half Agricultural and Half Industrial), *Shakaigaku Hyōron*, vol. 1, no. 1.

Suzuki, Ginichirō (1977), 'Damatte ite wa Dame Da: Shintai Shōgaisha wa Kenjōsha to Kurabete, Arayuru Men de Sabetsu o Sarete wa iruga, Semete Bōnasu Gurai wa Konjōshu to Byōdō ni Moraitai' (Something That Should Not Be Hushed Up: The Handicapped Should Receive Bonuses Equal to those of the Nonhandicapped Even Though They are Discriminated Against in All Other Ways), *Rōdō Jōhō* (edited by Rōdō Jōhō Henshū Bu), no. 3, June 15, 1977, p. 17.

Suzuki, Ichizo (1949), *Shigunaru wa Kiezu* (The Signal Is Not Out), Tokyo: Gogatsu Shobō.

— (1979), *Shōgen Ni-ichi Zenesuto* (The Declaration on the February 1 General Strike), Tokyo: Aki Shobō.

— (1981), *Shimoyama Jiken Zengo* (Around the Shimoyama Incident), Tokyo: Aki Shobō.

Taira, Kōji (1977), 'Nihongata Kigyōbetsu Rōdō Kumiai Sanbiron' (In Justification of the Japanese-Style of Enterprise Union), *Chūō Kōron*, March, pp. 114–26.

Takagi, Ikurō (1984), 'Kokutetsu Kaikaku wo Meguru Rironteki Mondai', in *Zaisei Kaikaku to Rōdō Mondai*, edited by the Shakai Seisaku Gakkai (The Association for the Study of Social Policy) as its 28th annual publication, Tokyo: Ochanomizu Shobō.

Takahashi, Kō (1965), *Nihonteki Rōshi Kankei no Kenkyū* (Research on Japanese Industrial Relations), Tokyo: Miraisha.

Takano, Minoru (1952), *Rōdō Kumiai Unei Ron* (Theories on Directions for the Labor Movement), Tokyo: Kawade Shobō.

Takano Minoru Chosakushū no Henshū Iinkai (The Editorial Committee for the Works of Takano Minoru) (1976), *Takano Minoru Chosakushu – Daikan* (The Collected Works of Takano Minoru, vol. 2), Tokyo: Tsuge Shobō.

Takemae, Eiji (1982), *Sengo Rōdō Kaikaku* (Labor Reform in Postwar Japan), Tokyo: Tokyo Daigaku Shuppankai.

Takita, Minoru (1972), *Waga Kaisō* (My Recollections), Tokyo: Yomiuri Shinbunsha.

Tokyo Daigaku Shakai Kagaku Kenkyūjo (The Tokyo University, Social Science Research Institute) (1950), *Sengo Rōdō Kumiai no Jittai* (The Situation of the Labor Unions in Postwar Japan), Tokyo: Nihon Hyōronsha.

— (1973), *Sengo Kiki ni Okeru Rōdō Sōgi* (Industrial Disputes During the Postwar Crisis), Tokyo: Tokyo Daigaku Shakai Kagaku Kenkyūjo, March (an internal publication not for sale).

Tokyo Denryoku Rōdō Kumiai (1975), *Tōden Rōso Shi Zenshi* (A History From the Early Years of the Federation of Electrical Workers Employed by the Tokyo Power Authority), Tokyo: Tokyo Denryoku Rōdō Kumiai (an internal publication not for sale).

Tokyo Shimbun Rōdō Kumiai (The Labor Union at Tokyo Newspaper) (1977), *Nen-Nen Saisai Gogatsu no sora no Gotoku* (Like the May Skies Year In and Year Out), Tokyo: Minshūsha.

Tōshiba Rōdō Kumiai (The Tōshiba Labor Union), (1963), *Kumiai Undō Shi* (A History of the Tōshiba Union Movement), Tokyo: Tōshiba Rōdō Kumiai, (an internal publication not for sale).

Totsuka, Hideo (1977), 'Shihonshugi no Kiki to Rōdō Kumiai Undō no Kiki' (The Crisis of Capitalism and the Crisis of the Unions), in *Rōdō Kumiai Undō no Kiki* (The Crisis of Labor Unions), edited by Rōdō Undō Kenkyūsha Shūdan (The Group of Specialists on the Labor Movement), Tokyo: Nihon Hyōronsha, pp. 1–32.

Totsuka, Hideo and Inoue, Masao (1982), 'Chūshō Kigyō no Rōdō Sōgi' (Labor Disputes in Small and Medium Sized Firms), in *Tenkanki ni Okeru Rōshi Kankei no Jittai* (Industrial Relations at a Turning Point), Tokyo: Tokyo Daigaku Shuppankai.

Tsutsui, Tokio (1961), *Densan Chūgoku Rōdō Undō Shi* (A History of Densan's Labor Movement in the Chūgoku Region), Tokyo: Nihon Rōdō Kyōkai.

Ujihara, Shōjirō (1966), *Nihon Rōdō Mondai Kenkyū* (Research on the Labor Issue in Japan), Tokyo: Tokyo Daigaku Shuppankai.

— (1966), 'Daikōjō Rōdōsha no Shakaiteki Seikaku' (The Social Characteristics of Workers in the Large Factories), in *Nihon Rōdō Mondai*

Kenkyū (Research on the Labor Issues in Japan), Tokyo: Tokyo Daigaku Shuppankai, pp. 351–401.

Unyu Shō (Ministry of Transportation) (monthly), *Kaiji Tōkei Geppō* (Monthly Maritime Statistics).

— (monthly) *Zōsen Kikai Tōkei Geppō* (Monthly Report of Statistics on Shipbuilding and Related Machinery).

Vogel, Ezra (1979), *Japan as Number One: Lessons for America*, Cambridge, Mass.: Harvard University Press.

Yakabe, Katsumi (1985), *Zenminrōkyō no Kenkyū* (Research on Zenminrōkyō), Tokyo: Nihon Seisansei Honbu.

Yamamoto, Kiyoshi (1967), *Nihon Rōdō Shijō no Kōzō* (The Structure of Japan's Labor Market), Tokyo: Tokyo Daigaku Shuppankai.

— (1977), *Sengo Kiki ni Okeru Rōdō Kumiai* (Labor Unions in the Postwar Crisis), Tokyo: Ochanomizu Shobō.

— (1978), *Yomiuri Sōgi* (1945–46 Nen) (The Yomiuri Dispute: 1945–1946), Tokyo: Ochanomizu Shobō.

— (1981), *Jidōsha Sangyō no Rōshi Kankei* (Labor-Management Relations in the Automobile Industry), Tokyo: Tokyo Daigaku Shuppankai.

— (1982), *Nihon no Chingin-Rōdō Jikan* (Wages and Hours of Work in Japan), Tokyo: Tokyo Daigaku Shuppankai.

— (1983), *Tōshiba Sōgi (1949)* (The Tōshiba Dispute of 1949) Tokyo: Ochanomizu Shobō.

Yokohama Gakkō Rōdōsha Kumiai (Union of School Workers in Yokohama) (1977), *Tomo ni Iki, Tomo ni Tatakawan – Iribune Shogakkō Shobun Hantai Tōsō no Shōri to Shiseru Nikkyōso Kara no Bunretsu* (Living Together, Fighting Together – The Victory Over the Disciplinary Measures at Iribune Primary School and the Break from the Dying Nikkyōso), Tokyo: Rokusaisha.

Yokoyama, Yoshio and Onogi, Yoshiyuki (1971), *Kōgai Hasseigen Rōdōsha no Kokuhatsu* (An Exposé on the Workers at The Source of Pollution), Tokyo: San-ichi Shobō.

Zenkinzoku Motoyama Tōsō no Kirokū Henshu Iinkai (The Committee to Record the Struggle of the All-Japan Union of Metal Workers at Motoyama) (1974), *Rōdō Kumiai no Shi to Saisei – Zenkinzoku Motoyama Tōsō no Kiroku* (The Death and Rebirth of a Union: A Record of the Struggle of the All-Japan Union of Metal Workers at Motoyama), Tokyo: Tsuge Shobō.

Zenkyūshū Denryoku Rōdō Kumiai (All-Kyushu Union of Electric Power Workers) (1979), *Nijūnen no Ayumi* (A Twenty-Year History), Fukuoka: Zenkyūshū Denryoku Rōdō Kumiai.

Zennippon Zōsen Kikai Rōdō Kumiai (All Japan Union of Shipbuilders and Marine Machinery Workers), ed. (1981), *Mitō e no Chōsen* (The Challenge of the Future), Tokyo: Rōdō Junpōsha.

Zenzōsen Kikai Rōdō Kumiai (The National Union of Shipbuilding and Machinery Workers) (1974), *Zenzōsen Kikai 25 Nenshi* (A Twenty-Five-Year History of the National Union of Shipbuilding and Machinery Workers), Tokyo: Zenzōsen Kikai Rōdō Kumiai.

Index